VIEW FROM THE RIGHT

VOLUME I: HERITAGE AND FOUNDATIONS

ALAIN DE BENOIST

VIEW *from* THE RIGHT

A Critical Anthology of Contemporary Ideas

VOLUME I
Heritage and Foundations

Translated by Robert A. Lindgren

ARKTOS
LONDON 2017

Printed in the United Kingdom.

ORIGINAL TITLE	*Vu de droite: Anthologie critique des idées contemporaines* (Paris: Copernic, 1977)
ISBN	978-1-912079-76-6 (Paperback) 978-1-912079-97-1 (Hardback) 978-1-912079-96-4 (Ebook)
TRANSLATOR	Robert A. Lindgren
EDITOR	Jason Reza Jorjani
COVER AND LAYOUT	Tor Westman

www.arktos.com

CONTENTS

To Jean-Claude Valla

Translator's Preface

This present work is, in many respects, a series of intellectual engagements with a surprisingly wide range of contemporary scholarly publications, from palaeontology to postmodernism. In the course of this undertaking, Alain de Benoist cites a wealth of French works, as well as a considerable number of French translations of works by foreign authors. As a translator, I had to make a number of decisions on how to deal with these citations, especially because they are not simply relegated to the status of footnotes, but form a major part of the primary discussion.

My approach has been as follows:

Where an English edition of a particular book exists, I have attempted to render the book by its known English title, while referencing the French edition cited by Benoist in the footnotes. Where an English edition does not exist (or is unable to be sourced), I have rendered the French title in the body of the text as given by Benoist, and glossed the translation of the title in the footnotes.

For books that are originally written in a foreign language (e.g. German), but which are cited in French translation, I have, wherever possible, cited both the original edition and the French edition in the footnotes, while rendering the title in English in the body of the text. Exceptions to this occur where Benoist specifically cites the original foreign-language title, or where no English edition of the cited foreign-language work can be found. Any relevant clarifications, translations, or editions are contained in the accompanying footnotes.

In several places, Benoist also cites lengthy passages from Greek, Latin, or German authors in French translation. Where time and resources have permitted, I have either sourced and translated the original texts directly, or sourced and adapted existing English translations. Where time and resources have not permitted, I have simply translated the French translation as given in Benoist's text.

I would like to thank John Morgan for inviting me to translate this fascinating work, while acknowledging, on my part, that a translation is by no means an endorsement of the author's views, nor those of the publisher. I would also like to express my sincere thanks to my friend and colleague, Sylvain Saboua, for assisting me with certain aspects of the translation that I found especially difficult. Any errors or shortcomings in the translation of course remain my own.

ROBERT A. LINDGREN

Preface to the New Edition (2001)

The first edition of *View from the Right* was published in 1977, twenty-five years ago. In the years which have followed, this book has seen five successive reprints, with an international print-run of around 25,000 copies. It was translated into Italian and Portuguese in 1981, into German in 1983–4, and into Romanian in 1998. In June 1978, it also received the Grand Essay Prize from l'Académie française, under circumstances which I have had occasion to speak of elsewhere.[1] The work is composed of over a hundred articles, nearly all of which were originally published in the weekly magazine, *Valeurs actuelles*[2] and the monthly periodical, *Le Spectacle du monde*,[3] but whose substance has been largely revised and expanded. The articles are grouped under broad rubrics designed to facilitate reading. The subtitle, 'Critical Anthology of Contemporary Ideas', aptly expresses the intention that presides over this redaction: to prepare a portrait of the intellectual and cultural landscape of the moment, to establish the state of affairs, to signal the tendencies, to open the pathways and provide benchmarks to aid (and incite) the task of thinking in a world that is already in the process of considerable change.

The author is obviously ill-placed to judge the causes of the success, relative but certain, that this book has known. But what is most striking today is the extent of the echo made at the time by this release from a publishing house (Éditions Copernic) which itself only occupied a marginal position. The act of releasing a book apparently identifying as 'right-wing' posed no obstacles to the publication of numerous reviews in the mainstream press. The testimonies and extracts of literary criticism published in the appendix of this re-edition are a testament to this. A quarter of a century later, this tendency is brutally

---

1   An interview on the affair in *Figaro-Magazine*, forthcoming through L'Âge d'homme, in Dossier H consecrated to Louis Pauwels.

2   *Current Values.* — Tr.

3   *The Spectacle of the World.* — Tr.

reversed. The rise of 'uniform thought',[4] exploited by those whose interests it could best serve, has done its work. I have been but one victim among many. The unjust attacks and accusations have created a zone of increasing ostracism and prohibition which spreads further and further, in regularly expanding circles. A number of authors published in the seventies by the greatest publishing houses are today relegated to marginal publishers. A number of writers and intellectuals willingly welcomed to the open forum by the great evening newspapers are now requested to express themselves elsewhere. The catalogues of the great publishing houses have been purged to satisfy the demands of the 'politically correct'. Conformity, intellectual laziness, and lack of curiosity have done the rest.

The title of this book has been the origin of many ambiguities. Two years later, during the summer of 1979, a vast press campaign would establish the international notoriety of the 'New Right'.[5] The expression had already been in the air for some time. Having hesitated for a long time on the choice of the title, I had nevertheless striven to dispel these ambiguities from the outset. 'For the time being', I had written on the first page, 'the ideas supported in this work are *to* the right; they are not necessarily *of* the right. I can still quite easily imagine some situations where they could be *to* the left. It is not the ideas that have changed; the political landscape has evolved'. Later on I would express the wish that 'one attains a position in which one is, at the same time, *both* right *and* left'. This is a way of taking note. Apparently there has been scarcely any acknowledgement of this.[6] But the fact is that at the time, the 'right' was becoming fashionable. Political men who until then restricted themselves to saying that they were 'not of the left', began to admit they were 'of the right' without difficulty. The ideas of May 1968 were already more or less relegated to the background, for better or worse, even by those who had loudly proclaimed them ten years earlier. In a book which knew a certain notoriety, two talented journalists, André Harris and Alain de Sédouy, did not hesitate to ask: 'Who is not of the right?'[7] We would effectively see the right resurface during the

---

4   *pensée unique.* — Tr.

5   *Nouvelle Droite.* — Tr.

6   Cf. the preface to Alain de Benoist, *L'écume et les galets, 1991–1999. Dix ans d'actualité vue d'ailleurs*, Labyrinth, Paris 2000.

7   André Harris and Alain de Sédouy, *Qui n'est pas de droite ?*, Seuil, Paris, 1978.

course of the following decades under two different forms: the neoliberal variant, symbolised by the era of Ronald Reagan and Margaret Thatcher, and the
national-populist variant, illustrated by various tribunes who talk loudly but
think superficially. These two variations which, in the era of Berlusconi and
Haider, do not tend to be more than one, have no correspondence whatsoever
to the idea that I had in 1977 of a 'right' engaging the realities of a nascent postmodernism. I had hoped to see the birth of a movement of thought (and action) defending the cause of the people, a right with a difference, participative
democracy, and the primacy of free values over commercial values. Instead
I have seen the right teach the logic of profit and the principle of exclusion.
Today as we witness the complete obsolescence of the right-left split, I do not
regret being shut out.

*

One of the passages from the introduction to *View from the Right* that has been
cited most frequently is this: 'I hereby define *the right*, by pure convention, as
the consistent attitude to view the diversity of the world, and by consequence
the relative inequalities that are necessarily the product of this, as a positive
thing; and the progressive homogenisation of the world, extolled and effected
by two-thousand years of egalitarian ideology, as a negative thing'. This phrase
summarised my way of viewing things, and even today I still recognise myself
well enough. This profession of 'anti-egalitarian' faith, mixing together the
contiguous but distinct notions of diversity and inequality, and homogenisation and equality, was also somewhat ambiguous. The obvious risk in making
the struggle against egalitarianism the principal objective was to appear to
legitimise practices of exclusion (in the name of the presumed inferiority of
such and such a group) or of elitist liberal practices (the inequality of conditions as the just result of equalities of nature, social justice as 'illusion'). I
would like to take the opportunity presented by this reedition to return to this
problematic complex in more detail.

The equality between A and B (A = B) means that A is either similar or
identical to B (that is, it does not differ), or that they are equivalents according
to a precise criteria and according to a determined relationship. It is therefore
necessary to specify this criteria or to identify this relationship. 'If it only has
equality according to one determined relationship', writes Julien Freund, 'the

same entities and the same things can be different or unequal according to other relationships'.[8] The result of this is that equality is never an absolute given, that it does not designate a relationship in and of itself, but that it depends on a convention, in this case the selected criteria or the chosen relationship. Articulated as a principle sufficient in itself, it is void of content, for equality and inequality only exist in a given context and through relation to factors that allow it to be situated in order to be appreciated concretely. The notions of equality and inequality are therefore always relative and, by definition, are never exempt from arbitrariness.

It is significant that inequalities (in the plural) are currently opposed to equality in the singular. Through the unicity of the concept, the notion of equality itself tends towards homogeny, that is to say, towards uniformity.[9] However, this conceptual unity does not have its counterpart in an identity of empirical forms that it evokes. The forms of equality are not equal among themselves. To the degree that it does in fact has an absolute value, the notion of equality additionally becomes contradictory. A unique value does not exist, for a value only has worth in relation to others which do not have worth (or which are worth less). To value necessarily implies the creation of hierarchy, which is what happens each time equality is posed as a supreme value. But in creating hierarchy, one already violates the principle of equality, which contradicts every idea of hierarchy. (This is the equivalent of the contradiction that pacifists find themselves placed in when they are constrained to wage war against those who do not share their point of view). 'Egalitarianism', adds Julien Freund, 'theoretically denies a hierarchy which it implies practically. Indeed, it accords a superiority and an exclusive value to equality in all its forms, and by consequence it reduces to the rank of inferior values all relationships which are not equal [...] As a consequence, it judges reality according to the order of lower and higher, that is to say, within its concept it includes practically a hierarchy that it claims to deny and condemn theoretically'.[10]

When it intends to show an equivalence, even the notion of value is ambiguous. When one says that two things are of the same value, one does not say that they are the same thing, but that one is valued as much as the other

---

8   Julien Freund, 'Pluralité of égalités et équité', in *Politique et impolitique*, Sirey, Paris 1987, p. 180.

9   For contextual reasons detailed below, *l'unique* has been translated as 'uniformity'. — Tr.

10   Ibid., p. 183.

despite what distinguishes them. However, the very fact of accentuating what renders them similar, no matter how dissimilar they may otherwise be, has the effect of shifting their dissimilarity to the background. Two things which are 'the same' are valued the same. It is easy to conclude, based on what they are worth, that they are the same.

Mathematical or algebraic equality, as distinguished from proportional equality, therefore contains in itself a principle of non-differentiation. Applied to human beings, it means that no difference exists between them that is of such a nature as to relativise what does not distinguish them. Understood in this way, equality leads to the elimination of every immeasurable part that specifies the human subject. But abstract equality is also a fundamentally economic notion, for it is only on the economic terrain, in relation to the universal equivalent of money, that it can be situated, measured, and verified. Economics, along with moral philosophy (but for different reasons), is the preferred domain in which equality can be appreciated because its unit of account, the monetary unit, is by definition interchangeable. One Franc or one Euro is worth any Franc or Euro. Only the quantity, the specified quantity, varies. Political or legal equality is a completely different thing. As to equality which is neither economic, political, or legal, it is not susceptible to any precise definition. Any doctrine which claims that this is so is a metaphysic.

In the modern era, human emancipation has long been associated with the desire for equality more than liberty. Inequality was posed as an *a priori* oppressive structure (which has actually often been the case); liberty, however, was in some way condemned to deny itself to the extent that, by allowing, indeed aggravating inequalities, it lead to the creation of new oppression. It is in reference to this that certain authors, like Norberto Bobbio, have been able to see the ideal of equality as the central operator of the left-right divide. 'Those in favour of equality', writes Bobbio, 'generally think that the vast majority of the inequalities which outrage them and which they would like to eliminate are of social origin and, following from this, that they can be suppressed, whereas those in favour of inequality generally think that these inequalities are by contrast natural, and therefore inescapable'.[11]

---

11   Norberto Bobbio, *Destra e sinistra. Ragioni et significati di una distinzione politica*, Donzelli, Roma 1994 (trad. fr.: *Droite et gauche: Essai sur une distinction politique*, Seuil, Paris 1996).

Is this still true today? It seems to me that in the opinion of people of all persuasions, it is henceforth better to realise that the equality of conditions is not highly possible, nor even strongly desirable. We believe less and less that all inequalities are of a social origin. Conversely, we can certainly see that too many financial inequalities are politically and socially unsupportable, without having to believe in the natural equality of individuals. (Moreover, it is a commonplace in classical thought to assert that too much wealth destroys virtue). We also realise that the cultural increase in volume and standardisation carried out in the name of equality and under the cover of 'democratisation' has more often served the interests of large corporations than the ideals of democracy. We aim for an equality of opportunity more often than an equality of results. We attempt to make the distinction between just and unjust, tolerable and intolerable inequalities, which is tantamount to admitting that inequality in and of itself, as well as equality, no longer means anything.

More than equality, the accent is now placed on equity or fairness, which consists not in giving the same thing to everyone, but in making sure that each gets his due as much as possible. Even in economic matters, the left, rather than aspiring towards equality itself, seeks the sustainable maximisation of the minimum (*maximin*), that is to say, a compensation or a redistribution that allocates the most possible to those who possess the least, all the while taking account, in their own interest, of the positive effect that certain economic disparities can have on the incentive to invest or save. John Rawls has been one of the first to present in a systematic manner — but it is true, from an essentially procedural perspective — a theoretical basis for the need for equality to be subordinated to the need for equity.[12] 'Equity', writes Julien Freund, 'is the form of justice that accepts from the outset the plurality of human activities, the plurality of ends and aspirations, the plurality of interests and ideas, and which strives to operate by compensation in the unequal game of reciprocities.'[13]

In regards to democratic equality, so poorly understood, for different reasons, by the right as well as the left, it is first necessary to comprehend it as an intrinsically political notion. Democracy implies the political equality of its citizens, and not at all their 'natural' equality. As Carl Schmitt remarks, 'the

---

12   John Rawls, *Théorie de la justice*, Seuil, 1987.

13   Op. cit., p. 186.

equality of everything "that has a human face" is incapable of providing the foundation for a state, a state form, or a form of government. No distinctions or demarcations can be derived [...] Nothing distinctive can be deduced in morality, religion, politics, or economics from the fact that all people are human [...] The idea of human equality does not furnish any legal, political, or economic criteria [...] An equality that has no contents except for the equality common to all men will be an apolitical equality, because it lacks the corollary of a possible inequality. All equality draws its significance and its meaning from its correlation to a possible inequality. This equality becomes all the more intense and important as the inequality opposing it grows. An equality without the possibility of inequality, an equality that one has intrinsically and that one can never lose, is without value and indifferent".[14]

Like any political notion, democratic equality indicates the possibility of a distinction. It sanctions a common membership in a precise political entity. The citizens of a democratic country enjoy equal political rights, not because their competencies are the same, but because they are equally citizens of their country. Likewise, the universal right to vote is not an endorsement of the intrinsic equality of the voters (one man, one vote). It no longer has the purpose of determining the truth. It is the logical consequence of this that the voters are equally citizens, and have a duty to express their preferences and to allow the record of their consent or disagreement. Political equality, the condition of all the others (in democracy, people represent the constituent power) therefore has nothing abstract, it is to the highest degree substantial. Already among the Greeks, *isonomia* did not mean that the citizens are equal in nature or competency, nor even that the law must be equal for all, but that everyone possessed the entitlement to participate in public life. Democratic equality therefore implies a common belonging, and by means of this contributes to the definition of an identity. This term 'identity' refers at once to that which distinguishes — the singularity or uniqueness — and to that which lets those who share this singularity identify themselves. 'The word "identity"', remarks Carl Schmitt, 'characterises the existential aspect of political unity, in contrast to any normative, schematic, or fictional forms of equality'.[15]

---

14   Carl Schmitt, *Théorie de la Constitution*, PUF, Paris 1993, pp. 363–365.

15   Ibid., pp. 372–373.

The first consequence that results from this is that 'the essential notion of democracy is the people and not humanity. If democracy must remain in a political form, then there are only peoples' democracies and not a democracy of humanity'.[16] The second consequence is that the corollary of the equality of the citizens resides in their non-equality with those who are not citizens. 'Political democracy', continues Schmitt, 'cannot rest on the absence of a distinction between all men, but only on the quality of belonging to a particular people, a belonging which can be determined by a diversity of factors — the idea of a common race, a common faith, a common destiny and tradition. The equality that forms part of the very essence of democracy only therefore applies itself to the interior (of a State) and not to the exterior: within the democratic state, all nationals are equal. The consequence of this for the political question and for that of the public right is: whoever is not a citizen has nothing to do with this democratic equality'.[17] It is in this sense that 'democracy as principle of political form opposes itself to the liberal ideas of the individual's freedom and equality with every other individual. If a democratic State recognised the ultimate consequences of universal human equality in the domain of public life and of public right, it would strip itself of its own substance'.[18]

It would therefore be a serious error to oppose abstract equality with a simple principle of inequality. Inequality is not the opposite of equality, but its corollary: one only has meaning in relation to the other. The opposite of equality is incommensurable. Moreover, as we can only be equal or unequal within a specified relationship, there is no equal or unequal in a pure sense. A society where only inequality would reign is also unthinkable, and would be as completely unliveable as a society in which there was only equality. Every society contains and can only contain hierarchical relations and egalitarian relations simultaneously, and both are also necessary to its proper functioning. As Julien Freund writes, 'equality is one of the normal configurations of social relationships, as is hierarchy. Egalitarianism, by contrast, regards the entirety of these relationships under the exclusive or predominant aspect of equality'.[19] Freund continues: 'Egalitarianism is the ideological doctrine that attempts to

---

16   Ibid., p. 371.
17   Ibid., p. 365.
18   Ibid., p. 371.
19   Op. cit., p. 19.

make believe that there would be a uniform and universal relationship capable of subsuming the diverse relationships of equality which engender a plurality of equalities [...] A uniform, exclusive, and universal relationship implies that there would be a uniform point of view that will be the reason for all points of view. Now the idea of a uniform point of view, exclusive and universal, is contradictory to the very notion of a point of view'.[20] That which is best in equality is in fact known as reciprocity: mutual assistance, concrete solidarity, a system of giving and receiving.[21] Equality and inequality are based in some sort of reciprocity.

*

'I hold the history of the world and of societies', writes sociologist Paul Yonnet, 'to be wholly interpretable according to two broad principles: the principle of equalisation, and that of differentiation (or the tendency towards similitude and the tendency towards variance), and between these two principles, relationships of rebalancing are always established, as well as relationships of compensation (whether true, false, symbolic, or real), and even of consolation'.[22] I share this point of view, and it is why I think that, behind the egalitarian rhetoric, it is actually necessary to read something else: the rise of the aspiration towards homogeneity, towards the reabsorption of differences; the rise of what we could call the ideology of the Same.[23]

The ideology of the Same proceeds from what is common to all men. It proceeds by only taking account of what is common to them and by interpreting them as the Same. In the absence of a precise criteria allowing them to be concretely appreciated, equality is but another name for the Same. The ideology of the Same therefore poses universal human equality as an equality in and of itself, disconnected from any concrete element that would allow us to precisely confirm or deny this equality. It is an ideology allergic to everything which is specific, which interprets all distinction as potentially devaluing,

---

20 Ibid., pp. 181–182.

21 *dons et contre-dons*, literally 'gifts and counter-gifts', or 'offers and counter-offers'. A process of reciprocal exchange is indicated by the context: thus 'giving and receiving', or perhaps 'giving and returning'. — Tr.

22 Paul Yonnet, 'Diversité, différence', in *Une certaine idée*, 4ᵉtrim. 2000, p. 94.

23 *Le Même*, 'the Same' or 'Sameness'. When used in a philosophical sense, it is often contrasted with *l'Autre*, 'Otherness'. — Tr.

which holds differences as contingent, transitory, inessential, or secondary. Its driving force is the idea of Uniformity.[24] Uniformity is that which cannot bear Otherness, and which aims to bring everything back to unity: a uniform God, a uniform civilisation, a uniform way of thinking. The ideology of the Same remains largely dominant today. It is at once the basic norm (in the sense of Kelsen's *Grundnorm*) from which all the others proceed, and the sole norm of an era without norms that does not want to know any others.

This ideology is meant to be both descriptive and normative, since it poses a fundamental identification of all men as an established fact and as a desirable and realisable goal — without ever (or rarely) questioning the origin of this disparity between what is already here and the reality to come. It thus seems to proceed from that which is to that which must-be. But in reality, it is on the basis of its own normativity, of its own conception of what should be, that it postulates an imaginary unitary existence, a simple reflection of the mentality which inspires it.

To the degree that it asserts the fundamental identification of individuals, the ideology of the Same naturally clashes with everything that, in concrete life, differentiates them. It must therefore explain that differences are only fundamentally insignificant secondary specifications. Mankind may certainly differ in appearance, but he is nonetheless the same. Essence and existence are thus disjointed, like soul and body, spirit and matter, and even rights (posited from the attributes of 'human nature') and duties (which are only exercised within a social relationship in a precise context). Concrete existence is no more than a deceptive covering that prevents us seeing the essential. It follows that the ideology of the Same is not itself unitary in its postulate. Heir to the myth of Plato's cave as well as to the theological distinction between created and uncreated being, it is of a dualist structure and inspiration, in the sense that it

---

24 *L'Unique* generally means 'only, single, sole' as well as 'unique', but here it clearly has the sense of 'uniform', or 'uniformity' (rather than 'uniqueness'). Frequently capitalised in Benoist's French, *l'Unique* is contrasted with the idea of *l'Autre*. The word *autre* simply means 'other', but when capitalised and taking the definite article — *l'Autre*, 'the Other', 'Otherness' — it situates itself within a long tradition of philosophical usage, from Hegel to Saïd. The opposition between *l'Unique* and *l'Autre* thus evokes the related polarity of 'Sameness' and 'Difference' (*le Même* and *la Différence*), also frequently employed by Benoist. *L'Unique* as 'Uniformity' thus emphasises the sense of homogeneity (rather than uniqueness) implied in this context. That which is uniform has only one single form; it is opposed by difference and otherness: a diversity of forms. — Tr.

cannot assert the perspective of the Same without basing itself on something exterior to or transcendent of diversity.

In order to eradicate diversity, in order to lead humanity to political and social unity, the ideology of the Same has the most frequent recourse, in its profane formulations, to theories that place the cause of these distinctions that they regard as a transitory evil in the social superstructure: the effects of domination, the influence of education or environment. (We note in passing that the theories in question identify the immediate causes of the state of affairs that they deplore, but do not question the cause of these causes, that is to say, their initial origin, or the reasons why they constantly re-emerge). Evil (*fons et origo malorum*)[25] is thus placed outside of man, as if the exterior was not primarily the product of the interior. In modifying the external causes, the inner being of man can be transformed, or his true 'nature' can be made to appear. In order to achieve this, recourse is sometimes had to authoritarian and coercive methods, sometimes to social conditionings or counter-conditionings, sometimes to 'dialogue' and the 'appeal to reason', without however obtaining better results in one case or another — the failure never being attributed to an error in the original postulates, but to the still-inefficient character of the means employed. The underlying idea is that of a pacified or perfect society, or at least of a society that would become 'just' as soon as one could make all the exterior contingencies disappear that impede the advent of Sameness.

The ideology of the Same was first formulated on the theological plane. It appeared in the west with the Christian idea that all men, regardless of their own characteristics, regardless of what the particular context of their own existence might be, are bearers of a soul in equal relationship to God. All men are by nature equal in the dignity of having been created in the image of the one and only God. This is the reason why Christian society, so widespread that it has been able to endure through the ages, develops from the ideal of One collective body (and power). Hence the observation from Hannah Arendt on 'the monotheistic representation of God — of the God from which man is supposed to have been created': 'From here, only man can exist, men being only a more or less successful repetition of the Same'.[26] The corollary, which has been developed at length by Augustine, is that of a humanity which

---

25   Latin: 'source and origin of misery'. — Tr.

26   Hannah Arendt, *Qu'est-ce que la politique ?*, Seuil, Paris, 1995, p. 42.

is fundamentally one, whose components will all be called to evolve in the same direction by realising among them an ever-greater convergence. It is the Christian root of the idea of progress. Brought down to earth, through the slow process of secularisation, this idea will give birth to that of a common reason for all — 'one and complete in everyone', Descartes will say — which all mankind participates in by very reason of his humanity. 'Thanks to the representation of a world history', adds Hannah Arendt, 'the multiplicity of mankind is melded into a human individual that we call Humanity'.[27]

This is not the place to examine the way in which the ideology of the Same has engendered in the midst of western culture all the normative/repressive strategies so well described by Michel Foucault. Recall only that the Nation-State, in the course of its historical trajectory, is less concerned to integrate than to assimilate, that is to say, to reduce differences even more by making global society uniform. This movement has been furthered and accelerated by the Revolution of 1789 which, faithful to the spirit of geometry, imposed the suppression of all intermediary bodies that the Ancien Régime had allowed to subsist. We no longer want to know anything but humanity and, together with this, a citizenry whose function is conceived as participation in the universality of public affairs. Jews become 'citizens like the others', women become 'men like the others'. That which specifies them in particular, belonging to a gender or to a people, is deemed non-existent or is obliged to make itself invisible by confining itself to the private sphere. 'The form of the One, from the age of heteronomy', remarks Marcel Gauchet, 'will command even the most radical versions of autonomy. The ultimate promise with which the future will be charged will be the restoration or establishment of the collective unity [...] The driving question of the ideologies, from this angle, may be summarised in the following manner: how to produce the One collective that produced religion by a means other than religion'.[28] In effect, the great modern ideologies dream variously of the unification of the world by the market, of a 'homogenous' society purged of all 'foreign' social negativity, or of a humanity reconciled with itself by having finally come into its own. The political ideal will be the

---

27   Ibid.

28   Marcel Gauchet, 'Croyances religieuses, croyances politiques', in *Le Débat*, May–August 2001, p. 10.

progressive effacement of borders that arbitrarily separate men. We will say: 'citizens of the world', as if the 'world' was (or could be) a political entity.

But the ideology of the Same has not only cast the theoretical foundations for egalitarianism. It has also permitted colonialism (in the name of the entitlement of those who are further developed along the path of human convergence to make those who lag behind 'progress'), while inside Nation-States, they legitimise repression against all kinds of supposed deviations from 'general' norms. In the modern era, this tendency toward homogeneity has been pushed to the maximum in totalitarian societies by a central power installing itself as the only source of possible legitimacy. In western postmodern societies, the same result has been obtained by the commodification of the world. It is a gentler yet more effective process: the degree of homogeneity of current western societies largely exceeds that of the totalitarian societies of the past century.

The universalist focus, which tends toward unity, is always correlated with individualism, which leads to separation and dissociation. The ideology which aims the most at the unification of the world is thus the very one that engenders the most division. Such is the strongest contradiction of the ideology of the Same. The universalist focus is necessarily linked to individualism, for it can only present humanity as fundamentally one by conceiving it as composed of individual units envisaged as abstractly as possible, that is to say, outside of any context or form of mediation. This is why it aims to make everything that puts a veil between the individual and humanity disappear: popular cultures, intermediary bodies, differentiated ways of life. We see here that difference and division must not be confused. The ideology of the Same extends its grip by destroying differences, but also by destroying that which ordains these differences, the supple structures, themselves differentiated, in which they inhere. By attacking differences that are always organically ordered, it evokes fragmentation and division at the same time. In the absence of an integrating framework, the fever of the One leads to the dissolution of social cohesion.

The rise of individualism, for which the liberals congratulate themselves, has thus engendered by a perfect logic the advent of the welfare-state, which dismays them. The more the communal structures collapse, the more the State will come to take charge of the security of individuals. Conversely, the more it secures them, the more it deprives them 'of the maintenance of family or communal belongings, which were previously indispensable protections'.[29] Dialectical movement and vicious circle: on one hand, the differentiated society defeats itself; on the other, the homogenising state progresses at the same rate as individualism. The more isolated individuals there are, the more the State can treat them uniformly.

Being both concurrent and opposed to each other, the great clash of modern ideologies has further aggravated the divisions and dissociations produced by the spreading of individualism. The paradoxical result has only made them stronger in their ambition: facing the spectre of 'anarchy', of 'social dissolution', of class struggle, of civil war or social anomie, they have only pleaded with greater force for alignment in the present and levelling in the future. 'The very ones who assiduously cast into relief the scale and the inexpiable character of the antagonisms that stir the societies of their times', Marcel Gauchet further notes, 'do so in order to emphasise by contrast the promise of resolving the contradictions that the future bears. This is typically the case with Marx. The spectacle of the convulsions that tear the present only serve to reinforce the faith and hope in the unity to come'.[30] The problem is that the ideology of the Same can only demand the radical exclusion of that which cannot be reduced to the Same. Irreducible alterity becomes the prime enemy, which must be eradicated forever. This is the resort of all the totalitarian ideologies: it must eliminate these 'excessive men' who by their very existence are the obstacle to the advent of a homogenous society or a unified world. Whoever speaks in the name of 'humanity' inevitably places his adversaries outside humanity.

The conflicting logic of universalism and individualism is not the only contradiction operating in the ideology of the Same. The latter, for example, sometimes argues from the idea of 'human nature' — of a 'human nature' reconstructed on the basis of its own postulates — and sometimes by asserting that natural determinations are secondary and that man never assumes his humanity better than when he frees himself from these contingent determinations. These two affirmations contradict each other — and the second is equally contradictory in relation to scientist ideology, according to which man

---

29 Marcel Gauchet, *La religion dans la démocratie. Parcours de la laïcité*, Gallimard, Paris 1998, pp. 68–69.

30 Art. Cit., p. 10.

can be integrally explained as no more than a natural object, such that 'there is nothing to know of him that the natural sciences cannot one day unveil'.[31]

The corollary of abstract equality is the principle of in-difference. The logical consequence is that, if all men have value, all their opinions have value too. From here arises contemporary relativism and the liberal theory of the necessary neutrality of the State for everything at the level of values and finalities (the 'good life' in the Aristotelian sense). But this neutrality can only be apparent, for the very fact of choosing to be neutral has nothing neutral about it. What is more, the liberals obviously do not admit that anti-liberal theories can have the same value as liberal theories. And the opinion that all opinions are valid is clearly not prevented from mobilising itself against some opinions, beginning with the statement that all opinions are not valid.[32]

There is an obvious contradiction between planetary homogenisation and the defence of the cause of nations, which implies the recognition and the maintenance of their plurality. We cannot defend both the ideal of a unified world and the right of peoples to self-determination, for nothing guarantees that they will determine themselves in the sense of this ideal. Equally, one cannot defend pluralism as the legitimisation and respect for differences while advocating for the equalisation of conditions which will reduce these differences. Finally, and above all, if all men on earth are 'the same as each other', what good is it to proclaim the inalienable rights of unique individuals? How can one celebrate both what makes us singularly irreplaceable and what renders us virtually interchangeable? Certainly, we can always dance around it with formulas, such as 'equality in difference'. But this expression has no meaning: it only refers to an in-different difference. One cannot sustain the right to difference while thinking that the thing that makes people the Same is fundamentally more constitutive of their social identity than that by which they distinguish themselves from each other. Pietro Barcellona has very aptly spoken of the 'tragedy of equality' in order to qualify the paradox according to which one could, by resorting to the notion of equality, at once disqualify all forms of hierarchy and guarantee 'diversity, the unique character of individuals'.

*

---

31   Alain Supiot, 'La function anthropologique du droit', in *Esprit*, February 2001, p. 153.

32   Cf. on this subject the book by Philippe Béneton, *Les fers de l'opinion*, PUF, Paris 2000.

Even though it will be vain to oppose abstract equality with an inequality that is likewise just as abstract, it will be erroneous in my opinion to attempt to oppose nationalism or ethnocentrism to the ideology of the Same. Historically, both have actually realised, on a small scale, what the ideology of the Same has realised at large. Both of them remain predominantly locked in what Heidegger, who makes it the most essential feature of modernity, rightly calls the metaphysics of subjectivity.

Nationalism and ethnocentrism see the people or the nation like liberalism sees the individual: as a fundamentally 'free' being, drawing its rights as well as its attributes from its unlimited 'liberty', who could only be constrained by its own will within the horizon of selfish action and the search for the best interest. The independence to which they aspire, conceived as absolute freedom of movement, as a position in which one does not depend on anything, where one could arbitrarily choose everything that one wants, is itself modelled on the liberal ideal of the autonomy of individuals. From this perspective, the universal struggle of nations and people is only a projection on a vaster scale of inter-personal competition, where the court of history plays the role of the market. The dogma of the sovereignty of the State is also tied to this metaphysic of subjectivity, tending in the final analysis towards solipsism, which places the individual, the self, at the centre of the world, and only sees in this world an object of the self's will and representation. Here, the 'self' or 'me' is simply replaced by 'we'. An ethnocentric people is only interested in itself. It judges events and situations only by the good or bad results that it can expect. It is obviously the negation of all justice and all truth. But it is also the opposite of organicism, for the same principle of organicism is democratic solidarity and social reciprocity, in contrast to the principle of association based solely on common interests. Just as universalism is only an ethnocentrism expanded to the limits of the universe, so too is nationalism only a collective individualism. In both cases, what is ignored is the sense of particularity and of concrete universals.

Ethnocentrism is also founded on a faulty conception of identity. Identity is not an essence, but a substance that is constructed every day. It is not that which never changes, but that which maintains itself amidst change. It is ultimately always reflexive, which means that the constitution of the self always takes place through exchange with others. This is why the defence of identities can only truly proceed on the basis of a comprehension of alterity.

Like universalism, ethnocentrism is wholly allergic to the Other and always has the tendency to regard it as an 'excessive' entity. The only difference is that ethnocentrism is more brutal. Whereas universalism tends to deny alterity by reducing the Other to the Same, ethnocentrism tends to reduce diversity by eliminating the Other or by keeping it radically separated. In both approaches, alterity is considered devoid of interest, and diversity devoid of value. Conversely, the positive conception of alterity consists in recognising difference without using it as an argument to submit the existence of some to the desires, the interests, or the reason of the others. Oppression does not only deny the liberty of the oppressed, but also that of the oppressor. This is what Marx meant to say when he wrote that 'a nation cannot become free and at the same time continue to oppress other nations'.[33] We know the dialectic of the master and the slave: the two roles are inevitably exchanged. Whoever has colonised should not be surprised to be invaded in turn. Whoever destroys the identity of another does not reinforce his own, but renders it more vulnerable, even more threatened in a world that has just lost a little more of its diversity.

The principle of diversity is better suited to oppose the ideology of the Same. A principle draws its power from its very generality. The diversity of the world constitutes its only true wealth, for this diversity is foundational to the most precious good: identity. Nations are no more interchangeable than people. To say that no one inherently possesses more or less value than another is not to suggest that they are the same — the Same under various guises — but that they are all different. Tolerance, if this word has any meaning, does not consist in looking at the Other in order to see the Same in it, but to understand what constitutes it as an other, that is to say, to grasp the alterity, a reality irreducible to all 'comprehension' by the mere projection of self. Differentialism does not prohibit the bearing of value judgements, any more than it condemns a relativism ignorant of truth. But it forbids itself from mentally fixing on an overarching abstract position, from placing itself as the dominant instance (because "universal" or because "superior") through which it will be possible, indeed necessary, to impose a way of being on other nations

---

33 Karl Marx and Friedrich Engels, 'On Poland', originally published in the *Deutsche-Brüsseler-Zeitung*, December 9, 1847. — Tr.

which is not theirs. When Aristotle defined the best form of government as that in which all the citizens participate both in the enacted and undergone dominion,[34] he admittedly states a general principle that goes well beyond the borders of the Greek city, but which does not exclude the ability for other people to give different laws.

It is not a matter of falling into naïve idealism.[35] Identities can clash with one another; differences can assert themselves at the expense of others. In this instance, it is perfectly normal to defend the identity that one belongs to as a matter of priority. But this is a very different thing from defending its identity against an abusive self-affirmation (colonisation, immigration, etc.) perpetrated by another, and of assuming that the only identity that has value is the one to which it is attached. The principle of diversity is not disputed by the first attitude, but it is by the second.

It is no longer a matter of passing from one excess to another by privileging what differs to the point of neglecting what is common. The difference alone is more important. It is more important firstly because it is that which specifies, which defines the identity, which makes of each person or each nation an irreplaceable being. It is more important secondly because belonging to humanity is never immediate, but on the contrary always mediated: one exists only by virtue of the fact that one belongs to one of the cultures or constituent collectives of humanity. ('I have seen in the course of my life men of all kinds', Joseph de Maistre once said, 'but man as such I have never met'). It is more important, finally, because it is from the singularity that one can access the universal, and not the inverse, which would consist in deducing from a universal posited *a priori* an abstract idea of the singularity. All concrete existence turns out to be indissociable from a particular context, from one or many specific belongings. All belonging is certainly a limitation, but it is a limitation that releases us from others. The dream of the unconditioned is only a dream.

'Men fear the Same, and there lies the source of racism', Jean-Pierre Dupuy has noted. 'That which men fear', he adds, 'is non-differentiation, and this because non-differentiation is always the sign and the product of social disintegration [...] Equality, negator in principle of differences, is cause for mutual

---

34 *République* VIII, 11, 557c.

35 *angélisme.* — Tr.

fear'.[36] In effect, men fear the Same at least if not more than the Other. The dominant ideologies peacefully believe that the homogenisation of the world could only have a pacifying function because it allows a better 'understanding'. On the contrary we see how, everywhere, it evokes in turn identitarian tensions, the reawakening of secular irredentisms,[37] and the creation of convulsive nationalisms. Even within societies, the ideology of the Same further generalises the imitative rivalry so well described by René Girard, exacerbating the desire to distinguish itself with all the more force that it forbids distinction. The Same thus proves to be profoundly polemogenic.[38] At best it generalises indifference and boredom. At worst, it leads to violent reactions and unleashes the passions.

The incommensurability of individuals or cultures is not synonymous with incommunicability. It simply entails the recognition of what irreducibly distinguishes them. The ideology of the Same aspires to total transparency, but the social always implies an opaque part. Opacity lies in the incommensurable. Some think that the affirmation of differences can only make men radically estranged from each other (these are generally the ones who automatically interpret identity as a confinement), but the opposite is true. Exchange presupposes the Other. It only makes sense in so far as it is placed in the presence of an Other. An exchange of the Same with the Same can only be a monologue. Dialogue, dialogism (Martin Buber), requires alterity. Not only does the upholding of differences fail to prevent dialogue or exchange, it is the primary condition for it. It would be wrong in this regard to oppose difference, supposedly aggressive and elitist, to diversity. Diversity entails harmonised differences.

A society in which there would only be people who are 'like each other' would be a society in which individuals would become interchangeable to the point where the disappearance or elimination of any one of them would only assume a thoroughly relative importance from the viewpoint of global society. It is completely the opposite in a differentiated society. Difference,

---

36 *Différences et inégalités*, Découverte, Paris 1984.

37 *irrédentismes*, from Italian *irredento*, 'unredeemed', referring to the political desire to redeem (i.e. reclaim, reoccupy) a lost territory. — Tr.

38 French *polémogène*, something that 'generates conflict', from Greek *polemos*, 'war, polemic' + -*gen*, 'something produced'. Cf. German *Polemogen*. — Tr.

furthermore, is a factor of resistance, and therefore of liberty. If individuals and nations were fundamentally the same, or if they were completely malleable, they would be all the more vulnerable to propaganda and conditioning. That their diversity reappears without cease, that the human species will also be strongly polymorphic, shows that they are anthropologically resistant to homogenising models. Difference, ultimately, is a factor of tolerance and harmony. Societies that recognise the reality and the value of differences are also the ones that are the most capable of integrating those who are bearers of these differences. Societies which do not recognise differences, or which hold them to be insignificant, are on the contrary destined either to exclude everyone that does not correspond to the particular model chosen, or to undermine the social bond by voiding it of its organic, composite, and differentiated character.

*

The history of modernity can be comprehended, at least in part, as one of a gigantic process of uniformisation. Induced by philosophico-moral or political universalism, and by the diffusion of more effective techniques for modelling attitudes than the most centralised of dictators, it is translated in the west by the progressive eradication of differentiated modes of life, and in the third world by the acculturation and imposition of the western myth of 'development'. This process seems to reach its apogee with globalisation. The ideology of the Same today becomes 'globality' (Paul Virilio) to the degree that it tends to give birth to a world without exterior, where fluxes circulate in every sense in 'time zero'. 'Pluralism' and even 'multiculturalism', which such a great deal is made about these days, are no more than the shadow and the caricature of former particularisms, coated today by tendencies and attitudes that are more and more homogenous. Already in western countries we dress, we eat, we speak, we dwell, we distract ourselves, we live, and ultimately we think more and more in the same way. We consume the same products, we see the same shows, we listen to the same programmes. Specific cultures, linked to a professional political or religious membership, have practically disappeared. Regional cultures and languages are threatened. Modes of life inherited from the past are only conserved as spectacles for tourists, generators of gain. These are frozen memories, artificially maintained traditions, souvenirs relegated to folklore or museum displays. The only differences that subsist are connected to the level of revenue: they play upon quantities, but change little in the nature of choices and aspirations. Alongside this, uniform thought disqualifies any project that avoids the dominant norm as a dangerous utopia or a harmful form of thinking. The entire media system is itself designed to celebrate the existing reality, implicitly presented as the best (or least bad) of possible worlds, indeed as the only possible world. Its principal function being to justify adaptation to the norms of unlimited consumption, it strives to 'homogenise needs, demands, expectations, and desires'.[39] Despite the economic and social disparities, which continue to increase, the planet is united under the economic and moral horizon: on one side, the ideology of the 'rights of man', on the other, the monotheism of the market.

At the same time, in a world marked by the generalised crisis of institutions and of great systems of social integration, the collapse of the model of the Nation-State, and the increasing insignificance of territorial borders, we see the reemergence, in the form of communities and networks, of an impressive thirst for returning to one's roots. Civil society restructures itself spontaneously by recreating groups and 'tribes' which seek remedies to the increasing non-differentiation of roles, to widespread circulation, to the systematic flattening of basic sociabilities, by reintroducing alterity into daily and local life, by resorting to direct democracy and to the principle of subsidiarity. This very phenomenon, by its rapid 'viral' expansion, shows that we have already departed from modernity. The desire for equality, superseding the desire for liberty, was the great passion of modern times. Those of postmodern times will be the desire for identity.

This postmodern preoccupation takes the form of a will to see recognised in the public sphere — and no longer merely in the private sphere, where modernity had restricted them in the name of republican universalism or of an ideal of axiological 'neutrality' — one or more aspects of collective belonging that are considered constituents of identity. This reclamation bears upon forms of belonging (cultural, ethnic, linguistic, regional, religious, sexual, etc.) that are inherited or chosen, enduring or transient; yet in all cases it is no longer primarily tolerance that is sought, but recognition and respect. Whereas the Nation-State fixed itself tendentiously on the object of abolishing all distinctions, all intermediary bodies which prevented it from being the exclusive incarnation of the social whole and the guarantor of its unity, it now

---

39 Pierre-André Taguieff, *Marianne*, 21 May 2001, p. 68.

recognises associations and communities and allows them to permanently develop themselves on their own, either because they are by nature irreducible to any political handling, or because their principal purpose is their very self-existence. This type of aspiration shows well that communities, far from aiming to confine themselves, want to become constituents in full right of the global society. At the same time, it contradicts a political model that only conceives of the social contract as something concluded among individuals who were not previously united by anything. The growing place of the identitarian question in postmodern democracies thus pushes to open up the space of political democracy to the collective identities themselves. Identity becomes (again) one of the conditions of the practical application of citizenship.

Modernity has been the era of the total mobilisation of the masses, a substitute for the evangelisation of the crowds. The postmodern era pushes for the affirmation of dispersed identities, as much on the individual plane as on the collective. But this tendency is not lacking in ambiguity. Independently of the fact that it develops on the basis of unprecedented social homogenisation (end of peasantry, disappearance of domesticity, reassimilation of working conditions, growing alignment of masculine-feminine social roles), it sometimes recovers a 'pluralism' which has scarcely any connection to genuine diversity. A typical example of this false pluralism is the multiplication of different brands to market the same product. More generally, false pluralism is what brings the democratic game back to the competitive action of established pressure groups. The multiplication of micro-differences, of artificial or superficial differences, can give the illusion of pluralism while losing sight of the deeper meaning of the notion of difference. The idea that a particular people can possess a vision of the world, a way of experiencing its presence in the world in a manner radically distinct from our own, then becomes increasingly unintelligible.

Postmodern identities, on the other hand, differ significantly enough from traditional identities. They have lost their 'naturalness' or 'objectivity'. 'A genuinely accustomed order, an order lived as wholly received', observes Marcel Gauchet, 'is an a-subjective order from the point of view of the identity of those who inhabit and implement it. [Today] it is rigorously to the contrary: the appropriation of collective characteristics is the vehicle of a personal singularisation. Belonging is subjectifying because it is reclaimed and vindicated, and it is cultivated for the subjectification that it produces'.[40] In other words, identities are now based less on objective data than they are on the result of a subjective decision. In the past, belongings, by the very fact of their anteriority/authority, prohibited the ability to truly choose them. Today, even inherited belongings are also chosen belongings to the degree that they only become effective when we decide to recognise them. They have no other power than that which we agree to attribute to them.

However, the general problematic has not changed. It is always a matter of knowing whether the ideology of the Same will eventually prevail. And it is here that I add what I wrote in 1977 in the introduction to *View from the Right*: 'What is the principal menace today? It is the progressive demise of the world's diversity'. Today we rightly emphasise the importance of biodiversity. But biodiversity cannot only concern the animal and vegetable species. It is also valid for cultures and peoples.

*

I have not changed a word of the text of *View from the Right*. This book, which already speaks a lot about 'cultural power' and the necessary battle of ideas, remains essential for current events. But it also represents a step in a personal itinerary, and honesty obliges me to say that today I would write some of the chapters completely differently. My feelings on subjects such as technology, the city, or ecology, for example, have profoundly evolved. I also think I have been unfair to authors such as Herbert Marcuse, Ivan Illich, or Edgar Morin. Such as it is, the work nevertheless remains a sort of panoramic guide consecrated to the men and debates of the seventies. Ten years later, the historian of ideas that I became would have obviously made reference to other names. Twenty years later, even more would have been cited. In consulting these pages, I am reminded that at the time that *View from the Right* appeared, what one then called the 'thought of the right' was still represented in France by the true intellectual masters: Thierry Maulnier, Louis Rougier, Jules Monnerot, Bertrand de Jouvenel, Raymond Aron, Pierre Gaxotte, Georges Dumézil, François Perroux, Julien Freund, Stéphane Lupasco, Raymond Ruyer, Raymond Abellio. I have the impression that none of them have been replaced.

ALAIN DE BENOIST

---

40 *La religion dans la démocratie*, op. cit., p. 92.

Introduction

From the right? Indeed.[41] A French chief of state has said that our fellow citizens wanted to be governed 'from the centre'. But from the centre of what? From the centre of the left? And how would there even be a left without a right? For the men of the left, the very refusal to speak of the right is a characteristic of the men of the right. The title of this book seems to escape this rule. In reality, this is only half true. Personally, the question of knowing whether I am of the right or not is completely irrelevant to me. For the time being, the ideas supported in this work are *to* the right; they are not necessarily *of* the right. I can still quite easily imagine some situations where they could be to the *left*. It is not the ideas that have changed; the political landscape has evolved. We will see this happen over time. On the other hand, we cannot perpetually sit on the fence. We thus accept this term, *right*; for words, after all, are not things. And saying that in France, at the end of the 1970s, during an era in which the entire world, or seemingly so, speaks from the left, to be 'of the right' is still the best way to be *somewhere else*.

Jean-François Revel has defined the doctrine of the right as 'one which by principle and without dissimulation bases authority upon something other than the inalienable sovereignty of the citizens' (*Lettre ouverte à la droite*, Albin Michel, 1968).[42] This definition seems a little brief to me. It gives rise to the understanding that in the regimes of the left, authority always belongs to the 'sovereign people'. We have good reasons for doubting this (and Revel certainly has them too). Indeed, it should be admitted that the doctrines of the left develop from those of the right once they have passed into the realm of fact — but that would be unfair. I will not define the right any more by a taste for order and authority. All human society rests on these notions (whatever

---

41 Here Benoist appears to play on the word *voire*, 'indeed' and the verb *voir* 'to see, view' which alludes to the title of the book: *Vu de Droite*, literally 'viewed from the right'. — Tr.

42 *Open Letter to the Right.* — Tr.

1

may have been said previously by those who established them), all *power* implies a governed minority and a governing majority, and this desire seems the most common thing in the world to me. Ultimately, I will not retain the distinctions made by René Rémond (*La droite en France*. Aubier-Montaigne, 1963),[43] between a traditionalist, monarchist right, a liberal, 'Orléanist' right, and a plebiscitary and Bonapartist right. Although they still correspond to a certain reality, these distinctions will not be of any use here.

The *minimum minimorum* will evidently be to define any current that rejects the left in an *explicit* manner as being of the right. I would like to introduce a restrictive nuance, however. I hereby define *the right*, by pure convention, as the consistent attitude to view the diversity of the world, and by consequence the relative inequalities that are necessarily the product of this, as a positive thing; and the progressive homogenisation of the world, extolled and effected by two-thousand years of egalitarian ideology, as a negative thing. I call *of the right* those doctrines that believe that the relative inequalities of existence induce the *relations of force* of which *historical becoming* is the product — and which deem that *history must continue* — in short, that 'life is life, that is to say a *combat*, for a nation as for a man' (Charles de Gaulle). In other words, in my eyes the enemy is not 'the left' or 'communism' or even 'subversion', but rather this *egalitarian ideology* whose formulations, religious or lay, metaphysical or supposedly 'scientific', have continued to flourish for over two thousand years, whose 'ideas of 1789' were but a step, and of which communism and the current subversion are the inevitable outcome.

Of course, this does not mean that all inequality will necessarily be just, in my view. On the contrary, there are numerous inequalities that are perfectly unjust; and often these are ones that our egalitarian society allows to subsist anyway. To profess an anti-egalitarian conception of the world is to believe that diversity is a *fact of life*, and that this diversity leads to actual inequalities; that society must take these inequalities into account and admit that the value of people in relation to different things is incommensurable from one person to the next. It is to deem that in social relations, this value is essentially measured by the responsibilities that each assumes, relative to their concrete aptitudes; that liberty resides in the effective possibility of fulfilling these responsibilities;

---

43 *The Right in France.* — Tr.

that these responsibilities correspond to proportionate rights, and that the result is a hierarchy based upon the principle *unicuique suum*.[44]

In a country where everyone recognises that, with rare interludes — the Popular Front, the Mendès-France experiment, etc. — the left has never occupied *political* power, rare are the men who declare themselves of the right. 'Maintained for over a century by parties, considerable periodicals, and eminent theoreticians', observes Gilbert Comte, 'the right itself no longer offers any readily admitted official representation'. He adds, not without reason: 'The reluctance of the current right to wear its proper colours certainly does not deceive anyone. Beyond the opportunism, the versatility of individuals, it betrays the persistence of a deep problem, of a kind of moral fracture, even within contemporary France' (*Le Monde diplomatique*, January 1977).[45]

The reticence of the right to define itself as such has numerous causes. The most noble, we will be tempted to say, is an implicit refusal to appear as the representative of a *part* of the reality of things. The right deeply feels the division of the national community into *parts* (and *parties*) as the beginning of what it contests — the commencement of civil war. Consciously or not, it rejects the tendency to give reality a *single* explanation. It rejects all the great *reductive unilateralisms* founded on economics, sexuality, race, class warfare, etc. It does not like to put the world in equations. It does not believe in the coherence of a castrated worldview when contrasted against the possibilities of perception that we have — nor does it believe that there is a *destiny* for *divided* nations. In the attribution of such labels, it detects a hidden castrating manoeuver. An aftertaste of hemiplegia.

It has been said that the key words of the right's vocabulary have been discredited by the various fascisms. Let us say instead that this discrediting has been cleverly created and maintained by factions experienced in the diffusion of *debilitating* and *condemning* myths. We must be clear about this. We are not in the presence here of an *analysis*, but of a *propaganda*. This propaganda consists in assimilating every doctrine that the right affirms, with some vigour, to 'fascism', and as a corollary, to define as 'democratic' only those regimes that conceive liberty as some kind of statutory free pass for the revolutionary

---

44   Latin, 'to each his own'. — Tr.

45   *The Diplomatic World*. — Tr.

undertakings of the extreme left. By extension, this assimilation to Fascism is applied retrospectively. We thus see Ernest Kahane, from the Union rationaliste, affirm that the *œuvre* of Gobineau 'borders on crime' — which is about as intelligent as accusing Jean-Jacques Rousseau of being responsible for the gulag. Our society thus offers the surprising spectacle of a right that cannot affirm itself as such without being tarred with the brush of 'fascism', and a left, and an extreme left, that can at any moment call itself socialist, communist, or Marxist, all the while affirming, of course, that their doctrines have nothing to do with Stalinism, nor indeed with any form of historically *realised* socialism. Now, if the supporters of diverse varieties of socialism do not feel *committed* to any of the concrete experiments that have preceded them — and notably to the most criminal among them — I do not see why the modern right, which formally rejects every totalitarian temptation, should have to chastise or justify itself. Before the tremendous nerve of the partisans of a doctrine in whose name more than fifty million people have already been massacred, and who present themselves as nothing less than the defenders of freedom (holding a rose to their heart), liberty herself responds by laughing freely — and continuing on her way.

The right, unfortunately, is most often mute. I have followed numerous televised debates. They always — or almost always — follow the same scenario. Stage right,[46] the 'man of the right', usually a gentleman of a certain age, well dressed, well groomed, always smiling, full of good intentions, completely unconscious of the *stakes* of the discussion. And stage left, some young wolves of the extreme left, bearers of a worldview having *its own* consistency, refusing the least concession, versed in the art of dialectic, in the play of paradigm and syntagm, who tear their interlocutor to pieces. I think that current society is a reflection of these debates.

All of this happens in truth as if the right had lost the desire to defend itself. Criticised, harassed, scolded in every way, they remain purely passive — and practically indifferent. Accused, it has retreated into itself. Not only does it no longer respond to its adversaries, not only does it no longer seek to define itself, but it grants almost no attention to this shifting of ideas, to

---

46 *Côte cour* and *côte jardin* ('court side' and 'garden side') are French theatre terms corresponding to our 'stage right' and 'stage left'. The directions are implicit in French, but can only be translated explicitly in English. — Tr.

current controversies, to new disciplines. Or rather, it has lost interest in this development of ideas because they move away from what could strengthen it. It neglects the recent results of ethology, genetics, historiography, sociology, and microphysics. In England, the United States, and Germany, more than sixty books have appeared recently on the social and political implications of the new life sciences. In France — nothing, or scarcely anything. The book by A. S. Neill on 'anti-authoritarian' education, *Summerhill: A Radical Approach to Child Rearing*,[47] sold more than 260,000 copies. There were numerous refutations abroad. But here, silence. On Konrad Lorenz, on Dumézil, on Althusser, on Lévi-Srauss, on Gramsci, the right seems to have *nothing* to say. The right could rely upon the writings of Jules Monnerot, Raymond Aron, Debray-Ritzen, Louis Rougier, etc., but curiously, one has the feeling that it is above all by the left that they are read, by *adversaries* who are more attentive than the presumed enthusiasts. Parallel to this, the left *itself*, enacting its own perpetual process of calling everything into question, obtains results that the right should have unlocked by its own process of reflection. It is therefore the left, not the right, who critiques the myth of an absolute 'progress' linked to the absurd idea of a meaning to history. It is the left who, after having supported the idea that celebration is essentially revolutionary (the thesis of Jean Duvignaud, *Fêtes et civilisations*. Weber, 1973)[48] discerns today that it is above all conservative (the works of Mona Ozouf). It is the left who, after having exalted the hope of equal opportunities in schools, now sees it as a 'mystification' (Christopher Jencks, *Inequality: A Reassessment of the Effect of Family and Schooling*. Basic Books, New York, 1972). It is the left that highlights the limits of a reductive, pseudo-humanist rationalism, and observes that the spirit of the masses is more transitional than revolutionary, and so forth. Little by little, the right is dispossessed of its themes and of its mental attitudes. And it even happens that the right criticises these ideas — without exploiting the contradiction of which they are the *instance* — when they are rediscovered in the ranks of the adversary, without understanding that these ideas have been drawn from their own. At the same time, the right opens the field to all *recuperations*. Having become dead or frozen, its thought is mended, restored to health, and finally annexed by a left which then becomes more *credible* than its traditional legacy;

47 Benoist cites the French translation: *Libres enfants de Summerhill* (Maspéro, 1970). — Tr.

48 *Celebrations and Civilisations*. — Tr.

it busies itself, not without success, by annexing the right's themes — themes now 'neutralised', and upon which the left performs an *inversion of meaning*.

In an extremely interesting article on 'le droite livrée au pillage' (*Le Monde diplomatique*, January 1977),[49] Paul Thibaud, director of the review *Esprit*, remarks: 'certain themes which classically belong to the right reappear with intensity in contemporary thought. The hatred for a falsely universalist abstraction which inspired Burke arose on all sides; the realist feeling for limits, and first of all of death, is a collective obsession that imposes an ecological threat; the value of rootedness in a cultural or geographic particularism has become a commonplace. But this reversal of tendencies appears to proceed without any gain for the intellectual right. All of this occurs within the left. The left plays all the roles, it formulates theses and makes objections to them, launches methods and attacks them. The intellectual contents can only be admitted in connection with the left. All nationalism must be revolutionary, all regionalism can only desire to be socialist. (…) Nothing is more characteristic than the change of status of certain authors today subject to rereading. In confronting their most virulent critics, or marginal ideas, the left renews itself. We henceforth see conferences by the left, or by leftists, on Chateaubriand, Balzac, or Péguy. Sorel comes back from the left wrapped in the baggage of Gramsci. Tocqueville becomes a reference for workers' self-management.[50] The failings of the left seem to be at the root of a new intellectual vitality, an anti-dogmatism that opens striking fields for them which were until then forbidden'.

The sociological right has always manifested a certain reticence before doctrines. And yet, in the best of cases, we have still been able to see a healthy enough reaction against a consistent form of intellectualism that only views life from the perspective of *problematisation*. Or, as the American *social workers* say so well (or so badly) — *what's your problem?* But today the struggle is unequal. Facing an adversary who advances into battle armed with a fully flourishing ideological *corpus*, the man of the right is decidedly *helpless*.

Without precise theory, no effective action. We cannot create the economy without an *idea*. And above all, we cannot put the cart before the horse. All the great revolutions of history have only served to *transpose into facts* an evolution

---

49   'The Right Delivered from Plunder', *The Diplomatic World*. — Tr.

50   *autogestionnaires*. — Tr.

already realised, in an underlying way, in the spirit. We cannot have a Lenin without having had a Marx. This is the revenge of the theoreticians — who are only the great losers of history in appearance. One of the tragedies of the right — from the 'putschist' to the moderate — is its inability to comprehend the necessity of the *long term*. The French right is 'Leninist' — without having read Lenin. It has not grasped the significance of Gramsci. It has not seen how *cultural* power threatens the apparatus of the state; how this 'cultural power' acts upon the implicit values around which the consensus indispensable to the *duration* of political power crystallises. It has not realised how direct political attack harvests the fruits of the ideological war of position. A particular kind of right peters out in little groups. Another, parliamentarily strong, always attends to what is most pressing — that is, to upcoming elections. But each time, it loses a little more ground. Due to playing the short game, the right finishes by losing the long game. As to the left, it progresses consistently. It owes this progress to the activity of its parties and its movements. But it owes it even more to the *general climate* that it has succeeded in creating *metapolitically*, and by comparison, its *political* discourse rings more and more true. Now such a task is only possible when a theory has been produced, when a distinct line with precise references has been established. In this there is a 'theoretical practice',[51] to speak with Althusser. A no before the theory = two nos before the pure application. It would be a grave error to imagine that a right that doesn't dare to speak its name can maintain its power in the long term, when its silence has let the psychological soil in which it is rooted disappear.

One of the causes of the current malaise is the progressive elimination of the substance of the State. The State depoliticises itself. Not in the sense of 'politicking' or 'party politics',[52] more present than ever. But in the meaning *of* politics. Of the essence of politics. The State becomes purely administrative. At the same time, it places itself in the position of being reversed by the powers that form themselves outside of it — and against it. The State denies its proper principle, which is a principle of authority and sovereignty, to concern itself essentially with economic and social problems. But people do not live solely for their purchasing power. They live for everything else. Never have we lived in a society so rich. Never has the standard of living of the greatest number

---

51   *pratique théorique.* — Tr.
52   *politique politicienne.* — Tr.

of people been so elevated. Never has education been so *widespread*. At the same time, however, never has unease been so great, never has protest been so strong, never has anxiety reigned so much. The state has become a prisoner of the 'pleasure principle': instead of appeasing the demand, every satisfaction given to those who demand makes it more acute. This is why the State has confined these demands to economic and social spheres. In the spiritual domain, the State no longer *says* anything, no longer offers anything, no longer exudes anything. It does not trace the outline of any *destiny*. I say that men, once their elementary needs have been met, aspire to a destiny, aspire to an authority that justifies a *project*. For only a project can give *meaning* to their lives. But the State gives no *meaning*. It furnishes no reasons for living — merely means of existing. (Nothing has value anymore, but everything has a price). And provided this role is no longer fulfilled by the State, it falls to sects, parties, pressure groups, and philosophical societies[53] to fulfil it, in disorder and confusion. Expelled from its natural sphere, politics arises everywhere.

In *Le complexe de droite* and *Le complexe de gauche* (Flammarion, 1967 and 1969),[54] Jean Plumyène and Raymond Lasierra go beyond the simple quip that the man of the right has a completely different gastronomy to the man of the left. They affirm, effectively, that no domain escapes ideology, or rather, escapes the *worldview* that one inherits or chooses. Everything is neutral outside of man. But within human society, *nothing is neutral*. Man is an animal that gives *meaning* to the things that surround him. There are different ways of seeing the world and of being-in-the-world[55] (the modes 'of the right' and 'of the left', as we have it), and they encompass both pure forms of knowledge, as well as intuitive beliefs, emotions, implicit values, daily choices, artistic sensibilities, etc. Let us be clear. I do not truly believe that there are *ideas* that are of the right and of the left. I think that there is a *way* of sustaining these ideas that is of the right and of the left. (The defence of 'nature' is no longer of the right or of the left, but there is a way of apprehending the *concept of nature* from the right and from the left). The arts, literature, fashion, symbols and

---

53 *Les sociétés de pensée* is a term that derives from the work of historian and sociologist, Augustin Cochin, specifically: *Les Sociétés de Pensée et la Démocratie: Études d'Histoire Révolutionnaire* (Plon-Nourrit et Cie., 1921). The expression literally means 'societies of thought', but is usually translated as 'philosophical societies'. — Tr.

54 *The Complex of the Right*, and *The Complex of the Left*. — Tr.

55 *Être-au-monde*, cf. Heidegger's *In-der-Welt-sein*. — Tr.

signs, nothing escapes the interpretation that a specific worldview is prone to give. In general, the individual of the left has understood this, and this is what furnishes their methodological superiority. They know what they should think, *from their point of view*, about the relations of production in the feudal era, about abstract painting, *cinema vérité*, quantum theory, or the forms of public housing. Or at least, they know that on these points as on any other, the theory that they lay claim to has something to say. The man of the right, however, is too frequently content to shrug his shoulders. He does not want to *see* so that he does not have to *do*. I feel that the right will have progressed immensely when it has: (1) understood the necessity of declaring what it is; (2) identified its 'principle enemy', that is to say, egalitarianism, the denier and *reducer* of the world's diversity; and (3) admitted that nothing in existence is 'neutral', and that it must produce its own discourse on every subject.

Before these repeated failures, a certain kind of right cowers in mere denial. This is not in its nature. The natural calling of the right resides in *approbation* — the tragic acceptance of this world and what happens here. The man of the right, constrained to denial, has generally become naïve, and no longer notices the adverse manoeuver, or else he becomes embittered, seized by the plague of *hypercriticism*. Let's be absolutely clear: instead of the best aspects of national character — the exaltation of a certain *style* — the French right has too often hypertrophied the most questionable: individualism, 'empty verbosity',[56] xenophobia. The right has neither known nor has it planned to analyse facts as fundamental as the rise of the third world to political decision-making, the Sino-Soviet conflict, the geopolitical situation created by the new division of forces, the collapse of constituted doctrines, the structural transformations of western society, the evolution of the United States, the formation of Euro-communism, etc. To these new facts, they too often answer with agreeable words and simple slogans. There is a right afflicted by Mephisto. By hypercritical derision. It is the right of rancour, bitterness, and bad temper. It believes to have won a victory on the night of General de Gaulle's death. Its sentiments are foreign to me.

---

56 *le comportement «verbomoteur»*. — Tr.

The right has become 'massist'.[57] It reassures itself by the idea of a 'silent majority' — a new avatar of the Maurrassian[58] 'real country'. It does not see that this mass is silent *prior* to being the majority — or rather, that it is only a majority in its silence. It avoids the opportunity to address the problem of the nature of the *decision-making centres* and how to access them. It believes that we have become weak because we have been 'subverted'. However, the opposite is the case: we have been 'subverted' because we have become weak. The left is only strong because of the weaknesses of the right, because of its doubts and hesitations. Admittedly, the areas of discontent in the current world are certainly not lacking. But this is not a reason to restrict ourselves to complaints. The right, with its *lamento*, contributes to an error of the left: attributing one's own responsibility to *others*. A look of lament is not an analysis. It only confirms a misunderstanding. To perform a diagnosis requires first identifying the *causes*. But the right does not identify the causes. Sometimes it even seems like it balks or grumbles. Or it reverts to the immediate causes, which are actually the effects. The right speaks of 'subversion'. And it is true that subversion is at work. But what is it exactly? To *speak* of subversion requires more than listing the symptoms. The right has abandoned its explanatory role; it has left this to the pedagogues, whose profession it is. However, the pedagogues have succumbed to subversion.

And yet, the ideology of the right exists. Inside. The right often overlooks what it carries within itself. It has never completely realised, on a formal level, everything that its aspirations imply. Its message is implicit. All the work lies in bringing it to the surface. We need a Professor Freud.

The left, for its part, beyond the proliferation of theories, seems to be dominated by the influence — admitted or not — of 'Gramscianism' (on the methodological level) and of the Frankfurt School. And the *negative critique* preached by Horkheimer and Adorno is always exercised with such virulence. The extreme left has understood that in a social structure where everything fits (where the arrangement of society is the reflection of a mental structure), no *reform* is possible. There is only a revolution, which will be the questioning of everything. Ecology, Neomarxism, Neofeminism, Freudo-Christianity are within the bounds of their *interior logic* when they demand the abolition of all

---

57   *massiste.* — Tr.

58   *maurrassien*, a partisan of Charles Maurras; cf. *Maurrassisme.* — Tr.

the *history* that our culture has been the conduit for; when they denounce the institutions (*every* institution) as 'alienating', and power (*all* power) as 'repressive', when they strive towards the dissolution of the State, the questioning of technology, the rehabilitation of madness, etc. It is the increasing implementation of the well-known agenda of Pierre Dac: 'to be for everything that is against, and against everything that is for'.

The extreme left dances upon the ruins of a power that denies itself. It hunts down its traces and vestiges everywhere. It finds unconscious deceptions. Jacques Attali (*Bruits*. Seuil, 1977)[59] claims to liberate music from the 'norm' — to liberate it (the unfortunate thing) from the alienation of the scale and counterpoint. In his inaugural lecture for the Collège de France, Roland Barthes declared: 'Language is neither reactionary nor progressive, it is all simply fascist'. What he means by this is that language *compels us to speak*, it constrains all speakers to mould their thought into the *form* of a given language. Thus, that which is specifically human — conceptual thought and syntactical language — is 'fascist'. All society, in so far as it *takes the form* of a social body, is 'fascist'. The State is 'fascist'. The family is 'fascist'. History is 'fascist'. *Form* is 'fascist'. It is but a small step to admit: the human phenomenon is 'fascist', since always and everywhere, it imposes *meaning, form, order,* and strives to make them endure. But at the same time, 'critical theory' only leads to perpetual frustration. If all language is 'fascist', what is there to do but be silent? If all power is 'fascist', what is there to do but renounce action? And if 'celebration' crystallises itself into Eternal Return, what does the reunion of being with itself become? All that is left is *absolute denial*. 'Horizontal' communities, 'space' music,[60] *art informel*, drugs, severance from the world and from adherence — by any means — to the universe of spiritual fraternities,[61] universal 'love', and metaphysical abstractions. Meanwhile, as the structuralists proclaim to us, man vanishes. This is how the extreme left has 'advanced'.

Another characteristic trait of the current world is the *rupturing* of established systems. Rigid schools of thought no longer hold. The church undergoes

59 *Noise: The Political Economy of Music* (Minneapolis: University of Minnesota Press, 1985). — Tr.

60 *musique «planante»*, conventionally translated as 'space music', a genre at the time the book was written. — Tr.

61 *essences fraternelles.* — Tr.

its *aggiornamento*.[62] The USSR has had its Twentieth Congress. Psychoanalysis fragments into a thousand sects. We 'reread' Marx in the light of Freud, and Freud in the light of Marx. We seek to revive medieval Christianity — or that of the catacombs. In a sort of fever, each seeks to renew what has *already* been. On the other side of the political horizon, in the world of *realities*, a prudent pragmatism dominates. Governments of western nations increasingly avoid referring to a given system. Statesmen 'fly by sight',[63] and only make tentative agreements at regular summit meetings. Speculations on the monetary system, on the world economy, or on nuclear deterrence, become hyper-abstract calculations that nobody really knows how to handle anymore. The latent crisis of political, economic, and social structures is augmented by a deep undermining of every acquired certitude. *Doubt*, fed by an increasingly systematic process of calling everything into question, corrodes the most elementary of convictions. The myth of a 'natural order' is revealed for what it is. There is no longer agreement on anything.

To me this confusion seems to be an established fact. There is no use in deploring it. But what we can do is concern ourselves with *what is to come*. From this inadequacy, which is more and more evident in ready-made formulas and ideologies, a feeling emerges. The yearning for a *synthesis*. Many are those who *intensely feel* the necessity to cross the lines of current divisions. The way in which, for some years, certain themes have passed from the right to the left (or from the left to the right) is one of the *signs* of such a yearning. But it is precisely here that things run into difficulty. It must not be concealed: what the end of the century needs is a synthesis of positive aspirations which, until now, have appeared in a scattered manner. This synthesis equates to a *surpassing* of the current stage of the human condition. I believe in the possibility of such a synthesis. But I am not sure we will have enough *audacity* to put it into effect. I fear that egalitarian ideology prevents us from realising it.

Today we *know* more than previous humanity has ever known. But it seems that we are *understanding* less and less. One of the great errors of our time — and it lies at the base of the egalitarian conception of education — is to believe that by accumulating knowledge, we automatically know how to use

---

62   Italian, 'bringing up to date, modernisation', per the Second Vatican Council. — Tr.

63   The expression *piloter à vue* means 'to fly by sight', i.e. without using instruments; it also has the sense of 'to fly by the seat of one's pants'. — Tr.

it. But the inverse is true. Without the Ariadne's thread of thinking, without a clearly formed worldview, the accumulation of knowledge is inhibitive and paralysing. Due to an increase in knowledge both for and against everything, without having the means to *discriminate* or *decide*, we can no longer do anything. I know people who are so knowledgeable that they can no longer write anything: when they set a sentence to paper, they immediately perceive so many counter-arguments that they give up trying to saying anything at all. Globally speaking, I believe our society is in the same predicament. It seems to me that in the past, we had certitudes in proportion to our doubts. Today, we mainly have doubts. And most of all we are scared of being wrong. And so we no longer judge and instead say that 'everyone is right'. This is where egalitarianism intervenes: if all people have equal value, all opinions have equal value too. I consider this kind of doubt fatal — for above all it corresponds to a false idea of 'truth'. In terms of *historical becoming*, there is no metaphysically established truth. That which is true is that which comes into the position of existing and enduring. That which should be, *will be*. That which deserved to be, *already is*. If false in the abstract, as the most damaging ideologies can be, they become 'true' to the extent that they constitute the daily reality that surrounds us and in relation to which we define ourselves. Marxism can be the 'truth' of tomorrow. But it is a 'truth' that we rightfully reject in order to oppose it with a stronger one. That which seemed to be the truth to us yesterday was but a rejection of the doubt — or sometimes a disregarding of the doubt. Where there is a will, there is a way. We do not ask ourselves if this way was conformed to an abstract truth. We *create* the way, and the rest follows. 'Knowledge' has little to do with this creation. This is because knowledge is not unambiguous, whereas creative energy exists by necessity. Our contemporaries behave like there is an absolute truth that exists outside of them to which they must closely conform. At least this is the impression that we take away from their terror at discovering that 'everything is convention'. The hypercritical extreme left proclaims that nothing, neither words, signs, or science, etc., nothing is *innocent*. Perfectly obvious! No, *nothing is innocent*. And why should things come to be this way? As soon as man is *there*, he finds meaning *here*. For man alone, the gaze that he places upon the world gives *meaning* to it. And this meaning *varies* according to his gaze. And this meaning only comes from him. And this meaning only endures through him. No, things are not 'innocent'. Fortunately.

Man inherits a natural gift that he transforms according to his discretion and from which he creates the laws that he deems the most appropriate to the order that he intends to institute. Hobbes: *Auctoritas non veritas facit legem*.[64] No law carries within itself the evidence of its own principle. But it is an obvious fact that no society can live without laws, and that these laws have validity, not by their moral intentions or their judicial coherence, but *first* because they put people in shape, because they contribute to the creation of an order. Law is the means of order, it is not the cause.

I do not believe in objectivity, but I believe in the need to strive for objectivity. I do not believe in pure truth — that terrible truth in whose name we have attempted to transform the world through genocide, instilled racism, or the Inquisition. I believe, like Malraux, that in the matter of historical design, the real world only exists like picture frames hung on the hook of myths.[65] I believe that the object in itself is inaccessible to understanding as to perception, but that it suffices for one and the other that they can construct themselves as the data or objects of a subject. I believe most of all that because pure truth cannot be determined, that it must, more than ever, be constructed 'heroically' — like man has always done.

I heard someone say on the radio one day: 'Each has his truth. I do not want to be judged. In our era, we can no longer judge anyone'. The left that discovers that the social order has no ultimate cause unless we *choose* to institute one by convenience — to be able, quite simply, to *live* — while also deducing that *all order* must be rejected, cannot reason otherwise. I say that this discourse is one of *pure regression*; that the left which notes the 'conventional' character of institutions and yet itself refuses to create, denies its own consideration as a *human* consideration. I say that it is at precisely this moment that man discovers that he is the master of himself and of his destiny, and that he must personally forge a destiny. It is the moment when the old 'absolutes', unmasked as conventions, appear as they are, which demands, *as always*, the creation of new norms, new 'conventions' with enough strength that in their turn they will seem just as 'natural' to future generations as those known to

---

64   Latin, 'Authority not truth makes the law'. — Tr.

65   *encadrement d'images et accroche-mythes*. — Tr.

our predecessors. Finally, I say that the only price of such an audacity — the audacity to institute a new objectivity from a subjectivity that knows itself as such — is that we can continue to progress. Unless of course thinking regresses towards the undifferentiated, where, as Hegel says, 'all cows are black'.[66]

The formula 'if God does not (or no longer) exists, everything is permitted' is only a literary expression: *no one* behaves as if everything is permitted. To (re)establish an order, to (re)create social norms, thus comes down to asking: what are we going to (re)institute as a final instance or as an ultimate means. This challenge is at the heart of the crisis of the contemporary world. *Who* today would dare to say, like Pericles: 'our boldness has forced a path over land and sea, raising imperishable monuments to itself everywhere, whether for good or for evil'?[67] I think that a new right could answer this challenge. A right whose true strength would consist not in possessing truth, but in being fearless before its manifestations.

Excesses proceed in pairs. I'm gaining some idea of a *third way*: that which rejects, from either side, extremisms and unilateralisms. A just line is always nuanced. What I mean by this is an approach that takes into account what is fair or correct in each system or from each point of view. Only this kind of approach can lead to synthesis. But I do not believe any more that a third way will be a 'middle way', a kind of compromise — which is only a transitory step towards either of the existing systems. Every true synthesis is a *surpassing*. It is not a little of this and a little of that, in succession, but this *and* that, with the same intensity, *at the same time*. It requires that we never let ourselves be locked in one alternative, and that we adopt a mental logic of the *included third* or *middle*. And of course, the result of this approach 'from the right' can only be the reabsorption into a single whole of the notions of 'right' and 'left' as we currently conceive them. We can be more precise. I do not mean by this that we will be 'neither of the left nor of the right' — which means nothing. But that we attain a position in which we are, at the same time, *both* right *and* left. I believe that the future belongs to those who will be able to *simultaneously*

---

66 Benoist says '*toutes les vaches sont grises*' (all cows are grey) but I have translated directly after Hegel (*Phänomenologie des Geistes*. Bamberg/Würzburg 1807, Sämtliche Werke II, 22) who says '*alle Kühe schwarz sind*'. The context is Hegel's likening of the dissolution of determination to a night in which 'all cows are black' — Tr.

67 Thucidides, *The History of the Peloponnesian War*, 2.41. Cf. Nietzsche, *Genealogy of Morality*, 1.11. — Tr.

think what, until now, has only been thought *contradictorily*. Heraclitus said: 'God is day and night, summer and winter, war and peace, satiety and hunger'. Paracelsus declared: 'Everything is within you and nothing can come to you from outside or above'. I believe that man is the quintessence of everything, and that he can realise the unity and the supersession of contradictions. *Coincidentia oppositorum*.

What is the principal menace today? It is the progressive demise of the world's diversity. The levelling of people, the reduction of all cultures to a 'global *civilisation*' built on what is most *common*. Already, from one end of the planet to the other, we see the construction of the same kinds of buildings, the establishment of the same mental habits. From the Holiday Inn to Howard Johnson, we see the emerging contours of a universally grey world. I have travelled widely — over many continents. The *joy* that one experiences when travelling is to behold the varied modes of life still deeply-rooted, to see different peoples living according to their own rhythm, to see another skin-colour, another culture, another mentality — people who are proud of their *difference*. I believe that this diversity is the treasure of the world, and that egalitarianism is killing it. It is for this reason that it is important not merely to 'respect others' — half-heartedly — but to arouse everywhere the most legitimate desire possible: the desire to assert an identity that is unlike any other, to defend a heritage, to govern oneself according to that which one is. And this implies the struggle, head on, against a pseudo-antiracism that denies differences, and against a vicious racism which is also only the refusal of the Other — the denial of diversity.

We live today in a *blocked* society. On a global level, we are just beginning to identify the means of departing from the order instituted at Yalta. On a national level, as always in times of peace, the division between political factions has been equally vivid. On the philosophical and ideological plane, we continually oscillate between opposing extremes without finding any equilibrium. The cause as well as the remedy for this situation finds itself in man. To say that our society is in crisis is a commonplace. Man *is a crisis*. He is tragedy itself. For him, nothing is ever definitively *said*. Man can always find within himself the thread of a new discourse corresponding to a new way of being-in-the-world, a new *form* of his humanity. Man has been in crisis ever since he existed. The originality of our time does not lie here. The originality — the sad originality — of our time resides in the fact that, for the first time, man recoils before the implications of what his desire and will would require of him in order to resolve the crisis. For the first time, man believes that the problems surpass him. And they effectively surpass him *to the degree to which he believes this*, whereas the problems are born from him, are equal to him and to the solutions that he carries within him.

We are no longer in the age where men kill one another because they are born on different sides of a border. Wars today no longer oppose nations (or, more exactly, only oppose them *secondarily*) but rather different worldviews, ideologies, and opposed ways of being. The fight for which the world is currently the theatre, the fight of which only one protagonist is *fully* known at this time and to which, also for the first time, the entirety of the planet participates, opposes different ways of perceiving the world, of conceiving it, and of seeking to *reproduce* it. A differentialist way and a universalist way. An anti-egalitarian way and an egalitarian way. A way which aspires to an organic society, founded and governed by increasing diversity, and a way that aspires to a mechanistic society, where increasing homogeneity reigns.

I think, finally, that we are entering the prelude to war. Since around 1965–1968, the principal political events have been direct prolongations of the situation created in 1945. Christian democracy, the cold war, decolonisation and so forth have all been more or less *residual* phenomena. The events that we live today do not end or 'complete' an age. They announce a new one. They are already forming another. They are forerunners. Of what? Of what we want the end of the century to be. Since 1974–1975, we have entered the 'decisive decade' — where things settle, where the waters separate, where new factions are put into place. I am convinced that the lines of division to come will be very different from those that still exist today. I believe that this decade, which was discussed in *L'épée de Damoclès* (Plon, 1967)[68] by General Gambiez, then-director of l'Institut des hautes études de Défense nationale (IHEDN), will ruin many of the predictions of the 'futurologists'. It will also restore its importance to foreign policy — the only policy, ultimately, that truly counts. Ernst Jünger said: 'there was no creation at the beginning, but it is possible for each age to ignite itself in its own time'. I still believe that we can 'ignite' ourselves.

---

68 *The Sword of Damocles.* — Tr.

This book attempts to provide an account of the movement of ideas since the beginning of the 1970s. More precisely, it takes into account the majority of the debates that have developed here and there in the wake of the great vogue of structuralism (following that of existentialism in the 1950s). Unfortunately its scope does not, of course, cover the debates in their entirety. From Montherlant to Cioran, passing through Dumézil, Mircéa Eliade, Raymond Aron, and so on, there are many 'gaps' that I regret not having filled. It serves as an *anthology*, not a true encyclopaedia — although at the end of the day a comparable enough concern to the encyclopaedists of the eighteenth century would be equally at work. But I have not entirely chosen my subjects. They have often been dictated by current events. I have essentially based myself on the books published in recent years, which have appeared to be either the most important or the most notable for developing an edifice that is receptive to *serving* a right of these times.

Within these pages we will express a double *critique*: an ideological critique of the left, and a methodological critique of the right. Throughout these texts, I have sought to trace the features of a *possible* right. I do not pretend — nor do I wish — that every man of the right will recognise himself. I have above all wanted to contribute to the clarification of a debate, the departure from confusion, and the assessment of ideas and men — beyond words and labels — in light of the same style and sentiment. I have striven to present 'openings'. The paths will follow. This book presents a great number of arguments, and yet it does not truly seek to *convince*. I do not think 'convincing' people is important. And while I don't disdain them, I do not believe in those great intellectual constructions that only address themselves to reason. One does not *create* a sensibility, but one can, at times, *awaken* it. Such is the ultimate goal of this work: to awaken a certain form of sensibility, to give birth to the conscious grasp of a certain allegiance of spirit, to provide a text to *read* where someone can recognise the *form* that they have never truly ceased seeking.

ALAIN DE BENOIST

HERITAGE

The Roots of Civilisation

The great cultural revolution took place here 35,000 years ago. If not earlier. 'It seems', writes Professor Marshack, 'that in an age as remote as 30,000 years before our era, during the glacial period, the western European hunter had made use of a previously evolved, complex system of notation whose tradition might go back many thousands of years. This notation proceeded from a cognitive technique that was time-factored and time-factoring'.

It is probably one of the most important discoveries of the century in matters concerning prehistory.

Everything started at the beginning of the sixties. Alexander Marshack, solid, jovial, short haired, researcher at the Peabody Museum of Ethnology and Archaeology at Harvard University, investigated the problem of 'origins'. He would seek to determine the nature of mental processes among the most ancient humans.

'Within the limits of the evolution of the species', he observed, 'the brain has remained a constant for one to two-hundred thousand years'. There is thus no 'progress of humanity', but a continued transformation of the world by a humanity who has remained the same since the remotest of times. If the human phenomenon forms a whole, 'culture' is also equally as old.

'I therefore pose as a hypothesis', continues Marshack, 'that pre-historical man, man of the glacial period, did not differ greatly from contemporary man. What differs most of all are the facts, the ideas and the relations inculcated in his brain, but not his manner of functioning, his aptitudes, his capacities, or his intelligence'.

In other words, *Homo sapiens* would not have simply been a 'maker of tools', he was also capable of recognising and employing forms. He would have been conscious of notions of 'consequence', of symbol, and time. The author qualifies this by a term: his activities would have been 'time-factored'.

Nevertheless, he still needed to prove the sound foundations of this hypothesis. Alexander Marshack thinks he has succeeded. He deciphers inscribed bones.

Lunar 'Phrases'

Up until now, prehistorians, when they discovered signs engraved on bones and small stones, contented themselves to speak of 'decorative motifs' or 'hunting marks'. It was necessary to take a closer look.

Between 1965 and 1970, professor Marshack had studied more than a thousand prehistoric objects from nine European countries and subjected them to meticulous analysis: photographs, mouldings, duplications, microscopic examinations. The results surpassed his expectations: details have appeared that no one has ever noticed.

On most of the objects, the notches, points, and striations were found arranged in lines or groups which were carved 'at different times, from different angles, and with different tools upon which one has exerted different pressure'. Certain marks reveal the sign of a single stroke, others many. The techniques also vary: simple impressions, partial turnings of the tool, large shallow holes, deep and narrow holes, etc. It is difficult to speak of coincidence. One notes a precise intention. But what is it?

'These marks', notes Marshack, 'have not been made at the same time with the same rhythm, the same thought, or the same tool. They are therefore "time-factored"'.

Continuing his work, Marshack has observed that the marks are not arranged randomly. We generally find a multiple number of twenty-nine or thirty, which immediately allows us to see a relationship with the months of the lunar cycle (the easiest to observe). Now, in the middle of the same 'sequence', the 'sub-groups' of the carved signs correspond exactly to different phases of the moon. We thus obtain what Marshack calls 'an almost perfect lunar phrasing right down to its subdivisions'.

In his copiously illustrated book, Marshack gives innumerable examples of such 'phrases' and presents digitally verified diagrams.

He also cites characteristic pieces: the bone from la Marche (21 cm) whose 221 marks correspond approximately to seven lunar months; the bone of Abri-Blanchard in Dordogne, which bears on its principal face a double line of sixty-nine rounded wells, during the tracing of which the tool-tip has been changed twenty-four times; the Barma Grande pebble, etc.

The Great Hunters

Prehistoric man thus had a 'visual memory aid of the seasons and lunations' at his disposal; a system of notation common to the whole Upper Palaeolithic in Europe, and a technique already more evidenced than certain attested systems of the historical era, notably among the Indians of North America.

In the second part of the book, Professor Marshack brings this evidence together with the notation system of the great rock engravings. More specifically, with representations of animals, feminine silhouettes and the vulvic symbols proper to the Aurignacian. Microscopic examination seems to suggest that these figures were also composed over time and that they too are therefore 'time-factored'. This enables us to situate them in a context of 'dramatic-narrative' and ritual.

Commenting on these discoveries, Henri de Saint-Blanquat has written in *Sciences et avenir*:[69] 'The representations of animals can provide a testimony of their method. One of the horses visible on the bone of La Marche reveals itself upon examination to possess three ears and three eyes, two manes, and two back lines. The three ears have been carved with three different tool-tips, and the same is true for the three eyes and two manes. The stratigraphy of the marks shows that two of the ears were carved after one of the manes. Everything appears to suggest that the horse had been 'used' many times, each 'use' corresponding to the addition of organs to the carving'.

'If we suppose', adds Marshack, 'that a first month tells the story of a lunar hero who gets devoured by some spirit animal, this story could belong to its own season. A second month could then recount the adventures of the same hero with another seasonal animal or some divine spirit. The notation could therefore emphasise the narrative or symbolic time of these adventures, etc.'.

Due to the essentially seasonal rhythm of Palaeolithic life, we consequently see the contours of a religion of great hunters, where the rites of pregnancy, for example, are associated with the animal 'ancestors' of the clan: the mammoth, the reindeer, the bison, the rhinoceros.

In the process, Marshack rejects the 'sexual' or psychoanalytic interpretations that satisfy some prehistorians. 'The magic of fecundity', he writes, 'is only one of the forms of participation in history and myth which surround

---

69   *Sciences and the future.* — Tr.

pregnancy and birth (...) The vulva itself is to a certain degree a "non sexual" symbol, that is to say, non-copulative and non-erotic, representing the stories of processes that include birth and death, menstruation and the time-factored cycles of nature'. How far does this system of notation go back in time? It is difficult to know. Marks made on the bone of Pech-de-Lazé (–230,000 years), the most ancient of the bone carvings discovered to this day — it was discovered in 1968, close to Sarlat, by the prehistorian François Bordes — open fantastic perspectives which are yet to be explored.

The tradition, in any case, is maintained through to the Mesolithic and Neolithic. Perhaps even to the dawn of history. In regards to a lunar calendar carved on the mattock of Urgerlöse (Denmark), Alexander Marshack writes:

'This calendar could explain the presence of a tradition of notation and observation in northern and central Europe in an age where the distant agrarian cultures of the south practiced a different regional tradition. It could explain the origin of calendric wands and runic calendars discovered in northern Europe in the modern historical era. It is equally possible that this European tradition would not be unfamiliar to the extremely late megalithic alignments of Stonehenge.

A Revolutionary Role

Prehistory and writing have been contradictory terms up until now. But linguistics and archaeology have already allowed us to breach the wall separating us from the 'silent millennia'. Marshack now speaks of the 'roots of science and writing'.

'We would then have', notes de Saint-Blanquat, 'something like a pre-writing, a pre-numeric notation, in sum: the substructure upon which, much later, true writing and true numeration has been built'.

'This ability to note and to symbolise', he adds, 'seems proper for the time of the European cultures of the Upper Paleolithic (...) The ancient European cultures could thus have played a relatively dynamic role, formative and revolutionary in relation to subsequent cultural developments'.

From here on out, prehistoric man transforms before our eyes. The 'primitive' hominid, crouching before his fire, cutting flint all day long, fades to leave in its place a 'finished' man, possessing a practical knowledge of time, of place, of direction, of the limits of his territory, capable of describing his experiences and of expressing them with symbols. A man, remarks Marshack, of a 'level of evolution and sophistication that we could call proto-modern'.

Hominisation thus appears linked to a sense for *difference in duration*. The 'human fact' characterises itself by the appearance of a perception 'in two stages': man is animal who is conscious of having consciousness. The *historical* dimension is the human dimension par excellence.

To the simple Darwinian notion of man fabricating tools, working by natural selection and the survival of the fittest, is now added the idea of 'time-factoring man'. Archaeology risks becoming an 'obsession of the collector' (Glyn Daniel). It becomes an auxiliary science of ethno-sociology.

*

Les raciness de la civilisation, a study by Alexander Marshack.[70] Plon, 415 pages.

*

Since the 1970s, the theses of Professor Marshack have continued to inspire impassioned discussion. After the publication of *Racines de la civilisation* in the United States (*The Roots of Civilisation: The Cognitive Beginnings of Man's First Art, Symbol, and Notation*. McGraw Hill, New York, 1972), the controversy extended to many disciplines, such that the press assured the work considerable publicity (cf. notably *The New York Post*, 16 May 1972; *The Washington Post*, 17 April 1972; *Mosaic*, autumn 1972; *Antiquity*, December 1972; *The Boston Globe*, 2 December 1972; *Newsweek*, 18 December 1972). Numerous specialists, such as Hallam L. Movius Jr, from Harvard University, and Gerald S. Hawkins (author of *Stonehenge Decoded*) from the Smithsonian Astrophysical Observatory, have declared themselves convinced. 'It is not only anthropology, but our entire conception of man's past that finds itself called into question', observes Lewis Mumford, author of *La cite dans l'histoire* (Seuil, 1972).[71] 'A revolutionary document', adds Professor Carleton S. Coon (*The Origin of Races, The Living Races of Man*).

In November 1972, Alexander Marshack presented an important communication to the Anthropological Congress of Toronto. He also updated his works in three articles of premiere importance: *Cognitive Aspects of Upper Paleolithic Engraving* (in *Current Anthropology*, June–October 1972), *Upper Paleolithic Notation and Symbol* (in *Science*, 24 November 1972) and *Exploring the Mind of Ice Age Man* (in *National Geographic Magazine*, January 1975).

In France, where he had undertaken the study of numerous prehistoric sites (Pech-Merle, Cougnac, Rouffignac, Niaux, etc.), Marshack published a highly technical monograph as early as 1970, which unfortunately passed by almost unnoticed: *Notations dans les gravures*

---

70   *The Roots of Civilization: the Cognitive Beginning of Man's First Art, Symbol, and Notation* (New York McGraw Hill, 1971). — Tr.

71   *The City in History: Its Origins, Its Transformations, and Its Prospects* (New York: Harcourt, Brace, and World, 1961). — Tr.

du paléolithique supérieur (Imprimirie Delmas. 6 place Saint-Christoly, 33000 Bordeaux).[72] This work was patronised by the Institut de préhistoire of the Université de Bordeaux. On the reception of *Racines de la civilisation*,[73] we can refer to the article by Henri de Saint-Blanquat, in *Science et avenir* ('Un pithécanthrope dessinateur' Febuary 1973), and to the *Monde* of 27 December 1972. Cf. also the interesting work by Maxime Gorce, *Les pré-écritures et l'évolution des civilisations* (Klincksieck, 1974).[74]

The works of Professor Marshack inscribe themselves in the framework of a general re-evaluation of antiquity and of the importance of the pre- and proto-historical cultures of western and northern Europe, a re-evaluation principally developed in Anglo-Saxon countries from 1965–1970. The key works in this regard are those of Colin Renfrew on chronology and dating (*Before Civilisation, The Emergence of Civilisation*), by Alexander Thom on prehistoric astronomy (*Megalithic Lunar Observatories, Megalithic Sites in Britain*), and by John Dayon on technology and metallography (*Minerals, Metals, Glazing, and Man*).

Colin Renfrew and Alexander Marshack were present at the IXème congrès de l'Union internationale des sciences préhistoriques et protohistoriques,[75] which was held at Nice from 13–18 September 1976.

---

72 *Notations in the Engravings of the Upper Palaeolithic.* — Tr.

73 I.e. the French translation of Marshack's book. — Tr.

74 *Pre-Writings and the Evolution of Civilisations.* — Tr.

75 The Ninth Congress of the International Meeting of Prehistoric and Protohistoric Sciences. — Tr.

The World of the Indo-Europeans

Almost 450 million representatives of the species *Homo sapiens* currently live in Europe. Inheritors of the same culture, they possess a common origin. Their ancestors are known as the Indo-Europeans.

The term 'Indo-European' is a linguistic term. It has been used since the nineteenth century, an age which saw the publications of Franz Bopp, Alexander von Humboldt, and Jacob Grimm on the comparative study of the language systems of the principle European speakers (with exceptions made for Hungarian, Finnish, Basque, and Sami). Proceeding from a correlation of form, this *comparative* method derives (by means of a process of equivalence analogous to the calculations of arithmetical proportions) a lineage positing the logical necessity of a common origin. In other words, it allows the recovery of the 'unknown' that establishes, through its relationship to the current European 'daughter-languages', a lost 'mother-language': common Indo-European. A capital discovery that restores the most ancient past at the heart of the immediate present.

Thanks to the effort of linguists, we have been able to successively establish the grammar, the syntax, and the lexicon of common Indo-European. By convention, we distinguish three successive stages of this language: Proto-Indo-European, Middle-Indo-European (the phase preceding the first dispersions), and Old European or Late-Indo-European, probably spoken in the northern part of central Europe in the third millennia before our era. Besides certain languages that are no longer spoken today (Illyrian, Macedonian, Hittite, Luwian, Tokharian, Thraco-Phrygian, etc.), the family of languages derived from common Indo-European incorporates the ancestral forms of the Indo-Aryan languages (Sanskrit, Hindi, Old Persian), as well as Greek, Albanian, and all of the Slavic, Baltic, Celtic, Germanic, and Romance languages.

Researchers have been very quick to preoccupy themselves with the origin of the people who used these languages emerging from prehistory.

'We envisage therefore', writes P. Borsch-Gimpera, 'the existence of a primitive people (the *Urvolk* of the German school), whose cradle or homeland

(*Urheimat*) could have been most likely situated in Asia, speaking an original language (*Ursprache*), source of the dialects from which the historical Indo-European languages derive'. (*Les Indo-Européens*. Payot, 1961).[76]

Two Theses on the Original Homeland

Countless controversies, from which ulterior political motives were not always absent, have been raised concerning the location of the original homeland.

Linguistics, fortunately, provides valuable indications. 'Common Indo-European', observes Nicolas Lahovary, 'includes terms designating the fauna, flora, and climate of temperate regions, more humid than dry, and more cold than hot' (*Les peuples européens*. La Baconnière, Neuchâtel, 1946).[77] In the book that he contributed to the anthropology of Europe, John Geipel adds: 'Numerous Indo-European languages use similar words to designate animals: bear, wolf, beaver, squirrel; trees: birch, beech, willow; or even for honey, bee, snow, winter, ice, cold. This strongly suggests to us that the Indo-European dialects were, before their dispersion, spoken by individuals living in a temperate, forested, continental region'.

The idea of an 'Asiatic' origin of the Indo-Europeans, advanced in 1888 by Max Müller, followed by H. d'Arbois de Jubainville, C. F. Keary, and William Ripley, is no longer defended today by anyone. Two theses remain current.

The Nordic or Germanic thesis relies first of all upon the physical characteristics attributed to the Indo-European populations by ancient texts. These characteristics (blonde hair, blue or light eyes, tallness of stature, slender hips, fine lips, prominent chin, dolicocephaly) are specific to the Nordic and Falic sub-races formed from a cromagnoid substrate in a territory comprising the shores of the North Sea and the Baltic as well as their hinterland. In 1878, Theodor Poesche situated the *Urheimat* in current Lithuania. Adding linguistic and archaeological arguments to the anthropological arguments, Karl Penka (*Die Herkunft der Arier*, 1886)[78] expanded this localisation to northern Germany and southern Scandinavia. He was followed by Isaac Taylor (1888)

---

76   *The Indo-Europeans*. The French edition cited here is translated from the Spanish original: *El problema indoeuropeo* (Mexico: Universita Nacional Autónoma de Mexico, 1960). — Tr.

77   *The European Peoples.* — Tr.

78   *The Origin of the Aryans.* — Tr.

and Herman Hirt (*Die Urheimat des Indogermanen*, 1892).[79] In 1902, Gustaf Kossina, founder of the journal, *Mannus*, proposed a primordial homeland situated in central Germany. The same Nordic-Germanic thesis would be reprised by Harold Bender, Hans Seger, Schachermeyer, Gustav Neckel, Ernst Meyer, Julius Pokorny, Stuart Mann, etc. It has been renewed recently by Nicolas Lahovary (1946), Paul Thieme (*Die Heimat der indogermanischen Gemeinsprache*, 1953)[80] and Ram Chandra Jain (*The Most Ancient Aryan Society*, 1964).

The second thesis is that of an *Urheimat* situated in central Europe or southern Russia. Otto Schrader supported it for the first time in 1890, followed by V. Gordon Childe (*The Aryans*, 1926), Georges Poisson (*Les Aryens*, 1934), Walter Schulz (1935), R. A. Crossland (1957), etc. In 1961, P. Bosch-Gimpera wrote: 'The aggregation that would lead to the formation of the Indo-European peoples manifests itself in the Neolithic milieus, probably in the fifth millennium. This role is perhaps played by ethnic groups from the centre of Europe'. In 1962, Giacomo Devoto (*Origini indeuropee*)[81] arrived at the same conclusions.

The idea of a primordial homeland in southern Russia has been defended in particular by the archaeologist Marija Gimbutas, whose principal works have appeared from 1956. According to Gimbutas, the 'kurgan culture', whose bearers came via the Danube valley, came to an end around −4,000 in the Old European Balkan civilisation (which was developed from around −7,000, independently from the cultures of the European northeast as well as from those of Arabia and Mesopotamia, ranging from Sicily, the Adriatic coasts, the basins of the Don, the Dniester, and the Dnieper, to the islands of the Aegean Sea), were of Indo-European nature and their representatives must be considered the first Indo-Europeans.

The two theses are not necessarily irreconcilable. Authors like Ward Goodenough ('Evolution of Pastoralism and Indo-European Origins', in G. Cardona, H. M. Hoenigswald and A. Senn, ed. *Indo-European and Indo-Europeans*. University of Pennsylvania Press, Philadelphia, 1970) have proposed viewing the Kurgan people as a simple pastoral extension of an Indo-European culture which was first developed in northern Europe. It is one part

---

79   *The Primordial Homeland of the Indo-Europeans.* — Tr.

80   *The Homeland of the Common Indo-Germanic Language.* — Tr.

81   *Indo-European Origins.* — Tr.

of these people who, having destroyed the Old European civilisation, would have descended towards the south, diffusing on their way the techniques of bronze metallurgy, giving rise to the Luwians, the historical Hittites, and the Mycenaean Greeks. The other part, by mixing with the elements of the culture that remained in central Europe, would have furnished the constituents of a later diaspora. This theory, apparently very convincing, is reconcilable with that of Hans Krahe, who distinguished on the linguistic plane between Old European (*alteuropäisch* — not to be confused with the Old Europeans of which Gimbutas speaks) and Indo-European (*indogermanisch*) properly speaking. It is cited favourably by James P. Mallory, author of one of the most recent studies on the question ('A Short History of the Indo-European Problem', in *The Journal of Indo-European Studies*, vol. 1, no. 1, 1973, Hattiesburg, Miss.). The primordial homeland could thus be situated in a zone circumscribed by the Elbe and the Vistule, extending north to Jutland and south to the mountainous region terminating in the Carpathians.

Social Structures

'Attested historically' towards the second millennium before our era, the Indo-Europeans already have a long history behind them. 'Archaeology has traced them back them to the beginning of the Neolithic', elaborates P. Bosch Gimpera, 'the roots of these ethnic formations are situated in the Mesolithic'. Authors such as Bulgare Georgiev even suggest of the end of the Paleolithic.

'Around 8,000 years before our era', recalls Geipel, 'the Scandinavian glaciers retreated definitively towards the north. The British Isles separated themselves from the continent. The Baltic made its junction with the North Sea. The tundra was covered with dense forests. From that point forward, Europe enjoyed a temperate climate'.

From the second Neolithic, groups of Indo-European had become semi-sedentary. Men dedicated themselves to raising animals, while women and the young practiced a rudimentary form of agriculture. This new type of economy succeeded another way of life, that of the great hunters who roamed nomadically over quite a large territory and whose members were principally assembled on the basis of their age groups. As a result, there was a demographic explosion which was accompanied by a complete transformation of the social life.

It is at this time, as a matter of fact, that the *genos*,[82] the great families of an exogamous nature — the name comes from *eg-, a reconstructed Indo-European term designating the idea of 'oneself'; cf. Latin *ego* — began to combine themselves in order to preserve common hereditary properties and to prevent the dispersion of young and able-bodied men. Each *genos* established or reinforced the exogamous rule and the patrilocal organisation that characterised it within the framework of a tribal association with other clans or *genoi*, with whom alliances were sealed by marriage according to a relatively rigid structure based on reciprocal benefits and obligations. Including only free men, 'well-born' ('ingenu' = *in-genos*),[83] the *genos* thus becomes a 'community of blood'. As such it is distinguished from the economic community, the *domos,[84] which is the whole formed by the *genos* and the new class of non-proprietaries, slaves, or liberated serfs. At a higher level, a distinction seems to be established between the *wenos (a term derived from *we-, 'we, us'; cf. German *wir*), or a community by alliance resulting from the association of three clans or *genoi*, and the corresponding economic community, the *weikos (cf. Latin *vicus*, French *village*, English 'village').

Subsequently, more complex social structures (independent cities, kingdoms, etc.) will be established on the same basis, the *people* defining themselves simply as a vaster 'we' — the ensemble of men and women linked together by alliance. Equally, the notion of *ethnos* (*sw-edh-nos) derives directly from *swe-, that is, from the community of blood whose exchange of women inside the *wenos assures and guarantees its maintenance.

At its basis, the social system is fundamentally patriarchal. The *genos* defines itself by identification with the paternal *ego*, representing a lineage that goes back to *deiwos-pèter (*dieu-père*, 'divine-father'). Whereas in certain primitive societies of the agrarian type, a murder ritual, the 'sacred murder of the king' (cf. the murder of the father in Freud's doctrine) signifies the destruction of the paternal lineage and assures the validity of the sole matrilineal descendants, among the Indo-Europeans, the 'role of the father' in the

---

82   *Genos*, from the Greek, 'race, stock, clan, kin, offspring', as well as 'gender, kind, class', etymologically related to a range of words for birth (e.g. *genesis*). cf. Latin *genus*. — Tr.

83   Benoist is drawing attention to the etymological connection of French *ingénu* (innocent, simple, ingenuous) to Greek *genos*. — Tr.

84   Presumably connected to Greek *dēmos*, 'people, the common populace'. — Tr.

lineage is assured by a rite derived from the 'couvade'.[85] The father symbolically 'engenders' and *acknowledges* the child by taking it upon (that is between) his knees: a simulation of birth or delivery. In the vocabulary of common Indo-European, it is said of the mother that she 'brings into the world'. Only the father *en-genders*, that is to say, brings into the *genos*. This explains how words that at first glance look so different — *genos, knee*,[86] *engender*, etc. — are all derived from the same root: **gen*.

Elected Sovereign

When the circumstances that bring about the *genos* endow it with a general authority, it is necessarily one of the *peters* or fathers, one of the leaders of the *genos*, that carries the decision. 'The king is in the same relationship to his subjects as the head of a family is to his children' (Aristotle). The leader is *elected* by his peers, in particular when he proceeds to appoint a **reg-s*, that is, a king (Latin *rex*, Gallic *rix*, Sanskrit *raja*, French *roi*). It is only in the historical era that this delegation of power, which is provisional, will become permanent, thus implementing hereditary monarchy. Originally, the king submits to the control of the *peters*, the fathers, within an assembly analogous to the *sabha* of the Indo-Aryans, the Greek *gerousia*, the Roman *senatus*, the Germanic *thing*, the Icelandic *althing*, etc. Thus the elementary form of sovereignty among the Indo-Europeans is able to be defined as a sort of aristodemocracy, where the monarch exercises a function at once religious and political. All Indo-European society is therefore a sublimation of the *genos*, where the social cohesion is realised by the projection of this original structure upon a religious and political superstructure — the two terms are inseparable, since among the Indo-Europeans, the society of gods is a projection of human society, while the civic cult itself results from a projection of the domestic culture placed under the responsibility of the father.

Priests, farmers, and warriors, the Indo-Europeans worked pottery and practiced metallurgy. 'Men rode wild horses and used cattle as beasts of burden', writes Geipel. Herds of cattle were the symbol of prosperity. The

---

85   A *couvade* is a kind of 'sympathetic pregnancy', referring to a practice among certain cultures in which the husband takes on some of the behaviours of the pregnant woman. — Tr.

86   While French *genou* 'knee', is visibly closer to *genos* and *engender*, the English word 'knee' is also in fact cognate with the words Benoist enumerates here. — Tr.

Indo-European term *peku, which we rediscover in the Italic, Germanic, and Indo-Iranian languages with the primary meaning of 'personal wealth' (cf. Latin *pecunia*, French *pécule*), has ultimately come to designate livestock: Latin *pecus*, Sanskrit *pashu*, French *pécore*. (Cf. Gothic *faihu*, 'fortune', and Old High Germanic *fihu*, 'cattle, livestock').

Worldview

The works of the Indo-Europeanists, especially those of Georges Dumézil, have demonstrated the existence — even before the first dispersions — of a common Indo-European 'ideology', that is to say, of a *specific mental structure* conformed to the same worldview and manifesting itself notably by a particular conception of the religious reality, of society, of sovereignty, and of the relationship between men and gods, as well as by a common theology, liturgy, poetry, and epic literature. This 'ideology', writes Dumézil, is the 'work of thinkers, of whom the brahmans, the druids, and the sacerdotal Roman colleges, are, for a part, the heirs' (*L'idéologie tripartite des Indo-Européens*. Latomus, Bruxelles, 1958).[87]

In the specific domain of poetry, the works of Antoine Meillet and Roman Jakobson, followed by Calvert Watkins and Donald Ward, have revealed structural analogies in the realm of Greek, Vedic, Slavic, and Irish that can only be explained by a common heritage, and which allow us to presume the existence, among the first Indo-European communities, of a body of 'singer-poets' very similar to the Irish *fili* and the ancient Scandinavian skalds.

In regards to Indo-European society, Donald Ward ('On the Poets and Poetry of the Indo-Europeans', in *Journal of Indo-European Studies*, vol. 1, no. 2, 1973, Hattiesburg, Miss.) has taken up the fruitful distinction, introduced by Margaret Mead (*Cooperation and Competition among Primitive Peoples*, New York, 1937), between shame cultures and guilt cultures. In shame cultures, the fundamental notion is that of honour: the ability to look someone in the face. This *ethic of honour* implies a direct link with the sociocultural milieu. By a despicable act, one can dishonour his name and as a consequence the ancestors and descendants of his lineage. In guilt cultures, the guilt is objectified by recourse to a third party, which interiorises and individualises the sanction; its revealed dogmas define a *morality of sin*. According to Ward, the notion of

---

87   *The Tripartite Ideology of the Indo-Europeans*. — Tr.

'shame' common to the Greeks, Romans, Irish, and Scandinavians is typically Indo-European, in contrast to the notion of 'guilt' characteristic of the great universalist metaphysical systems.

Specific Characteristics

The entire ancient history of Europe is formed around two great waves of Indo-European migrations: one around −2,200–2,000, the other around 1250 BCE. From here proceed the Iranian and Vedic societies, the Hittite empire and the kingdoms of the Anatolian plateau, the historic civilisations of the Greeks and Romans, and of the Celts and Germanic peoples. To the west, the Indo-Europeans populated Gaul, the Iberian Peninsula, England, and Scandinavia. To the south, according to traditional chronology, the city of Rome was founded in April 753. In the east, the Indo-European peoples advanced as far as China, where their influence would be felt in the 'barbarian kingdoms' of the country's north. According to Hans Jansen, the Chinese words *mi*, 'honey',[88] *ch'yan* 'dog',[89] *yen*, 'goose', *ma*, 'horse', among others, were originally Indo-European.

Thanks to horse-breeding, the use of metals, and war chariots, the Indo-European peoples therefore spread, in successive waves, to conquer the world. (For a long time, one of the characteristic traits of a well-born man would be the possession of the horse, as testified by the respect accorded to the Roman or Gallic *equus*; cf. the words *cavalier* and *chevalier*, *Reiter* and *Ritter*, etc.[90] 'However', writes Nicolas Lahovary, 'these conquests should be considered the result of greater energy and superior military virtue. Here again it would not be in the material considerations, but in certain psychological qualities, in the force of character of the individuals and as a consequence their ethnic group, that the secret to the prodigious success of the Indo-Europeans should first be sought, including their upper hand over intelligent people whose civilisation was much more developed than theirs'.

After having traced the history of these migrations in a quite cursory and at times confusing manner, John Geipel examines the distribution of some of

---

88   The connection is more transparent in French: *miel*, 'honey'. — Tr.

89   Again, more transparent in French: *chien*, 'dog'. — Tr.

90   French *cavalier* (rider, horseman) and *chevalier* (knight); German *Reiter* (rider) and *Ritter* (knight). The connection also pertains between French *chevalier* and English 'chivalry'. — Tr.

the physical characteristics proper to the ancient Europeans: stature, eye and hair colour, cephalic and facial indications, etc.

Some of his observations lead to unexpected survivals. 'It is perhaps significant, for example, that the only parts of Europe where the vertical superposition of the jaws still exists, and which have only been recently supplanted by the advancement of the upper jawbone, are precisely those regions where the dental sibilants (the English 'th' sound) are still used in the phonetics of the local language'.

The ethnological kinship of the European people is further confirmed by the specific distribution of blood types O (45–75% of subjects), A (5–40%) and B (4–18%).

John Geipel also studied the physiognomy of Europeans today before launching himself into 'research on the races of Europe', a task to which he resigned himself with very little scientific reticence.

'The man who arrived in Europe long ago was a mixed breed', he reminds us at every instant, 'and we, his descendants, are no different'. But every individual is a 'mixed breed' to the extent that he issues from a certain number of cross-breedings, beginning with those of his parents. And Geipel overestimates the naivety of his audience if he believes that he can confuse them by revealing that racial characteristics are always relative.

Race is a dynamic, evolving, statistical notion. It is defined by the mean frequency of a certain number of genes that determine, for a given population, physical, pathological, and psychological predispositions or characteristics. To propose, with Professor Livingstone, to replace this term with 'line of frequency' thus reverts to wordplay — since it is precisely in the combination of 'lines of frequency' that anthropologists see the racial definition of the great branches of humanity.

George Montandon was the first, in 1933, to substitute the idea of 'racial homogeneity' with that of 'pure race', an ambiguous expression without scientific value — and otherwise easier to refute. 'Evolution characterises itself by a greater and greater differentiation', he observed elsewhere (*La race, les races*, Payot),[91] there is every reason to suppose that 'the undifferentiated is originally a primitive'.

---

91   *Race, Races.* — Tr.

Geipel also affirms that language and ethnicity 'exert absolutely no influence upon one another'. It is well known that African Americans speak English. But the reappearance of the morphology proper to the African languages (agglutination) in Caribbean speakers or in 'black English' (the language of the black ghettoes in the United States) is no less revealing.

It can no longer be doubted that the context varies from one era to another. The event of the 'Neolithic revolution' would cause the encounter of human groups who had previously remained isolated during the entire period of racial formation. 'This isolation conditioning the racial differentiation', writes Giorgio Locchi, 'is doubled by a linguistic isolation to which corresponds an extreme differentiation of language. From this fact, it is not hazardous to suggest that at the end of this era of humanity, each racial group corresponded to a specific language' ('Linguistique et sciences humaines', in *Nouvelle école*, April-May, 1968).[92]

Some Publications

With exceptions made for the principal works of Georges Dumézil (*Mythe et épopée*, Gallimard)[93] and Emile Benveniste (*Vocabulaire des institutions indo-européennes*, Minuit),[94] we only find a scarcity of recently published works in France consecrated to the (neglected) beginnings of Indo-European civilisation, such as those by P. Bosch-Gimpera (*Les Indo-Européens*. Payot, 1961),[95] V. Gordon Childe (*L'Europe préhistorique*. Payot, 1962),[96] Sigfrid de Laet (*La préhistoire de l'Europe*. Meddens, 1965),[97] Guido A. Mansuelli (*Les civilisations de l'Europe ancienne*. Arthaud, 1967),[98] and Jacques-Pierre Millotte (*Précis de protohistoire européenne*. A. Colin, 1970).[99] And yet some of these titles prove to be strongly disappointing, while most of the works of the great contemporary Indo-Europeanists still wait to be translated. The university itself is completely

---

92 'Linguistics and the Human Sciences'. — Tr.

93 *Myth and Epic.* — Tr.

94 *Vocabulary of Indo-European Institutions.* — Tr.

95 Spanish original: *El problema indoeuropeo* (Mexico: Universita Nacional Autónoma de Mexico, 1960). — Tr.

96 *Prehistoric Europe.* — Tr.

97 *The Prehistory of Europe.* — Tr.

98 *The Civilisations of Ancient Europe.* — Tr.

99 *Summary of European Protohistory.* — Tr.

disinterested in the subject: no course on the origins of our civilisation figures in the programmes of schools and faculties.

Despite (certain) shortcomings, Geipel's work nevertheless comes at the right time. For, contrary to what its author affirms, the 'hunt for the ancestors' is neither sterile nor derisory. On the contrary: the most distant past inspires the most powerful future.

*

L'anthropologie de l'Europe, a study by John Geipel.[100] Laffont, 356 pages.

*

Since the publication of the book by John Geipel, the only major works published in France on the Indo-Europeans have been those of Georges Dumézil, notably *Idées romaines* (Gallimard, 1969), *Fêtes romaines d'été et d'automne* (Gallimard, 1975), as well as vol. 2 and 3 of *Mythe et épopée* (Gallimard, 1971 and 1973).[101] A special number consecrated to the work of Dumézil (with texts by Jean-Claude Rivière, Robert Schilling, Mircéa Eliade, Georges Charachidzé, etc.) has also been published by the journal *Nouvelle école* (No. 21–22, winter 1972–1973).

In English and German speaking countries, as well as in Eastern countries, Indo-European studies are clearly more successful. In the United States, an important quarterly periodical, *The Journal of Indo-European Studies* (Suite 108, 1785 Massachusetts Avenue N.W, Washington, D.C. 20036), has appeared since 1973 under the direction of Dr. Roger Pearson.

---

100 *The Europeans An Ethnohistorical Survey* (London: Longmans, Green and Co., 1969). — Tr.
101 *Roman Ideas. Roman Festivals of Summer and Autumn. Myth and Epic.* — Tr.

Heligoland: Atlantis?

So many stupid things have been written on Atlantis that serious people have ended up relegating the problem to the same category as extra-terrestrials, flying saucers, and the cave of Ali-Baba. It is necessary to put an end to these convoluted ramblings.

Jürgen Spanuth — sixty-five, convincingly eloquent, wearing *Herr Doktor* glasses — has investigated the problem of Atlantis for thirty years. Born in Austria, he studied at the Universities of Berlin, Vienna, Kiel, and Tübingen; in 1931 he was named Professor of Theology, History, and Ancient Archaeology. Since 1933 he has been the pastor of Bordelum, a small village in Northern Friesland, Germany.

His first book, *Das enträtselte Atlantis* (Stuttgart, 1953),[102] appeared in French translation through Plon in 1955. *L'énigme de l'Atlantide*, published in France almost twenty years later, is unfortunately only a condensed version of a larger work of almost seven-hundred pages, entitled *Atlantis* (Grabert, Tübingen, 1965), which has attracted passionate debates.

'Like many people', remarks Spanuth, 'I had long believed that it was a myth. And then in 1933, while I was working on the antiquity of the Near East, I discovered the inscriptions of Medinet Habu'.

The royal temple of Medinet Habu was recovered in 1927 on the site of former Thebes by researchers of the Oriental Institute of the University of Chicago. It was constructed on the order of the pharaoh Rameses III (1200–1168 BCE) in order to celebrate the victory of Egypt over the mysterious invaders that historians designate by the name 'Sea Peoples' (or 'People from the Seas to the North'). The text of the mural inscriptions that relate the event in great detail was published between 1934 and 1954.

Spanuth was therefore surprised to notice that this text closely matched the account of Atlantis transcribed by Plato in two of his later dialogues, the *Critias* and the *Timaeus*.

---

102 *Atlantis — The Mystery Unravelled* (New York: Citadel Press, 1956). — Tr.

Around 570 BCE, relates Plato, the lawmaker Solon went to Egypt to 'gather information on past ages'. Thus did he learn, from the mouths of the priests, about the very ancient kingdom of Atlantis, whose capital had been submerged by floods following a great natural catastrophe, and whose inhabitants, ejected from their home, launched an assault on the Mediterranean lands.

'Solon was above all inspired by the heroic role played by Athens, his native town: it had been the only one at the time to conquer the inhabitants of Atlantis who, proceeding from Europe with a very powerful army, penetrated into Greece and occupied many other states'.

The 'Sea Peoples'

Having returned to Athens, Solon transmitted this account to his friend Dropides, the great-grandfather of Critias the Younger, a contemporary of Socrates (as portrayed by Plato).

The bas-reliefs of Medinet Habu are indeed of the greatest interest. They describe the attacks of the 'Sea Peoples', how the assailants were repelled, and what the scribes learned from their prisoners. Now, Plato did not know anything about Medinet Habu. And those after him, who would situate Atlantis in every location on the planet, were even more ignorant.

The ancients willingly ascribed an extremely remote date to the events of their history because they considered them all the more important. Plato, who was no exception, placed the arrival of the Atlanteans on the Greek coasts at around 9,000 years before his own time, a date which is obviously impossible to retain, since during this era the town of Athens was still far from being founded.

By contrast, archaeologists know that in the last third of the eighteenth century BCE, Athens actually suffered an attack from 'Sea Peoples'. The 'Pelasgic wall', built in complete haste, consequently protected the citadel of the Acropolis. The Greeks fought under the direction of King Codros, who would claim the victory, but lose his life. 'This heroic action', writes Plato, 'has remained unknown because it is very ancient, and because the men who accomplished it disappeared a very long time ago' (*Timaeus* 21d).

Repelled by the Athenians, the 'Sea Peoples' occupied Peloponnesus, Crete, Cyprus, Rhodes, and part of Asia Minor. Finally, having crossed Palestine and

Syria, they arrived at the borders of Egypt, where in 1192 BCE, they attacked the army of the pharaoh. The fight was terrible. Rameses eventually won.

The invaders then receded towards Europe and the Near East, crossing the terrain like a hurricane.

'Some of them would install themselves upon the Palestinian coast', writes Spanuth. 'It was by the tribe of the "Pheres", which we know under the name Philistines (following the Hebraic pronunciation, *Pheles*, from the word Pheres). The Wenamun papyrus indicates that the "Saksar" fixed themselves on the west coast of Syria, whereas the "Dori" (the Dorians) colonised Peloponnesus, Crete, Rhodes, and the islands of the Aegean Sea'.

Considering what we know of the great Indo-European migrations, Jürgen Spanuth is attempting to discover the origin of these people, which the Egyptian papyrus designates with the term *Haunebu* (a term that the Greeks translated as 'Atlantes'). Here again, he makes use of the lessons of Medinet Habu.

The bas-reliefs of the royal temple actually depict, with great precision, the physical aspect of the invaders, the horned helmets and crowns, carp's tongue swords, the round shields that they used, the slender vessels bearing heads of swans or dragons on the prow as well as the stern, which they took into battle. These traits, Spanuth emphasises, correspond neither to the equipment nor the customs of the Ancient Near East. However, they irresistibly evoke Europe, and most especially Northern Europe of the Bronze Age.

'There is every reason to think', he writes, 'that the point of departure of "Atlantis" must be situated in northern Germany or southern Scandinavia between the 52nd and 58th degrees of northern latitude. This region also corresponds to the "ninth sphere"[103] of Egyptian cosmology, from whence the prisoners came, according to the scribes, whose testimony they received'. It also corresponds to the place that the Greeks considered the 'pillars of the world', as it is recounted in the myth … of Atlantis.

---

103 *neuvième courbe*, literally 'ninth curve'. Benoist is citing Spanuth in French translation. I have rendered it 'ninth sphere' as Egyptian (and Egyptian-influenced) cosmologies frequently enumerate a series of concentric circles or spheres (as did Plato's description of the capital of Atlantis). 'Curves', however, seems out of place, while 'ninth parallel' does not make any geographic sense in this context. — Tr.

The three principle tribes of the 'Sea Peoples', the 'Pheres', the 'Saksar', and the 'Denen', would thus be the distant ancestors of the Frisians, the Saxons, and the Danes.

On the Rediscovery of the Ancient Basileia

The Atlanteans, Plato tells us, used a precious material called *orichalcum*. It was most probably yellow-amber, which two thousand years before our era, was an object of intense trade by Northern Europeans. Wasn't the god Apollo, whose cult was borne in Greece by the Dorians, supposed to return every year to Hyperborea, where on the banks of the Eridanos (the Eider), his sisters cried tears of amber? 'Now there is only one place', Spanuth underscores, 'where yellow amber was extracted in antiquity. It is precisely on the coastline of Schleswig-Holstein, between the North Sea and the Baltic'.

It is also there that the Elbe, the Weser, and the Eider converge, rivers whose courses were brutally modified by great natural catastrophes that occurred precisely in the eighteenth century BCE. These catastrophes, which caused the collapse or subsidence of the rivers of the North Sea and the Baltic, can be placed in relation to those which caused the ruin of the Cretan civilisation and the eruption of the volcano of Thera, Santorini, ravaging the Hittite empire in Asia and the Mycenaean kingdom in Greece, of which the Bible bears testimony with the episode of the 'seven plagues of Egypt' and the seaquake that allowed the dry crossing of the Red Sea.

'All of this', continues Spanuth, 'brings us to the vicinity of the isle of Heligoland, in the North Sea, which corresponds exactly to the description given by Plato of the sacred capital of the Atlanteans, the ancient Basileia.

Etymologically, moreover, Heligoland (*heiliges Land*) means 'sacred land'. In antiquity, it bore the name Basileia, then Balcia and Abalcia. Even today, old legends report that a temple 'of glass' or a fortress of 'yellow-amber' was engulfed by a marine pit off the island, and transformed into a seaside resort.

All that remained for Spanuth was to prove his thesis. In 1953, two underwater excavation campaigns had been undertaken to the east of Heligoland. At the place that had been indicated to them, the divers retrieved some plaques of bronze identical to those of which Plato spoke, as well as imposing murals of a lost city.

After the publication of *Atlantis*, Jürgen Spanuth received more than 16,000 letters from readers, including numerous scholars. Many felt that he had opened a serious pathway. More serious in any case than the far-fetched thesis of an 'Atlantic Atlantis', for which geological proofs are completely deficient, and whose adherents forget quite simply that the name of the Atlantic Ocean was only given to it much later, in 1665, by the Jesuit Athanasius Kircher.

'The mystery of Atlantis', Spanuth declared in Paris on 10 June 1971, 'can be considered resolved'.

*

L'énigme de l'Atlantide, a study by Jürgen Spanuth.[104] Published by Vie Claire (Périgny-sur-Yerres, 94520 Mandres-les-Roses), 156 pages.

*

In a new book, *Die Atlanter. Volk aus dem Bernsteinland* (Graubert, Tübingen, 1976),[105] Jürgen Spanuth puts together a dossier on Atlantis incorporating new data and a critique of localities proposed, more or less to date, by different authors (the Atlantic, Azores, Crete, Thera-Santorini, etc.). Some of these additions have already been the subject of articles published in the journal *Deutschland in Geschichte und Gegenwart* (Tübingen). The book is under translation and scheduled to appear through Éditions Copernic.

The controversy to which the hypotheses of Pastor Spanuth have given rise is revealed in an essay by Gerhard Gadow, *Der Atlantis-Streit. Zur meistdiskutierten Sage des Altertums* (Fischer, Frankfurt/M., 1973).[106] The author, who in a previous work (*Erinnerung an die Wirklichkeit*. Fischer, Frankfurt/M., 1971)[107] had violently attacked the fanciful claims of Erich von Däniken, feels to the contrary that the hypotheses of Spanuth have every chance of corresponding to reality.

On the history of Heligoland, there is a book by Jacques Mordal (*Héligoland*. Presses de la Cité, 1967), which, at least on the question of origins, remains relatively superficial. In the German domain, we find more precise information in a study by Werner Lorenzen, *Helgoland und das früheste Kupfer des Nordens* (Niederelbe-Verlag, Otterndorf, 1965).[108] On the cartographic history of northern Frisia, cf. also: Arend Lang, *Kleine Kartengeschichte Frieslands zwischen Ems und Jade* (Heinrich Soltau, Norden 1962).[109]

---

104 *The Mystery of Atlantis.* — Tr.

105 *Atlantis: People from the Land of Amber.* — Tr.

106 *The Atlantis Controversy: The Most Debated Tale of Antiquity.* — Tr.

107 *Memory of Reality.* — Tr.

108 *Heligoland and the Earliest Copper of the North.* — Tr.

109 *A Small Historical Map of Friesland Between Ems and Jade.* — Tr.

Linear B was from Greek

He was called Michael Ventris. He died in 1956 at 34 years of age. Upon learning of his death, Georges Dumézil, historian of religions, would write: 'Before the centuries, his work is done'.

His work was the decipherment of 'linear B', an achievement that enjoys a comparable role in relation to the study of Greek as the translation of the Rosetta Stone by Champollion does for Egyptology.

The story traces back to the last century. In 1876, an innovative German travels through Greece, *Iliad* in hand. He believes that Homer had spoken truly. He had good reason. Six years after having discovered the ruins of Troy on the Anatolian site of Hissarlik, Heinrich Schliemann discovered, in the northwest of Peloponnesus, in a wild and mountainous region, 'cyclopean' murals from the fortress of Mycenae. And then the Treasury of Atreus and the royal grave circle.

Mycenae is not the capital of the 'Mycenaean' world, but it is the most celebrated and best-known site. The founders of the Mycenaean civilisation are the Achaeans. Arriving from the north, they came to Greece at the beginning of the second millennium BCE, passing through Macedonia and Thessaly. In the same period, the 'battle-axe people' (*Streitaxvölker*), ancestors of the Germanic people, imposed themselves on the megalithic populations of northern Europe. The Hittites laid the foundations of an immense empire. The Indo-Aryans lead themselves towards the Indus Valley.

The Achaeans, colonising the Aegean Sea, installed themselves at Lipari, Cyprus, and Sicily, establishing strongholds in northern Syria, and destroyed Troy, guardian of the Hellespont (Bosphorus), key to the wheat trade. They subdued the autochthonous Mediterranean populations, and imposed their language upon them, derived from common Indo-European.

In Schliemann's time, the Achaeans were still poorly understood. The leading question was the origin of their power.

In 1900, a British scholar, Sir Arthur Evans, born in 1841, believed himself to have found the answer. Crete, barely liberated from Turkish rule, was fully effervescent. Excavating the ruins of the royal palace of Knossos, Evans discovered a brilliant and even refined civilisation: a palace with complicated structures, sumptuous frescoes, painted ceramics. It was the 'Minoan' civilisation (named after King Minos, builder of the legendary Labyrinth).

In the course of his digs, Evans also found some clay tablets, seemingly 'baked' due to a fire, which bore a mysterious, non-alphabetic writing. Incapable of deciphering it, the specialists nevertheless recognised two neighbouring systems: Linear A, traced from left to right, which is the most ancient (1750–1450 BCE), and Linear B (1400–1200 BCE). The tablets composed in Linear B are more numerous. More than three thousand would be discovered.

A 'Psychological Divide'

From this moment, Evan's opinion was arrested. The ruins of Knossos, he affirmed from 1909 (*Scripta Minoa I*), are those of an ancient Aegean civilisation of a Mediterranean or Semitic type. Mycenae, apparently, is merely a 'Minoan province'. The 'barbaric' Achaeans, students of the Cretans, had been the subjects of a great colonial empire founded on naval and commercial domination. Greece is the spiritual heir of the orient.

However, this diagnostic did not satisfy the entire world. In 1924, Forrer discovered Hittite texts that speak of a powerful '*Archaiwoi*' whose sovereign is considered equal to the pharaoh. Alan J. B. Wace contrasted the palace of Minos, tortuous and confused, to the royal palaces of Mycenae and Tiryns, which have a vigorous art organised around the hall of the throne and the *megaron*. Some pieces of 'Aegean' ceramic uncovered in Egypt reveal themselves to be Helladic and not Minoan; and vases exhumed at Knossos as simple imitations of an art originally from Corinth, in continental Greece. The 'psychological divide' which separates the Achaean civilisation from that of Crete appears increasingly deeper. But the researchers who attempt to diminish the rift run into violent opposition. Wace, notably, was forced to abandon the direction of the English School at Athens. The spirits were only seemingly appeased after the death of Evans, which occurred in 1941 when the Wehrmacht invaded Crete.

More or less around the same time, the American Professor Carl W. Blegen discovered six hundred tablets at Pylos in the ruins of a palace of another Homeric monarch, old Nestor. Some ingenious yet extravagant hypotheses were advanced to decipher 'Linear B'. As usual, Basque, Etruscan, and Hebrew were all evoked. Always without success.

An Archaic Dialect

It was thus in 1952 that a veritable thunder-strike resounded in the heavens of Hellenic studies. A thirty-year old philologist, Michael Ventris, made a staggering revelation: Linear B, the language from the height of Crete, is none other than Greek.

Son of a former officer in the Indian Army, Ventris had had a passion for archaeology since his childhood. A lecture by Sir Evans, which he heard when he was fourteen years old, had been a revelation for him. Thenceforth, he only spent his holidays at the British Museum. In 1940, he published his first article on the 'Minoans' in the *American Journal of Archaeology*. He concealed his age.

For a long time Ventris has been persuaded the Linear B belonged to Etruscan. It was only gradually that the Greek solution appeared to him as 'inevitable'. In June 1952 he declared to the BBC:

'After many years of work, I have come to the conclusion that the tablets of Knossos and of Pylos must, in the final analysis, have been written in Greek; a difficult, archaic Greek, to the extent that they are five hundred years older than Homer and written in quite an abridged form. But it is indeed Greek.'

With his friend John Chadwick, Ventris treated Linear B as a secret code. In the absence of any bilingual document, he had to demonstrate meaningful occurrences using the 'combinatory' method, setting up 'syllabic grids'. In 1953 he summarised his efforts in an article for the *Journal for Hellenic Studies* ('Evidence for Greek Dialects in Mycenaean Archives'), which offered the interpretation of some sixty-five of the ninety signs already identified. Three years later, a book followed up on the article: *Documents in Mycenaean Greek*.

Chadwick mastered his subject so well that he was able to write in Linear B: 'John to Michael, Greetings! Today I am going to give the book to the printer. Good luck!'

Gradually, the educated world surrendered to the evidence. As early as 1953, the *Times* celebrated those who had surmounted the 'Everest of Greek archaeology'! Linear B is a system of the syllabic type (words are 'di-vi-ded'). It also includes some ideograms for common vocabulary (man, woman, bronze, chariot, wheat). Numbers correspond to the decimal system, and there were special signs for fractions. As to the difficulties of 'translation', they adhere to archaisms, and to the fact that the signs were not originally conceived for the Greek language; they are only a 'phonetic transcription' of it.

'We note indeed', writes François Chamoux, 'that the values attributed to the different signs of the syllabary must admit a certain play to lead to a coherent transcription in a Greek dialect, even of a strongly archaic type. Most of the diphthongs are not notes as such, the distinction is not made between short and long vowels, between l and r, etc.' (*La civilisation greque*. Arthaud, 1963).[110]

The tablets are for the most part 'compatible pieces' deriving from stewardship services from the palace of Knossos, Pylos, or Mycenae. But they are of immense descriptive interest. They 'take us back' to the Mycenaeans like the Salic law takes us back to the Franks or the *Domesday Book* to the Anglo-Normans.

Beyond the inventories of goods and furniture, or the status of cultic fees, a system of feudal inheritance from the more ancient Indo-European past is also described: a patriarchal civilisation practicing agriculture, stockbreeding, and bronze metallurgy. Imposing fortresses were richly ornamented with hunting and battle scenes on the walls. Fleets submitted to the authority of a prince (*anax*). Cities were run by a leader, assisted by a 'retinue' of companions (analogous to the Germanic *Gefolgschaft*)[111] and by a council of Elders. These were the Achaeans of Menelaus and Agamemnon. The civilisation of which Homer had sung.

Ten years before Pericles, the Greek pantheon was already complete. On the tablets we find the names of Zeus, Hera, Poseidon, Athena, and perhaps also Dionysus attested by a probable genitive. A dedication is even present 'to all the gods' (*pa-si-te-o-i*).

At Mycenae as in Crete, at Pylos as in Thebes, masters and servants bore Greek names, spoke Greek, and kept their records in Greek.

---

110 *Greek Civilisation.* — Tr.

111 *Gefolgschaft*, 'allegiance, fealty, loyalty', indicating a reciprocal relationship of loyalty and protection established between a lord and his retinue of warriors. — Tr.

A Period of more than 3,500 Years

Since then, the perspective proposed by Evans has found itself suddenly reversed: it is Greece who imposed its domination upon the Cretans in the fifteenth century BCE. The absence in the administrative inventories of any mention of insular Cretan dependencies sounds the death-knell of the highly imaginary 'Minoan thalassocracy'.[112]

The Greek Dark Age is no longer a chasm between two different worlds, but a point of connection continuing the same mentality. The Mycenaeans are not the 'pre-Hellenes'; they come wholly from the Greeks.

'We need to admit', writes François Chamoux, 'that the history of Greek civilisation no longer began in the eighteenth century, but at the moment that the first decipherable texts appeared, that is to say, in the middle of the second millennium, towards the end of the fifteenth century, if not even sooner. All Mycenaean civilisation now departs from Hellenism, not merely as a preface, but as the first chapter of its history, which started at least six hundred years earlier than we had believed'.

The Greek language is thus known to us by texts extending over a period of more than 3,500 years. The only other comparable language is Chinese.

The Mycenaean civilisation was replaced by that of the Dorians, who founded Sparta and brought with them the cult of Apollo and the metallurgy of iron. Was the destruction of the palace of Knossos and of Mycenae linked to the natural catastrophes that accompanied the arrival of the 'Sea Peoples'? The hypothesis has some consistency. It nevertheless runs into a chronological error, since the end of the palatial civilisation is habitually placed around 1450–1400 BCE, whereas the Sea Peoples have scarcely appeared in the Aegean region until around 1,200 BCE. But this difference, perhaps, does not correspond to reality. It could result from the juxtaposition of two different chronologies, one applying to Europe, and the other to Egypt and the Near East. It is also in the process of being 'reduced'. According to Professor L. R. Palmer, the eruption of the volcano at Thera-Santorini, the invasions of the Sea Peoples, the collapse of the Mycenaean culture at the end Cretan palatial civilisation, as well as the arrival or the Dorians, were indeed situated in the same era. 'As far as the writing and the language are concerned', he observes, 'the tablets of Knossos, dated to around 1,450 BCE, are quite similar to those of

---

112 Thalassocracy, from *thalassa* (sea) + *kratein* (to rule); empire at sea, naval supremacy. — Tr.

Pylos, which date from around 1,200 BCE. Is it possible that the language had remained static during those centuries?'

This hypothesis explains the conservation of tablets and the uniform character of the inscriptions. 'It was the enormous heat of the final accident,' recalls Chadwick, 'which had cooked most of the clay tablets, giving them the hardness of brick or ceramic that allowed them to survive down to our own time'.

Linear A

The Greek poet Menander said: 'Those who are loved by the gods die young'. The life of Michael Ventris ended on the night of 6 September 1956, near Hatfield. A car accident. The decipherer of Linear B was killed on impact.

The spark was ignited. After the 'breakthrough' of 1952, all subsequent works confirmed the conclusions of Ventris and Chadwick. In France, the linguist Michael Lejeune and the philologist Pierre Chantraine were among the first to catalogue them. Tablets are still discovered each year. Thebes, Sparta, and Pleuron still remain to be excavated. (Incidentally, in 1963–1964, it was verified that Sir Arthur Evans had somewhat 'embellished' his findings, and that pieces as celebrated as his 'Prince of the Lilies', his 'Three Cretans', his 'Seated Goddess', and his 'Goddess with Serpents' were all simply false).

The book by Chadwick was published in Great Britain in 1958. It has taken fourteen years for it to cross the Channel. But it is lively, precise, and conducted like a police investigation. The postface, dated to 1967, adds some new summaries. There is one discordant note: a fairly pointless preface in which Pierre Vidal-Naquet, who was part of a small group of Marxising Hellenists (Jean-Pierre Vernant, Moses I. Finlay) continues to denounce the 'Homeric illusion'.

As to Linear A, it is still undeciphered. But the hypotheses are going strong. It cannot be excluded that this script records an Indo-European language from Asia Minor; 'Luwian', says Professor L. R. Palmer (*Mycenaeans and Minoans*, London, 1965), while Professor Simon Davis from the University of Witwatersrand thinks that it is from a dialect derived from Hittite. Stay tuned. We await a new Ventris.

*

Le déchiffrement du linéare B, a study by John Chadwick.[113] Gallimard, 238 pages.

---

113 This is the French translation of Chadwick's *The Decipherment of Linear B* (Cambridge University Press, 1959). — Tr.

Homer and the Homeric Epic

'The unequal struggle between spiritual values and materialism leads to chaos and despair', declares Eleftherios C. Mamounas, founder of the International Society of Homeric Studies. More and more, the young restrict their ideals to dubious and degrading pleasures. This deviation is clearly depicted in the Homeric writings. Doesn't the first verse of the *Iliad* begin with the word 'wrath'? Homer has been the witness of men's weaknesses. By keeping his work alive, we also understand how to defend the values of our own civilisation.

15,693 verses + 12,110 verses: the *Iliad* and the *Odyssey*. More than a masterpiece. One of the most ancient monuments of western literature. Not a legend, but a *myth* embroidered upon a reality.

Not one author from Antiquity has ever contested the reality of the Trojan War. Plato himself, who rejected the 'ethics' of Homer, casts no doubt on the event itself. Besides, it is found in other texts (of which there is a previous account wrongly attributed to Dictys of Crete). 'The very fact', notes Jean Bérard in his preface to the Pleiade edition (Gallimard, 1961), 'that in the *Iliad* and *Odyssey*, the unusual episodes of the two poems are mentioned by simple allusions is significant: it implies that this legend was known by the poet as well as by all those to whom he addressed himself'.

The date of the storming and burning of Troy is still uncertain. It generally goes back to the vicinity of −1270, the thirteenth century BCE. In 1870, on the mound of Hissarlik (Anatolia), the German archaeologist Schliemann found the ruins of the city of King Priam.

The world of Homer is the Mycenaean world that scholars have restored for us. The Atreidae and the golden fleece. The establishment of Rhodes and the destruction of Thebes. Achilles and Patroclus, Helen and Paris. The crime of Aegisthus and Clytemnestra. This universe was destroyed around 1200 BCE. After the Trojan War, Homer tells us, the descendants of Heracles, at the head of the Dorians, established themselves in the Peloponnesus. Thus, with the 'return of the Heracleidae', the time of ancient heroes came to an end.

Due to essentially ideological motivations, some authors have sought to deny the identity of the Homeric world and of the Mycenaean civilisation. Moses I. Finley, followed by Pierre Vidal-Naquet, never fail to place Homer's name in quotation marks, and to ensure that ancient Greek society 'incontestably recalls the other societies of the same age from the Near East' (*Le monde d'Ulysse*. Maspéro, 1969).[114] Jean Bérard responds: 'It can no longer be doubted that the Age of Heroes, to which the epic legends of Greece refer, answers to the archaeological realities of the Mycenaean epoch that the excavations have revealed to us'.

The Sacred Books of Ancient Greece

From the Trojan War, which lasted ten years, Homer retains only two brief episodes: the battle of Achilles and Agamemnon and that which follows; the long wandering of the cunning Odysseus after the sacking of Ilion. Exemplary destinies. Odysseus lives to a ripe old age and reaches his end after a long journey. Achilles has the brief existence of heroes. (One cannot have, at the same time, both *endurance* and *intensity*). For one, adventure and love. For the other, war and friendship. The fox and the lion.

The technique of composition is ultra-modern. The first song of the *Iliad* begins when the war is reaching its end. The *Odyssey* takes Odysseus from his departure from Calypso, where he remained for seven years. It is only in a secondary episode that the reader is invited to 'return'. Homer invents the *flashback*.

The poet sings of exploits, and above all exploits of war. But the clash of weapons does not exclude psychological analysis nor emotional heights. The harshest customs are also the least crude. 'Achaean society of the heroic age, however it might appear to our modern eyes, is in no way a primitive society. The brilliance of material civilisation and art, as notably testified by the carved gold cups from Vaphio or Dendra, are already linked to a great moral refinement'. (Jean Bérard).

A wealth of images: 'In the heart of the countryside, where one is without neighbours, the brand is hidden under ash and ember to conserve the seed of fire so one doesn't have to seek it elsewhere: thus was Odysseus hidden under its leaves'.

---

114 *The World of Odysseus.* — Tr.

Some constants appear in the *Iliad*: the sense of honour, the joy of liv-ing, the taste for affirmation, virile values, love of friendship. The society of gods reflects those of men, with the same qualities and shortcomings. Homer, who conceived them in his image, portrays them with a 'disregard' that would scandalise Plato. 'The gods of Homer are not pure spirits', writes Professor Albert Severyns from the University of Liège. 'Given a sensible form compara-ble to that of the human being, they conduct themselves as mortals would in an earthly society' (*Les dieux d'Homère*. PUF, 1966). These are not jealous or severe gods. They are gods who laugh.

It is perhaps for this reason that that the *Iliad* and the *Odyssey* were truly, in Flacelière's terms, the 'sacred books of Greece'. For the Greeks of Antiquity, Homer was 'the Poet'. He was unique. But he was also more: repository for the old Hellenic spirit in its purity, master of all wisdom, guardian of traditions. In Athens, Solon and Pisistratus made his work both liturgy and textbook. Every four years, on the occasion of the Great Panatheneia, the two poems were read from end to end. 'We perhaps forget', writes Flacelière, 'that the capacity of ancient audiences was much stronger than ours. At the dramatic competitions of the Great Dionysia alone, held at Athens, the spectators heard probably around eighteen-thousand verses over three consecutive days. The twenty-eight thousand verses of the *Iliad* and *Odyssey*, without lyrical division or choral developments, could have been recited at this pace in four days'.

After the Homeric period, the bards[115] dispersed throughout the islands and coasts of Ionia, ensured the diffusion of the *Iliad* and *Odyssey*, and composed new poems. These are the Homerides. To them we owe a series of accounts that constitute the Epic Cycle. In the Greek world, they provided not only the texts, but also the rhapsodists or reciters.

In the first centuries of our era, the decline of ancient culture lead to the eclipse of Homeric studies. These would only be revived in the tenth century, in Constantinople. In the fourteenth century, they flourished again in Europe. The first printed 'Homer' appeared in Florence in 1488. The Renaissance, and then the Enlightenment, were each inspired in turn. Exegeses and critiques proliferated. In the twentieth century, Anglo-Saxon and German universities competed in knowledge and ability.

---

115 Benoist uses the term *aèdes*, derived from the Greek *aoidoi* (singular, *aoidos*), the bards, singers, chanters; epic poets of the oral tradition. — Tr.

Almost as many books have been published on Homer as on Goethe and Shakespeare, Atlantis, and the pyramids of Egypt. In France, Victor Bérard has attempted to recover the geography of the Achaeans (*Les navigations d'Ulysse*, 1927–30). Emile Mireaux (*Les poèmes homériques et l'histoire grecque*. Albin Michel, 1948–49) has sought the secret of Homer in 'colonial antagonisms' and the trade of tin. Charles Autran (*Homère et les origines sacerdotales de l'épopée grecque*. Denoël, 1939–43), who portrays the mysterious castes of Hellenic priests, has seen in the Trojan War an 'act of purification' destined to efface a 'detested impiety'.

All of Antiquity attributed the *Iliad* and the *Odyssey* to the same author. The 'analysts' have been more sceptical. They have given us ingenious theories which sketch the uncertain contours of a 'Homer in the plural'. But most of the Homerists have returned to the hypercriticsm that was popular last century among the Anglo-Saxons and the Germans. From 1930, Victor Bérard wrote: 'Today one is considered the last of the ignorant if they dare cast into doubt the idea that the *Iliad* and the *Odyssey*, from their first verse to their last, were composed by the blind poet' (*La resurrection d'Homère*. Grasset, 1930).[116]

Blind, Homer was perhaps not. According to the Ancients, 'material' blindness was frequently associated with 'spiritual' clairvoyance, with the prophetic gift, and with divination. In myth, Oedipus acquired the gift of prophecy the instant that he punctured his eyes. Georges Dumézil has noted other examples of 'qualifying mutilations': Odhinn and Horatius Cocles, Tyr and Mucius Scaevola, etc. 'The greatest of poets *must* therefore be blind', writes Robert Flacelière, 'but in fact, we do not know if he was'.

If we are to believe Herodotus, Homer would have lived around 850 BCE. He possibly composed other, minor works, such as the *Hymn to Apollo* spoken of by Thucydides.

Seven cities contend for the honour of having given birth to the poet. The island of Chios, in Ionia, cited by Pindar and Semonides of Amorgos, appears to be the best 'situated'. The place is celebrated for its landscape and its beauty. It owes its name to Chioni, daughter of one of the first kings who was pledged to marry Orion once he had ridden the country of the serpents that infested it. Homer, said Herodotus, would have lived in the village of Pytis, which is

---

116 *The Resurrection of Homer*. — Tr.

today called Pytios. A body of Homerides (the best known being Cynethos of Chios) worked there for a long time. Here we see the 'olive trees of the master' and drink an age-old wine, the 'nectar of Homer'! In the Museum of Chios one finds the head of Homer discovered by the archaeologist Anderson, the Homeric epitaph discovered by Professor Kondoleon-Stephanou, and various other vestiges from Antiquity.

Pilgrimage to Chios

A location near Chios features 'Homer's stone' (or Daskalopetra), a former cult site close to a rocky alcove. Tradition would have it that Homer publicly read the *Iliad* and *Odyssey* here. In 1960, during a voyage here, Eleftherios C. Mamounas was inspired to create an organised movement for the study of Homeric 'philosophy'.

Thus was the International Society of Homeric Studies born. 'It envisages today', writes Marc Michel in the journal *Europe Sud-Est* (Athens), to 'transform the peaceable Island of Chios into a Mediterranean Stratford-upon-Avon'.

Besides Mamounas, its Cultural Committee is composed of numerous renowned Hellenists: Professors François Chamoux (France), Hugh Lloyd-Jones (Great Britain), Erick Havelock (United States), Reinhold Merkelbach (Germany), Theseus Tzannetatos, Andreas A. Potamianos, A. Skiadas (Greece). The French Committee, presided over by Chamoux, also includes Professor Edouard Delebecque, of Aix-en-Provence.

In London, a powerful union of shipowners from Chios have decided to finance the construction of an open air theatre and a 'Homeric Centre'. Chios will thus become a place of international gathering and a centre of pilgrimage for the spiritual sons of those who died at the siege of Troy.

*

International Society of Homeric Studies: Kanari 8, Athens.[117]

*

At the end of the last century, the English writer Samuel Butler (*On the Trapanese Origin of the Odyssey*, 1893; *The Authoress of the Odyssey*, 1897) had advanced the idea that different authors were responsible for the *Iliad* and the *Odyssey*, and that the true author of the *Odyssey* was a young woman originally from Trapani, in Sicily. This hypothesis has been

---

117   As far as I have been able to ascertain, this society no longer exists. — Tr.

reprised by a modern disciple of Butler, Raymond Ruyer, in *Homère au féminin* (Copernic, 1977).[118]

On the historical background of the Odyssey, the most audacious theories continue to be advanced. At the beginning of 1977, Professor Karl Bartholomäus of the University of Essen had proposed a new itinerary of Odysseus' peregrinations. Charybdis and Scylla correspond to the ruins of Gibraltar; the island of Thrinacia to Teneriffe, and Ogygia, home of Calypso, to one of the islands of Azores. As to the island of the Phaeacians, it is identified with Heligoland (which links to one of the hypotheses of Jürgen Spanuth).

The International Society of Homeric Studies organised a symposium from 18–19 October 1976 at the University of Alexandria, in which several Greek and Egyptian Hellenists participated.

---

118 *Homer in the Feminine.* — Tr.

Zoroaster

The good empire must be chosen.
It secures the most advantageous fate for the one who acts with zeal. Through
Justice, O Sage, by these actions,
he will reach the sovereign good (Yasna 51).[119]

These words were pronounced more than twenty-five hundred years ago by Spitāma Zarathustra, the reformer of the ancient Iranian religion to whom Europe gave the name Zoroaster.

During the course of the third millennium BCE, the Indo-European peoples, departing from a homeland reaching from the Baltic to the Aral Sea, slowly moved towards the east, the west, and the south.

A few centuries later, the 'oriental' branch subdivided into several groups. One of them, via Punjab and Kashmir, would colonise the Indian subcontinent: these are the Indo-Aryans. Another occupied Asia Minor and established themselves at Azerbaijan, and after that, in the country to which they would lend their name: Iran, i.e., the 'Aryan region'.

In this place, the Indo-Iranians found some Asiatic populations, the Elamites, who submitted to them without difficulty. They then organised a National State based on the representatives of the clans and lineages.

Herodotus described the first Persians as men of great height, as strong as they were proud. He recounts how the children of the noble family are raised at the court of the king to 'learn to ride the horse, draw the bow, and speak the truth'. Xenophon praised the stature of their men and the beauty of their women. Heraclides called them 'the bravest of the barbarians'.

---

119 The translation rendered here is from the French edition cited by Benoist (*Il faut choisir le Bon Empire. Il procure le sort le plus avantageux à celui qui agit avec zèle. Par la Justice, celui-ci accèdera, pour ces actions, ô Sage ! au souverain bien »*.) For comparison, D. J. Irani's English translation of Yasna 51 from *The Gathas: The Hymns of Zarathustra* (Center for Ancient Iranian Studies, 1998) reads: 'A righteous government is of all the most to be wished for, Bearing of blessing and good fortune in the highest. Guided by the law of Truth, supported by dedication and zeal, It blossoms into the Best of Order, a Kingdom of Heaven! To effect this I shall work now and ever more'. — Tr.

In the first millennium, the Indo-Iranian cult, already strongly transformed, evolved towards a new form, Mazdaism, of which Zoroaster became the propagator.

Three French figures stand at the origin of modern knowledge about this enigmatic character, who would enjoy a certain vogue in eighteenth century Europe, even though, at the time, it was merely a fanciful idea: Anquetil-Duperron, who went to India in 1754 in order to collect the text of the *Avesta*; Eugène Burnouf (1801–1852) who first explained this text according to a philologically sound method; James Darmesteter, whose translation of the *Avesta*, published in 1892 (and recently reissued in three volumes by Adrien-Maisonneuve) continues to have authority.

Jean Varenne, Professor of Sanskrit at the University of Aix-en-Provence, author of a Sanskrit grammar and various translations of the *Vedas*, the *Upanishads*, and the *Brahmanas*, had already published a work entitled *Zarathoustra et la tradition mazdéenne* (Seiul, 1965). In his study of Zoroaster, he returns to the problem from a new angle.

The name of Zoroaster (Zarathustra) belongs to a dialect from the northeast of Iran. His entire career, moreover, unfolds between the outskirts of Sogdiana and the Sistan Basin. He thus most likely came from this region, which adjoins the plateaus of Afghanistan, and not, as a tradition dating from the Sassanians would have it, from western Iran, i.e. current Tehran. More precisely, he would be born in Bactria, in the region of the lower Oxus, where soviet Turkestan is currently located.

The dates are poorly attested. Tradition situates the life of Zoroaster on the eve of the foundation of the Persian Empire by Cyrus the Great (546), but the archaisms of the *Gāthās* instead incline one to place him at the very beginning of the first millennium BCE.

This is not a man of the people but a man of a princely stock. Perhaps he was born in a family of warriors: doesn't the first part of his name, Spitāmā, mean 'to the brilliant attack'?[120] However, he was raised within the purview of a sacerdotal profession. 'Knowing thousands, perhaps even the tens-of-thousands of stanzas by heart', observes Varenne, 'it would not have been difficult for him to compose his own later'.

---

120 Or perhaps 'to attack brilliantly' (*à la brillante attaque*). — Tr.

His sermonising began around the age of thirty-six. Four years later, he was received by Balkh's sovereign, Vishtāspa (who some have falsely considered the father of Darius the Great), and he successfully made Vishtāspa embrace the reformed religion. Henceforth, the success of the new cult was assured. Zoroaster became the king's priest, and the entire court converted.

Zoroaster would spend the rest of his life close to Vishtāspa. He seems to have died at the age of seventy-seven, possibly in a violent manner (assassinated, it is said, by the Turanians), after being married and having many children.

What we know of the Iranian religion before Zoroaster comes to us from Herodotus. This religion was very similar to that of the Indo-Aryans, since the two peoples had lived together for a long time in Central Asia before separating. 'Alongside the commonality of language', specifies Varenne, 'a commonality of civilisation and therefore of ideology is also manifest'.

Among both of them, therefore, we find the same gods (*deva* in Sanskrit, *daeva* in Iranian): Vāyu, Indra, Mitra, Bhaga, etc. The society of gods is divided into two clans or factions: those of the Asuras or 'forces of life', and those of the Devas proper, or 'beings of light'. These factions date back to the common Indo-European period and correspond, among the Germanic peoples, to the distinction between the Vanir and the Aesir. But here their 'destiny' is different. Whereas among the Germanic peoples, the two clans, at the end of a 'war of foundation', join to form a harmonious society ruled by the Aesir, among the Aryas the conflict results in a completely different theological situation. In India, the Devas become the only true gods, while the Asuras are qualified as demons. In Iran, it is the opposite: Zoroaster makes himself the champion of the Asuras (Ahuras in Old Persian) and retains the Devas as the forces of evil (in Iranian, the word *daeva* will ultimately come to mean 'demon').

This choice by Zoroaster is based upon motives that remain obscure. An ancient rivalry between the Indo-Iranians and Indo-Aryans is spoken of, which would have had current-day Afghanistan as its theatre. This is still to be proven.

The 'Mazdaean' Archangels

The Mazdaean religion rests on a fundamental antagonism between two principles that the Avesta (the Mazdaean texts) portrays as being in perpetual war. One is responsible for all that is beautiful, pure, luminous, and living; the other, for everything that is evil, impure, deadly, and dark.

The supreme god, Ahura Mazdā ('the Great Creator') is assisted by seven abstract entities or 'beneficent immortals' (*Amesha Spenta*) who form the Heptad, that is to say, the aspects of the Divinity worthy of reverence.

The first of these 'archangels' (a term suggested by Georges Dumézil in *Naissance d'archanges*, Gallimard, 1945), Spenta Mainyu ('Holy Spirit'), son of Ahura Mazdā, has a twin brother, Angra Mainyu ('Evil Spirit'), who since the origin of the world, struggles to pervert creation. At the beginning of the cosmic cycle, the two Mainyu brothers were 'neutral', but when they had to choose between justice and deception, they were each articulated with a different meaning: Angra Mainyu suggests Lucifer, another luminous fallen angel (*lux-fero*, 'I bear the light').

The six other archangels are always enumerated in a constant order: 1. Asha Vahista (Right Order). 2. Vohu Manah (Good Thought). 3. Kshatra (Empire, Power). 4. Haurvatāt (Integrity, Health). 5. Ameretāt (Immortality, Deathlessness). 6. Ārmaiti (Sacred Devotion).[121]

The meaning and the exact role of these entities have been investigated for a long time. In 1945, Georges Dumézil had been able to demonstrate by meticulous analysis that the two premier archangels correspond to the first function among the Indo-Europeans (the prescriptive ordering of the world, and juridical sovereignty); the third, Kshatra, to the second (warrior) function; Haurvatāt and Ameretāt, to the third function (fecundity and longevity), symbolised among the Indo-Aryans by the Nasatya twins, givers of life and health. As to the last entity, Ārmaiti, she represents a divinity that takes on a 'synthesis' of the three functions, whose equivalent is found in Saravasti among the Indians or Athena among the Greeks.[122]

---

121 I have transliterated the names of the Amesha Spenta according to current English conventions. A few points of clarification are nevertheless helpful regarding Benoist's usage. For *Asha Vahishta*, Benoist uses the alternate transliteration, *Arta*, and glosses it as *l'Ordre* (Order); its broader range of meanings encompasses 'truth, existence, and [that which is] right' (cf. Vedic *rta-*). For Haurvatāt, Benoist uses the alternate form, Sarvatāt. Armaiti is glossed as *la Pensée pieuse*, literally 'Pious Thought', but I have followed the convention in Zoroastrian scholarship of rendering it as 'Sacred Devotion'. — Tr.

122 Benoist has 'Saravasti' here, but possibly means Sarasvati (Saraswati), a Hindu river goddess associated with the flow of wisdom, knowledge, and speech (cf. the Vedic goddess, Vāc). — Tr.

The nature of Mazdaeism is therefore much more complex than it appears at first glance.

First of all, this apparent dualism is a monotheism. Ahura Māzdā is qualified as the only supreme god and there is never any doubt as to his final victory. The religion of Zoroaster does not have a 'good god' and a 'bad god'; both have equal power; but an emanation (a 'son') of Ahura Māzdā struggles with another emanation, which is turned towards evil. 'The teaching of the Iranian reformer', emphasises Jean Varenne, 'is less dualistic than Christianity, where it is God himself in the person of his son who confronts Satan'. Evil is no longer identified with the 'veil of tears' of earthly existence, while the good is in the 'kingdom of heaven'. On the contrary, if Mazdaism opposes light with darkness, it is to place the first in this world and the second beyond it.

On the other hand, the identification of the archangels with the symbolic survivals of the three functions shows that the Zoroastrian 'heaven' is a space that is rustling with activity. Ahura Māzdā does not differ fundamentally from the supreme god of the Indo-Europeans: Jupiter among the Romans, Zeus-Pater among the Greeks, Diyuh-Pitā and Varuna among the Aryans. Varenne's conclusion: 'Zoroaster was more conservative than revolutionary'.

The Mediating Fire between Men and Gods

Zoroaster has not left a systematic exposition of his thought; the only documents at our disposal on the subject are the religious hymns that he authored: the *Gāthās*. These furnish us with some precise indications as to the customs, social organisation, habits, and ethics of the Old Persians.

Their tone is not lacking in aggression. At every instance, the author uses the same 'military' vocabulary that in India is found in the *Rig Veda*. He insists on justice more than mercy or grace. The Good Religion, he says, must be diffused by every means: it is the purpose of temporal power to establish, if necessary by force, Beneficent Order in this world.

Zoroaster condemns all forms of renunciation: fasting, celibacy, etc. His three principle commandments are: 'Good thoughts, good speech, good actions'. In leading a life of righteousness, conformed to courage and to a sense of honour, man increases the power of Good (Ormazd) and diminishes that of Evil (Ahriman).

After death, man will be accountable for his actions. His soul will pass the 'Sifting Bridge' (*Chinvat*). If it has done Good, he will cross this passage without any difficulties. If the opposite is the case, the bridge will appear as thin as a hair, and he will plummet into an infernal abyss.

Liturgy takes on a considerable importance. The sacred fire (*Atar*) is in some way the mediator between men and the gods: it transmits the prayers and conveys the smoke of the sacrifices prepared by the priests (*hotar* in Sanskrit, *zaotar* in Iranian). Even there, Zoroaster has resumed an older practice. In Indo-Iranian paganism, fire has the rank of divinity. Zoroaster strips it of its divine character, but conserves for it a central place and goes so far as to make it a representation of Ahura Māzdā.

Ultimately we are dealing with a community-based, 'national' cult. Any reliance upon 'missionaries' is rejected. Mixed marriages are prescribed and Zoroaster goes as far as advocating consanguineous unions.

The influence of Mazdaism on later religions (Christianity and above all Islam) is likely. We have been able to see the Iranian *magi* in the 'magician-kings' who, according to Matthew (2.1–2), came to Bethlehem bearing gifts for the new-born Christ.

It is certain that the Achaemenids (from Cyrus the Great in 559, to Darius II in 330) were not all Zoroastrians. However, under the Sassanid dynasty, from 226 CE, the reformed religion triumphed and became the State Cult. The *Gāthās*, augmented by numerous commentaries, were thus translated into Pahlavi. But in one stroke the faith froze into a rigid orthodoxy. The influence of oriental currents made itself felt. In 639, Mazdaism collided with the Muslim conquest. Noble families were hunted down. Many emigrated to India, where they formed the Parsi community. Only the Guebres were able to remain in Iran despite persecutions.

Today, the Parsis ('Persians') or modern Zoroastrians live in the region of Bombay. Descendants of families hunted by the Arabs who arrived in India in 716 or, more simply, heirs of the Iranian 'counters'[123] from the west coast, they have carried with them the sacred fire, which they venerate as the symbol of the Light that shines in the heart of man.

---

123 Fr. *comptoirs*. — Tr.

Proponents of the immortality of the soul, they nevertheless rejected the doctrine of reincarnation. They are divided into two sects: the Shahanshahis and the Kadmis. Their cult underwent the influence of Hinduism. Having become hereditary, the priesthood contained three degrees. In the nineteenth century, a movement of 'return to the *Gāthās*' lead to a veritable cultural and political renaissance. In 1941, there were a little less than 115,000 Parsis. Their economic and social status is currently far superior to that of the average indigenous person: many Indian businessmen are Parsis.

The survival of Mazdaism in our day, and the existence of a prosperous Parsi community, pose an enigma. According to Varenne, the eschatological optimism of Zoroaster's religion, as opposed to the metaphysical pessimism of Buddhism, Brahmanism, or Manichaeism, is not unrelated to this.

*

Zoroaster, a study by Jean Varenne. Seghers, 258 pages.

The Etruscan Mystery

'Not only do the Etruscan people speak', affirms Zacharie Mayani, 'they joke, they use irony, they sing, they exalt the gods, they pray and address their exhortations to the shadows of their ancestors, and all of this in the language of Alexander the Great, of Pyrrhus, and of Maecenas. It is a terse language with a jagged rhythm, but full of vigour'.

Will the Etruscan mystery ever be resolved? And first of all, who are the Etruscans?

The Indo-Europeans arrived upon the Italian peninsular around 1,200 BCE, at the height of the Bronze Age. The founding of Rome, which is attributed to the Umbrians, dates to April, 753. Two centuries later, the Romans clashed violently with the inhabitants of Etruria, a territory situated between Umbria, the island Elba, and Latium. The most ancient chronicles report the war against the Etruscan king Porsenna in 507, and the legendary exploits of the one-eyed Horatius Cocles and the one-armed Mucius Scaevola, who were shown by Georges Dumézil to be 'historical avatars' corresponding to the Germanic gods, Odhinn and Tyr.

The Etruscans were expelled from southern Italy in 471. Their capital, Veius, was taken in 405. In 261, a year before the first Punic War, they submitted themselves definitively. Sicily was conquered in 241.

Stendhal, when he was consul at Civitavecchia, was seized with passion for the Etruscan question. In October 1834, he wrote: 'I have joined a society that is going to dig up the Etruscans'.[124]

We are always 'digging' them up. Two theses still confront each other on the origin of this mysterious people. According to some, the Etruscans are autochthonous. They descend from the survivors of the Italian Stone Age, and their language is lost to the darkness of time. For others, who represent the opinion of the ancients (Livy, Tacitus, Herodotus, Pliny, and Seneca), the Etruscans are 'foreigners' who arrived in Italy between the thirteenth century and the eighth century BCE.

---

124 Literally 'stir up': *Je me suis mis d'une société qui va remuer les Etrusques.* — Tr.

Where did they come from? Asia Minor, says Herodotus, and more specifically, from Lydia. 'The observation of lightning, the inspection of the entrails of victims by the haruspices', writes Raymond Bloch (*L'Art et la civilisation étrusques*. Plon, 1955),[125] forms an essential part of the Etruscan discipline, and with this we are irresistibly brought back towards the Asiatic East'.

Adventurous Hypotheses

The Etruscan alphabet, issued from the Greek alphabet, does not present any particular difficulties. We know the phonetics thanks to the names of the gods and heroes figuring in the votive inscriptions. But our knowledge stops there: we read Etruscan without understanding it.

The researchers have more than 10,000 inscriptions at their disposal, the most famous of which is the 'book of the mummy' (1,500 words written on the bandages of a mummy preserved at the Museum of Zagreb).[126] But these inscriptions are very short. Beyond proper names, we have only been able to translate the words which recur most frequently, like *clan*, 'daughter', *puia*, 'woman', *lupu*, 'he is dead', etc. Unfortunately, we do not have any bilingual document, like the celebrated Rosetta Stone that allowed us to decipher the Egyptian hieroglyphs.

Hypotheses are legion. The works of Professor Pallotino from the University of Rome, of Raymond Bloch and Michel Lejeune, to cite but a few, are well known. But the results are deceiving. The Danish linguist Louis Hjemslev, in his book on *Le langage* (Minuit, 1966),[127] rejects the classification of Etruscan into any of the six great linguistic families of the world.

In 1961, Zacharie Mayani, an orientalist trained at l'Ecole du Louvre and at the Sorbonne, published a work entitled *Les Etrusques commencent à parler*.[128]

'Contrary to what certain authors think', he claims, 'the Etruscan language is an Indo-European language. The Etruscans may well have come from Asia Minor, but this does not make them "Oriental"'.

Published simultaneously in New York and Moscow, the book was a sensation. A year later, Mayani revealed the details of his conclusions at the

---

125 *Etruscan Art and Civilisation.* — Tr.

126 *Liber Linteus Zagrabiensis.* — Tr.

127 *Language.* — Tr.

128 *The Etruscans Begin to Speak.* — Tr.

International Albanological Conference of Tirana. Some scholars immediately approved. Others (like R. P. Raymond Bloch) violently denounced his 'adventurous hypotheses' and his 'extrapolations'.

In *La fin du mystère étrusque*,[129] Mayani took up the case again. He studied the inscriptions discovered between 1963 and 1968, maintaining his position and participating in a war against the proponents of 'autochthonism'.

'Those who fight against the recognition of Etruscan as an Indo-European language', he says, 'act under the influence of a prejudice. They do not constitute a school, but a sect'.

Towards 1,300 BCE, Aegean Asia Minor (Ionia, Lydia, Anatolia, Phrygia, Caria) was partly populated by Thracians and Illyrians from the Balkans. 'The Macedonian Bryges thus became, in Anatolia, the Phrygians. And it is in Anatolia that a tradition retained by Herodotus situates the Etruscans' point of departure for Italy'. As a consequence, the Proto-Etruscans were no other than the 'Tursha', an Indo-European population who emigrated from the Balkans to the territory of present-day Turkey during the period of the Trojan War. They would participate in the great invasions of the 'Sea Peoples' and share their destiny. Embarking upon the assault of Rameses III's Egypt under the leadership of an aristocracy from the north, the 'Tursha' withdrew, after being defeated, to Sardinia, Sicily, and northwest Italy. And the myth of Aenaeus, related by Virgil, intervened as a myth of foundation concurrent with the account of Romulus and Remus, which would guard the memory of this distant past.

In order to demonstrate that 'Etruscan exudes an archaic, Balkan Indo-Europeanism', Zacharie Mayani appealed to three sources: the Illyrian words that we find today in the names of people and places; the dialectical survivals of the 'Illyro-Etruscan' language, notably Apulian; and lastly, Albanian.

'Albania', he recalls 'is ancient southern Illyria. The Albanians have been there for at least two millennia. The numerous and incontestable Illyrian words are found as much in Etruscan as in Albanian. These elements allow us, in large measure, to decipher the Etruscan language.'

The work also contains a glossary. The author cites several hundred Etruscan words like *clen*, 'to exist', *atranes*, 'fathers', *ha*, 'to eat', *iu*, 'god', *setirune*,

---

129 *The End of the Etruscan Mystery.* — Tr.

'calf', *mir*, 'beautiful', etc., which come close to the Albanian words having the same meaning: *klēnë, atër, ha, hie, shterunë, mir.*

He then attempts to decipher certain inscriptions. The results that he obtains correspond very little to the traditional idea that we have of the Etruscans. These people, who are said to be severe, instilled with sorrow, scarcely concerned with anything but the cult of the dead, would have inscribed on the recently discovered fragments messages such as 'Here is life', 'Drink to endure' (*pi peri snati*) or 'place yourself among the wine-drinkers and you will smash the underworld'!

The thesis of the Indo-European character of Etruscan does not properly belong to Mayani. It has also been sustained by F. Schachermeyer (*Etrüskische Frügeschichte*, 1929),[130] G. Buonamici (*Studi etruschi*, 1921),[131] Paul Kretschmer (*Die Herkunft der Umbrer*, 1933),[132] Paulé, Muller, Deeke, etc. They have been taken up again by the Belgian Sanskritist, Carnoy, author of an important *Dictionnaire étymologique de proto-indo-européen*[133] (1955), by the American philologist Ernst Pulgral (*The Tongues of Italy*) and, more recently, by the Bulgarian, Vladimir Georgiev.

At the beginning of 1971, in fact, Moscow's Tass Agency announced that Georgiev had 'definitively penetrated the secret of the Etruscan language'. But then it said no more.

Vladimir Georgiev started writing on the Etruscan problem in 1941–42 in collaboration with Italian researchers. In the 1960s, he published a variety of articles in the journal of the Academy of Sofia, *Balkansko Ezikoznanie*.[134] He is also the author of an *Introduzione alla storia delle lingue indeuropee*[135] (L'Ateneo, 1966), released in Italy as part of the collection of the Centre of Mycenaean Studies by the University of Rome.

The interest of the works of Georgiev resides in the fact that their author does not base his approach solely on phonology (relationship to consonance), but also on morphological facts (relationship to structure).

---

130 *Etruscan Protohistory.* — Tr.

131 *Etruscan Studies.* — Tr.

132 *The Origin of the Umbrians.* — Tr.

133 *Etymological Dictionary of Proto-Indo-European.* — Tr.

134 *Balkan Linguistics.* — Tr.

135 *Introduction to the History of Indo-European Linguistics.* — Tr.

In his opinion, Etruscan would be a kind of 'late Hittite dialect'. This is an assertion that we can accept with some nuances: Etruscan is perhaps, ultimately, a late form of an Indo-European language from Asia Minor, of which Hittite itself would be one of the dialects.

Zacharie Mayani does not hesitate to conclude: 'the Etruscan people were of a lively and spontaneous character, alongside the Greeks and Romans, a remarkable pioneer of western civilisation'.

*

La fin du mystère étrusque, a study by Zacharie Mayani.[136] Maloine, 452 pages.

*

Despite the constant progress of Etruscology, agreement is far from being reached among the specialists in regards to both the origin of the Etruscans as well as the decipherment of their language. On this last point, two methods are employed: the first, deductive, seeks to relate Etruscan to already-known languages of the same script. The second, inductive, consists in engaging similar formulas or phrases in order to extract, using the comparative method, the meaning and value of the words. But until now, each remains sure in its position. A good exposé on the status of the argument can be found in the book by James Wellard, *The Search for the Etruscans* (Thomas Nelson, London, 1973; pp. 170–92).

A *Corpus inscriptionnorum etruscorum (CIE)*[137] has appeared in instalments since 1893. This undertaking is realised under the aegis of the Academy of Berlin, with the assistance of the Institute of Etruscan Studies in Florence.

---

136 *The End of the Etruscan Mystery.* — Tr.
137 *Corpus of Etruscan Inscriptions.* — Tr.

Carthage versus Rome

In *The Interpretation of Dreams*, Freud relates how when he was a child, he identified with Hannibal. 'When we studied the Punic Wars', he writes, 'my sympathy went not to the Romans, but to the Carthaginians'. For a long time he recalled 'the scene where Hamilcar swore to his son, in front of his house altar, that he would take his vengeance upon the Romans'. 'Since then', he adds, 'Hannibal held a great place in my imagination'.

It also held a place in that of Jean-Paul Brisson, a historian influenced by Marxism whose heart beats for Carthage and for whom no love is lost for the Romans.

Carthage (*Quart hadasht*, 'the new city') was founded in 814 (traditional date), or more probably during the seventh century BCE, by the Phoenician populations from Tyr. These populations were lead, according to legend, by Elissa (Dido of the Aeneid), the sister of King Pygmalion. Today the site is found in the large suburban area of Tunis. It is a peninsula that terminates in a rocky promontory rising 150 meters above the sea.

The Phoenicians, a people of the Canaanite group with the same origin as the Hebrews of the pre-Mosaic period, had previously established other cities in the region: notably Hadrumetum and Utica. At Carthage they associated with the people of Cyprus. 'The Punics were not averse to marriage with foreigners, explains Madeleine Hours-Miédan. Orientals, Greeks banished from their own country, the inhabitants of Malta and Sicily, all found a warm welcome among them'. All, however, 'were deeply bound by a civilisation, a religion, and a language that was Semitic' (*Carthage*, PUF, 1959).

The cults celebrated at Byblos and at Sidonia also flourished at Carthage. The Punics adored the goddess Tanit, emanation of the Great Mother, and above all Ba'al Hammon ('the master of stelae'), identified with El, chief of the Phoenician pantheon.

It is to Ba'al that the priests, the *Kohen*, sacrificed the firstborn sons or daughters according to Canaanite tradition. The children were burnt alive at night in the arms of the statue, amidst the din of dancing and the sounds of lyres and tambourines. Urns containing their ashes were subsequently placed in the *Tophet* (sanctuary) of Salammbó, in the suburbs of the city; thousands have been discovered. Justin has told us that, by means of these sacrifices (*molk*), Carthage sought to assure its prosperity.

Other deities inhabit a *baetylus* — a stone anointed with oil — like the one venerated today at Mecca. No images of this have come to us. The religion forbids figurations being cut from wood or stone, a prohibition which is found in the Bible.

Luxury and 'Gravitas'

For Carthage, city of merchants, commerce is at once a means and an end. Their entire civilisation organises itself around this preoccupation. 'Here the Phoenicians came, those avaricious seamen, with a thousand trinkets in their black vessel', writes Homer in the *Odyssey* (XV.415). These merchants are bold. They do not recoil from any expedition as long as it helps them gain exclusivity in the coveted markets, such as those of tin or gold. They take economic control of Sardinia, the Balearic Islands, Malta, and southern Sicily. They soon establish stalls at Gades and at Lixos, on both sides of the Straights of Gibraltar, as well as in Crete and the Nile delta. One of their navigators, Hannon, cruised from Africa to the Gulf of Guinea. From his voyage he brought back the skins of two female pygmies which he hung up like trophies in the temple of Tanit.

Carthage, Hours-Miédan adds, does not seek colonies, but points of sale: 'They desire first and foremost the flow of merchandise to raise the level of life of those whom it administers, thus creating and expanding their needs'.

This 'luxurious' attitude contrasts with the rigour, the gravitas, and the sobriety of Senatorial Rome.

For many centuries, the two cities ignored each other. One was continental, European, and warlike; the other maritime, African, and mercantile. But Rome and Carthage, precisely because of everything that distinguished them, could only clash. In addition, the Carthaginian thalassocracy had extended itself to the Greek coasts. In Sicily, the disputes between the Greek and Punic cities were incessant. Rome, having conquered Magna Graecia, also had its eyes on Sicily. A rivalry between Messana, its ally, and Syracuse, backed by Carthage, forced them to intervene. In total, three wars, known as the 'Punic' wars, took place between the two rivals. Rome imposed itself and its victory was complete.

The most celebrated war was the second, that of Hannibal.

Peace was restored in 241. During the truce which followed, the general, Hannibal Barca, one of the Carthaginian leaders, became the object of great popularity: he had subdued some revolting mercenaries. This plebeian support would trouble the Senate of Carthage, who in the past were always mistrustful of the military. ('The Senate', writes Hours-Miédan, 'had taken the attitude of resolving exterior difficulties by diplomatic transactions and financial sacrifices, only using military power when constrained by force').

Hamilcar had to go into exile in Spain. He embarked upon the conquest of the hinterland and carved himself an Empire.

His son, Hannibal, raised with hate for the Romans, inherited the command of the army at the age of twenty-seven. He immediately resumed hostilities.

In 219, in contempt of the treaties, he attacked the city of Saguntum, protected by Rome and situated north of the Ebro (the Jucar), which he had vowed not to cross.

Besieged, the city soon became indefensible. The leaders of the Roman faction were put to death. The others surrendered. Negotiations opened. The Punics gained the advantage by surprising the vigilance of the guards, and put the inhabitants to the sword. To this day, the bad faith of the Carthaginians has become proverbial in Rome, where Good Faith (*Bona Fides*) was precisely the object of a cult.

An excellent strategist trained in the school of Greek military leaders, Hannibal soon exploited his advantage. He traversed the Pyrenees and southern Gaul, crossing the Rhone and then the Alps. At Trebia and lake Trasimene (217) he crushed the Romans. Exhausted by his victory, he withdrew to Capua where he awaited reinforcements. But the Senate of Carthage, envious of his success, denied him. His brother, Hasdrubal, who attempted to help him, was killed in 207 on the borders of Metaurus. Hannibal subsequently occupied the south of Italy. Rome opposed him with the scorched earth strategy.

Shortly thereafter, Scipion, previously in Africa, launched an offensive against Carthage. Changing their attitude, the Senate called Hannibal to their aid. He abandoned Calabria, where he was entrenched, and attempted to carry out the order. But his efforts were in vain. Conquered at Zama in 202, he had to ask for peace. (A refugee in Syria with King Antiochus, he attempted to unite all the enemies that Rome had amassed in the orient. His plan having failed, hunted by the Romans, he would kill himself in Bithynia in 183).

Carthage, twice submitted, is obligated to completely destroy its fleet and to dismiss its army.

The End of Punic Power

Not for very long. Having resumed its commercial activities, the Phoenicians soon recovered their former splendour. According to Strabo, its population increased to 700,000 souls. During a voyage through Africa, Cato the Elder (Marcus Porcius) becomes concerned; he is disturbed to see the Romans neglecting the aristocratic and martial virtues that created their grandeur. Upon his return, he released his famous cry:

'Carthage must be destroyed'.

The hostilities resume in 149. This time, things are very quick. Attacked by Scipion Aemilianus, Carthage cannot resist the organised assault of the legions. Its troops are decimated, its navies burned. In 146, the city is besieged, taken, and razed. The proud Punic power has seen its day.

The remaining fortifications and the citadel (Byrsa) were discovered in 1949 by General Duval.

Jean-Paul Brisson, 56 years of age, Professor at Nantes, had previously published an apology of sorts for *Spartacus* (Club français du livre, 1959), and then, with Maspéro, an essay on Virgil (1966). In 1969, he had also approached the question of the Punic Wars in a collective work published under his direction (Mouton, La Haye).

The Example of Regulus

Despite a certain erudition, his bias is obvious. It also radiates throughout his conclusion, where Brisson admits that in his eyes, the work of the historian can only have one object: 'To recall that Punic Carthage was far more valuable than Latin Rome'.

To be explicit, the author thus proclaims himself to be aligned with the Carthaginians, who he identifies with in order to demonstrate 'pacifism' and 'fairness', which he contrasts to the 'democratic ideal' of Antiquity's Prussia, Ancient Rome. He reproaches Cato for having supressed the cult of Dionysus, which opposes itself to the ethic of the city. ('Men and women, rich and poor, masters and slaves find themselves with equal rights before a god who does not make any distinction between them'). All of his judgements are oriented to the future. The Romans are 'cynical', and their 'bellicose pretensions' naturally prefigure European imperialism. The Senate is attached to its 'privileges'. The aristocracy fosters 'ambitious plans'. The only thing that animates them is 'the thirst for a certain military prestige', etc.

'For the Roman aristocracy, members of the Senate, and citizens of the first class of the census', writes Brisson, 'war is the essential source of necessary prestige'. Carthage, by contrast, completely occupied with its markets, 'engages in war without enthusiasm'.

Generations of schoolchildren have seen the same example of devotion and loyalty in consul Marcus Attilus Regulus. He had been imprisoned during the first Punic War by Xanthippus, a former Spartan mercenary in the service of Carthage. In 250, the Punics sent him to Rome to negotiate an exchange of captives, upon his promise to return after he had placed himself in their hands. Regulus would advise the Senate against softening and yielding. Then, faithful to his word, he returned to Carthage against the advice of the priests and his own family. The Carthaginians, after cutting off his eyelids, threw him in a barrel full of nails to die.

Brisson of course claims that this account is only a 'legend'. Better, he sees in Regulus 'a particularly distinctive representative of a certain form of foolish arrogance'.

In order to maintain balance, he also denounces the Punic oligarchy, which he contrasts against Hannibal's brilliance.

Peace would have been possible, he concludes naively, if Rome had ceased to be Rome, 'in order to take the model of Carthage'.

It was not. But in the second century of our era, Carthage became the most important Christian community in Africa. Tertullian lived there, as did Saint Augustine's friend, Aurelius. There were no less than thirty-two councils. Today, on the site where the king, Saint Louis, died in the year 1270, a cathedral stands.

*

Carthage ou Rome?, a study by Jean-Paul Brisson.[138] Fayard, 437 pages.

---

138 *Carthage or Rome.* — Tr.

Celtic Civilisation

'If the excellence of the races had to be appreciated by the purity of their blood and the inviolability of their character, no one, it must be admitted, could dispute the nobility of the vestiges of the Celtic race that still remain'. Such is the opinion of Ernest Renan.

These 'vestiges of the Celtic race' have continued to inspire researchers. Jean-Jacques Hatt, curator of the museum of archaeology at Strasbourg, published a study entitled *Celtes et Gallo-Romains*.[139] The young archaeologist Guy Rachet published studies on *La Gaule celtique* and *La Gaule romaine*.[140] The journal *Nouvelle Ecole* consecrated two special editions to Celtic civilisation. Jacques Harmand (lecturer at the faculty of literature at Clermont-Ferrand), in collaboration with Fernand Nathan, also published a work on *Les Celtes*.[141] The Bretonian Surrealist Jean Markale, forty-three years of age, professor of literature in Paris, author of *Celtes et civilisation celtique* (Payot, 1969), has made primary source texts available to the French public via books such as *L'épopée celtique d'Irland* and *L'épopée celtique de Bretagne*.[142] He gives strongly contested interpretations, but the texts have not been translated since Arbois de Jubainville (*L'épopée celtique en Irlande*, 1892) and Georges Dottin (*L'épopée irlandaise*, 1925).[143]

Natives of Bohemia and Thuringia

For the Ancients, the Celts were men who came from the cold. 'Those who exist beyond Iberia', writes Aristotle, 'live in a climate so cold that the donkey cannot survive there'.

Of the inhabitants of Gaul, the Roman historian Ammianus Marcellinus (fourth century CE) says that they form 'a people called Celts, from the name

---

139 *Celts and Gallo-Romans.* — Tr.
140 *Celtic Gaul* and *Roman Gaul.* — Tr.
141 *The Celts.* — Tr.
142 *The Celtic Epic of Ireland* and *The Celtic Epic of Brittany.* — Tr.
143 *The Celtic Epic in Ireland* and *The Irish Epic.* — Tr.

of a beloved king, or Galatae, from the name of the mother of this same king. From this name, the Greeks have made that of the Gauls or Gaulish.[144]

It is around −2,200 that the first Indo-European tribes, bearers of Corded Ware and the battle axe, make their appearance in the east of France. They introduce the wheel and the horse.

Around −1,500 (Middle Bronze I), we see the multiplication of funerary *tumuli* dedicated to the first ancestors of the Proto-Celts.

Eventually, around −1,250, the great Celtic migrations cover Belgium, Holland, England, France, Switzerland, and Spain. This dispersion is probably linked to the extension of the civilisation known as the 'Urnfield culture' into central Europe, or even to the natural catastrophes, of which the legend of Atlantis and of the Ville d'Ys, engulfed by floods, perhaps preserve the memory.

Speaking of the population of Gaul, Ammianus Marcellinus actually mentions 'people from the regions across the Rhine driven from their homeland, whether by the vicissitudes of war, a permanent state of these countries, or by the inundation of the stormy sea.'[145]

'It is possible', writes Rachet, 'that here we have the echo of certain coastal inundations of the Bronze Age, like those of the German shores of the North Sea, and those that caused the neighbouring settlements of the island of Heligoland to be engulfed, which had undoubtedly been the cause of the migrations of people from these regions who had escaped the cataclysm'.

The cradle of the Celts properly speaking situates itself between Bavaria and Lusatia, more specifically in Bohemia-Thuringia.

In the eyes of the Ancients, Germania was little more than a subdivision of the Celtic realm.

'Compared to the Celts', writes Strabo, 'the Germans offer a few small differences. They are, for example, more savage morally, greater in size, and blonder. In all other respects they resemble each other strongly, and the same traits are found among them, and the same way of life. This is what made the Romans give them the name that they carry, for they recognise them as the brothers of the Celts and so have called them Germani, a word which, in

---

144 Ammanius Marcellinus, *Roman Antiquities*, 15.9. — Tr.

145 Ammanius Marcellinus, *Roman Antiquities*, 15.9, adapting John C. Rolfe's translation (Loeb, 1939–1950). — Tr.

their language, designates brothers born from a same father or from a same mother'.[146]

In regards to the Celtic epoch, specialists distinguish, two great periods corresponding to two particularly important sites: Halstatt, in Austria, from 900 BCE, and La Tène, in Switzerland, from −600.

The Celtic Empire

Situated near Lake Neuchâtel, La Tène is an ancient Celtic encampment which had undoubtedly served as a tollgate. Jewels, weapons, and harnesses have been found. It is during this second period that the Celtic empire was formed. Around −600, the Celts of La Tène set out towards the south and the west. They repelled the Illyrians towards the lower Danube, invaded Thrace, Macedonia, Anatolia, and northern Italy. They founded the city of Singidunum (today Belgrade) and plundered Delphi with 150,000 men. In 381, they took Rome and the Capitol. Their empire soon extended over immense territories. But due to lack of organisation, its existence was brief.

'When their waves of expansion are described by the Mediterranean people', remarks Harmand, 'we notice that it only took the Celts a decade at most to travel over half of Europe, or to pass from the Danube to Egypt'.

All over we find the trace of the 'Gaels' (Celts): in the Gallic countries, in Gaul, in Spanish Galicia, in Russian Galicia, in Gallic Turkey, among the Galatae, but also (via the alteration of *Gal-* into *Wal-*: *Wales*, the 'Country of Wales') in Wallonia, in Walachia, etc.

To the east and to the west, the Celts clashed with the Iberians and the Ligurians, who retreated before them. We know only a few things about these people. Their lineage, notably, is not substantiated. Among the Iberians, we have sometimes seen the Proto-Indo-Europeans, sometimes the descendants of the Berberids, who occupied the western coasts from England to north Africa. According to other researchers, they were Indo-Europeans from the coasts of the Black Sea who would emigrate to Spain before passing into

---

146 Strabo, *Geography*, VII, 1.2. In the last line, the French translation cited by Benoist differs significantly from the English translation of Horace Leonard Jones (Loeb, 1924), which for comparison reads: 'And I also think that it was for this reason that the Romans assigned to them the name "Germani", as though they wished to indicate thereby that they were "genuine" Galatae, for in the language of the Romans "germani" means "genuine". — Tr.

Gaul. The origin of the Ligurians, small farmers with round skulls, is no less uncertain.

In Gaul, the period of La Tène is initially situated in the second Iron Age, from around 475 to the *pax romana*. It first appeared in Champagne ('Marnian' civilisation), then in Burgundy, the region of Paris, and in Britany.

The personality of the 'continental' Celts quickly asserts itself. Under their influence, Gaul is transformed. The indigenous population submits. The marshlands are dried up. The Celts proceeded to clear and exploit the tremendous Hercynian Forest, which had remained virgin for centuries. They made remarkable developments in the utilisation of iron for agricultural equipment.

The countryside is rich in minerals. Gold flows in abundance. Iron mines multiply. Gaul situates itself at the crossroads of the great commercial thoroughfares of Antiquity: the Amber Road, which connected the North Sea and Schleswig; and the Tin Route, which connects the Cassiterides (the Isles of Scilly, at the southwest tip of the Cornish peninsula) to the Mediterranean basin.

Their livestock includes poultry, sheep, cattle, and above all pigs, an animal that is never put under cover, which according to Strabo, grants them such a vigour that even the wolves refrain from attacking them!

The Hammer God, the Goddess of Horses

J. -A. Mauduit, a seventy-year-old specialist in prehistoric art, and author of a study on *L'épopée des Celtes*,[147] sees in the Celt 'someone who is unstable in the process of settlement, rather than a nomad'.

He adds: 'Contrary to the Mediterranean man of the city, the Celt was a man of the country, in direct contact with the forces that originated him. His religion was a religion of the earth'.

It was also one of the sky. But a sky strongly connected to the earth. The principle god of the Gaulish pantheon, Teutates, is of the same class as the national divinity. His name comes from *tuah*, 'tribe', and *tatis*, an ancient form of Gaulish *tad*, 'father'. One could almost translate it as '(little) father of the people'!

---

147 *The Epic of the Celts.* — Tr.

Figuring among the other Celtic gods are Esus, Lugh, Dagda, Taranis, a thunder god carrying the solar wheel, Brigid (Saint Brigitte in the Christian tradition), Epona, goddess of horses and harvests, etc.

Sucellus, god of the mallet (closely related to Thor, the 'hammer god' of the ancient Germans and, without doubt, of Perkunas, the Balto-Slavic lightning god) seems to have played a special role, as numerous survivals suggest.

'In Britany, even to the last century', signals Mauduit, 'the tradition persists of the "hammer of good death". This was a heavy mallet whose only purpose was to abate painful agonies. The most senior of the village elders, after having informed the moribund person, raised the hammer above his head and pretended to smash his skull; the dying person then gave up their last sigh. We also know that the death of a pope is determined by striking him on the forehead with a mallet; only after this is the formula pronounced: "The pope is dead"'.

Saint Patrick and Ossian

The principal festivals are four in number. Imbolc, the first of February, has survived in Candlemas. Beltane, the first of May, corresponds to the famous 'Walpurgis Night' once celebrated in Germany and all of central Europe. The first of August is Lughnasadh, festival of the god Lugh, which in the era of Augustus was confounded with that of the emperor and would become the great 'national' festival of Romanised Gaul. Finally, Samhain, the first of November, the day where the dead irrupt into the world of the living, obviously corresponds to All Saints' Day, the Eve of the Dead.

Contrary to what is often believed, druidism only appears in the sixth or fifth century BCE, under foreign influences.

'It is a fact', notes Guy Rachet, 'that the druids are unknown to the Celtic communities of central Europe and the Orient. However, in the time of Caesar they are fully established in Gaul, which became their domain, along with the south of England. It seems therefore that they are the heirs of a very old sacerdotal caste, which the Celts would have known when they arrived in Great Britain.'

'More precisely', he adds, 'why wouldn't they be the heirs of the Hyperboreans of which Diodorus speaks, who inhabited a large island facing the Celtic Sea (which can only be England) and who regarded themselves as the priests of the Hyperborean Apollo who they celebrated each day by hymns and chants in a circular temple adorned with rich offerings? This temple seems to be none other than the megalithic monument of Stonehenge'.

As throughout Europe, paganism and Christianity clashed fiercely with one another in ancient Celtic culture. The Irish love to recall the legendary dialogue waged between Ossian and St. Patrick. Ossian lamented the adventures of ancient times, the hunts, the sound of the horn, the old kings. 'If they were still here', he said to Patrick, 'you would not roam the countryside with your chanting flock'. And further: 'Hear my account: although my memory weakens and worry gnaws at my being, I want to continue to sing of the deeds of the past and to live the ancient glory. Now I am old. My life freezes over and all my joys disappear. My hand cannot hold the sword, nor my arm the spear. Among the clerics my sadness endures a final hour, and the psalms now replace the victory songs'.

Renan writes: 'I do not know a more curious spectacle than this revolt of the masculine sense of heroism against the feminine sentiment that reached the brink of fullness in the new cult. Indeed, what exasperates the old representatives of Celtic society is the exclusive triumph of the peaceable spirit of men dressed in linen and singing psalms, whose voice was sorrowful, who preach fasting and no longer know the heroes'. (*Essais de morale et de critique*).[148]

The last pagan king of Ireland was Loegaire. Patrick was never able to convert him. He wanted to be buried standing up, fully armed. But Arthur, having relinquished his divinity, ended by reciting the Lord's Prayer. Ossian concluded his days in a cloister. Merlin himself submitted to the arguments of Columbanus.

The Celts would have their revenge. Christianity had influenced their myths. They would influence its myths. From here arises the long struggle of Britany's churches against Roman claims related by Augustin Thierry. From here arises Scotus Eriugena, Duns Scotus, and the intellectual radiance of the Irish monasteries.

Gaelic and Brythonic

The Celtic languages represent the westernmost branch of the Indo-European languages. They include the Gaelic languages or 'Q-Celtic' (which preserves

---

148 *Moral and Critical Essays.* — Tr.

the 'q', or the Indo-European *kwe-*, as in Latin *equus*, 'horse') and the Brythonic languages or 'P-Celtic' (which transform the *kwe* into 'p', as in Greek *hippos* or Irish *epos*, which also mean 'horse').

In the first group we find Irish, Scottish, and Manx (spoken in the Isle of Man). The language of the Celtiberians, who we only know by very short and obscure inscriptions, is also placed here. The second group includes Welsh, Cornish, and Breton, as well as the language of the ancient Picts and 'ancient continental Celtic', commonly called Gallic, even though it has been spoken well beyond the limits of historic Gaul.

Continental Celtic very quickly disappeared from Central Europe, and then (under the influence of Latin) from Gaul and Galatia. Traces, which are less numerous than one would think, are nevertheless discovered in France, notably in the toponomy.

Other languages have survived. Some are revived today under the influence of political and cultural tendencies towards preserving roots. Whereas French had been instituted as an obligatory language seven years after the annexation of Britany (1532), the Breton language is still used daily by 750,000 people, 25,000 of which are monolingual.

'The Breton language', writes Paul Sérant in *La Bretagne et la France*,[149] has never been spoken in the totality of the Armorican peninsula. But until the tenth century, it was the only language spoken to the east of a line running from Saint-Brieuc to Paimboeuf. Today, its domain includes the totality of the Finistère region, a third of the Côtes-du-Nord region, and half of the Morbihan'.

The legends of the Celtic people mirror their art: completely interwoven. The stories are full of convolutions; the heroes have complex personalities. Collected by the Irish poets, the *filid*, and by Christian monks, who censored numerous passages, Irish literature is composed of historic and mythological cycles (the Ulster Cycle, the Fenian Cycle, the Royal Cycles, etc., depicting the ancient gods of Ireland, the Tuatha de Danaan, and legendary heroes like Conchobar and Cuchulainn.

'From the ninth century', explains Markale, 'the Irish monks transcribed into Gaelic most of the pagan Celtic legends that had been transmitted to

---

149 *Brittany and France.* — Tr.

them orally or even by previous manuscripts'. However, 'the monks have not hesitated to modify what they no longer understood or else what shocked their Christian zeal. We therefore have a profusion of texts, some of which are incomplete or deliberately truncated'.

The most important character in the Gaelic tradition is a Celtic Hercules figure named Cuchulainn. A mystery hangs over his birth. His father would turn out to be none other than the god Lugh, the pan-Celtic divinity honoured on the first of August who gave his name to the city of Lyon (*Lugdunum*, 'the fortress or hill of Lugh').

The Great Literary Texts

Cuchulainn occupies a comparable enough place in the Irish tales to that of Lancelot du Lac in the Brythonic cycle of Round Table romances popularised by Champenois Chrétien de Troyes in the twelfth century.

'From its appearance around 1155', writes Joseph Bédier, 'the prose novel of Lancelot du Lac was considered as the Mirror of all chivalry, as the Sum of all courtesy, as the Romance of romances'.[150] The adventures of Merlin, Arthur, Galahad, Gawain, and Guinevere the beloved Lady, of Perceval, and Galehaut have remained justly celebrated. They have been recently republished in three volumes from the edition that Jacques Boulenger published in 1941, which bases itself on the English text in the British Museum, established from the first French *Lancelot*.

The old Celtic legends were compiled between the ninth and fifteenth centuries. Works of prose, romantic poetry, bardic literature, great epic gestures, all these masterpieces form an integral part of the European patrimony. The Middle Ages has bequeathed 'the four branches of the *Mabinogi*', Welsh texts known by late manuscripts that give a perfect description of ancient Brythonic society. In the ninth century, the *Voyage of Saint Brendan* (a Latin account containing the voyages of a certain Brendan in search of the Island of Paradise) comes to point where he relays the *Voyage* of the Celtic hero Bran and his quest for the Land of the Fairies, which is not without parallels to the Argonauts and the *Odyssey*. Renan will see in this 'one of the most astonishing creations of the human spirit, and perhaps the most complete expression of the Celtic idea'.

---

150 French *roman* means 'novel' (narrative), but in the literary context of High Medieval chivalry, is usually translated as 'romance'. — Tr.

In 1155, Robert Wace composed the first history of Arthur in French. In the fourteenth century, the works of the Welsh poet Dafydd ap Gwilym (1320–1380) knew an immense success. In the sixteenth century, Breton poetry is no less renowned: Marie de France cites the 'lay of Laüstic' (from Breton *eostig*, 'nightingale').

However, these texts only make their entry very late in the literary anthologies. 'There was a time', writes Jean Markale, 'where Celtic literature was considered non-existent: it would have been inconceivable to claim a comparable position for a Celtic or Germanic work'. It was necessary that the people of the north should be barbaric, only touched late by civilisation. *Ex oriente lux.* Of the ancient Irish literature, J. -P. Mahaffy says in 1899: 'Where it is not dumb it is indecent'!

It is thanks to romanticism that these works, forgotten but transmitted in small cenacles from generation to generation, will be rediscovered. Madame de Staël would undergo the influence of Ossian, as would Napoleon. In the nineteenth century, we will even witness a wave of 'Celtomania'. Then come the archaeologists, the historians, and the linguists.

Like the Romans, the Celts 'thought their history mythically'. In their accounts, as in those of the Germanic sagas, the themes of Greek tragedy are rediscovered: the ethic of honour, a sense of duty, the inexorability of destiny. Many authors have been struck by these analogies.

'It may be necessary to seek their origin in the font of common Indo-European', writes Markale, who adds: 'After all, the Hellenes, especially the Achaeans, left the Aryan stem at around the same time as the Gaelic Celts. Both have carried with them, in addition to the language, the traditions, beliefs, and also a certain way of seeing things'.

The font is far from being exhausted. Irish storytellers and Breton bards, Johnathan Swift, George Russel, James Joyce, Beckett, Yeats, Flaherty, Padraid Pearse, and Alain Guel — all have drunk deep draughts from this wellspring. 'We retrieve in this epic literature', Markale concludes, 'the myths that interest us. And we place our own myths there. And this is what bears fruit'.

Impassioned War Enthusiasts

Among the characteristic traits of the Celtic civilisation, Guy Rachet cites the aristocratic regime and the role of nobility, the diffusion of cities, blood alliances, the custom of giving, the system of 'customers', etc.

Among the Celts of the continent, the authority of the father is very strict. The monogamous patriarchal family structure is the rule. In Great Britain and Ireland, the morality appears more free. In the fourth century, this will provoke the indignation of Saint Jerome. 'In Ireland', he will write, 'no one is married, no Irish person has only one woman, each abandons himself to his passions in the same way that animals do'. Pious exaggeration.

The Gallic woman followed her husband everywhere. 'When a Celt went into battle', relates Ammianus Marcellinus, 'and he was accompanied by his wife, whose eyes flashed brighter than his, a whole band of foreigners would scarcely be able to resist them, for she was endowed with even more strength than he was'![151]

Plutarch, in his treatise *On the Bravery of Women*, cites the example of the Gallic Chiomara, wife of Ortiagon, who decapitated the Roman centurion who had violated her, and threw his head at the feet of her husband. 'Wife', said Ortiagon, 'fidelity is a beautiful thing'. 'It is even more beautiful', she responded, 'when there is only one living man to whom I have belonged'.[152]

This warlike attitude is no surprise. The Gauls were impassioned war enthusiasts. The ancient authors have emphasised their courage while also deploring their lack of discipline, which contributed to their defeat.

'The appearance of the Gallic army, and the noise that they made, terrified the Roman soldiers', writes Polybius. 'The number of horns and trumpets was incalculable; at the same time, the army made such clamour that one no longer heard only the sounds of the instruments and the cries of the soldiers; the surrounding countryside, returning the echo, also seemed to add its voice to the din'.[153]

---

151 Ammanius Marcellinus, *Roman Antiquities*, 15.12, adapting John C. Rolfe's translation (Loeb, 1939–1950). — Tr.

152 Plutarch, *De Mulierum Virtutibus*, 2.22. Note that where Benoist has 'Gallic' (*gauloise*), F. C. Babbitt's translation (Loeb, 1931) has 'Galatian'. I have not compared the original Greek. — Tr.

153 Polybius, *Histories*, 2.29, adapting W. R. Paton's translation (Loeb, 1922–1927). — Tr.

'All the people belonging to the Gallic race', notes Strabo, 'are war-mad, and both high-spirited and quick for battle, although otherwise simple and not ill-mannered. And therefore, if roused, they come together all at once for the struggle, both openly and without circumspection, so that for those who wish to defeat them by stratagem they become easy to deal with'.[154]

As soldiers, they made for highly-sought mercenaries. In the third century BCE, Justinus affirms that 'the kings of the east wage no wars without having an army of Gallic mercenaries'.[155]

Having fought *en masse*, they perished *en masse*. The cries of war will be followed, little by little, by the sobs of funeral songs and evocations. As it is said in the legend:

'Cuchulainn started to laugh, and this was the last time that Cuchulainn laughed. The shadows of death surrounded him. He went out towards a small lake nearby and bathed'. Emerging from the lake, the hero clung to a pillar of stone so that he wouldn't fall, and died standing.

Many centuries later, the Breton Chateaubriand would evoke 'these wandering warriors in the midst of the ashes, clouds, and phantasms' with sorrow and respect.

*

Les romans de la Table ronde, texts published by Jacques Boulenger. UGE-10/18, 883 pages (three vols).
La Gaule celtique (des origins à 50 av. J.-C.), and *La Gaule romaine (50 av. J.-C–500 ap. J.-C.)*, studies by Guy Rachet. Culture Art Loisirs, 256 and 258 pages.
L'épopée celtique d'Irlande, texts published by Jean Markale. Payot, 204 pages.
Celtes et Gallo-Romains, a study by Jean-Jacques Hatt. Nagel, 335 pages.
Les Celtes, a study by Jacques Harmand. Fernand Nathan, 172 pages.
La Bretagne et La France, a study by Paul Sérant. Fayard, 441 pages.
L'épopée des Celtes, a study by J. A. Mauduit. Laffont, 282 pages.[156]

*

Among the numerous works recently consecrated to Celtic matters, mention must be made of the important work by Myles Dillon and Nora K. Chadwick, *Les royaumes celtiques*

---

154 Strabo, *Geography*, 4.4.2, adapting H. L. Jones's translation (Loeb, 1917–1932). — Tr.

155 Marcus Junianus Justinus, *Epitome of the Philippic History of Pompeius Trogus*, 25.2. — Tr.

156 *The Romance of the Round Table*, Boulenger. *Celtic Gaul (From its Origins to 50 BCE)* and *Roman Gaul (50 BCE to 500 CE)*, Rachet. *The Celtic Epic of Ireland*, Markale. *Celts and Gallo-Romans*, Hatt. *The Celts*, Harmand. *Brittany and France*, Sérant. *The Epic of the Celts*, Mauduit. — Tr.

(Fayard, 1974),[157] whose French translation is augmented by a chapter on Gaul in the Celtic world thanks to Christian J. Guyonvarc'h and Françoise Le Roux. This work covers nearly all the sectors of ancient Celtic civilisation, from its prehistoric origins to the invasion of Brittany, and by presenting a panorama, distinctly situates itself beyond the fray of legends, distortions, and fantasies. The translator, Christian J. Guyonvarc'h, oversees the journal *Ogam-Tradition celtique* (B.P. 574, 2 rue Léonard-de-Vinci, 35007 Rennes Cedex);[158] he is also the author of a *Dictionnaire étymologique du breton ancien, moyen, et moderne,*[159] which currently appears in instalments.

Another interesting title: *Die Kelten. Das Volk das aus dem Dunkel kam* (Econ, Düsseldorf, 1975), by Gerhard Herm, author of numerous documentary films on Mediterranean civilisation made for west German television. This book has also appeared in England (*The Celts: The People Who Came out of the Darkness.* Weidenfeld and Nicolson, London, 1976).

---

157   *The Celtic Kingdoms.* — Tr.
158   *Celtic Ogham-Tradition.* — Tr.
159   *Etymological Dictionary of Ancient, Middle, and Modern Breton.* — Tr.

Roman Gaul

'At the moment when so many voices denounce the misdeeds of colonialism, where the colonising nations themselves are frightened by their unpopularity, Roman Gaul offers the precedent, unfolding over more than four centuries, of a successful colonial enterprise in which the colonised as well as the coloniser have ultimately yielded the greatest profit'.

Jean-Jacques Hatt, a fifty-eight-year-old Professor at the Department of Literature at the University of Strasbourg, originates from a large family of Alsatian brewers. He is an archaeologist. On Sunday he roams the countryside and the excavation sites with the methodical look of a hunter on foot. Coordinator of the Musée d'Epernay, conservator of the Strasbourg Archaeological Museum, former director of historical and prehistorical antiquities, he has previously published studies on the Gallo-Roman tomb, Celtic religion, and Strasbourg in the time of the Romans. To him we notably owe a beautiful interpretation (expanding on Dumézil's work on the tripartite ideology of the Indo-Europeans) of the motifs figuring on the silver plaques of the celebrated Celtic cauldron of Gundestrup.

Before him, others have written on the Gauls: Albert Grenier, Paul-Marie Duval, Fernand Benoît, recently deceased. And also Camille Jullian, whose work still holds authority, even though the eighth volume of his monumental *Histoire de la Gaule*[160] dates from 1926. Excavations such as those at Vix near Châtillon-sur-Seine (Côte d'Or), which in 1953 brought to light the princely tomb of a young Gaul of the Halstatt era, along with a treasury containing a magnificent archaic bronze crater of Greek origin, obviously remained unknown to him.

In four hundred pages, Jean-Jacques Hatt, utilising both historical testimonies and archaeological discoveries, provides an update on the subject. His *Histoire de la Gaule romaine*[161] covers a period from 120 BCE to the year 451.

---

160 *History of Gaul.* — Tr.
161 *History of Roman Gaul.* — Tr.

The work is dedicated to the rebels of Gergovia that repelled the legion-
naires of Caesar. But the conqueror does not appear any less a noble figure.
The author does not share the opinion of Livy, who considers the campaigns
of the Roman proconsul against the Swiss and the Germans, and then the conquest of Gaul, as personal initiatives undertaken in opposition to the 'pacifists'
of the Senate.

'De Bello Gallico'

'If his movements had been free', writes Jerôme Carcopino in the preface,
'Caesar, who was obsessed with the noble vision of the Roman Empire recruiting less subjects than affiliates, would have attempted to realise in Gaul an
opus similar to that which Pompey had previously built in Asia: it would be
restricted to surrounding the pre-existing province of Narbonne by a belt of
Celtic tribes who, promoted to the rank of protected cities by Rome, would
have continued, under this aegis, to enjoy a regime that would be defined
today as internally autonomous'.

Fate would decide otherwise. In the year 58 BCE, Caesar is called on for
assistance by the inhabitants of Narbonne, who are troubled by Celto-Ligurian
and Gallic raids. The protectorate that he attempted to install was a failure.
Rebellion rumbled. Some Roman negotiators are massacred at Cenabum. This
is the beginning of the insurrection: *De Bello Gallico*.[162]

Should we conclude that the priests of the Celtic cult were no strangers to
the initiation of hostilities? The great pilgrimage to the Celtic gods used to take
place for many years among the Carnutes, at the location where the Cathedral
of Chartres now stands. And the one responsible for the uprising was a certain
Gutuater, who the Roman chronicles present as a hothead. 'Gutuater', explains
Jean-Jacques Hatt, 'is a common name which means great priest, or chief of
the priests. He was without doubt the chief of the druids'.

The following year, the Arverni arise in their turn. Their chief, Vercingetorix,
took lead of a coalition against Rome. He enacted the scorched earth tactic.
The beginning of guerrilla warfare.

Caesar counted on the legions. Vercingetorix reasoned by 'resistance'. The
Aidui and the Bellovaci joined in the resistance movement. But Caesar called

---

162 *Commentarii de Bello Gallico* (Commentaries on the Gallic War), Julius Caesar's firsthand
    account of the Gallic Wars. — Tr.

on the knights of Germania. And the cohorts are finally overcome by the rebels. This is the episode of Alesia, the siege, the capitulation.

The tribes who participated, in −52, in the defence of Alesia came from the farthest regions of Gaul. Inspection of coins found on the battle site have confirmed this. These coins are now displayed in the National Museum of Antiquities of Saint-Germaine-en-Laye, in the château built by François I, which Napoleon III, in 1862, made a Gallo-Roman museum. In 1965, more rooms consecrated to Gaul were opened to the public. In 1970, René Joffroy, conservator in chief (also the author of a book on the treasure of Vix), unveiled five rooms on the civilisation of La Tène.

Hermann the Cherusker

In the room consecrated to the conquest, a scale model shows the plan of the labours deployed by Caesar around Mount Aixois (Côte-d'Or), the war machines, the mobile towers, the ramparts, the spears. Numerous iron arrow heads, called 'socketed', discovered during the excavations conducted under Napoleon III, attest to the effort of the besieged.

In 51–50, the resistance is definitively liquidated with the submission of the Armoricans, the Carnutes, and the Aquitans. We know the fate of Vercingetorix: woe to the vanquished!

Fifteen years later, the conquest is an established fact. Romanisation has born its fruits. As the borders are stabilised, the Gauls offer absolute fidelity to the Flavian dynasty. They defend it wherever it is threatened. Gaul has become Roman.

Four centuries would pass before it would become Merovingian.

The Germanic peoples, themselves, are intractable. Via the Rhône corridor, the legions raised an assault on the people of the Rhine, but weren't able to subdue them. Flux and reflux. In winter, the Germanic tribes took back the advantage lost during the summer. Between Metz and Strasbourg, scattered coins and defeated camps punctuate the contours of the battles.

A Roman general of middling rank, Quinctilius Varus, is pressured by the Cheruscer Arminius (Hermann), a noble Germanic who had served as an officer in the Roman army before returning to his people. Beset on all sides, the troops are worn down between the swamps and the forests. The final assault takes place in the region of Detmold. No high Roman officer survives. Three legions and nine auxiliary bodies, 20,000 men, two thirds of the army of the Rhine, are consumed by the defeat. Germania eludes the Senate.

'Varus, Varus', cries Augustus in his nightmares, 'give me back my legions!'

In the year 14 CE, Germanicus, nephew of Tiberius sent to avenge Varus, proceeded to wage a campaign of massacre and devastation between the Rhine and the Lippe. The most celebrated sanctuary of all Germania, that of Tamfana, is destroyed. But two years later, the fleet of Germanicus is wrecked near Heligoland. The Germanic peoples do not give up an inch of their independence. Today the statue of Hermann the Cherusker stands in the Teutoburg forest.

Rome, ultimately, will be destroyed by those who they weren't able to conquer. But the first invasion of the Alani and the Vandals would only take place in 352. For three centuries, the Germanic tribes did not seek at any moment to exercise reprisals on their enemy.

Jean-Jacques Hatt makes the observation: 'If we refer to the recent difficulties experienced by the French army for the "lockdown" of Algerian borders, it is stupefying to note that with four legions and a complement of auxiliary troops, that is to say around 50,000 men, the Roman army would manage to hold the border of the Rhine for a hundred and fifty years, from the North Sea to the sources of the Danube. We are forced to conclude that the Germanic tribes did not want to force these defences, and that they preferred to live in mutual understanding with their neighbours'.

The contrast between the attitude of the Gauls and that of the Germanic tribes is striking. Only the Gaul had recognised the benefits of Romanisation, while fully retaining certain characteristic traits of its own personality for quite some time.

'How did the Gauls, so fiercely independent between 58 and 50 BCE, become for the most part, and from the reign of Nero, loyal and faithful subjects of the Roman Empire?'

The 'Provincial' Spirit of the Conquered Gaul

J.-J. Hatt answers by recalling that Gaul, at the beginning of our era, was already the theatre of significant cultural and commercial changes.

'Hellenism had opened the way to Romanisation, and this is the cause of how the Gauls so rapidly become Roman citizens.

After having suffered under Caligula, Gaul breathed under Nero. 'The reign of Nero may well have been marked by a systematic reaction against the western provinces', Jean-Jacques Hatt emphasises, 'the progress nonetheless having continued in Gaul, in the sense of economic and cultural assimilation and of political integration (…) It develops within itself a provincial spirit, which is no longer indigenous nationalism at all, but is simultaneously made of Roman consciousness and of a reaction against the excesses of the capital and imperial milieu'.

Marcus Aurelius (161–80)[163] is one of the last great Roman emperors. A Stoic philosopher, he represents an ideal 'that paganism had elaborated in the combination and selection of what was best among pagan religions and Greek philosophies'.

Shortly after, some Christians are persecuted at Lyon. The population pays no attention. A letter addressed by the Christian part of the Lyonnaise to their eastern brothers 'proves that the Christian community, still few in number in this period, were essentially recruited among the Orientals, notably the Asiatics and Phrygians'. Eusebius nevertheless mentions ten martyrs, including the bishop Pothinus, deacon of Vienna. It is the beginning of a confrontation between the nascent cult and Gallo-Roman paganism. Evangelisation commences at the end of the second century with Saint Irenaeus.

After the assassination of Caracalla in 217, the Roman empire degenerates. Macrinus is absorbed in devotions and debaucheries. The Syrian Elagabalus, high priest of Baal, is proclaimed supreme god of the Empire. Exotic princesses rule over Cato's city. The economy is in crisis. Slaves revolt. Once the Severan dynasty disappeared, periods of anarchy followed. Rome is no longer in Rome. With each *pronunciamento*, the army rushes from the Rhine to counter the perils, stripping the border and opening Gaul up to the Franks and Alemanni.

A Gallic Empire is planned in north and northeast Gaul. The country is divided into a diocese of Gauls to the north of the Loire, with Trier for the capital,[164] and a diocese of Vienna, which covers Aquitania, Narbonne, and the Alps to Geneva.

The coming of Constantine, along with the Edict of Milan, inaugurated a new period of troubles. But Julian, having re-established calm, imposed

---

163 These are the dates of his rule; he lived from 121–180. — Tr.
164 Also known as Trèves. — Tr.

himself immediately on Gaul. 'He was gladly received by the city of Vienna', details Hatt. 'The inhabitants of the city of Isère saw in him a tutelary genius, capable of warding off the troubles of their time'. The Apostate redressed the political, economic, and financial situation. He reinstituted justice in its rights. Gaul loves its Caesar. It compared him to 'a sun, which expands serenity in the sky and dissipates the horror of long darkness'.

Roman Gaul saw its last beautiful days under Gratian (375–383). But the situation degraded again. Decadence follows its course. On the borders, the Alemanni are stirred. In the City, the old Roman spirit is no more than a memory. Saint Martin initiates the evangelisation of the countryside. The cities are acquired by the bishops. However, the farmers or peasants,[165] the *pagani*, refuse to abandon the faith of their fathers, remaining loyal to the divinities of the springs, trees, and streams. Theodosius prohibits paganism under pain of death. Parishes, churches, and monasteries are established to make it through the long medieval night intact.

During the fourth century, the frontier of the Rhine collapses. Little by little, Gaul fragments under the excesses of imperial authoritarianism. Hatt states: 'It is not Gallic nationalism that is the cause, but the flaws in the system of the Late Empire'. In 406, the irruption of the Vandals, Suebi, and Alani put an end to speculations. Gaul ceased to be Roman. It would soon be Merovingian.

*

Historique de la Gaule romaine, a study by Jean-Jacques Hatt.[166] Payot, 405 pages.

*

Since the celebrated study by Camille Jullian (*Vercingétorix*, Hachette), whose first edition dates back to 1921, several books on Vercingetorix have been published in France, notably by Jean-Jacques Rochard (*Vercingétorix le Gaulois*. Table ronde, 1967)[167] and Jean Séverin (*Vercingétorix*. Pensée universelle, 1975). Maurice Bouvier-Ajam has also released a useful and very personal work on *Les temps des empereurs gaulois* (Pavillon, 1976).[168]

In *Avec César en Gaule* (éd. d'Artrey, 1970),[169] Raymond Schmittlein attempted to rehabilitate the proconsul of Rome, and attacked the virtually classic thesis according to which

---

165 French *paysans*, which carries the resonance with *pagani*, 'pagans'. — Tr.
166 *History of Roman Gaul.* — Tr.
167 *Vercingetorix the Gaul.* — Tr.
168 *The Times of the Gallic Emperors.* — Tr.
169 *With Caesar in Gaul.* — Tr.

Caesar would have invaded Gaul by pure ambition and reignited the war each time that it was extinguished in a basic spirit of pillage and profit. (The book is prefaced by Alain Peyrefitte).

Outside of specialised journals, *L'Anitquité gauloise* (B. P. 119–05, 75224 Paris Cedex 05),[170] a quarterly publication founded by Christian Pacaud, has striven to make the national past better known with a view to broad popularisation. Guy Rachet occasionally participates.

The society of friends of the museum of the château of Saint-Germain, presided over by Jean-Paul Palewski, has published the bulletin *Antiquités nationales* since 1969.[171]

---

170 *Gallic Antiquity.* — Tr.
171 *National Antiquities.* — Tr.

Structures of Nordic Mythology

'It is regrettable that a people in whose veins Frankish blood flows, upon the territory in which the Germanic dialects are today still spoken (notably in Flanders and Alsace), and who possess a province called Normandy, have forgotten their Nordic heritage and do not know to place the Edda and the Icelandic Saga next to Virgil and Tacitus'.

Renauld-Kranz includes these lines at the beginning of his *Anthologie de la poésie nordique ancienne*, published by Gallimard in 1964.[172] It is a labour in which he intends to make one of the richest poetic traditions of all time available to the French public by restoring for the first time the great Eddic and skaldic texts (drawn from the Edda of Snorri Sturluson and the works of the 'skalds' or Scandinavian bards) in a rhythmic system similar to the original.

On the basis of ancient Nordic literature, Renauld-Kranz is currently attempting to deepen the character of the principal Germanic gods, and to establish the structures of Germanic religion, that is to say, the organising, constitutive forms that cannot be reduced to simple historic processes.

Nordic mythology perpetuates in its broad lines a common Germanic mythology which the authors of antiquity (Tacitus) and the Middle Ages (Adam of Bremen, Saxo Grammaticus) relied upon, and which modern authors (Jakob Grimm, Jan de Vries, Georges Dumézil, Otto Höfler) have afforded improved knowledge.

'Scandinavia', writes Renauld-Kranz, 'is effectively the only Germanic country (and one of the few countries in Europe) whose literature still bathes in paganism. If we exclude the runic inscriptions, the first monuments of this literature date from the ninth century and the last documents of religious significance from the thirteenth. At this time, Scandinavia had been Christian for around two hundred years (in Iceland, the official conversion to Christianity was only proclaimed in the year 1,000). But it is very probable that the pagan tradition was still alive then'.

---

172 *Anthology of Ancient Nordic Poetry.* — Tr.

It survives even today in the local cults, pagan family traditions, and popular costumes.

The Three Functions

The dominant figures of Scandinavian mythology are as follows: on one hand the gods Tyr and Odhinn (Wotan in southern Germany), then the god Thorr, all three of the Æsir; on the other hand, a collection of divinities (notably Njordhr, Freyr, Freyja), the Vanir, with less distinct features, who patronise the same field of activity.[173]

This pantheon articulates itself around three functions, which are the basis of the Indo-European ideological structure as established by Georges Dumézil: sacredness and sovereignty (cosmic plane, first function, with Tyr and Odhinn), the warrior power (human plane, second function, with Thorr), fecundity and productivity (social plane, third function, with Njordhr, Freyr, and Freyja).

At the origin of the harmonious society of the gods, Germanic myth places a 'war of foundation' which opposes the Æsir and Vanir. (The same theme is found among the Romans, in a historicised form, with the Etruscan wars; and among the Indians, in the *Mahābhārata* epic). The cause is a Vanic goddess, Gullveig (that is to say, 'gold-drunk'). Divided, the Æsir are first defeated and the Vanir invade their territory, Asgard ('the enclosure of the Æsir', cf. German *Garten*, French *jardin*, 'garden'). But the Æsir prevail in the end, for their chief Odhinn, who knows the secret of the runes and watches over the order of the world, manages to 'domesticate' the assailants thanks to the binding power of his magic.

In the unified society that follows this period of discord, the Æsir acquire the functions of sovereignty (Odhinn) and of combat (Thorr), whereas the Vanir take on the economic function: they are charged to produce wealth. Such is the nature of the 'social contract' among the Indo-Europeans.

The function of sovereignty contains two aspects: one 'judicial' and religious, and the other 'political' and administrative. The fact that they are closely associated shows that, in the society of the gods (and by extension, that of men), they must necessarily go together. The political aspect establishes the

---

173 The orthography that Benoist uses here for the names of the gods follows that of Old Norse: Óðinn, Þórr, Njörðr, Freyr, and Freyja. — Tr.

relationship of authority, indeed of constraint; the judicial aspect furnishes, with the notion of *law*, the justification for this authority, and at the same time assures social cohesion and the smooth functioning of the world. Among the ancient Norse, leadership entails support and protection in return: a fundamental relationship, pivoting on 'fidelity' (*Treue*), of which we could cite many examples, from the *Pax Romana* (subdued and protected cities) to the feudal system (relationship of vassal to suzerain).

The Union of Reason, Passion, and Work

An entire historicist tradition has wanted to see in the myth of the Æsir and Vanir the more or less deformed memory of two different peoples, one living by hunting and gathering, the other by agriculture; they would have fought, and after, overlapped with each other. Archaeologists have put forward the names of the *Megalithenvölker* (people of the megaliths) and the *Streitaxvölker* (people of the battle axe). But Dumézil, in *Les dieux des Germains* (PUF, 1959),[174] writes: 'we do not think that the duality of the Æsir and Vanir is a reflection of these events; it is a matter here of two complementary terms of a unitary religious and ideological structure, two terms which imply each other, and which have been brought together, already articulated, by those Indo-Europeans that became the Germans'.

In a study entitled *Histoire et société*, published in *Nouvelle école*,[175] Giorgio Locchi adds: 'In essence, the Æsir and the Vanir effectively represent two different modes of life: on one hand an ancient tradition of great hunters, and on the other hand a new one: the producers or growers who could have infiltrated the midst of Indo-European societies by acculturation'.

The ideal society therefore recognised the union of intelligence (reason), force (passion), and the virtues of appetite (work). The Æsir occupied a dominant position; the Vanir a subordinate position. But this hierarchy forms a *harmonious* whole. And all the gods unite to combat Utgard, the ensemble of monsters and giants. 'The gods are opposed to the giants', notes Renauld-Kranz, 'like the civilised to the wild, but also like the parent to the child!'

---

174 *Gods of the Ancient Northmen* (English edition, ed. Einar Haugen, University of California Press, 1973). — Tr.

175 *History and Society*, in *New School*. — Tr.

The principal gods are Thorr and Odhinn. The first is associated with air and wind, the second with fire and thunderbolts (the Vanir being earth and water).

Odhinn is the creator or at least the shaper of the world. It is he who ensures (with Tyr) the proper order of the cosmos. God of kings, he is also the king of gods. Like his Indo-European homologues (Zeus-Pater, Juppiter, Varuna), his power rests upon knowledge and magic. And his ecstasies themselves are of a spiritual order.

Thorr, god of war and storm, is the son of Odhinn, just as the lightning flash is the son of the sky. But just as the thunderbolt falls to earth, so too is it on the human plane that his activity unfolds. His power comes to him not from wisdom but from physical force, symbolised by his hammer. He incarnates the virtues of the heart and action: courage, generosity, loyalty.

'Between "Red-beard" and "Grey-beard", that is to say, between Thorr and Odhinn', Renauld-Kranz states, 'there exists a binary structural relationship demonstrated by several documents'.

'This', he writes, 'is why Odhinn is the god of intellectual functions, which have their seat and their symbol in the head, while Thorr is the god of active functions, which have their seat and their symbol in the heart and at the same time their means of expression and application in the body. Odhinn thus represents the power of the spirit and Thorr the force of the body, and so the pair Odhinn-Thorr expresses the same polarity as the pair spirit-body'.

In the Vedic religion of the Indo-Aryans, we find an analogous relationship between Varuna and Indra. Hinduism preserves a very distorted echo in the opposition between Shiva and Vishnu.

At the same time, the relationship between Thorr and Odhinn translates an original relationship between the two age classes. Father and son. By contrast, the third function, which deals with (human) fecundity and (economic) productivity, is on one hand related to the *feminine* element, without distinction for age, and on the other to the greater multitude: the plebeians, the masses, the Third-Estate.

The Guardian of the Sanctuary

From the High Middle Ages, the cult of Thorr seems to overtake that of Odhinn. His patronyms are more frequently encountered in the names of people and places. And in the great pagan temple at Uppsala, according to Adam of Bremen, it is the god of the hammer who had primacy of place. The time was indeed one of conquests. And of retaliation.

'That Thorr remains down to the end of paganism the warrior and the defender of the gods, the "guardian of the sanctuary", has no better proof than the common invocation of which he is the object by pagans against invading Christians. It is around him that the holders of the ancient faith would rally; it is him, and not Odhinn, that they opposed to Christ, to Saint Olaf, and to the converters'.

Renauld-Kranz concludes: 'Some idea of the personality of the ancient Scandinavians, their knowledge of man's powers, of a specific image of man, is guaranteed; and it is this image which is reflected in their mythology. Man thus projects himself into the universe by the same movement by which he attempts to explain it. And so one could, in the final account, define this mythology as a cosmic anthropology'.

*

Structures de la mythologie nordique, a study by Renauld-Kranz.[176] G. P. Maisonneuve et Larose (11 rue Victor-Cousin, 75005 Paris), 234 pages.

*

A new French translation of the *Eddas* has appeared in *Les religions de l'Europe du Nord* (Fayard-Denoël, 1974),[177] an important collection of texts presented by Régis Boyer, Professor of Scandinavian Language and Literature at the University of Paris-IV (Sorbonne) and Eveline Lot-Falck. This translation differs from that of Renauld-Kranz to the extent that it does not seek to render the Nordic poems in a French poetic form, but selects the original texts, transcribed in a literal manner, according to religious criteria. The introduction by Boyer covers 'the sacred among the ancient Scandinavians' and emphasises the importance of Destiny and the heroic values among the Nordic people.

Régis Boyer has also translated several sagas into French. (*La Saga de Snorri le Godi*. Aubier-Montaigne, 1973; *Le Saga de Njall le Brûlé*. Aubier-Montaigne, 1976), as well as the text of the 'Landnàmabok' (*Le livre de la colonisation de l'Island*. Mouton, La Haye, 1974).[178]

The problem of Indo-European tripartition has been the object of a meticulous examination, as much on the religious and 'cosmic' plane as on the social and 'human' plane, in the edition of *Nouvelle école* (Nr. 21–22, winter, 1972–73) that was dedicated to Georges Dumézil.

---

176 *Structures of Nordic Mythology*. — Tr.

177 *The Religions of Northern Europe*. — Tr.

178 *The Saga of Snorri the Godhi. Burnt Njall's Saga. The Book of the Colonisation of Iceland.* — Tr.

On ancient Scandinavian cosmology and its kinship with the Indo-European account of the origins of the world, we find some concise but clear indications in the text by Magnus Magnusson, adapted by Marcel Bougaran: *Les Vikings* (Atlas, 1976).[179]

The journal *Heimdal* (B. P. 124, 14402 Bayeux Cedex), directed by Georges Bernage, takes as its subject the study and rediscovery of the 'Norse heritage in Normandy'. It has published several articles (of popularisation) on Nordic mythology.

---

179 *The Vikings.* — Tr.

The Vikings in America

E very year, on the 9th of October, America commemorates Leif Erikson Day — three days before Columbus Day. This results from a debate which took place on the 4th of March 1964 at the United States Congress, in the course of which the senator Thor Tollefson launched to the podium and proclaimed:

'I am Norwegian like Leif Erikson. My father has given to me the name of a brother of Leif, Thorwald Erikson, who was killed by the Indians in Massachusetts. And I am proud of him'.

At the end of the debate, at the suggestion of senator Hubert H. Humphrey, to whom the book by J. Kr. Tornöe, *Norsemen Before Columbus* (Allen & Unwin, London 1965) is dedicated, President Johnson decided to set the 9th of October as the date for the true discovery of America.

More than four centuries after Christopher Columbus, the Americans thus confirmed that the Genoese navigator had had illustrious predecessors: the Vikings.

It was a summer morning in the year 982. A robust ship sways on the waters of the Breidi Fjord on the northwest coast of Iceland. The vessel is loaded with materials and provisions. Forty men are on board, including fifteen rowers. The sharp-eyed captain stands at the prow.

This is duke Erik the Red.[180] Born in Norway, outlawed in his country, he leaves for the unknown.

Rich in detail, highly colourful, the accounts of the Viking expeditions feature in the collections of Sagas bequeathed to us by the European North: the *Landnàmabok* or 'Book of colonisations', the *Flateyarbok* (cf. the English *Annals*), the *Hauksbok*, etc., all set down in the fourteenth century.

The *Landnàmabok*, the book containing the national Icelandic epic, relates how, towards the year 900, a Norwegian named Gunbiorn, sailing towards Iceland, was diverted far to the west where he glimpsed a large unknown island.

---

180 Benoist describes him as a *duc*. — Tr.

In 982, Erik the Red, searching for this mysterious land, discovered Greenland, which had not yet been covered by ice (hence 'green land'). Returning to Iceland, Erik chartered a veritable fleet: twenty-five boats, six hundred men, a sufficient quantity of livestock. Only fourteen vessels will arrive in safe harbours. Thus begins, in 996, the colonisation of Greenland.

During the same period, the Icelander Bjarni Herjulfson gets lost in fog while making his way to Greenland and ends up travelling as far as Labrador. Following the coasts for nine days, he thinks he has found an island. Weary of struggling, he returns to the north where he rejoins the Greenlandic encampments. But he recounts his adventure. And imaginations are enkindled.

Leif Erikson, son of the outlaw, is a friend of Bjarni. Captivated by his accounts, he cannot resist the call of the sea. In 999, he too quits Norway for Greenland.

In 1003, he raises his first expedition. Forty men accompany him. Following the route indicated by Bjarni, Leif successively discovers Helluland ('land of flat stones'), Markland ('land of forests'), and Vinland ('land of wine', or 'land of the vine').

The first two of these lands correspond to Baffin Island and Labrador. The third is situated between Boston and New York, on the site of New England: the remains of an encampment (*Leifbudir* in the Sagas) have been discovered on the small island of Chappaquiddick, on lake Menemsha.

Having spent more than a year in Vinland, the Scandinavian explorers return to Greenland. Leif takes the place of his father, who had died in the interim. He will not leave again.

In 1006, one of Leif Erikson's brothers, Thorwald, organises a second expedition. He is killed by Indians the following year. A third brother, Thorstein, consequently decides to search for his body. But he fails to reach Vinland and dies shortly after his return.

His widow, Gudrid, is remarried to an Icelander recently arrived in Greenland, Thorstein Karselfni. He also embarks in turn, in the spring of the year 1011.

The expedition includes 160 people, including two women: Gudrid, and a natural daughter of Erik, Freydis. Arriving in Vinland, the immigrants set up a permanent camp. This time, the colonisation of America genuinely begins. It spreads rapidly.

When Leif Erikson died in 1025 at the age of forty-six, colonies are already installed on a good part of the continent, from Labrador to Virginia. Some expeditions have been undertaken to the interior of the land, in the direction of the Great Lakes, to current North Dakota and Minnesota. In total, more than four thousand people are scattered across Vinland, living primarily by trading.

The *Grœnlendinga* Saga even records the nomination of the first 'bishop of Greenland and Vinland', Eirik Gnupsson, who would have taken up his duties towards 1115.

From Cartography to Ethnography

C. W. Ceram writes in *Le premier Américain* (Fayard, 1972):[181] 'The fact that the Vikings have disembarked in North America before Columbus has been acknowledged as early as the last century'. This conviction is substantiated by numerous material proofs.

The first and foremost is cartographic. As early as the fourteenth century, the map by the Italian Pizzigano includes the outline of the east coast of North America. The one by Martin Waldseemüller, drawn at Saint-Dié in 1507, reveals a map traced with astonishing precision. We find the same richness of detail in the planisphere of Sebastian Cabot (1544), currently at the Bibliothèque Nationale, and in the map of the Danish geographer Sigurd Stephanson, which dates from 1570.

The map of Vincent de Beauvais and Jean de Plano Carpini, which would have been prepared around 1245, before being recopied around 1435–40, is even more remarkable. Indeed, it mentions the name Vinland (*Vinlanda*) and includes several annotations on the voyages of Leif and Bjarni.

Its discovery in 1957 in a manuscript on Mongolia (the *Tartar Relation*), and its publication in 1965 by Thomas E. Marston and R. A. Skelton (*The Vinland and Tartar Relation*. Yale University Press, New York), aroused vivid emotions and provoked a polemic. In 1966, forty experts gathered in Chicago to discuss it. This was the 'The Vinland Map Conference', whose proceedings were published in 1971 by the University of Chicago. But since then, the authenticity of the map has been cast into doubt: we are practically sure today that it is a forgery (cf. Eila Campbell, 'Verdict on the Vinland Map', in *The Geographical Magazine*, April 1974).

---

181 *The First American.* — Tr.

There are, however, many other confirmations of an ethnological and archaeological order.

In the sixteenth century a Frenchman, Louis Jolliet, reveals the presence of 'white Eskimos' in Labrador. Jacques Cartier in 1534, Samuel de Champlain in 1615, some fur-traders[182] and trappers (La Verendye, Coudreau, Crevaux, Homet, Fawcett) speak of 'white Indians' living to the west of the Great Lakes. In 1630, the wood-runners,[183] Jean Nicolet, attempted to make contact with them. In 1738, the Governor of Canada identifies them. They are the Mandan Indians, who live in the regions of North Dakota and Montana. Their physical type is strange. Could they be the descendants of the Vinland settlers?

In 1850, Dr. Mitchell, director of the Bureau of Indian Affairs, declares: 'The Mandans differ from all the other Indians of North America. They are distinguished by their language and their customs, but also by physical particularities. Many among them have hair tending towards red, and eyes that are light brown or blue'.

These Mandans unfortunately disappeared last century, following a terrible epidemic of smallpox.

As early as 1930, the remains of Viking encampments have been discovered by Canadian archaeologists at Brattahlid. But it is in Quebec that the most spectacular results have been obtained.

5 November 1963, Dr. Helge Instad from Oslo, an expert of the arctic regions, announced the discovery of the vestiges of a Viking village at L'Anse aux Meadows, at the north of Newfoundland. The news hit like a bomb. Guided by the contours and undulations of the terrain, Helge Instad discovered the typical foundations of a Scandinavian house, a blacksmiths workshop, slag, fragments of worked iron, tools, the remains of boats, and even a distaff — all dating from around the year 1000.

This time, it is necessary to face the facts:

'If judged according to the full range of available evidence', notes Dr. Instad, 'the Normans who stayed around 1000 years ago at l'Anse aux Meadows can be

---

182 French *voyageurs*, literally 'travellers' (voyagers), indicates in this context French Canadians involved in the fur trade who would transport animal furs by canoe over long distances. — Tr.

183 French *coureur de bois*, 'wood-runners', indicate those engaged in the fur trade generally, rather than those focused on transportation. — Tr.

identified as the Vinland explorers of the Icelandic Sagas. It is also likely that Leif Erikson built his "large house" here.

Some other remains of Viking habitations have been discovered since: notably on the banks of the Charles River, near Cambridge, in the Bay of Brador, in Newfoundland, and near the Payne Lake, northeast of the province of Quebec.

Previously, in Ontario, some pieces of iron had been unearthed, along with some weapons (including a rounded shield[184] and a battle axe) and some tools; in Massachusetts, some wooden spoons and silver objects; and at Fall River, in 1831, the skeleton of a warrior was found, armed from head to toe, unfortunately lost today. (The Indian *tumuli* of Massachusetts have also furnished some objects of the Scandinavian type, doubtless trophies taken from combat).

At Newport (Rhode Island), a mysterious stone tower has been found which has not been able to be dated. Some have seen in it a replica of the Church of Saint-Olav of Tunsberg (Norway).

In 1898, while clearing one of his fields, a farmer in Kensington (Minnesota) discovered a stone bearing an inscription in runic characters.

Deciphered in 1907, the inscription reads: '(We are) eight Goths and twenty-two Norwegians, on an expedition from Vinland towards the west. We have camped on the edge of a lake. We left for a day to fish. When we came back, ten (denos) companions were lying on the ground, bathed in their own blood. AVM (Ave Maria), Save (us) from peril ...'. On the reverse, a date: 1362.

From 1908, a polemic of rare violence would be established on the issue of this 'Kensington stone' (which would be displayed for a long time at the Smithsonian Institute). Some researchers, such as Erik Wahlgren (*The Kensington Stone. A Mystery Solved*), assert that it is a forgery: the inscription would have been carved in the last century by Swedish immigrants, very numerous at the time in Minnesota.

Other experts, such as Hjalmar R. Holand (*Westwards from Vinland*) will fight with their last breath to demonstrate its authenticity.

'In 1948', asserts René Guichard in his study on the Vikings, 'Professor Johannes Bronstedt, director of the National Museum of Copenhagen, was invited to Washington to study the inscriptions borne on the stone. He

---

184 Fr. *coupelle de bouclier* — Tr.

concludes, after a serious study of the runic signs, that the inscription was authentic.'

In 1969, two Americans, Alf Mongé and Ole G. Landsverk, have released new hypotheses making appeal to runic cryptography. After having submitted the results of their works to a computer, they have also declared in favour of its authenticity. But they are still far from having convinced the scholarly world.

The Arrival of White and Bearded Gods

The decline of Vinland began around 1300.

King Erik VI of Norway restricts trade with the distant colonies and creates a State monopoly. In the Mediterranean, the freeing of the Muslim yoke opens new pathways. After the sinking of a royal vessel, exchanges between Scandinavia and America will soon be interrupted.

During this time, in Greenland, the cooling of the climate, scurvy, and increasingly frequent clashes with the Eskimos, lead to the progressive extinction of the Scandinavian community, formerly some ten-thousand men strong.

In Vinland, the indigenous people (Eskimos or Indians, called *Skraelings* in the Sagas) become bolder.

Freshly Christianised, Scandinavia now has another subject of concern: The Crusades, the Hundred Years' War, the Black Death. Little by little it forgets its pioneers.

In 1340, the principal establishment of Vinland is overwhelmed by the Eskimos. Departing in 1354, a salvage expedition commanded by the Norwegian Paul Knudson finds nothing on the site but abandoned houses and roaming cattle. A great number of settlers have been killed. The others have left.

Now in this period, Jacques de Mahieu affirms, the Vikings have already explored and colonised an important part of the South American continent. And this for three centuries.

Jacques de Mahieu, seventy-one-year-old former Dean of the Faculty of Political Science at Bueno Aires, directs the Institute for the Science of Man in Argentina. For years he has been committed to collecting traces of Viking penetration into the American continent upon the fourfold plane of archaeology, historical tradition, mythology, and anthropology. He thinks that the Scandinavians have gone much further than we imagine: as far as Latin America and Polynesia.

'The white racial element of Pre-Columbian America', he writes in *Le grande voyage du dieu-soleil*,[185] plays a fundamental role in the development of the great Nahuatl, Maya, and Quechua cultures'.

Countless chronicles actually speak of the arrival of 'white gods' in Latin America and, curiously, situate this arrival between the tenth and twelfth centuries CE.

The Muiscas of Columbia call themselves the descendants of a 'white god come from the north'. In Peru, this god carries the name of Huiracocha (Viracocha in the Spanish chronicles). In Mexico, he is called Quetzalcoatl. Among the Incas, sons of the Sun, the eighth sovereign of the royal dynasty, represented in the form of a white, bearded man, will take the name Viracocha.

Among the Quiché Mayas (Mexico), the god Itzamna is an old man with a sharp nose, god of the rising sun, who passes for the inventor of writing. The *Popol Vuh* (People's Book?) recounts that the ancestors of the Aztec sovereign Montezuma come from the land of Dawn, that is to say, the east. It is in 987 that Kukulkan would have arrived in the peninsula of Yucatan (Mexico), where he would have given new vitality to Mayan civilisation, then in full decline. The Tzendales of Chiapas (the southeastern point of Mexico), themselves also Mayans, knew him under the name of Votan or Uotan (Wotan?). Elsewhere, he carries the name of Ollin Tonatiut (Odhinn, Donar, Tiu?).

'The Votan (Odon) of Central America and of Peru', writes Alexander von Humboldt, 'is identical to the Scandinavian Wotan (Odin)'.

In the same period, Bochica, the 'white god' of the Chibchas, would have landed in Venezuela.

Everywhere we discover the same theme of the birth or rebirth of a civilisation under the influence of divinities or of mythic heroes come from elsewhere. And these events are situated more or less at the same time.

One fact is certain: the sudden appearance of the Pre-Columbian cultures has posed a problem to scholars for quite some time. Some support autochthony: the Mexican and Andean world developed itself separate from all exterior influence. But for some time now, this thesis has been considered unsatisfying.

---

185 *The Sun God's Great Journey.* — Tr.

Successively, the Polynesians, the Chinese, the Indians, the Hebrews, and the Phoenicians, indeed the Basques, the Bretons, and the Atlanntes, have all been presented as the 'founding fathers' of South-American civilisations. (Without forgetting the 'extra-terrestrials', who always have their supporters!).

The Power and Wisdom of Tezcatlipoca

It is likely that the coasts of South America were recognised and then explored very early by seafarers from eastern China and southeast Asia. In his book, C. W. Ceram reveals numerous common cultural traits. Between the pyramids of Tikal at Guatemala, and the edifices of Angkor in ancient Indochina, the analogies are particularly strong.

The 'Phoenician' thesis, sustained by Professor Cyrus H. Gordon from the Brandeis Univeristy (*L'Amérique avant Christophe Colomb*. Laffont, 1973),[186] which Frederik J. Pohlmakes references, seems very much to be the most unrealistic. Professor André Dupond-Sommer, a prominent specialist of the Near East, has formally contradicted it.

The thesis of an ancient association between Egypt and Pre-Columbian America is pure fabrication. 3,500 years separate the construction of the Egyptian pyramids and those of Mexico (the most ancient were constructed in the seventh century CE). Furthermore, the design of the two groups of monuments is completely different.

That leaves the Vikings.

Certainly, recourse to 'civilising heroes' does not explain the development of Olmec civilisation (Gulf of Mexico); the great periods of classical Mayan culture (Honduras, Guatemala, Yucatan); the first civilisation of Teotihuacan (Mexico); the cultures of Chavin, or those of the Mochica and the Nazca (Peru). However, their influence appears certain, in Mexico, on the Toltec and Aztec civilisation, and upon the culture of the post-classical Mayans (Yucatan); in Peru, on the Tiahuanaco culture and the Inca Empire.

In all these regions, the 'white god' has left traces, distorted by time, altered in the course of invasions and mixing, but still identifiable today.

Quetzalcoatl (the 'feathered serpent') is the wisest of the seven chiefs from the north who invaded Mexico from the 'land of seven caverns', at the head of seven armed detachments. Warrior god, 'Lord of the Sunrise', the

---

186 *America Before Christopher Columbus.* — Tr.

traditions describe him as having white skin, broad forehead, and a majestic beard. Civiliser of the Anahuac plateau, he brings with him a religion, laws, a calendar, new agricultural and metallurgical techniques. He forbids human sacrifices. Under his reign, the Toltec Empire became prosperous.

But Quetzalcoatl runs into the hostility of the priest caste, reduced to joblessness by the new cult. Quetzalcoatl faces a violent conflict, and as a result he is conquered. Forced into exile, he embarks, with four young nobles following him, on a boat that sets course for the east. They promise to return.

'When the time has come', he declares to them, 'I will return to your midst by the eastern sea, accompanied by white and bearded men'.

Transmitted from generation to generation, this 'prophecy' explains the welcome reception that the conquering Spaniards received when they landed in Mexico. Cortès and his *conquistadores* were honoured as 'the heroes that we have awaited'. Those among them who were blond, such as Pedro de Alvarado, one of the lieutenants of Cortès, became the object of a cult. Motecozuma II (Montezuma) ordained the provision of all their needs. Later, the Emperor Maximillian was the object of the same veneration.

In Peru, the civilising heroes known under the name of Huiracocha (Viracocha) had arrived at Arica on the north coast of Peru during the ninth century. He had organised the Aymara culture and founded on the High-Plane[187] in proximity to Lake Titicaca, the great solar city of Tiahuanaco.

The etymology of the name Huiracocha has long remained an enigma. Bertrand Flornoy, in *L'aventure inca* (Perrin, 1963),[188] proposes 'foam of the sea'. De Mahieu advances the translation 'white god' (*huitr* or *witt*, 'white'); *koch* or *gott*, 'deity').

In the thirteenth century, internal struggles devastated the High-Plane. The heroes of the civilisation of the sun are defeated. They escape via the Pacific, announcing that one day they will return.

Shortly after, still in Peru, appears the legendary founder of the Inca Empire, Manko Cápak, first of twelve kings of the dynasty. The foundation of the city of Cusco is attributed to him.

---

187 Altiplano in Spanish (*Haute-Plateau*). — Tr.

188 *The Inca Adventure*. — Tr.

He was also a 'foreigner'. 'According to the myths', writes Rafaël Karsten (*La civilisation de l'empire inca*. Payot, 1972),[189] 'the dynasty of monarchs who later called themselves Incas originated from four brothers and four sisters created by Viracocha, and who came from a large cave situated around seven leagues east of Cusco. The myths designate this cave by the name Paqariq Tampu (…) It is likely that there is a grain of historical truth to this. It could be that the Incas effectively drew their origin from four brothers who, departing from a place called Paqariq Tampu, penetrated via Wanakawri into the valley of Cusco, where they established their law and imposed it upon the indigenous population'.

The Temple of the Sun and the 'Enclosure of Gold' of Cusco

'The term *inca*', adds Jacques de Mahieu, 'is neither Quechua nor Aymara. So where does it come from?' In the old Germanic languages, the *ing* declension served to designate the members of a single lineage, and we still find it, with the same meaning, in French words such as *mérovingien*, *carolingien*, and *lotharingien*. It is therefore not by chance, nor by error, that the Spanish chronicles write *inga* instead of *inca*, as it is done today: the letter 'g' does not exist in Quechua'.

Come from the 'land of the Rising Sun', the Incas carried with them the cult of the sun, of which they declared themselves the sons.

'Wherever they extended their authority', writes Karsten, 'they also extended the cult of the sun, prudently however, and without employing violence'. It is a matter here of an original contribution, for in the mountainous regions of Bolivia and Peru, we find few traces of it before the Inca period. Having arrived with the foreigners, the new cult would also disappear with them. 'It is in vain that in our days we would seek survivals', adds Karsten, 'made all the more remarkable as we encounter many vestiges of a cult of the sea goddess and other kinds of primordial nature cults'.

The centre of the solar cult is installed in Curicancha ('the enclosure of gold') of Cusco. After having pillaged all the treasures, the Spanish destroyed it entirely.

---

189 *The Civilisation of the Inca Empire.* — Tr.

In 1523, the last Inca, Huayna Capak, warned his people of the future return of the 'white gods'. He asked them to serve them. In 1527, Pizarre landed
at Tumbes. The same scenes witnessed at Mexico were reproduced. Seeing the
face of Huiracocha sculpted on the Gate of the Sun at Tiahuanaco, some *conquistadores* believed to recognise the effigy of Saint Bartolemeo. To all those
who have blond or red hair, the indigenous give the same name of Huiracocha.

In the final analysis, Pizarre conquered the Andean Empire with only 177
men!

'The Incan aristocracy', writes his brother Pedro in his *Relacion del
Descumbrimiente y Conquista de los reinos del Peru*,[190] 'has whiter skin than
that of the Spanish, and hair the colour of ripe wheat'.

Jacques de Mahieu has brought to light other astonishing facts.

'In Peru', he reveals, 'the year was divided into four seasons by the solstices
and equinoxes, with corresponding festivals. Now the festival of the new Fire
is celebrated in June, as in Europe, while the inversion of the seasons would
have required it to be performed in December. It is this which demonstrates
the northern origin of the rite'.

Among the peoples of Anahuac (Aztecs, Toltecs), the presence of two
calendars, one religious, of 260 days, and the other civil, of 365 days, gives rise
to the idea that the second calendar had been brought from outside, at a later
date.

A stele from the island of Apara, on Lake Titicaca; the bearded head from
Rio Balsas (in Mexico); the frescoes of the temple of the warriors of Chichen
Itza, in Yucatan, portray figures with distinctly European traits.

Conversely, the Scandinavian tapestry of Ovrehodgal (end of the eleventh
century) includes a certain number of animals strongly representing llamas.

The *codices* from Mexico are even more revealing. Among those conserved
in Paris in the Mexican collections of the Bibliothèque nationale (Aubin
Collection), the Tonalamatl represents several individuals with blond hair: the
navigator Thor Heyerdahl has personally counted more than a hundred. 'The
fresco of the Temple of the warriors', summarises Paul Rivet in his study on
Les origins de l'homme américain (Gallimard, 1957),[191] 'represents a struggle

---

190 *Account of the Discovery and Conquest of the Kingdoms of Peru.* — Tr.
191 *The Origins of American Humanity.* — Tr.

between the indigenous people and assailants from the sea who have pale skin and blond hair'.

In Peru and Chile, ancient sepulchres, notably those from the caves of Paracas discovered in 1925 by Tello and Lothrop, have delivered mummified bodies, in perfect state of conservation, of young women with long blonde, light chestnut, and red hair. These mummies have been studied by Reiss and Stübel, Busk, Dawson and Trotter. De Mahieu publishes some photos in the German edition of his book (*Des Sonnengottes grosse Reise*. Grabert, Tübingen, 1971),[192] which is more rich than the French edition in regards to illustrations.

The Mystery of the 'White Indians'

Anthropology also provides its testimony. At the beginning of the nineteenth century, the French naturalist Alcide d'Orbigny studied the 'white Indians' of Bolivinan Beni, as well as the Antis and the Yuracaré, tribes which lived in the same region but which have now vanished. Two missions (1969–70 and 1971–72) by the Argentinian Institute for the Science of Man, directed by de Mahieu, have permitted the identification of another: the Guayaki of Paraguay.

These Indians live in the subtropical forest of west Paraguay. There are scarcely more than four hundred of them: the race is in danger of extinction. Their physical type is distinguished from all other tribes: tall stature, pale skin, oval cross-section of the hair, strong pilosity, elongated face, etc. De Mahieu sees in them the descendants, very degenerated, of the Scandinavian settlers that were chased from the Andean High-Plane, who, after being displaced in the forests, would have mixed with the Guarani Indians.

In the course of their missions, the members of the Institute for the Science of Man have also brought to light a large number of designs and inscriptions on walls and pottery fragments (rock from Cerro Polilla in the sierra of Yvytyruzu, an encampment of Cerro Moroti near San Joaqui, to the west of Paraguay). According to de Mahieu, who has attempted to decipher them, some of the signs could be runic in nature (*Les inscriptions runique précolombiennes au Paraguay*. Bienos Aires, 1972).[193]

The conclusion of de Mahieu: 'In Pre-Columbian South America, in the midst of a mostly Amerindian population of Mongol origin, there are some

---

192 *The Sun God's Great Journey.* — Tr.
193 *The Pre-Columbian Runic Inscriptions of Paraguay.* — Tr.

groups of whites who, from the anthropological point of view, possess a Nordic European type'.

Foreign Migrations in Polynesia

In *L'agonie du dieu-soleil*,[194] de Mahieu asks: where have the white gods, Huiracocha and his companions, gone?

In 1947, the celebrated 'Kon Tiki' expedition carried out by Thor Heyerdahl, proved that the sea-journey from Peru to Polynesia was possible. At the same time, he had also provided a basis for the hypothesis of ancient contacts between South America and the Pacific Islands.

For his part, the ethnologist Jean Poirier, former Professor at L'École nationale de la France d'Outre-Mer, in a communication published in 1953 by the Society of Oceanologists of the Museum of Man (*L'élément blond en Polynésie et les migrations nordiques en Océanie*),[195] have gathered and presented a multitude of historical and ethnological testimonies concerning the presence of a 'blond' human type in the population of Polynesia.

For the anthropologists, Polynesian ethnicity arises from a stock belonging to Mongolia (perhaps an ancient specialisation of the Proto-Indo-European stock), upon which an important Caucasian branch would have been grafted, as well as a weaker negro element.

'But there is another element', writes Poirier, 'numerically much more important, which has also contributed to the formation of Polynesian ethnicity: it is a blond element, so qualified according to its most apparent characteristic, and which could also be called 'Nordic', without raising a dangerous extrapolation'.

Polynesia, moreover, also has its 'white gods': Kane and Wakea in Hawaii; Tangaroa and Tu in Niue (an isolated island between the Tonga and Cook archipelagos); Tama-ehu in Tahiti, etc.

When the navigator Cook would arrive at Mangaia in the eighteenth century, the indigenous people believed that he was a reincarnation of Tangaroa.

In Hawaii, local traditions make allusion to a 'land very far away', where the trees have fragile leaves and the rivers can freeze during winter. They

---

194 *The Death-throes of the Sun God.* — Tr.
195 *The Blond Element in Polynesia and the Nordic Migrations in Oceania.* — Tr.

report also that some 'white men' had come to Hawaii on three occasions: 'the arrival of Paao, the arrival of many men in canoes in the time of Opiri (son of Paao), the arrival of foreigners under the reign of Kahukapu'. The descendants of the foreigners, says the explorer Ellis, are distinguished 'by the colour of their skin'. He adds that to the Sandwich Islands (formerly of Hawaii), they are called 'ehu'.

At the same time, the problem of the mythic origins of the fabulous Easter Island resurfaces.

Situated in the middle of the Pacific 800 kilometres from the coasts of Peru, Easter Island had been discovered in 1722 by the Dutchman Rogeveen. Some local accounts mention 'white foreigners' who had come by sea. It is in their honour that the celebrated statues had been erected. In the seventeenth century, the foreigners and their adherents would have been exterminated during violent events whose trace has been preserved at various sites: scattered tools, burnt areas, incomplete statues at all stages.

At Paraguay, de Mahieu also discovered ideographic signs of the 'rongorongo' type, characteristic of Easter Island.

Bouganville (1729–1811), describing Tahiti, writes: 'The people of Tahiti are composed of two races of very different men, who nevertheless have the same language, the same morals, and who appear to circulate without distinction. The first produce the tallest men ... Nothing distinguishes their traits from those of the Europeans, and if they were clothed, if they lived less in the air and in the great sun, they would also be white like us ... The second race is of a medium size, has frizzy, hair, coarse like a horse; their colour and their traits differ little from those of the mulatto'.

Called to the side of the wife of a Tahitian chief, Dr. Maximo Rodgriguez noted that she had 'very fair complexion, blonde and curly hair, and blue eyes'.

In a memoir by Pedro Fernandez de Quiros, who was the pilot of Alvaro Mendana de Neira during the time when he discovered the Solomon Islands, we are able to read: 'The natives of Madalena Island are almost white; they have regular and agreeable traits, beautiful eyes, gentle features, white and well-formed teeth. Most have blond hair; they wear it long and flowing like the women; but some roll them up and twist them upon their heads' (cited by Claret-Fleurieu: *Voyage de Marchand*, 1809).[196]

Concerning the Sandwich Islands, the Maluku, the Marquesas, dozens of testimonies exist of this kind, from those of Jacob le Maire and William Schouten (1615) to those of Carl Frederick Behrens, Wallis, Bougainville, and Crozet, Cook, Parkison, Forester, etc.

Paul Huguenon reported as late as 1902: 'The families of the great chiefs of Nuka Hiva (one of the Marquesas Islands) call themselves Arri. Their complexion is more fair, their eyes are blueish, their hair has red in it'.

In his conclusions, Jean Poirier distinguishes 'two layers in the Polynesian blond element'. 'The first layer', he writes, 'goes back to an indeterminate past. It is contemporary with the formation of the Polynesian race: Neolithic, numerically the most important, came from the west; it has penetrated into Polynesia by sea, and into America by the Behring Straight, before descending the length of the western coastline. As to the second, the preferential presence of fair types (hair and, unusually, eyes) in the eastern archipelagos can only be explained by a recent contact with elements of the same type, that is to say of Nordic elements. Now, we know today that the Scandinavian migrants have penetrated deeply into North America. Henceforth, it is only logical to suppose an arrival of these elements in Polynesia'.

12 October 1492, Christopher Colombus arrives before a continent which he believes to be the Indies; he calls the inhabitants *Indios*.

24 June 1497, Jean Cabot from England, landed on Newfoundland. 24 April 1500, the Portuguese Pedro Alvarez Cabral arrived in Brazil. Around 1500, the Florentine Amerigo Vespucci explored Patagonia. In 1513, the conquistador Vasco Nunez of Balboa discovered the Pacific. In 1521, the Spaniard Sebastien del Cano, survivor of the Portuguese Magellan, brings the last ship back to the port. He was the first European to have made the tour of the world.

Finally, in 1532, François Pizarre undertook the conquest of Peru on behalf of the King of Spain.

Europe discovered America. Once again.

The Vikings founded the city of Kiev, the Norman kingdom of Two-Sicilies, the sovereign duchy of Normandy. Their *drakkar* go by north Africa

---

196 *Voyage of Marchand.* — Tr.

to Faroe, from Labrador to the Caspian. They appear as the greatest navigators of history.

A Nordic proverb says: 'Cattle die. Kinsmen die. And you, too, will die. But a noble name never dies'. The name of Leif Erikson has remained alive. Since 1887, the discoverer of America has had his statue at Boston. He looks out over the Ocean.

*

Le grand voyage du dieu-soleil, a study by Jacques Mahieu. Special edition, 205 pages. 25 Francs.[197]

L'agonie du dieu-soleil, a study by Jacques de Mahieu. Laffront, 228 pages.[198]

Les Vikings, créateurs d'États et découvreurs de nouveaux mondes, a study by René Guichard. Picard, 196 pages.[199]

*

Further vestiges of the Vikings' presence in America have been found over the course of the last several years. The most important discovery has been that of the ruins of three ancient Scandinavian 'longhouses' on Pamiok Island, in Ungava Bay (northern Quebec). The last of these buildings, brought to light in 1972, is absolutely identical to the Viking constructions of Iceland and Greenland. On the same site, a Thor's hammer and an iron axe identified as Nordic by metallographic analysis were unearthed in 1970. The excavations have been undertaken by Professor Thomas E. Lee from the Université Laval of Quebec, who has published the results in *Archaeological Investigations of a Longhouse Ruin, Pamiok Island, Ungava Bay* (Centre d'études Nordiques, Québec, 1974). Cf. also Dietrich Lüth, *Further Evidence of Early Norse Settlements in the Americas* (in *The Journal of Indo-European Studies*, vol. II, no. 1, spring 1974).

Like those of Helge Instad, these discoveries confirm the reality of the historical accounts contained in the Sagas, in particular the *Graenlendiga Saga* and *Eriks Saga*. In this regard we will refer to *The Vinland Sagas. The Norse Discovery of America* (Penguin Books, Harmondsworth, 1965) and to *Vinland the Good*, a work prefaced by Helge Instad (Johan Grundt Tanum, Oslo, 1966).

In England, the Viking Society for Northern Research (University of London, University College, Gower Street, London WC1), animated by Professors Peter G. Foote (*The Viking Achievement*. Sidgwick & Jackson, London, 1970) and G. Turville-Petre (*Myth and Religion of the North*. Weidenfeld and Nicolson, London, 1964) have published many works on the Viking expansion.

In his book on *La civilisation des Incas* (Famot, 1976),[200] Jean-Claude Valla provides his own take on the numerous hypotheses emitted by Professor Jacques de Mahieu, and brings

---

197 *The Sun God's Great Journey.* — Tr.

198 *The Death-throes of the Sun God.* — Tr.

199 *The Vikings, Creators of States and Discoverers of New Worlds.* — Tr.

200 *The Civilisation of the Incas.* — Tr.

new precision to the identity of the 'white and bearded' civilising heroes who, between 1050 and 1100, founded the 'kingdom of Tiahuanaco' on the banks of Lake Titicaca. 'These men who, from Mexico to Peru, altered from top to bottom previous cultures of manifestly Asiatic origin, established themselves as the ruling class and gave birth to kingdoms with a level of civilisation comparable to those of Europe, and who introduced a solar cult unknown before their arrival, who are they if not the Viking navigators come from the North' (Michael Marmin, 'Les Vikings en Amérique du Sud ?', in *Eléments* Nr. 21–22, April–July 1977).[201]

Professor Mahieu has himself followed these studies. He has documented the results in three new works: 'Drakkars sur l'Amazone' (Copernic, 1977), 'Le tombeau du dieu-soleil' (forthcoming), and 'La géographique secrete de l'Amérique avant Colomb' (unpublished).[202]

In the United States, O. G. Landsverk, who situates Vinland at the top of New England, has published (in collaboration with Alf Mongé) three books dedicated in large part to 'runic cryptography': *Norse Medieval Cryptography in Runic Carvings* (1967), *Ancient Norse Messages on American Stones* (1969), and *Runic Records of the Norsemen in America* (1974). These three titles are distributed by the Landsverk Foundation (Box 652, Rushford, Minnesota 55971).

---

201 'Vikings in South America?' — Tr.

202 *Drakkar on the Amazon. The Grave of the Sun God. The Secret Geography of America Before Columbus.* — Tr.

FOUNDATIONS

Philosophical

ZARATHUSTRA

H e said: 'The higher we soar, the smaller we appear to those who cannot fly'.[203]

The scene takes place in Switzerland, in the Engadine, at the beginning of the month of August, 1881. At the end of a path in the forest, Nietzsche stops at the foot of a rock on the banks of Lake Silvaplana. It is here, '6,000 feet beyond man and time',[204] where he first had the intuition of the Eternal Return. He would write: 'That day, Zarathustra assailed me'.

In the work of Friedrich Nietzsche (1844–1900), *Thus Spoke Zarathustra* is situated between *The Gay Science* and *Beyond Good and Evil*. Nietzsche went through a period of great interior suffering then. But it is also the time where he reveals himself to be the most fecund: the works follow one after the other like lightning strikes.

The first part of *Zarathustra* is written at Rapallo, at the beginning of 1833. On the 15th of February, Nietzsche learns of the death of Richard Wagner. He goes to Rome, then to Sils Maria. The second part is completed in spring. In autumn, Nietzsche left for Leipzig, where he attempts without success to offer some free courses at the University. After this, he departs again for Genoa and, from there, to Villefranche-sur-Mer. He finished the third part at Nice, during the winter. But the publication of the first sections, on which he had based such great hopes, encountered no response.

---

203 Where necessary, for reasons of fidelity, I have sourced and translated many (but not all) of the Nietzsche quotes cited in this chapter from the original German. In other instances, for stylistic reasons, I have remained closer to the French translations cited by Benoist. This opening citation, for example, remains closer the French (Plus nous nous élevons, et plus nous paraissons petits à ceux qui ne savent pas voler); cf. *Zarathustra*, I, Vom Wege des Schaffenden: 'aber je höher du steigst, um so kleiner sieht dich das Auge des Neides' (the higher you climb, the smaller you seem to the eye of envy). — Tr.

204 *Ecce Homo*, Warum ich so gute Bücher schreibe, Also Sprach Zarathustra, §1: '6000 Fuß jenseits von Mensch un Zeit'. — Tr.

More isolated than ever, Nietzsche resumed his peregrinations: Venice, Sils-Maria, Zurich, Menton, Nice. In 1885, having composed the fourth part, he decided to publish it himself. He secured the printing of forty copies. But he only found seven people to send them to. This drama summarises his whole life: those who interested Nietzsche scarcely understood his work, those who appreciated it most no longer interested him.

At the end of 1886, the publisher E. W. Fritsch from Leipzig united the first three parts of *Thus Spoke Zarathustra* together in a single volume. But it would have to wait until July 1892 to see the first edition corresponding to the complete manuscript appear, published by Naumann, also in Leipzig. (A French translation, by Henri Albert, would be released by Mercure de France in 1898).

Some Exaggerated Critiques

The most recent of the 'versions' offered to the French public form part of the Complete Works whose publication has been underway, for some years, by two Italian Professors, Giorgio Colli and Mazzino Montinari. This edition appeared simultaneously in Germany (Walter de Gruyter), France (Gallimard), and Italy (Adelphi). In our country, it is placed under the direction of Gilles Deleuze (*Nietzsche, Différence et répétition, Nietzsche et la philosophie*)[205] and Maurice Gandillac. The collection is comprised of nine tomes in some forty volumes, more than half of which have already been published. The project resumes the one conceived by Alfred Baeumler in 1933, which he had not been able to carry out due to lack of means.

Such a delay should not be surprising. In the aftermath of the Second World War, the USSR took hold of the Nietzsche Archiv and entrusted it to East Germany. They stored it at Weimar and forbid access to researchers. The prohibition was not lifted until 1950, when all the manuscripts were transferred to the Goethe und Schiller Archiv.

One of the particularities of the Colli-Montinari edition consists in the 'dismantling' of *The Will to Power*, a collection which brought together, in 1906, then in 1911 (Kröner edition), a certain number of fragments composed by Nietzsche between 1884 and 1888. The presentation and classification (by themes, in a non-chronological order) of these fragments has been the object

---

205 *Nietzsche. Difference and Repetition. Nietzsche and Philosophy.* — Tr.

of some criticism, notably by Karl Schlechta (*Le cas Nietzsche*. Gallimard, 1960),[206] who questions the 'abusive' influence of the philosopher's sister, Elisabeth Förster-Nietzsche. In reality, it can be observed, thanks to a comparative reading of the old and the new versions, that the stated criticisms are themselves strongly exaggerated.

'At the root', writes Jean-Michel Palmier, 'it (is necessary to) be of a singular naivety to imagine that even the image of Nietzsche could be modified. Adding some aphorisms, some notes and some supplementary drafts will not cause Nietzsche to be understood differently, unless one tries to make him say what he did not say' (*Le Monde*, 7 June 1969).

For each volume, all the variants, all the corrections, are noted and commented upon — which allows us to follow the development of the work in all of its permutations. However, the translations have been reviewed very closely. In *Nietzsche éducateur* (Buchet-Chastel, 1961), Christophe Baroni has already brought up many misinterpretations by Henri Albert.

Unfortunately, the text sometimes loses in clarity what it gains in word-for-word exactitude. An example taken at random, in *Zarathustra*: 'You want to "make" imaginable everything which is: for you doubt, with a justifiable mistrust, that it is already imaginable' (Henri Albert) becomes: 'All that is, first you want to "render" it thinkable, for you doubt, with justifiable mistrust, that thinkable this will already be'.[207] A surprising heaviness in the mouth of 'Zarathustra, the dancer, the light one'.

Thus Spoke Zarathustra is a philosophical poem with the rhythm of a musical composition. It has its themes, its *Leitmotive*, its variations. 'Compared to music', said Nietzsche, 'all communication by words is indecent'.

Zarathustra descends from the heights of the mountain. He goes to men like a hammer to the sculpting stone. He who carries the name of one of the

---

206 German: *Der Fall Nietzsche: Aufsätze u. Vorträge* (The Nietzsche Case: Essays and Lectures). — Tr.

207 We are necessarily dealing with translations of translations here: Nietzsche's German into French; and then the French translations cited by Benoist into our English. For proper comparison, the German of the passage in question reads: 'Alles Seiende wollt ihr erst denkbar machen: denn ihr zweifelt mit gutem Misstrauen, ob es schon denkbar ist' (Zarathustra II, 'Von der Selbst-Ueberwinding', 12). In Henri Albert's French: 'Vous voulez "rendre" imaginable tout ce qui est: car vous doutez, avec une juste méfiance, que ce soit déjà imaginable'; the more modern translation reads: 'Tout ce qui est, d'abord vous le voulez "rendre" pensable, car vous doutez, avec juste méfiance, que pensable ce soit déjà'.

first great moralisers (Zoroaster, reformer of the ancient religion of Iran) proclaims the death of morality, the coming of the Overman, and the certitude of the Eternal Return.

Against the 'Hinterworlds'

The whole work is completely solar in inspiration. Each page is bathed in the blinding clarity of an affirmation of life. 'I who am born on the earth', cries Zarathustra, 'I suffer the diseases of the Sun like an eclipse of my being and a cataclysm of my own soul'.

Already in *The Gay Science* we read: 'Who will sing us a song, a song to the high morning, so sunny, so light, so full that it does not chase away the crickets or the black moods, but instead invites them to sing and dance with it?'[208] And in the *Songs of the Prince Vogelfrei*: 'Let us chase away the murky skies, the world-darkeners, the cloud-bringers! Let us brighten the kingdom of heaven! Let us roar, oh free spirit of spirits!'[209]

Nietzsche too intends to be roaring.[210] 'I prefer noise and thunder and accursed weather to the staid and circumspect calm of cats', he writes. 'And among men I hate above all those who creep, half-and-halfers, doubting, hesitant drift-clouds'.[211]

Here again, the air is light which descends from the glaciers. The birds of prey circle in the azure skies, unconcerned by the approaching storm.

---

208 Nietzsche, *Die fröliche Wissenschaft*, V, § 383: 'Wer singt uns ein Lied, ein Vormittagslied, so sonnig, so leicht, so flügge, dass es die Grillen nicht verscheucht, — dass es die Grillen vielmehr einlädt, mit zu singen, mit zu tanzen?' Note that the word *Grillen* here means both 'crickets' and 'whims, freakish ideas', evidently with a negative connotation, as the Williams/Nauckhoff/Caro edition (Cambridge University Press, 2001, p. 248 n. 5) glosses it as 'bad mood', and the French translation (cited by Benoist) renders it as 'black ideas' (*les idées noires*). — Tr.

209 Nietzsche, *Die fröliche Wissenschaft* (Lieder des Prinzen Vogelfrei; An den Mistral): 'Jagen wir die Himmels-Trüber,/ Welten-Schwärzer, Wolken-Schieber,/ Hellen wir das Himmelreich!/ Brausen wir... oh aller freien/ Geister Geist'. — Tr.

210 Nietzsche's *brausen* is rendered as *retentissant* ('loud, resounding, tremendous') in French. — Tr.

211 Nietzsche, *Zarathustra*, III, Vor Sonnen-Aufgang: 'Denn lieber noch will ich Lärm und Donner und Wetter-Flüche, als diese bedächtige zweifelnde Katzen-Ruhe; und auch unter Menschen hasse ich am besten alle Leisetreter und Halb- und Halben und zweifelnde, zögernde Zieh-Wolken'. — Tr.

Zarathustra denounces the illusions of 'those of the hinterworlds (*Hinterweltler*), of the 'deceivers' who want to give a transcendental consistency to the world of phenomena. Without illusions, moreover. The idealist who 'condemns life because it is will to power and because it opposes itself to morality' (C. Baroni) is incorrigible: 'If one falls from his heaven, he makes of hell an ideal'.

Nietzsche attacks the 'despisers of the body'. It is clear, in his eyes, that the body and the spirit are one. 'The soul is only a word for a piece of the body'. He reproaches the great universalist religions for having denigrated the body, for having made it a miserable corpse, an inferior object, a source of temptations. Deploring the effects of an education which only treats things of the spirit, he calls for a return to the 'complete man' of Antiquity. 'Of all that is written', he declares, 'I love only what one writes with his blood. Write with blood and you will find that blood is spirit'.

Our body itself is principle of hierarchy: that which we value depends on the qualities of which it is the support. And just as the body and the spirit are one, all beings are linked in the specific milieu that is compatible with their worldview (*Weltsicht*): 'When man will have known all things, then he will know himself. Things, in effect, are only his own limits'.

'In maltreating the body', writes Nietzsche in *The Will to Power*, 'we produce favourable conditions for feelings of culpability, that is to say, a state of malaise demanding an explanation'. This explanation is given by the priest (he who, according to Nietzsche, 'changes the direction of the hostility'), when he affirms that the disease is not only an evil, it is a *punishment*. From *suffering sickness*, man is then transformed into *sinner*. He is the prey of *bad conscience*.

The Dwarf and the Giant

'This man of bad conscience has seized on religious presupposition in order to provide his self-torture with its most horrific hardness and sharpness. Debt towards God: this thought becomes an instrument of torture. In God he seizes upon the ultimate antithesis he can find to his real and irredeemable animal instincts, he reinterprets these self-same animal instincts as debt/guilt before God (as animosity, insurrection, rebellion against the 'master', the 'father', the primeval ancestor and beginning of the world), he pitches himself into the contradiction of God and Devil, he emits every no which he says to himself, nature, naturalness and the reality of his being as a yes, as existing, living, real, as God, as the holiness of God, as God-the-Judge, as God-the-Hangman, as the beyond, as eternity, as torture without end, as hell, as immeasurable punishment and guilt. We have here a sort of madness of the will showing itself in mental cruelty which is absolutely unparalleled'. (*On the Genealogy of Morality*).[212]

The danger, continues Nietzsche, is not the 'wicked' — for their wickedness can pass. It is the 'sick' — for their state dwells. 'The sick', he writes, 'are the greatest danger for the healthy'. This is because the sick hate (at the same time that they desire) this 'great health' which they do not possess, in the same way that the weak are horrified of strength. The weak would like it if the whole world was exhausted. The sick would wish that everything was attained. Thus their illnesses would appear lighter to them. The dwarf who fells a giant is still found to be small.

'The weak say: "We alone are the good, the just, we alone are the *homines bonae vonuntatis*". They walk in our midst like living reproaches, as if they would serve as warnings to us, as if health, robustness, strength, pride, and the feeling of power were simply vices which must be expiated, bitterly expiated, and they are thirsty to play the role of *hangman*!'[213]

Nietzsche gives the speech to the weak. He has them explain the causes implicit in their hate: '"Ah! If I could be someone else, no matter who!" Thus does his glance sigh. "But there is no hope. I am who I am: how would I know how to get away from myself? And also — I am tired of myself!"'[214]

In *Zarathustra*, Nietzsche surpasses the critique, now classic, of Judaeo-Christian morality and of the role of the priest that he developed in *The Genealogy of Morality* and *The Twilight of the Idols* in order to directly approach the problem of the creation of a 'new objectivity' on the very ruins of the notion of the absolute.

'Previously', he writes, 'blasphemy against God was the worst blasphemy; but God is dead, and with him all his blasphemers are also dead. The worst

---

212 Nietzsche, *Zur Genealogie der Moral*, II, § 22; *On the Genealogy of Morality*, ed. Keith Ansell-Pearson, trans. Carol Diethe (Cambridge, Cambridge Univerity Press, 2006), pp. 63–4. — Tr.

213 *Zur Geneaology der Moral*, III, § 14. — Tr.

214 *Zur Geneaology der Moral*, III, § 14. — Tr.

sacrilege at present is to blaspheme the earth'. Zarathustra is 'true to the earth'. But he also knows to withdraw. For Nietzsche, 'he must quit life like Odysseus would quit Nausicaä, with recognition sooner than with love'. He adds: 'the maturity of man is to rediscover the seriousness that he placed in games as a child'. And further: A man approaches genius when he can simultaneously love a thing and mock it'.

Friedrich Nietzsche proposes to replace the morality of sin with an ethic of honour in which life is only worth the price of being lived under certain conditions. 'My ego has taught me a new pride', declared Zarathustra, 'I teach it to mankind: no longer bury your head in the sand of heavenly things, but bear it proudly'. 'Nietzschean morality will therefore be a morality of life, it will only condemn enslaved and fallen lives' (Thierry Maulnier, *Nietzsche*. Gallimard, 1943).

Faced with inferior beings ('When they say "I am just", this always sounds like "I am avenged" …'), the superior man is caught by the trap of his human-ity: — 'Because you are mild and just, you say: They are innocent by their petty existence. But their narrow souls think: — All great existence is guilty'.

'A Rope Over an Abyss'

The decline of aristocracies has gone hand in hand with a process that has given power to those who Nietzsche calls 'the last men'. With this term, he denounces in advance the representatives of the society of consumption and the morality of merchants: those who think that the human *adventure* is too *risky*, that it must put an end to history, abolish tensions, give everyone the same *comfort*, submit politics to economics, and economics to society. 'We have invented happiness, say the last men, blinking'.

In fact, man is something that must be overcome. 'Man is a rope stretched between beast and overman, a rope over an abyss (…) What is great about man is that he is a bridge and not a goal'. We know the attention with which Nietzsche followed the works of Darwin on the evolution of the species. However, for him, the Overman (*Übermensch*) is not an inflation of man (*übermenschlich*). It is an entirely different being, with its own way of being, its own way of seeing the world and evaluating the meaning of things. The Overman is one for whom the affirmation of the self gives birth to a new spe-cies. One for whom the worldview is imposed *by itself* with such power that afterwards, one can no longer think outside of it. It is the culmination of a creative projection of the past into the present, the 'return' in another form of that which was. And at the same time an *achievement*: for the being who *realises* itself, at the same time overcomes itself.

The Meaning of the Eternal Return

For Nietzsche, man only has meaning if he attempts to go *beyond his condition*, that is to say, if he proceeds to pursue his own demise: the demise of his 'nature' for the benefit of the 'higher nature'[215] that it will be given. 'The overman corresponds to a goal, a goal given at every moment and which it is perhaps impossible to attain; better, a goal which, at the very instant it is attained, proposes another on a new horizon. In such a perspective, man is presented as a perpetual surpassing of man by man' (Giorgio Locchi, *L'histoire*, in *Nouvelle école* Nr. 27–28, autumn–winter 1975).

'The Overman is the meaning of the earth! Let your will say: let the Overman be the meaning of the earth!'

In order to express this necessity for surpassing, Nietzsche takes up the hammer of Eternal Return. In *Zarathustra*, the theme is illustrated by the enigma of the gate: 'See this gateway! It has two faces. Two paths come together here, which no one has yet followed to the end. A long path back, which lasts an eternity; and this long path forward — which lasts another eternity. They contradict each other, these paths, they lock heads: and it is here at this gateway that they come together. The name of the gate is written above it: "Moment".

'Everything comes and reaches out its hands and laughs and retreats — and comes back. Everything goes, everything comes back; the wheel of being rolls eternally. Everything dies, everything blossoms again, the year of being runs eternally. Everything breaks, everything is joined anew; the same house of being builds itself eternally. Everything separates, everything greets itself again; the *ring* of being remains eternally loyal to itself. In every Moment being begins; around every Here rolls the sphere There. The centre is everywhere. Crooked is the path of eternity'.

Here Nietzsche does not hide his debt to the Greeks of the Presocratic era: Heraclitus, Parmenides, Anaximander. But he also adds, in the same intuition,

---

215 Fr. *nature* and *surnature*. — Tr.

the incessant renewal of the seasons and of generations — and the discoveries of modern science: the carbon cycle, the oxygen cycle, etc.

In the same period that he formulated this idea, Gustave le Bon writes: 'If it is the same elements of each world that serves, after its destruction, to reconstitute other worlds, it is easy to understand that the same combinations, that is to say the same worlds inhabited by the same beings, must have been repeated many times' (*L'homme et les sociétés*, Vol. 2. 1881).

We know that Nietzsche studied much contemporary science, and that he once thought to demonstrate the concordance of atomic theory, then nascent, with the idea of Eternal Return. At the beginning of this century, Gabriel Huan wrote: 'The scientific character of the doctrine of Return is undeniable; perhaps it is even the only cosmological system that adapts itself to the most recent hypotheses of modern science' (*La philosophie de Frédéric Nietzsche*. E. de Boccard, 1917). Ten years later, Abel Rey confronted the theories of Nietzsche with the teachings of thermodynamics and the kinetic theory of gas. He remarks: 'The idea of the Eternal Return is ultimately only the affirmation that all evolution is relative. Considered over a sufficiently long time, it unfolds itself as if it could begin again' (*Le Retour Eternel et la philosophie de la physique*. Flammarion, 1927).

Since then, the idea of the Eternal Return has found a new justification in the notion of the discontinuity of the real elicited by microphysics. Disputing the universal extrapolations of Carnot's theorem — which is applied to complex results but not to molecular events — modern science tends to deny the idea of a generalised fundamental irreversibility, to return the irreversible to the reversible — and the generalised disorder to a *possible* order.

On a more directly philosophical plane, the Eternal Return is often poorly interpreted — when it is not considered 'marginal' in the work of Nietzsche. In reality, as Gilles Deleuze has remarked, identity refers less to the nature of what comes back than to the fact that difference returns eternally. This is the expression of a principle which is the reason for diversity and its reproduction, the reason for its difference and repetition. In his critique of the 'linear' conception of history (which implies that there is necessarily a *beginning* and an *end*, as well as a *meaning* to history), Nietzsche goes further than the simple cyclic conception of the Ancients — of which he himself expresses the limitations ('where does the diversity within a cycle come from?') by specifying that 'we do not go back to the Greeks'. He asserts that history is like a *sphere*: that in every moment dwells a possibility for the regeneration of time.

A Sphere Whose Centre is Everywhere

In order to understand the conception of history that Nietzsche proposes to us, it is necessary to place it alongside a *four-dimensional* perspective — for which we are indebted to the relativist conception of the physical universe. Whereas in Antiquity, *moments* were still seen as *points* following each other on a line, for Nietzsche, becoming is conceived as a *collection of moments* of which each forms, like a sphere, the interior of a 'four-dimensional supersphere' (one spatial dimension, three temporal dimensions), such that *each moment* occupies the centre in relation to the others.

From this perspective, indicates Giorgio Locchi (*L'«idée de la musique» et le temps de l'histoire*, in *Nouvelle école* Nr. 30, winter 1976–77), not only does the universe have neither beginning nor end, but the most appropriated image to express the idea of time is no longer the *circle* (as in the cyclic conception of the Ancients), but the *sphere*. Time *is* a sphere, in which, as Nietzsche says, the 'centre is everywhere'. The 'complete position' of the totality of forces is always destined to *return*, because each combination conditions an *infinity* of other combinations.

Destiny is a game of dice, observes Gilles Deleuze: 'If the dice that are thrown are the affirmation of chance, the dice which fall are the affirmation of necessity, the number or the destiny that brings the roll of the dice back down' (*Nietzsche et la philosophie*. PUF, 1962 and 1970).

This theme has an obvious ethical aspect. Of the thought of the Eternal Return, Nietzsche says that it is 'heavy and difficult'. In effect, the pressure that it exercises on man is not *elective*, but *selective*. It implies a selection of choices. Only that which has decided to return returns eternally. 'Only he who holds his life eternally capable of being repeated, remains'. Nietzsche deems that this thought — to live in such a way that one can will to eternally revive his life — is susceptible to transform man more actively than the myth of 'eternal damnation'. He makes this maxim: 'Impress on your life the image of eternity'.

For Nietzsche, a perspective established in history is all the more 'just' because it is expressed with a force that is more susceptible to realise it. It is for this reason that, in his eyes, the *will to power* is the 'very essence of life'. It is this, and not 'class struggle', that is the *engine* of the *causality* of history.

'I am a Man of Fatality'

Just as aristocratism does not consist primarily in rights, but first of all duties, so too the will to power, before the authority to take, first obliges us to give. Being pure affirmation in and of itself, it is necessarily creative: affirmation *adds*, it does not take away. The tragic heroes do not ask, like the 'bourgeois' (or the 'proletariat', as Marx defines it), what it can *take away* or *extract* from existence, but what it can *give* to life.

Following from this, history is not to be defined as a series of events or facts without links, like a simple succession of generations; it is no longer a 'spectacle' or a 'cult object'. It is the perpetual transformation of societies by a historical consciousness specific to man, served by the will to power which only gives *meaning* to history by imposing the strongest perspective upon it.

In this conception proposed to us by Nietzsche, man is the only one who *makes* history — not as a member of a class, or because he satisfies the prescriptions of a dogmatism, but as an undetermined individual free to choose, finding in *himself* alone the possibility to be *more than himself*. History is wholly his making: *faber suae fortunae*. His freedom consists in *always* being able to choose between different possible historical perspectives — the only situation in which this freedom is not a pretence.

Thanks to his action within (and upon) time, man overcomes the object by *everything* that cannot be reduced to it. Chaos is not that which was 'before' — all things have at once become and not-yet-become — but that which of all time is *unformed*: the 'chaos of all', also eternal, excluding the finality and the unequivocal ordering of history, the very condition of the 'spherical' movement of things within becoming. Freely creative, man is *creator of himself*: he is sufficient unto himself. (And what applies to individuals also applies to cultures and peoples).

In contrast to Marx, Nietzsche does not speak merely in terms of *society*, but in terms of *civilisation*. In socialism, he detects a profane reiteration of this 'gospel of the petty' which *renders* petty, a resurgence of this 'poison of the doctrine of equal rights for all' through which 'Christianity has destroyed our happiness on earth' (*The Twilight of the Idols*). To the *inescapability* of the society of equals, he opposes the permanent *possibility* of an aristocratic society, rendering to each according to his merits, where man will be the measure of all things, where life would find its own justification in itself—and which would enrich the world instead of impoverishing it.

'I am a man of fatality', he writes. 'For when the truth enters into conflict with the lies of a thousand years, we will have shocks like never before, convulsions and earth quakes, a shifting of mountains and valleys likes we have never dreamed. The concept of politics will then be completely consumed by spiritual warfare (…) There will be wars like never before on earth. It is only starting with me that *great politics* will exist on earth'.

Affirming that Europe will make itself, by itself, 'fatally', he adds: I would like to see Europe create itself by means of a new caste which would rule it, a unique will, tremendous, capable of following a purpose over thousands of years, in order to put an end to the too-long comedy/farce of its petty politics and its paltry and innumerable dynastic and democratic wills. These times of petty politics is passed, already the coming century predicts the struggle for the sovereignty of the world. And the irresistible push towards great politics' (*Beyond Good and Evil*).

Free from the unbearable tension resulting from the antagonism between morality and life, man bursts with laughter. Like the young shepherd from the vision of Zarathustra, when he has spat out the head of the serpent which was choking him, he finds innocence and joy at the same time.

All Joy Wants Deep Eternity

The theme of joy (or 'pleasure' in the translation of de Gandillac) bursts forth at the end of *Zarathustra* like in the Ninth Symphony, where the sky clears after the storm. Zarathustra, like all heroes, is above all joyous. In the midst of the path leading to the Overman, when the hour of the Great Noontide comes, he begins to sing a 'song of drunkenness'. For joy is more profound than toil. And this is why it is immortalised: 'Pain says: pass and finish! But all joy wants eternity. Wants deep, deep eternity'.

'What we do', writes Nietzsche, 'is never understood, but only praised or blamed'. He himself has not escaped this law. But the 'joyous messenger' does not intend to found a new religion. 'Now, I bid you to abandon me and find yourselves, for it is only when you have all denied me that I will return to you'.

Thus spoke Zarathustra.

*

Ainsi parlait Zarathoustra, by Friedrich Nietzsche. Gallimard, 449 pages.

*

Whereas in all countries we see a veritable flourishing of books on Nietzsche, the publication of the complete works in the great edition of Giorgio Colli and Mazzino Montinari continues actively. To the edition of Walter de Gruyter in Berlin, a total of around thirty volumes are projected, divided into eight parts. Always with Walter de Gruyter, Colli and Montinari have initiated a considerable œuvre: the publication of the entire correspondence of Nietzsche in some twenty volumes separated into three chronological parts (1844–1869, 1869–1879, and 1880–1889). The first volume of this edition, named *Kritische Gesamtausgabe von Nietzsches Briefwechsel (KGB)*[216] was released in 1975; it covers the period 1849–1864.

In *Nietzsche et la critique du christianisme* (Cerf, 1974),[217] Paul Valadier presents, from a Christian point of view, an in-depth analysis (without concessions to various attempts at the 'recovery' of Nietzschean thought) of an important aspect of Nietzsche's work.

In *Nietzsche: finalisme et histoire* (Copernic, 1977),[218] Pierre Chassard focuses more particularly on Nietzsche's 'anti-providentialism'. He summarises the Nietzschean philosophy of history in these terms: 'It demystifies and shows that the universe is not subjected to any omnipotence that would impose an end on it, and that men themselves make history. It reveals this, in its essential character, as resulting from a struggle between value systems expressing different human types, needs, and the interests of specific powers. It attempts to overcome an effective nihilism without prescribing mental evasion into the imaginary beyond, without recommending the de-realisation of the real, but by suggesting the acceptance of a world which does not have reason, and even to want it without reason. It attempts to give European history, depicted as a process of organic decadence ascribed to the Judaeo-Christian movement, a positive orientation by selection and multiplication of a type of man of great intellectuality and of strong will. It conceives, finally, a doctrine supposedly able to effectuate this vital ascension by replacing the so-called weakening values with values of increasing strength, and by substituting the morality that creates slaves with a morality that liberates'.

THE RETURN OF TRAGEDY

Karl Jaspers writes: 'Every action brings into this world consequences which the agent had not suspected' (*Philosophie*, 1932). With these words alone,

---

216 *Complete Critical Edition of Nietzsche's Correspondence.* — Tr.

217 *Nietzsche and the Critique of Christianity.* — Tr.

218 *Nietzsche: Teleology and History.* — Tr.

tragedy is revealed. At the same time it strips away the puerile illusion of a 'predictable' whole.[219]

In *Le retour du tragique*,[220] Jean-Marie Domenach explains: 'The tragic departs from tragedy, since it returns to provoke philosophical reflection and political action to the point that we can consider the most active philosophies and the most decisive revolutions of the modern era as efforts for confronting a defiance initiated twenty five centuries ago under the Greek sky'.

A great connoisseur of pre-Hellenic and proto-historic Greece, archaeologist Guy Rachet, in *La tragédie grecque*,[221] recounts how this defiance was launched.

Friedrich Nietzsche saw in tragedy the meeting and culmination of two great currents constitutive of Greek genius: Apollonian spirit, luminous and measured, and Dionysian instinct, wild and unchained — reason and excess (*The Birth of Tragedy*, 1878). He also connected tragedy to the 'spirit of music' as well as the dithyramb, by insisting on the importance of choirs. 'This vision', says Rachet, 'remains fruitful with regards to its psychological implications'.

Mircea Eliade, for his part, has emphasised the importance of religious *myth*, which tragedy allows us to refresh by *re-presenting* it at any moment.

One thing is certain: of Doric origin, tragedy has rapidly been transplanted in Attica, where it has found its chosen home. Unfortunately, many classical pieces have not come down to us, whether because they were lost, or because they were destroyed after the coming of Christianity. We only know seven tragedies by Aeschylus, who wrote eighty, and seven by Sophocles, to whom more than 120 are attributed.

Greek tragedy is first of all a religious representation: it addresses itself to spectators 'linked' together by the same conception of the world.[222]

It draws its inspiration from the old legendary sources of the Hellenes. The destinies of Hector, Odysseus, Achilles, Patroclus, and Iphigenia, are tragic destinies: the personages of tragedy are less the gods themselves than the

---

219 Literally « *prospective* » *totale*. — Tr.

220 *The Return of Tragedy*. — Tr.

221 *Greek Tragedy*. — Tr.

222 Benoist plays on the etymological connection between 'religion' (from *religare*, 'to bind fast') and 'ligature' (*ligare*, 'to bind'); the 'religious' (*religeuse*) are thus 'linked' or 'bound' (*reliés*) to the same conception. — Tr.

intimate life of the heroes. 'In the only tragedy that situates itself in the world of the gods', remarks Rachet, 'we find a confrontation between a god, Zeus, and a being who, immortality aside, assumes the character of a civilising hero: Prometheus'.

Misconduct, failure, crime, and malediction are the great dramatic well-springs of this 'literary' genre, for which the cultural history of humanity provides no equivalent.

From Greece to Germania

The oracle or diviner plays an essential role: they are intermediaries between the visible and the hidden. Through them, the law is unveiled and the drama congeals. The hero affirms himself. Prometheus defies the gods. Oedipus refuses to believe what the diviner Tiresias reveals to him. Creon remains obstinate in his decisions. Then the *deus ex machina* intervenes, that is to say, the god who descends upon the *mechane* in order to unravel a situation that has become inextricable.

Nature is also always present: in Aeschylus, the waves, the rivers, and all the elements weep over the sufferings of Prometheus.

Guy Rachet restricts himself to the analysis of only Greek tragedy. But the tragic sentiment is a constant of the entire European spirit. We even note an astonishing parallelism between ancient Greece and, for example, ancient Germania. In Scandinavian mythology, the gods themselves end by dying: the end of *this* world is also *their* loss. 'If the gods are ultimately powerless before evil', observes Edith Hamilton, 'men and women must be even more so' (*Mythologies*, Marabout).

Political action and literature, history, and philosophy thus interweave in an interior drama that pivots upon a contradiction. The universe is immense and infinite. Man is ephemeral and limited. Bringing this opposition clearly into awareness, yet struggling against what is inexorable, man expresses the tragic sentiment of life. Here we discover the idea of the Eternal Return: tragedy *re-presents* what we *always* await. (It is this, Domenach emphasises, which introduces it to history).

In relation to the universe, man becomes at once contained and containing: contained by his presence, containing by his consciousness. Not having *duration*, he strives to enjoy the *intensity*.

In the clear consciousness of this contradiction between our weakness (and the inevitability of our *end*) on one hand, and on the other, the strength that bestows upon us the power to *historicise* our existence — a power that we allow to *dominate the world* by giving it a *form* — Jules Monnerot, author of an admirable study on *Les lois du tragique*, sees an 'anthropological differential' characteristic of European man.

Utilitarian morality is absent from tragedy. Medea, having provoked the death of Creon and killed his children, escapes to Athens. Helen, who caused the misfortune of the Greeks and Trojans, completes her life happily at Sparta. 'Virtue', by contrast, conducts Antigone and Hippolytus to death.

The value of tragic theatre is also more instructive than morality. 'The power of the soul', writes Guy Rachet, 'this height from which events and its own destiny are viewed, this ideal that has been forged, which belongs to us and which we put all our efforts towards accomplishing, this virtue certainly appears as a *model* to imitate'.

Domenach observes: 'Good and Evil. Provisional vocabulary that must be discarded. Tragedy reduces us to these overly simplistic distinctions'. The tragic sentiment is not a 'moral' affair, but a *level of being*, of quality in destiny.

A Rage to Live Inhabits Beings

Destiny: 'This conqueror who is not a character' (Jules Monnerot). The entirety of tragedy is dominated by this notion; not the resignation of the Orient, but the *fatum* of the Romans. In the piece by Sophocles, it is 'necessary' that Oedipus kill his father and unite with his mother. It is 'necessary' that the curse of the Atrides be fulfilled, etc. And yet the hero, warned of the lot that is reserved for him, conscious that he cannot escape, acts as if he can escape.

'The sacred among the ancient Germans', writes Régis Boyer, 'is Destiny, the sense of Destiny, the countless configurations that Destiny takes'. He adds: 'The rock carvings of Bohuslän, the Merseburg spells, and the Edda of Snorri agree on this point: higher than the gods and the myths, stronger than time and the death over which it presides, looms Destiny. Nowhere does this obsession appear better than in the heroic *Nibelungenlied-Völsunga Saga-Edda* complex: not a single character is found who does not know his lot in advance, everything has been announced in detail, everything will be realised in detail. If we maintain a flat view of things, the whole Germanic religion appears as an enormous, overwhelming absurdity … what good is living? Wouldn't a frank nihilism be better? Now here is the miracle: the entire Germanic universe violently answers no. A rage to live inhabits beings. The spirit of struggle (*vighugr*) is upon them. Cowardice is infamy; suicide, unknown; scepticism, despicable (…) We see here the most original characteristic, the most astonishingly modern, of Germanic paganism: man does not submit to his fate, he does not attend his destiny as an interested but foreign spectator, it is given to him to accept and to accomplish — to take charge of it, on his own' (*Les religions de l'Europe du nord*. Fayard-Denoël, 1974).[223]

In the Nordic saga of Kara Halfdansdatter, the hero is protected by a swan which flies above him during battle. But one day, while fighting, he raises his sword so high that he kills the animal. That day, his destiny is severed.

The same sentiment impregnates the poems of Homer. In the Iliad, Helen says to Hector: 'Zeus has fashioned a hard fate for us so that we will be sung about by men to come'. We discover an echo in Herodotus and the pre-Socratic philosophers. Heraclitus declares: 'Man's character is his destiny'.

The individual upon whom destiny dwells fulfils its radical 'mission', which is perhaps the ultimate form of realism. The works that Clément Rosset (*La philosophie tragique*. PUD, 1960)[224] and George Steiner (*La mort de la tragédie*. Seuil, 1965)[225] have consecrated to it show that the tragic vision, the worldview that is connected to it, has the cold clarity of absolute lucidity.

But tragedy only exists, of course, if the hero is the artisan of his own loss. 'A man alone against everything', writes Jules Monnerot, 'is not necessarily tragic. He becomes tragic when "the enemy" is also within him'. Tragic action is inscribed *within* and *against* uncertainty. (Only the anti-tragic turns this uncertainty into meaninglessness; lack of meaning is only identified with the world's arbitrariness for the man doomed to suffer it). According to Jaspers, the tragic hero enters 'limit-situations' with open eyes. These 'limit-situations' (*Tod, Leiden, Kampf, Schuld*, in the view of Jaspers)[226] ensure that he is never defeated by *their* circumstances.

---

223 *The Religions of Northern Europe.* — Tr.

224 *Tragic Philosophy.* — Tr.

225 *The Death of Tragedy.* — Tr.

226 Death, Suffering, Struggle, Obligation. — Tr.

In order to be at the height of his destiny, the tragic hero is therefore accomplished in action. The certitude of final defeat is not a reason for him to surrender. On the contrary. If God is dead, if the world is a chaos in which only a voluntary action can make an organised cosmos, then man is *alone*. Alone to undertake and construct. Alone, since he is both subject and *object of himself*. It is only by relation to himself, by relation to the cultural and social ensembles in which he includes himself, which he can define the terms of a new objectivity — all while knowing, precisely, that this objectivity is but a convention produced by his *will*, that it has no absolute value other than that given by space-time. In this sense, we can say of the world today that by ruining the idea of a universal reason (which, in the previous belief, automatically gave a meaning to life), it has also provoked the existential void above which tragic thought can develop itself anew. To be conscious that death is inevitable, while doing everything to *become* immortal. To impose oneself on the inexorable by *willing* that which others are content (at best) *to accept*. To choose *one* form of life among a thousand other *possible* forms. To deeply feel both the ultimate futility of all action upon things, and the necessity of undertaking this action so as not to decay, etc.

The Conscious Will of What Must Be

The best die, also. But their name, once it has been portrayed, does not die: it is by their *example* that they reach eternity. For the hero, life is a destiny which cannot be stolen from them. The only freedom that they possess is to meet their requirements with or without honour. In height and affirmation, or baseness and anonymity.

In the song of the Nibelungen, Gunnar (Günther) takes himself to the court of Atli (Attila), even though he knows full well that an ambush awaits him. Heroism consists in pursuing a goal in regards to which we do not matter.

A Roman historian relates that in the first century the Cimbrians, threatened by a tidal wave, entered the water, sword in hand, to fight the sea. A model of excess.

The tragic maxim par excellence is that of Taciturnus: 'One need not hope in order to undertake, nor succeed in order to persevere'. It expresses itself in the celebrated engraving by Dürer: *Knight, death, and the devil*.

The tragic man is the one who loves the event for the event. He prefers situations, even bad ones, where something happens, to situations, even good ones, where nothing happens. He loves what happens. *Amor fati*, this maxim from Nietzsche, Montherlant has made his own. It is not a taste for the worst, nor simple acceptance of fate. It is the tenacious and conscious will of that which must be.

And that which must be is chance as much as necessity: 'Unlike the sage who eliminates it, the tactician who calculates it', writes Domenach, 'the Nietzschean hero throws himself wholly and immediately into chance'. He answers the challenge of death with the play of life.

With this behaviour, an intimacy with the world ensues, which reveals itself as a source of joy. For Nietzsche, who opposes Dionysus to Socrates, tragedy is worth the affirmations that it engenders, which create values. 'What does it matter if they conflict', summarises Domenach, 'if they are spoken from the viewpoint of life!' Tragedy is 'the joy which is born of multiple affirmation'. It is the consciousness wrested from the incompatibilities of being and the contradictions of becoming.

Thus, tragic man is the complete opposite of the man of quantity beloved by 'reductionist' theoreticians. In essence, he escapes the reassuring analyses of the 'human sciences'. These only trace an illusory curve: that which belongs to the mass. It remains silent on the exemplary few destined to be recorded in counterpoint.

That which tragedy brings into play cannot be measured by statistics. 'Nietzsche and Hegel have equally asserted', writes Domenach, 'that there is no "science of man". There is only history of man, who contains and overcomes all science'.

*

La tragédie grecque, a study by Guy Rachet. Payot, 285 pages.
Le retour du tragique, a study by Jean-Marie Domenach. Seuil, 300 pages.
Les lois du tragique, a study by Jules Monnerot. PUF, 128 pages.[227]

---

227 *Greek Tragedy* (Rachet). *The Return of Tragedy* (Domenach). *The Laws of Tragedy* (Monnerot). — Tr.

THE WORLD AS CHAOS

Either an *order* that exists in the universe, and the task of man is to conform himself to it: the establishment of public order is thus fused with the search for truth, and the essence of politics comes down to morality; or the universe is *chaos*, and the task of man is to attempt to give it *form*.

If there was a 'natural order', values and forms would be the same in all times and all places. Without reigniting the argument for Universals, it suffices to note that historical experience shows this is not the case. There exists a general relativity of lifestyles, ideas, moral regulations, aesthetic aspirations, etc. — and these *forms* are specifically human products.

Ernst Jünger said that 'at the centre of the cosmos, power is no longer sovereign, but anonymous'. To speak the language of Hobbes: the state of nature is civil war. The world is chaos.

A young philosopher by the name of Clément Rosset, thirty-nine years of age, specialising in Schopenhauer and Spinoza, teaches at the Faculty of Literature and Humanities in Nice. In 1965 he published a *Lettre sur les chimpanzés* through Gallimard,[228] which attracted considerable attention: a pastiche of social and Christian 'humanism', this advocacy for the recognition of the 'rights' of chimpanzees also became a mockery of Rousseau, Sartre, and Teilhard de Chardin. Since then, Clément Rosset has also written *La philosophie tragique*, *Le monde et ses remèdes*, *Schopenhauer, philosophe de l'absurde* (PUF), and under the pseudonym Roger Crémant, a vigorous pamphlet: *Les matinées structuralistes* (Laffont).[229]

In *La logique du pire*,[230] he proposes a worldview that rigorously contradicts the vision of Plotinus, for it contrasts the *plural* reality of a world of nuances, differences, and variety to ideologies that attempt to bring everything back to the *one*. This leads him to resume and to deepen the theme of tragic philosophy.

'What must be said and thought above all', he writes, 'is the tragic'.

Rarely taken into consideration, and even more rarely integrated, tragic philosophy is used to unveil the 'fundamental chaos' and the true quality of

---

228 *Letter on the Chimpanzees.* — Tr.
229 *Tragic Philosophy; The World and its Remedies; Schopenhauer, Philosopher of the Absurd; Structuralist Matinées.* — Tr.
230 *The Logic of the Worst.* — Tr.

reality generally concealed under the reassuring discourse of 'ideologies of happiness' and doctrines of consolation.

Tragic thinkers are the 'logicians of the worst'. 'To succeed to think the worst' is their preoccupation.

In the history of philosophy, tragic thought has primarily undergone critiques bearing on its most superficial aspects. Those who contradict it thus avoid going to the heart of it. An example cited by Rosset is the attitude of Plato faced with his opponents, the Sophists. That which Plato, father of idealism, fears among those who are mocked by the 'truth', is their tragic conception of man's nature and of his relations with the universe. However, in the *Protagoras*, he does not attack their scepticism, but their alleged vanity. Projecting upon them the inherent vice of his philosophy, sophistry, he thus reveals himself a 'calumniator of genius'.

Tragic philosophers refuse to portray situations as more pleasing than they are. For them, that which exists does not exist solely as a 'fact', but also as a reality to *will*. This does not mean that this reality cannot be changed. But that it can only be changed by *overcoming* it after having previously accepted it.

Affirmation of the world's constitution and what is produced within it, an authentic trait of tragic philosophy, above all characterises the thought of Lucretius, de Montaigne, and Nietzsche, but also that of Kierkegaard, Shestov, and Unamuno. The latter are 'pseudo-tragic' thinkers: they lack precisely this capacity and this will for affirmation of the real.

'The logic of the worst', writes Rosset, 'therefore teaches the necessity of the link between tragic thought and affirmative thought'.

Because the tragic does not add anything to the world, we could say that it begins where there is no longer anything to say or think. Because it is stripped of all rational and moral interpretation, it seems to be silent. Tragic discourse remains possible however, because it has at its disposal a word that allows it to 'speak without saying anything, or to think without conceiving anything'. This word is '*chance*'.[231]

For Clément Rosset, *chance* or *hazard* is not related to fortuitous encounters or to good and bad fortune. It simply designates the narrow field left to the disposition of tragic thought.

---

231 French *hasard* primarily means 'chance', but also 'coincidence, accident, hazard, luck, fate'. — Tr.

And yet it is necessary to distinguish the 'chance of events', which follows the constitution of nature, and the 'chance of origin' which precedes it. Only the second operates here. One discovers it among the Sophists and in Lucretius, Montaigne, Pascal, Nietzsche. The tragic is no other thing than chance thus understood.

The idea of 'affirmed chance' is translated by notions that characterise the tragic demeanour: tolerance, the creative faculty, a 'certain way of laughing'.

Man is *free* to the degree that he is capable of affirming and willing himself as he truly is — that is, to the degree that he assumes his tragic dimension.

Non-tragic doctrines, by contrast, are intolerant by nature: their standards are in contradiction to the adverse ideologies with which they are necessarily concerned. Thus, the intellectual mentor of the 'New Left', Herbert Marcuse, writes: 'Tolerance must henceforth be restricted to that which is tolerable'.

The Master of Forms

From this perspective, aesthetic creation can only be chance joined to chance. It anticipates chance and outplays it: art is tragic or it is not.

As to the laughter of tragic thought, foreign to the subtle games of 'sense' and 'non-sense', it represents the victory of the *reality* of chaos over the *appearance* of order, that is to say, the recognition of chance or hazard as the 'truth of what exists'. For there is no other order in the universe than that which we impose, by convention, for the convenience of analysis or for peace of mind. And this laughter is an *exterminator* to the degree that, by affirming everything that is, it also celebrates destiny.

Every society thus draws its configuration and its ordering from the *play* of relations and forms that bind and unravel. Order is not *received*; it is *created*. In other words, it only exists *as a result of the acts that establish it*, that is to say, by the form of the relational activity between individuals or groups of individuals, legal and natural persons, social bodies, and institutions. The correlation between order and form is therefore obvious: we institute a social *order* by being a master of social *forms*. 'Without formation', writes Julien Freund, 'knowledge is no more possible than action. Now, this formation consists in the organisation of the relations between things according to a principle or a sequence which is the condition of all intelligibility and all efficacy' (*L'essence du politique*. Sirey, 1965).

Not only does the human order owe as much to energy as to reason, it is also pure *convention*. Like art, it is *its own model*. It does not follow a plan established in advance; it does not fulfil a 'contract' to which man would only have the freedom to subscribe or not subscribe. He is no more the 'reflection' of a natural, anti-tragic arrangement of the world than he is an extension of law, morality, art, science, or economics. Along with politics, he is not an end in itself— but the result of an *activity* placed in service of a certain way of conceiving the relations between man and the universe, and the relations among men. It depends on the idea that one has of it, on the energy that one has available to realise this idea, and on the goal that one sets.

There is no absolute, but we cannot live without an absolute — without something that surpasses us and motivates us in our most essential attitudes. No man escapes the problem of *its* transcendence. But for the first time, we are *simultaneously* conscious of the *relativity* of norms, and of their *necessity*. From here it ensues that a new 'objectivity' can only be born from a 'heroic' subjectivity: from a subjectivity consciously affirmed as a norm by someone who has such power that this affirmation will appear *natural* to everyone.

Man is not master of his capacities, but he is master of the way they are used. He is the demiurge of forms, *der Herr der Gestalten*.[232]

'Tragic philosophy', says Clément Rosset, 'appeared the day that the Greeks celebrated life, hazard, and death in one single festival'.

*

La logique du pire. Eléments pour une philosophie tragique, a study by Clément Rosset.[233]
    PUF, 180 pages.

*

In *L'anti-nature* (PUF, 1973),[234] Clément Rosset has refined and developed some of the leading ideas of the *Logique du pire* by throwing a retrospective look upon the history of philosophy and by opposing, in a relatively systematic fashion, 'naturalist' philosophies, which create meaning where man does not exist, and 'artificial' philosophies, which exclusively connect the existence of meaning to human actions. In 1976, he also published a short essay entitled *Le réel et son double* (Gallimard).[235]

---

232 *The Lord of Forms.* — Tr.
233 *The Logic of the Worst. Elements of a Tragic Philosophy.* — Tr.
234 *Anti-Nature.* — Tr.
235 *The Real and its Double.* — Tr.

CULTURE AND CIVILISATION

Elias's book is entitled *La civilisation des mœurs*.[236] It would have been better to call it: 'Les mœurs dans la civilisation'.[237] It is in fact the first volume of a study entitled: *Sur le procès de la civilisation* (1939 and 1969).[238]

Norbert Elias, seventy-nine years of age, has done all of his studies in Germany. He completed his thesis in Heidelberg under the direction of Alfred Weber, after pursuing the philosophy and psychology courses of Hönigswald, Rickert, Husserl, and Jaspers. Afterwards he lived in France and then Great Britain. He teaches courses at Leicester and The Hague. In regards to the sociology of knowledge, his name holds authority.

His book takes up an idea familiar to modern sociology, to know that our day-to-day behaviour, even in its most simple, 'natural' forms (our way of eating, spitting, sleeping, blowing our nose, our sexual relations, our forms of aggression, etc.) constitute only one specific feature of our culture, which not only differs in strength from the behaviour of other cultures, but has also undergone important transformations over time.

The first part is of the greatest interest. It analyses an important but frequently unrecognised subject: the antithesis between the notions of 'culture' and 'civilisation'. This antithesis rests on two completely different conceptions of society.

Among the French and English, relates Elias, the word *civilisation* 'summarises in one single concept the topics of the nation's pride, the progress of the west and of humanity in general'. Among the Germans (and also among the Italians), it 'designates something of strong utility, certainly, but which is nevertheless of secondary importance: that which constitutes the exterior side of man, the surface of human existence. When Germany seeks to define itself, when it wants to express pride in its own realisations and its own nature, it employs the word *culture*'.

Therefore, from one side of the Rhine to the other, the same terms do not have the same meaning, nor do they refer to the same realities.

---

236 *The Civilisation of Manners.* — Tr.
237 Manners in Civilisation. — Tr.
238 *On the Process of Civilisation.* — Tr.

Spiritual Frontiers

Civilisation is concerned with 'recognised values' which every man born in a *civilised* country can rely upon without himself having achieved any concrete accomplishment. But it takes more than being born in a country of high culture to be *cultivated*: 'Culture does not designate the values of being a man, but the value and character of certain human productions'.

The idea of civilisation, continues Elias, implies and includes that of 'progress'. Thus, *civilised* man opposes himself to 'primitive' (previous) man. Civilisation 'is in effect related to something fluctuating, in constant progression'. In contrast, the idea of culture revives in the *present* an eternal *past*; the 'cultured' man does not fundamentally distinguish himself from 'original' man: he merely actualises him.

Furthermore, 'the notion of civilisation effaces to a certain point the differences between peoples; in the sensibility of those who use the term, it places the accent on what is *common* to all men, or at least what should be (...) By contrast, the German notion of culture emphasises national *differences*, the particularities of groups. (It is thanks to this function that it may have assumed an importance surpassing, in the domain of ethnology and anthropology for example, the German linguistic zone)'.

Norbert Elias relates this 'semantic' difference to the distinctive way that the French and German nations are formed.

'Civilisation expresses the complacency of a people whose national borders and specific characteristics have not been called into questioned for centuries because they are definitively fixed; whereas the notion of culture belongs to a people who, in relation to other western people, have achieved unification and political consolidation very late, and whose limits have fluctuated for centuries and still threaten to do so.'

'The notion of culture, henceforth, reflects the consciousness of a nation obliged to continually ask itself what its specific character consists in by ceaselessly seeking and consolidating its spiritual and political frontiers'.

For this reason, although 'the German may try to explain to the French and to the English what it means by "culture", it is incapable of making them feel the specific lived experience of the national tradition, the emotive halo which surrounds this word for them (...) And the discussion gets lost if the

German attempts to demonstrate why the notion of "civilisation" represents for them something of value, but a value of second rank.

In France, where it is the *State* that has created the *nation*, the *court* has been at once the complete cause and consequence of the irresistible tendency towards centralisation that has accompanied the successive expansions of the *'pré carré'*;[239] as such, the court has been the crucible of a *French civilisation* which has been gradually elaborated while the *regional cultures* perish. Drawn into this gilded prison that constitutes the court of Versailles, the provincial aristocracies, a permanent danger for the authority of French crown, progressively *polished* themselves by contact with refined fashions and manners, which however only concern the *exterior* aspects of the personality. At the same time, incrementally accentuating the urbanisation and the 'courtisation' (*Verhöflichung*)[240] of elites, the disparity between an urban milieu dominated by the bourgeoisie, and a rural milieu where landed aristocracy still live in symbiosis with the people, deepens.

The Antithesis Shifts Towards a National Context

In the seventeenth century, the radiance of 'French courtliness'[241] reached the whole of Europe. Princes from all the capitals came to 'polish' themselves in the salons where the intellectual spirit, if not the soul, flourished. To the foreigner, 'honest people' expressed themselves in French, the language whose use denotes belonging to a superior class (the same phenomenon will play out in nineteenth century France, accelerating the disappearance of regional dialects). 'Nothing is more vulgar than to write letters in German', asserted the fiancée of Gottsched in 1730 (a writer born near Königsberg). Leibniz himself wrote in French or Latin, rarely in German. In 1740, in his *Lettres français et germaniques*,[242] E. de Mauvillon remarks: 'There are some years that we do not say four words in German without adding two words of French'.

---

239 In the seventeenth century, *pré carré* referred to a double line of fortified cities which protected new borders in France; in modern times it refers to a zone or centre of influence. — Tr.

240 A neologism of Elias, *Verhöflichung* (*curialisation* in French) means 'rule from royal courts'. — Tr.

241 *curialité française.* — Tr.

242 *French and Germanic Letters.* — Tr.

Everything changes at the end of the century when the German literary movement appeared with Klopstock, Herder, Lessing, the poets of the *Sturm und Drang*, the young Goethe, early Schiller, etc. After having organised a 'competition on the universality of the French language', Frederic II is the first to become concerned with the 'deculturation' of Prussia. Alongside this (and contrary to what occurred in France, where the aristocracy had always defended national values), nationalism is reborn in reaction to the princes. It is an act of the middle class intelligentsia, conscious of expressing the hostility of the popular milieu against the 'good manners' of courtly society, which were deemed to be artificial and softening.

In the writings of the 'Hainbund' (a league of poets from Göttingen) we find 'manifestations of fierce hate against the princes, the aristocrats, the Gallomaniacs, the immorality of the courts, and cerebral rationalism'.

In the period in which he composed his *Götz von Berlichingen*, Goethe recounts: 'We were at Strasbourg on the French border, where we suddenly rid ourselves and became free of all things French. We have found their manner of living far too particular and aristocratic, we have found their poetry cold, their critique destructive, their philosophy abstruse and inadequate ...' (*Dichtung und Wahrheit*, book IX).[243]

Kant writes: 'We are cultivated to a high degree through arts and science, we are civilised to the point of satiety for all kinds of social grace and decency'.[244]

For the French, the Germans are 'heavy' and 'coarse'. They 'lack finesse'. Their language is 'barbaric'. Around 1790, numerous revolutionaries see the German language as a 'slave idiom'. At the meeting of the Convention on 8 pluviôse year II[245] (27 January 1794), Barère declares: 'Emigration and hate for the Republic speak German'. For Rousseville, zealous propagator of the ideas

---

243 The quote is from book XI: 'So waren wir denn an der Grenze von Frankreich alles französischen Wesens auf einmal bar und ledig. Ihre Lebensweise fanden wir zu bestimmt und zu vornehm, ihre Dichtung kalt, ihre Kritik vernichtend, ihre Philosophie abstrus und doch unzulänglich'. I have translated from the German original with reference to the French cited by Benoist. — Tr.

244 Kant, *Idee zu einer allgemeinen Geschichte in weltbürgerlicher Absicht*, Siebente Satz: 'Wir sind im hohen Grade durch Kunst und Wissenschaft cultivirt. Wir sind civilisirt bis zum Überlästigen zu allerlei gesellschaftlicher Artigkeit und Anständigkeit'. — Tr.

245 Pluviôse is the second month of the French Republican Calendar, which was implemented from 1793–1805. — Tr.

of 1789 at Strasbourg, 'the rude and difficult sound of German only seems fit for commanding slaves, expressing threats, and counting the blows of the stick'. (This did not stop the expatriate, Louis de Bonald, a catholic author and monarchist, from writing that of all the languages of Europe, German had been the one in which 'the child of atheism and philosophy' had made the most progress). For their part, the Germans reproached the French for completely sacrificing themselves to an 'artificial politeness', for lack of 'simplicity' and 'sincerity', for pushing social convention to the point of falsehood, and for exhibiting constant superficialities', etc.

Theodore Fontane writes in *Ein Sommer in London* (1852): 'England is to Germany what form is to content, what appearance is to being. Unlike objects which, anywhere but in England, have a quality oriented to the essential, men are judged according to form, according to their most exterior packaging! There is no need for you to be a *gentleman*, all you have to do is have the means of appearing like one and then you are. You do not have to be in the right, all you have to do is observe the legal forms and you are right!'

The antithesis culture/civilisation equally recovers, little by little, the opposition between the philosophies of life and the philosophies of the spirit. That is to say, between those of the 'soul' (*Seele*) and the 'spirit' (*Geist*), or interior sentiment and pure intellect.

In 1914, the French set out to defend *civilisation*. The Germans declare a fight for *culture*.

In 1929, the psychologist Ludwig Klages (1872–1955) published a book entitled: *L'esprit comme antagoniste de l'âme* (*Der Geist als Widersacher der Seele*).[246] Civilisation, he explains, is related to man and to society 'seen externally': to the degree of technical evolution and of scientific knowledge, to the rules of manners and decency, to the forms of behaviour, etc. Culture is related to man and society 'seen internally': to the people's soul, to deep sentiments, to essential values …

Oswald Spengler approaches the same problem from a different angle: 'I distinguish', he declares, 'the idea of a culture from its historical realisation. I oppose the first to the second, like the soul to the body'. In *Le déclin de l'Occident*,[247] his principle work, cultures are defined as veritable 'organisms'

---

246 *The Spirit as Adversary of the Soul.* — Tr.
247 *The Decline of the West* (*Der Untergang des Abandlandes*). — Tr.

of which universal history constitutes the 'general biography'. Civilisations are only the ultimate forms, rigid and decadent. If cultures — organic, natural forms — are notably characterised by the persistence of 'original countries', in civilisations it is by contrast the 'global village' that predominates. Size and volume oppose the quality of life. The 'soul of the culture' (*Kulturseele*) disappears. Massive expansion[248] engenders impotence. Society *exists*. But it no longer *lives*.

*

La civilisation des moeurs, a study by Norbert Elias.[249] Calmann-Lévy, 344 pages.

*

The antithesis culture/civilisation has been the object of a detailed analysis (notably concerning its historical aspects) in: Alain de Benoist, 'Culture' (in *Nouvelle école*, Nr. 25–26, winter 1974–75). The same text also examines the antitheses of culture/unculture, culture/nature, and culture/politics. It shows that history creates words at the same time as words create history. On the same subject, cf. also Philippe Beneton: *Histoire de mots: culture et civilisation*[250] (Presses de la Fondation nationale des sciences politiques, 1975).

The two other volumes that compose the work of Norbert Elias have appeared under the following titles: *La société de cour* (Calmann-Lévy, 1974) and *La dynamique de l'Occident* (Calmann-Lévy, 1976).[251]

GERMAN ROMANTICISM

'In Germany', writes Jacques Droz, Professor at the Sorbonne, 'Romanticism must not be considered merely as an aesthetic or as a philosophy of sciences, but as a *politic*, which situates it at the heart of the European counter-revolutionary movement'.

'We *feel* Romantic', asserts Sébastien Mercier, 'we do not define it'. For Paul Valéry, 'it would be necessary to have lost all spirit of rigour to attempt to define Romanticism'. At the end of the eighteenth century, Friedrich von Schlegel confessed to his brother that he had filled no less than 125 pages in search for such a definition. In this literary form, which is also a manner of

---

248 *massification.* — Tr.

249 *The Civilisation of Manners = Über den Prozeß der Zivilisation. Soziogenetische und psychogenetische Untersuchungen. Erster Band. Wandlungen des Verhaltens in den weltlichen Oberschichten des Abendlandes.* — Tr.

250 *History of Words: Culture and Civilisation.* — Tr.

251 *Courtly Society* and *The Dynamic of the West = Über den Prozeß der Zivilisation. Zweiter Band. Wandlungen der Gesellschaft. Entwurf einer Theorie der Zivilisation.* — Tr.

thinking, many have seen 'a permanent state of sensibility, not a historical phenomenon' (Paul Van Tieghem, *Le romantisme dans la literature européenne*.
Albin-Michel, 1948).[252]

The adversaries of Romanticism have not failed to exploit this imprecision.
In a still-famous study (*Politische Romantik*, 1925),[253] Carl Schmitt reproached
the Romantics for substituting God as the absolute instance (or supreme third-
party) for any other concept: whether the State, the people, the individual. (We
know the formula: 'Romanticism is subjectified occasionalism').[254]

In English, the word Romantic initially had the same meaning as French
romanesque, by which it was customarily translated at the beginning of the
eighteenth century. It is with Rousseau's *Rêveries*[255] that the adjective *roman-
tique* made its appearance. It therefore distinguishes itself from *romanesque*
by the fact that it is applied less to events that are engaged by action than to
characters and environments that are evoked to memory. Elsewhere, in the
same period, the sentimental novel or *roman*[256] begins to overtake the swash-
buckling *roman*. It would be necessary, however, to wait until the nineteenth
century to see the substantive, *romantisme*, enter into current usage. De Staël
currently employs it. It is opposed to the classical tradition in the same way
as *culture* is opposed to *civilisation*: *romanticism* is the adversary of *classicism*.

But this definition is no more satisfying than the others. Especially if one
relates it to German Romanticism, of which the character and evolution is
completely different to that which one has called, perhaps wrongfully, French
Romanticism and English Romanticism.

Far removed from the classics, the German Romantics begin by laying
high claim to Kant in philosophy and to Goethe in literature. Better, they
have the sense to perpetuate a tradition which, through the *Sturm und Drang*,
the Baroque, the works of Lessing, Herder, early Goethe, and young Schiller,
has never ceased to proclaim the sovereignty of passion, the cult of life, the
adoration of creative genius. Since 1770, it is true, the classics in Germany
have 'provided the theory and example of a spontaneous and direct lyric

---

252 *Romanticism in European Literature.* — Tr.

253 *Political Romanticism.* — Tr.

254 *l'occasionnalisme subjectivé*, or *subjektivierter Occasionalismus* in Schmitt's German. — Tr.

255 *Les Rêveries du promeneur solitaire* (Reveries of a Solitary Walker). — Tr.

256 In French as in German, *roman* means 'novel' (narrative).

poetry, of a drama free from barriers, varied and picturesque, of a critical and non-dogmatic historicism open to the most varied forms of art; in short, a literature of dissent for the regard of the traditional French Graeco-Latin ideal' (Paul Van Tieghem, op. cit.).

The great German mystics (Paracelsus, Meister Eckhart, Jakob Boehme), as well as Friedrich Christoph Oetinger, the theoretician of Pietism, also count among the 'ancestors' of Romantic speculation.

'The principle antagonist of Romanticism', remarks Erika Tunner, 'is not classicism, but the rationalism of the Age of Enlightenment' (*Aufklärung*).

Just as the Lutheran Reformation was a reaction against the Thomist rationalism linked to the rise of Scholasticism, so too does Romanticism appear as a 'response' to the rationalism, this time profane, stemming from the *Aufklärung*.

'Ineffable, Sacred, Mysterious Night'

We generally distinguish a first generation of Romanticism (*Frühromantik*), above all literary, with Novalis, Ludwig Tieck, the brothers Schlegel, Heinrich von Kleist, Jean-Paul, E. T. A Hoffman, Hölderlin; and a second generation (*jüngere Romantik*), more political, with Adam Müller and Görres, J. von Eichendorff, the brothers Grimm, Bettina and Achim von Arnim, Clemens Brentano, von Chamisso, Bonaventura, Mörike, Büchner, etc.

In total, the movement would last scarcely more than a quarter of a century: from 1795 until around 1825.

The first Romantic circles were formed in Berlin (1795–96) and Jena (1798–99), where the brothers Schlegel published the magazine *Athenaeum*. They try next Heidelberg and Dresden.

Novalis (by his true name Friedrich von Hardenberg) is the first to introduce into his poetry the theories of monarchic traditionalism and the admiration for the medieval conception of the State. He is influenced by Pietism, and above all by Jakob Boehme, who his friend Ludwig Tieck had introduced him to, and of whom Friedrich de la Motte-Fouqué, descendant of Norman Huguenots who had emigrated to Prussia after the revoking of the Edict of Nantes, had prepared a biography.

Novalis writes: 'The world must be romanticised. By giving an elevated meaning to what is common, a mysterious aspect to what is banal, the dignity of the unknown to what is known, an infinite halo to what is finite, I romanticise.'

In the eyes of their contemporaries, the Romantic authors often seemed to be frail imaginative poets of a sickly sensibility, almost always inadequate, cultivating impossible loves, prone to suicide and unfortunate by vocation. This cliché (the 'blue flower') only gives a very poor idea of the nature of the movement.

In reality, the first Romantics conceived the world as a 'dynamic infinity': an inexhaustible plenitude of ever-renewed forms.

To the Graeco-Latin ideal of *finite* perfection and of the completed form, they substitute the Faustian ideal of hyperbole and form in a state of *becoming* (the cult of the incomplete, of the infinite); to the *social* relationship, in which men associate with each other, they substitute the *cosmic* relationship, which connects man to the universe. Likewise in literature, to the systematic œuvre constructed without spontaneity, they prefer the 'fragment', the incomplete but *authentic* text, where the heart expresses itself in an original and creative form.

In the aesthetic domain they proclaim that the work of art is not the creation of a conscious intelligence, but that it is born in the manner of a living being by virtue of a quasi-organic process.

In the cult of the theory of I, they draw from the certitude that destiny belongs to some exceptional individualities powerful enough to liberate themselves from much-too-human realities by creating a new world, all the while remaining capable of surpassing it. Schlegel and Novalis speak of 'divine egoism'. 'An exceptional man', they say, 'can *be* humanity in its entirety. The man who participates in the œuvre of the universe becomes in some way a god. We discover here the idea of the 'spark in the soul' (*scintilla in anima*) presented in Meister Eckhart, and also of the *genius*, which in the *Sturm und Drang* movement, is already snatched from its Christian context.

The taste for nature, which they proclaim to be as primordial as the spirit, leads the Romantics to celebrate childhood, the 'blessed time' during which man is in immediate sympathy with the world.

'The ingenuity of the child is necessary to study nature', says Novalis. 'Childlike nature, more receptive, remains more intimately linked to action from above', observes Heinrich Schubert.

Another magic door leads to the state of childhood: the fairy tale (*Märchen*), which translates a whole universe of beliefs and popular sentiments into illustrated stories. In the fairy tale, everything is possible. Opposites no longer contradict each other: they meld together to give birth to new concepts. The creative imagination, at last liberated, takes precedence over the reason of the period.

The group from Heidelberg, with Görres, Brentano, the brothers Grimm, and Achim von Arnim, devote themselves more specifically to the discovery of forgotten songs and ancestral poetry.

In 1805, *The Boy's Magic Horn*,[257] a collection the popular songs compiled by Arnim and Brentano, enjoyed a staggering success. The *Children's and Household Tales*[258] by the brothers Grimm would go around the world.

At the same time, the Romantics discovered the virtues of darkness. Turning their backs on the day which betrays them, they threw themselves with abandon into the silence of the night. Only the moon, eternal and icy, illuminated their work. Love itself belonged to the kingdom of the night (cf. the Second Act of Wagner's *Tristan*). 'I turned myself towards the ineffable, holy, mysterious night', says Novalis in his *Hymns to the Night* (1800).[259]

The desire for nature and childhood, this nostalgia for a lost paradise, does not turn at any moment towards the egalitarian utopianism of a Rousseau. Once seduced by *Les confessions*,[260] the Romantics quickly turn away. They do not want to return to nature to discover a 'good' or 'better' man, but to be suffused by what makes them *authentic*.

The unconscious into which they plunge themselves is not, as per Freud, that 'backstage'[261] where the individual 'represses' the depravities of their nature, but rather the 'source of the soul', the intimate domain in which the personality discovers and enriches itself. 'Man must dive back into his unconscious', writes Goethe, 'for there lives the root of his being'.

---

257 German: *Des Knaben Wunderhorn*, French: *Le cor enchanté de l'enfant*. — Tr.

258 German: *Kinder- und Hausmärchen*, French: *Contes de l'enfance et du foyer*. More popularly known as the Grimms' Fairy Tales. — Tr.

259 German: *Hymnen an die Nacht*, French: *Hymnes à la nuit*. — Tr.

260 The *Confessions* of Jean-Jacques Rousseau. — Tr.

261 The word is *coulisse* (pl. *coulisses*), a theatre-term which indicates the 'screens' — the flat, moveable pieces of scenery or drapery — that hide the back areas of the stage from the audience. — Tr.

Far from confining itself to a simple literary exercise, the dream is a means of communicating with the invisible universe of a forgotten past. 'Thanks to the dream', observes Jean-Paul, 'the past is conjoined with the future in an eternal present'.

A particular place is reserves for music, hailed from the beginning as 'the most Romantic of the arts': *Keine Farbe ist so romantisch als ein Ton!* ('No colour is as Romantic as a note!'). This is because music opens a gate to the collective unconscious like a dream opens one up upon the individual unconscious. During the centuries of 'false clarity', it was the ultimate refuge for ancient feelings and rhythms.

After Beethoven, there is the blossoming of the *Lied* with Schubert, the flourishing of opera with Weber, then Schumann, Liszt, Brahms, and finally Wagner and Richard Strauss.

E. T. A. Hoffmann is at once poet and musician. Tieck places music above everything. Others attempt to write 'poetic symphonies', or seek 'musical effects' in their writings.

A New Religion

All of this is enveloped by a religiosity which is far from orthodox. Novalis, in his *Hymnes*, develops a kind of nocturnal pantheism. He proposes the founding of a church which would borrow at once from the secret societies, the mystics of the Middle Ages, the Jesuit Order, and pagan cults. He asserts that a 'new Catholicism' gain momentum in Germany and evoke the hour in which 'a Saviour like a pure genius will have his home among men'. On 2 December 1798, Friedrich von Schlegel writes: 'I intend to create a new religion; for it will come and will triumph also without me'.

This is also the opinion of Schleiermacher, for whom 'true Christianity' must reunite the richness of Protestantism and that of Catholicism. A formula summarises this acute sense of the sacred: 'Do everything with religion, do nothing by religion'.

Quite different from the first, which it nevertheless perpetuates, the second Romanticism is felt most deeply in the spirit of the times.

The work of Rousseau, then the Revolution, first raised the hopes of the Romantics. They are disenchanted when they discover in the ideas of 1789 the logical outcome of the 'enlightened' philosophies which they stood against.

The movement then looks on with horror at the execution of Louis XVI, the assassination of suspects, and the Terror. It gains the greatest publicity from the *Reflections on the Revolution in France*[262] which the Englishman Edmund Burke published in 1790, and who had considerable influence upon Novalis and Adam Müller. In the eyes of the Romantics, France is now the mother of democratic egalitarian ideas.

Ten years later, an immense shadow spreads across Europe. That of Napoleon. In reaction, German Romanticism will contribute to the formation of a nationalism that is still trying to find itself. (This *right-handed* outcome of a phenomenon that would have the exact inverse result in other countries, appears characteristic of the German temperament. We could evoke in this regard the fate of the *Wandervögel* movement and of the *Jugendbewegung* at the beginning of this century — and even wonder today about the *specific* future, in Germany, of a certain 'dispute').

'Imagine for a moment', notes Erika Tunner, 'what the Napoleonic invasion meant on the simple, material plane: dislocated families, separated friends, broken correspondences. The former centres of Romanticism find themselves neglected; at the head, Berlin: the Court resides from 1806 to 1809 at Königsberg — and the literary salons, generally of a free spirit and largely open to the great artistic problems of Romanticism, are closed'.

The Romantics are thus forced to put an end to their self-fulfilment.

In the first case, they no longer exclusively insist upon love or individual friendship ('Love', writes Schleiermacher, 'consists in making two people one, but friendship makes each of us two people'), but upon other privileged forms of 'sociability', such as 'symphilosophy' (or common philosophy) and 'reciprocal meditation', etc. Schlegel dreams of an international elite, of a 'hanse' or 'guild' of superior spirits. Schleimacher declares the desire to make university life a 'common scientific existence'. In the second case, 'sociability', emotionally speaking, becomes political. Most of the Romantics recognise that beings of quality have a need to form bonds with those similar to themselves and, following from this, that the development of the personality flows from the 'community' (*Gemeinschaft*) where social contacts occur.

---

262 Benoist cites the French edition: *Considerations sur la Révolution français.* — Tr.

Individualism is increasingly repudiated: the individual cannot be subtracted from his cultural environment nor from his heredity.

Pure sensibility is no longer found at the centre of the preoccupations of the second Romanticism, nor are the states of the soul or the restless humours; instead what is found is everything related to the *popular soul*: the history and science of language, the origin of beliefs, ancestral traditions and legends, the chivalric Middle Ages, ancient law, Germanic antiquities, folklore, script, etc.

Literature is therefore related to the arousal of enthusiasm and the galvanisation of energies. Erika Tunner notes: 'German Romanticism takes a distinctly political turn; the patriotic inspiration of the Heidelberg years emerges into a nationalist inspiration'.

A Call to Arms

The two centres of anti-Napoleonic resistance are Prussia and Austria.

In 1808, the year that Napoleon achieved his greatest triumphs, Goethe wrote the first *Faust* and Heinrich von Kleist published *The Battle of Hermann*,[263] a homage to Hermann (Arminius) the Cherusker, who defeated the legions of Varus in the Teutoburger Wald in the ninth year of our era. In the context of the contemporary period, the piece is a veritable call to arms. Censorship prohibits the portrayal.

Von Kleist also wrote his famous *Catechism of the Germans*,[264] in which a father questions his son upon the duties of patriotism in occupied Germany: 'Why do you love your homeland? — Because it is my homeland.'

This same year, 1808, Adam Müller, the most profound of the political theoreticians of Romanticism, published his *Elements of Statesmanship*,[265] while Schleiermacher conducted his celebrated sermons in which he made it a religious duty for his audience to become aware of their civic responsibilities.

Schlegel writes: 'Why so small as a nation, while we are so grand as individuals? The reason is simple and clear. We are a divided people'. And whereas Arnim places his pen at the service of his Prussian homeland, Hölderlin published a *Hymne à Allemagne*[266] which expresses a painful love:

---

263 German: *Die Hermannsschlacht*, French: *La bataille d'Arminius*. — Tr.

264 German: *Katechismus der Deutschen*, French: *Catéchisme des Allemands*. — Tr.

265 German: *Die Elemente der Staatskunst*, French: *Eléments d'art politique*. — Tr.

266 *Gesang des Deutschen* (Hymn to the Germans). — Tr.

O Sacred Heart of the People, O Fatherland!
All-enduring like the silent Mother Earth,
Utterly misjudged by all, even though strangers
have taken the best from your depths!
They harvest your thoughts and spirit,
They gladly pluck your grapes, but scorn you
malformed vine! You, erratic,
wild and rambling on the ground.
Land of high and solemn genius!
Land of love, I am already yours,
Often I raged in tears because you
Witlessly rejected your own soul.[267]

On 29 April 1809, Kleist quit Dresden for Prague, where he hoped to publish a journal called *Germania*. But his project failed. In January 1810 he returned to Berlin where he launched his *Evening Paper*,[268] a daily newspaper closely monitored by the censors and which, on 30 March 1811, had to stop publication.

In despair, Kleist kills himself on the shore of the Kleiner Wannsee at the gates of Berlin in November 1811. He was 34 years old.

This is the epoch where Clausewitz teaches at the Higher School of War,[269] where Ernst Moritz Arndt must flee because of his patriotic poems, where Ludwig 'Turnvater' Jahn rekindles popular enthusiasm thanks to the collective physical culture.

On 3 February 1813, King Frédéric-Guillaume III launches a 'call to the people' in Breslau. Numerous Romantics are engaged as volunteers for the war of liberation, notably Joseph von Eichendorff and the painter Philipp Veit. The young poet Theodor Körner, twenty-two years of age, falls in Mecklenburg. His songs are brought together under the title *Lyre and Sword*,[270] and set to music by Carl Maria von Weber.

---

267 Translated from Hölderlin's German: 'O heilig Herz der Völker, o Vaterland!/ Allduldend, gleich der schweigenden Mutter Erd,/ Und allverkannt, wenn schon aus deiner/ Tiefe die Fremden ihr Bestes haben!/ Sie ernten den Gedanken, den Geist von dir,/ Sie pflücken gern die Traube, doch höhnen sie/ Dich, ungestalte Rebe! daß du/ Schwankend den Boden und wild umirrest./ Du Land des hohen ernsteren Genius!/ Du Land der Liebe! bin ich der deine schon,/ Oft zürnt ich weinend, daß du immer/ Blöde die eigene Seele leugnest'. — Tr.

268 German: *Berliner Abendblätter* (Berlin Evening Paper), French: *Les feuillets du soir.* — Tr.

269 *Ecole supérieur de Guerre.* — Tr.

270 German: *Leyer und Schwerdt*, French: *Lyre et épée.* — Tr.

At Koblenz, Joseph Görres, eminent Catholic theologian, created *The Rhenish Mercury*,[271] which Napoleon will qualify as 'the fifth great power'. The journal will be banned on 3 January 1816.

The pioneer of this new attitude had been J. G. Fichte, whose fourteen *Addresses to the German Nation*[272] laid the foundations for what will later be called 'the German idea'.

The Era of the Fichte's Addresses

Fichte, whose idealist doctrine effected the transition between the rationalist reclamation of the eighteenth century and German nationalism, is not a Romantic. But he made large borrowings from Romantic thought. In his work we find the theme of the exclusivity of the *National Self*, conceived as an enclosed whole, the theme of the originality of national character, linked to the 'primitiveness' of the German language, the exaltation of history as a factor of regeneration, etc.

The *Addresses to the German Nation* are delivered in the aftermath of the Battle of Jena, during the winter of 1806–07, in the halls of the Berlin Academy. Napoleon, whose troops occupied the city, pays no attention, judging this literature 'insignificant'. (On 26 August 1806, however, he executed the 39-year-old librarian, Johann Philipp Palm, who was responsible for distributing patriotic pamphlets).

Fichte, who links his predication to that of Luther, reveals the theme of 'German predestination'. He asserts that the Germans have the privilege of speaking an 'original' language (*Ursprache*), which makes them a 'chosen people' called to dominate the world by virtue of an inherent historical necessity. The Spirit, in his eyes, being absolute, an absolute Self, is opposed not to another Self but to a *not-Self*; in the same way, the absolute People are not opposed to another group of people, but to a *non-People*: the *Foreigner*. 'For Fichte', remarks Jean-Edouard Spenlé, 'the Germans are the absolute people, those who exist "in and of themselves", that is to say, "the People pure and simple" (*das Volk schlechtweg*), those who do not draw their reality from history, but who, conversely, engender their being, their history, by their thought,

271 German: *Der rheinische Merkur*, French: *Le Mercure rhénan*. — Tr.
272 German: *Reden an die deutsche Nation*, French: *Discours à la nation allemande*. — Tr.

by the consciousness which they have of themselves' (*La pensée allemande*, 1934).[273]

A little-known poem by Schiller, *German Greatness*,[274] composed in 1801, already announces this idea. 'What constitutes German grandeur', says the poet, 'is precisely the current deprivation of the German people, the fact that their grandeur resides uniquely in its culture and in the moral character of the nation, a thing which does not depend at all on its political destiny. The German spirit is the only one for which "holy things exist". It alone communicates with the spirit of the universe' (J. A. Spenlé, ibid.).

In a celebrated passage, Fichte declares: 'All those who believe in the spiritual reality and in the liberty of this spiritual life, all those who believe in an eternal progress in spirituality by means of liberty, whatever their country of origin may be, and whatever language they speak, they are of our race, they form part of our people, and they will be reconnected sooner or later. By contrast, all those who believe in a fixed State or in regression, or in the circular dance, or even those who place an inanimate Nature at the helm of the world, no matter their country of origin or the language they speak, they are not German, they are foreigners to us, and it is necessary to wish that they will be completely removed from our people ...'

The influence exercised by the *Addresses* upon Romantic thought is considerable.

Hölderlin sees in the German people the *Urvolk*, the 'original people'. He observes that, of all the languages of Europe, the German language remains the closest to primitive Indo-European. Novalis writes: 'With its slow but steady pace, German precedes the [language of the] other European countries'. He declares: 'There are Germans everywhere'. In 1848, The Frankfurt Assembly will proclaim: *Was deutsch spricht soll deutch werden*. That is to say: 'Whoever speaks German will become German'.

It is the Heidelberg group, under the aegis of Arnim and Brentano, who are the most concerned with defining the new elements constitutive of nationality. 'These writers', observes Jacques Droz, 'have admitted that they could not have reawakened the German people if they did not become conscious of the artistic treasures which it concealed in its breast, if it did not substitute a culture

---

273 *German Thought.* — Tr.

274 German: *Deutsche Größe*, French: *La grandeur allemande.* — Tr.

reserved for an elite with a truly popular culture, if the individual did not seek to connect himself spiritually to the entire nation. They have therefore been lead to place the accent on a certain community or ethnic kinship, which has been called *Volkstum* or *Volkheit*,[275] cemented by the idiom that the population speaks, by cohabitation in a specific region, by common respect for certain customs, beliefs, legal traditions, and morals'.

To the cosmopolitan idea of the nation, the Romantics responded by a theory of the inevitability of national belonging.

Resuming the theses if the publicist Justus Möser (*German History*, 1773)[276] and above all of Johann Gottfried Herder (1744–1803), they make the notion of 'national genius' rest upon a collective spiritual entity which they call the 'people' (*das Volk*). This term does not designate any social class. It refers to the *totality of the national community*, finally become conscious of itself, which it represents for all eternity: it is only apprehended in its historical manifestations, but it is anterior to these.

Hence the astonishing admiration of de Staël: 'Some poems of Goethe and Burger are set to music, and you hear them repeated from the banks of the Rhine to the Baltic! Our French poets are admired by all wherever there are cultivated spirits among us and in the rest of Europe — but they are completely unknown to the common people and to the bourgeois, even in the cities ...' (*De l'Allemagne*. II, 11).

At the same time that they situate the people in their becoming, the Romantics rehabilitate history. In his dissertation *Some Remarks on the Study of the History of the Fatherland* (1808),[277] Heinrich Luden affirms that 'even science must have a nationality', and because they 'lost the meaning of history', the Germans experienced disasters. 'Historicity', he adds, 'is the criteria of all *humanity*'.

Systematically, the Romantics insist on originalities and diversities. To the *Aufklärung*, which examined the past in the light of universal history and sought to discover the laws of a constant *progress* of spirit, they oppose

---

275 'Folkdom' or 'Folkhood'. — Tr.

276 *Histoire allemande* in Benoist's French, possibly corresponding to *Osnabrückische Geschichte: Allgemeine Einleitung* (1768) or *Patriotische Phantasien* (1775–86). — Tr.

277 German: *Einige Worte über das Studium der vaterländischen Geschichte* (1810), French: *Sur l'étude de l'histoire de la patrie*. — Tr.

research into everything that allows the mentality of man and the genius of the people to be situated in space and time.

Joseph Görres places the accent upon the *Stammesgefühl*, the popular consciousness of the same ethnic origin, cemented by the use of the same language, attachment to the same countries, respect for the same customs, cohabitation in the same regions.

He writes: 'For a people, the most deplorable of all self-deception is to let its own originality be forgotten, to ignore its deep nature, to let itself become involved in foreign practices ... Everything that is foreign, everything that is introduced without deep reason into the life of a people, becomes the cause of disease for them, and must be eradicated if they want to remain healthy. To the contrary, everything that is essential or specific to them must be cultivated by them and pruned without respite.

It follows that 'every ethnic group has the right and the duty to jealously conserve its historical denomination, to which the memories of the past are linked'.

Maurice Barrès (1862–1923), whose thought is in part formed by the school of German Romanticism, will have this expression: 'the earth and the dead' (*The Uprooted*).[278]

The Holy Spirit and 'Medieval' Values

'Authenticity' for the Romantics is first of all ancient medieval Germany. They turn towards it with a burning nostalgia which goes hand in hand with an admiration for 'historical' Catholicism. One of the principal essays of Novalis, *Christendom or Europe*,[279] begins with the words: 'It was a bright and beautiful epoch, when Europe was a Christian land, when a single and unique Christendom lived upon this so characteristically human continent'.

Hence we find the desire, served by an impassioned nostalgia (*Sehnsucht*), for that which resembled a rebirth of the Germanic Holy Roman Empire.

The Romantic authors are thus lead to give a preponderant place to 'medieval' values: to the 'feudal exchange' of service for protection, to the given word, to honour, to courage, to discipline and freely consenting obedience. They aspire to a new nobility. They pronounce themselves for a patriarchal

---

278 'la terre et les morts' (*Les déracinés*). — Tr.

279 German: *Die Christenheit oder Europa*, French: *Le chrétienté ou l'Europe*. — Tr.

system, to a peasantry connected to the soil, a bourgeoisie limited in its economic ambitions, the inalienability of land ownership (the farm owner is 'married' with his land: a divorce is unthinkable).

Joseph Görres distinguishes the teaching profession (*Lehrstand*), the fighting profession (*Wehrstand*) and the nourishing profession (*Nährstand*). This is a return to the traditional division proper to Indo-European societies between those who know and direct (sovereign function), those who fight and defend (warrior function), and those who work and nourish (productive function).

The Organic State

The Romantics, in fact, desire to obtain a *synthesis* of opposites: the people and the nation, the State and the public spirit, Europe and its regions.

'There will come a day', Novalis assures us, 'where we will be universally convinced that no king can exist without the Republic, and reciprocally, that no Republic is appropriate without a king; and that each are as inseparable as soul and body'.

In the same way that dreams, the unconscious, and fairy tales help them to recover their childhood, the *chanson de geste* (the *Heldenlied*),[280] the epic, and the literature of the Minnesänger (the troubadours) allows them to place the 'people' in their distant origins.

Many of them go to Paris to study the texts of the Middle Ages at the Bibliothèque Nationale, and it is in Paris that Achim von Arnim wrote his epic, *Hermann and his Children*.[281] It is also in Paris that Friedrich von Schlegel, who lived at rue de Clichy, gained awareness of his nationality and his 'earthly homeland'. In 1803, he writes in the review *Europa*, which was published at Frankfurt: 'Perhaps the sleeping lion will awaken once again; and should we not see it ourselves, perhaps the history of the times to come will be filled with the exploits of the Germans'. In 1804, he creates a course on heroic mythology: he is above all interested in the epic of the Nibelungs, whose spirit and composition he admires. (The adaptation of this epic song by Fredrich de La

---

280 The 'Song of Heroic Deeds' or 'Heroic Song'. — Tr.

281 German: *Das Heldenlied von Hermann und seinen Kindern* (The Heroic Song of Hermann and his Children), French: *Hermann et ses enfants*. — Tr.

Motte-Fouqué in 1808, in *The Hero of the North*,[282] will furnish Wagner with one of his sources of inspiration).

The other Schlegel, August-Wilhelm, penned an apology for the Germanic Roman Empire: 'It is the people of the German race who have recreated and founded Europe, and if it is permitted of me to ask something about the national sentiment of the Germans, it is that they recognise that they are the motherland of Europe'.

He adds: 'The Eagle, this symbol of royalty, is for Germany a Roman inheritance'.

To the *mechanistic* attitude of the *Aufklärung*, which, taking *man* for a *thing*, extends the laws of the physical world to organic nature, Romanticism opposes a *dynamic* conception of life, which no longer only affects morality and religion, as with Lessing or Leibniz, but also nature and history.

Novalis denounces 'the miserable philistines, devoid of spirit and miserable of heart, the followers of the letter, who seek to hide the dullness of their thought and their inner deprivation under colourful appearances and behind the imposing mask of cosmopolitanism'. 'Everything that is absolute', declares Friedrich von Schlegel, 'is, by its very nature, inorganic, and tends to destroy the constituent elements. We can even say that the absolute is the true enemy of humankind'.

All of this results in an absolutely new conception of the state, which is no longer considered as a static concept (*Begriff*), but as a dynamic *Idea*.

The *Aufklärung* has seen in the state a necessary but transitory evil, a scandal for a reason. Romanticism sees it as a necessity in itself, a natural, organic reality independent of the arbitrary will (the 'social contract') of individuals, an entity which remains in service of the people, but which, being endowed with a life of its own, transcends and surpasses them by expressing all potentialities and specific values, and thereby *shapes* the people.

Adam Müller, in his *Elements of Statesmanship*,[283] writes: 'The State is not an invention of men destined for the utility or pleasure of the citizens' life; nothing exists for the citizen besides it. It is indispensable, inevitable, founded upon human nature'. He adds: 'The State is the fusion of human interests into an organic Whole'.

---

282 German: *Der Held des Nordens*, French: *Le héros du Nord.* — Tr.

283 German: *Die Elemente der Staatskunst*, French: *Eléments de l'art politique.* — Tr.

The same idea according to Novalis: 'Every citizen is an official of the State. Only in this capacity does he have his income'.

The Romantics noticed that the national community 'cannot be envisaged as the arithmetic sum of its equal members, but rather that it forms by itself a new, creative synthesis, mystically possessing an existence independent from those who compose it' (Jacques Droz, *Le romantisme allemande et l'Etat*. Payot, 1966).

This idea that the State is not a *composed whole*, but an *organic whole*, that it is no longer the simple 'sum' of its citizens just as an organism is not the simple sum of the organs that compose it, finds its origin in the thought of Schelling.

It is in his *Lectures on the Method of Academic Study* (1802)[284] that Schelling establishes the link between the philosophy of nature and the Romantic doctrine of the State. His interpretation, notes Droz, 'is accompanied by an aristocratic contempt for all forms of modern egalitarianism, as well as by a pronounced affirmation of the prerogatives of the monarch, without which the State remains "invisible" to its subjects'.

Fichte also wrote on this: 'In a product of nature, each part is only what it is in connection with the whole, and cannot absolutely be itself outside of this connection (...) In the organised body, each part ceaselessly maintains the whole, and by conserving it conserves itself. The same holds for the citizen in relation to the State'.

What is more, the State is justified by natural inequality, which supports freedom. 'If freedom is in fact only the general effort of differently endowed natures towards a more perfect development of their faculties', writes Adam Müller, 'there is nothing more contradictory than to deny the particularities, the diversities of these natures. Also the concept of freedom that I have defined has never been implemented in France. It is a false concept of freedom which, accompanied by equality, has characterised Revolutionary France (...) If the diverse elements of civil society were not different and unequal, there would be no State. For the State is not born once and for all from some kind of compromise, conciliation, or synthesis between the diverse forces which

---

284 German: *Vorlesungen über die Methode des akademischen Studiums*, French: *Conférences sur la méthode de l'enseignement académique*. — Tr.

oppose each other: it is *itself* the instrument of compromise, of conciliation, of synthesis between these forces'.

Finally, the State, being an end in itself, will not be submitted to international authorities. This is why the Romantics principally combat the doctrine of the 'equilibrium of forces', implemented by Metternich. 'An eternal peace', affirms Heinrich Luden, 'will be as pernicious to the human race as if storms disappeared from the atmosphere, leaving behind the swamps'.

Müller writes: 'If we place ourselves in the vantage of the state, we will see that war is the event in which the greatest momentum of the political life is manifested, where the State becomes conscious of its specific essence and puts the totality of its forces to the test in the presence of an adversary of equal size.

Joseph von Eichendorff, one of the most esteemed poets from the war of liberation, declares, in regards to the texts of the Constitutions: 'The paper is good for nothing. It is not in the dead letters that the sanctity of the contract resides, but in the loyalty, the unwavering will to uphold it'.

In 1814, the jurist Friedrich Carl von Savigny published *On the Call of our Time for Legislation and the Science of Jurisprudence*,[285] a work which would give birth to the historical school of jurisprudence.

Breaking with all juridical internationalism, Savigny affirms that 'law, like language, grows with the people, develops, and dies with them when the latter loses its profound peculiarities'. From here it follows that to want to interrupt the course of history is to go against life, that it is a 'crime' to want to impose institutions on a nation which are foreign to it, that the principle task of the jurist is not to codify and legislate, but to collect and formalise the elements of customary jurisprudence, only in accordance with the popular spirit or genius.

It is in this spirit that Savigny founded in 1815 the *Zeitschrift für geschichtliche Rechtswissenschaft*,[286] which would have considerable impact.

From the years 1812–16, Romanticism was developed above all in the south, notably in Vienna, which since 1809 had become the capital of Napoleon's adversaries, and also at Munich.

It is in Vienna that the Baron Joseph von Hormayr, born at Innsbruck in 1782, intends to make history serve the resurrection of national values.

---

285 *Vom Beruf unserer Zeit für Gesetzgebung und Rechtswissenschaft*, French: *De la vocation de notre temps pour la legislation et la science du droit.* — Tr.

286 Journal for Historical Jurisprudence. — Tr.

'History', he writes, 'is the unique depository of the originality of peoples'. It is also in Vienna that Adam Müller and Beethoven are based. Also at Vienna, August-Wilhelm von Schlegel, travelling in the wake of de Stäel, insists in his *Lectures on Dramatic Art and Literature*[287] upon the necessity of making the poetic *élan* coincide with the superior interest of the homeland.

In Bavaria, where the Romantics gathered around Joseph Görres and Franz von Baader, the penetration of the movement is linked to the fight for the Church's independence. It thus assumes an ultra-Catholic and particular-istic character which it never had elsewhere. Its centre is found in the new university, which Louis I had transferred from Landshut to Munich.

It is here that von Baader, Professor at the University and collaborator with the review, *Eos*, rediscovered the works of Meister Eckhart that had been eliminated from the centres of study since the condemnation of the great Rhenan mystic by the tribunals of the Inquisition, first at Cologne, then at Rome in 1328.

In Swabia, the most representative authors are Ludwig Uhland (1787–1862), the novelist Wilhelm Hauff (1802–1850), Gustav Schwab (1792–1850) and the poet Eduard Mörike.

Romanticism and Modern Science

Romanticism concludes, around 1827, in southern Germany, in the draft of a doctrine for Restoration and with an apology for the Christian State. Its last manifestations are stifled by the increase of ideas from the left, linked to the rise of the bourgeoisie liberal. (Heinrich Heine, theoretician of the Young Germany movement[288] and 'defrocked' Romantic, will come to see in Romanticism 'the most sustained proof of despotism'.)

In the world, however, the grip of Romanticism has only just begun.

In France, the work of Madame de Staël, *On Germany* (1810),[289] vigorously in favour of German Romanticism, has already provoked passionate contro-versies. From 1829, the *Revue de Paris* published the texts of E. T. A. Hoffman, Kleist, Jean-Paul, and Novalis. Alfred de Musset, Vigny, Aloysius Bertrand,

---

287 German: *Über dramatische Kunst und Literatur: Vorlesungen* (On Dramatic Art and Literature: Lectures), French: *Conférences sur l'art et la literature dramatiques*. — Tr.

288 *Junges Deutschland* (*Jeune Allamande*, Young Germany). — Tr.

289 French: *De l'Allemagne.* — Tr.

Baudelaire, and Rimbaud, followed by Apollinaire, Barrès, the Symbolists, and the Surrealists, will all draw elements of their own thought from Romanticism.

In Germany, Romantic literature has not contributed solely to national and political renewal. All the philosophers of life, from Schopenhauer and Nietzsche to Klages and Dilthey, have fed on it directly or indirectly. The brothers Grimm laid the foundations for modern philology. Thanks to Brentano, folklore and mythology have been renovated. Indo-European studies and linguistics have taken flight from the works of Schlegel and Franz Bopp, along with archaeology, ethnology, and palaeontology. The development of the German historical school, with Savigny, then Niebuhr and Raumer, of whom Leopold von Ranke was the eminent heir, formed a decisive step for historiography.

In 1821, Romantic music gained a victory with the first representation of the *Freischütz*[290] by Carl Maria von Weber.

At the beginning of the twentieth century, Oswald Spengler pushes the *organic* theory of culture and State to its ultimate consequences. Carl Schmitt will comment on the works of Savigny. The economist Ernst Wagemann will strive to lay the bases of an 'organic economy'. And the Viennese school, with Othmar Spann, will see in Adam Müller, the precursor of the 'spirit of community' (*Geist der Gemeinschaft*), one of the founders of sociology.

*

Romantiques allemands (vol. 1 et 2), collection presented by Maxime Alexandre, Erika Tunner, and Jean-Claude Schneider. Gallimard, 1,606 and 1,744 pages.[291]
Le romantisme politique en Allemagne, a study by Jacques Droz. Armand Colin, 211 pages.[292]

*

La Société des études romantiques[293] (27 rue Racine, 75006 Paris), whose secretary is Marie-Claude Chemin, publishes the journal *Romantisme* twice a year (through Flammarion).

---

290 The *Marksman* or *Free-shooter*. — Tr.
291 *German Romantics.* — Tr.
292 *Political Romanticism in Germany.* — Tr.
293 The Society for Romantic Studies. — Tr.

Scientific

WORLDVIEWS AND COSMOLOGY

I magine an observer equipped with the same astronomical instruments as us, but who is millions of light years from our solar system. 'If he looks far enough into the sky, the world that he will see will be similar to the world that we see. And even more similar the further he will look'.

This is not the least of modern cosmology's paradoxes.

Astronomy observes the stars and describes their properties. Astrophysics attempts to interpret these properties through the play of the laws of physics. Borrowing from each without confusing them with each other, cosmology deals with the universe considered as a whole.

From Aristotle to Einstein

Jacques Merleau-Ponty, sixty-one year old Professor at the University of Nanterre, first cousin of the philosopher Maurice Merleau-Ponty, and Bruno Morando, lecturer at the Sorbonne in Paris, editor-in-chief of the journal *L'Astronomie*, astronomer at the Bureau des Longitudes, have divided their work into three parts. Each consists of a 'philosophical presentation' and a 'scientific presentation' which cross-reference each other.

Three names are advanced which correspond to three great milestones in cosmology: Aristotle for Antiquity, Newton for the classical era, and Einstein for the contemporary period.

The alternation of day and night, the succession of the seasons, the movement of the sun, moon, and planets have struck the imagination of the ancients. The peoples of the Near East draw upon a hypothesis of chance: astrology; the Greeks, a science: astronomy.

Aristotle remarks that a shadow is cast upon the moon by the earth at the beginning and the end of eclipses, always in a circular form. He draws the logical conclusion: the earth is a globe. Thus is born the 'spherical cosmology', equally illustrated by Plato, Pythagoras, Eudoxus of Cnidus, and Ptolemy.

According to this conception, the universe is associated with prominent geometric forms. The earth is a sphere around which are arranged other celestial spheres, each eternally describing the same movement of an absolute perfection.

Two centuries after Pythagoras, Aristarchus of Samos imagines 'the hypothesis which makes the earth a planet like the others, turning both upon itself and around the sun'. The idea passed unnoticed. Seeking 'eternal truths', the theologians of the Middle Ages preferred to take the ideal views of Aristotle and Ptolemy.

Everything changes in the Renaissance with Copernicus (*De revolutionibus orbium coelestium*, 1542), Kepler, and Giordano Bruno. 'Copernicus, reviving Aristarchus whose work he knew well, showed that the heliocentric hypothesis, in which the sun is the centre of the universe, gives an even more satisfying explanation for the apparent movement of the planets than the system of Ptolemy. Fifty years later, Kepler discovered the exact laws of the movement of the planets around the sun'.

The spherical cosmology collapsed one tranquil night in the summer of 1609, when the lens of Galileo revealed a new world. The universe ceased to be the place for the election of 'absolute movements'. The stars, which the progress of optics allowed us to observe better, are described by irregular ellipses. The ideal spheres of the Empyrean where angels guide the planets in their course, the 'sublunary world' of Aristotle, and the 'crystalline heaven', disappear at the same time. The Church, deeply struck, protests. It is too late. The earth is no longer the centre of the universe. It is the beginning of the end of anthropocentrism.

But at the same time, the world ceases to be apprehended as a *whole*. The distribution of the stars is declared 'without necessary relevance to the framework in which objects are cast and events unfold'. In the eighteenth century, science centres its attention on the fundamental laws of celestial phenomena and seems to give up trying to solve questions touching on the structure of matter, the nature of space, and the limits of the universe. Newton speaks a priori of the 'infinity of the world'. The idea which is imposed is of a spatio-temporal framework which is void, homogenous, and infinite, peopled by bodies in interaction, but whose distribution remains approximately known.

Until the middle of the eighteenth century, two systems dispute the legacy of Aristotle: that of Descartes, built on abstract rationalism, and that of Newton, founded upon experiment. It is the second, supported notably by Voltaire, which prevails, thus consecrating the reign of classical physics.

'We owe to Kant', comment Merleau-Ponty and Morando, 'one of the first cohesive attempts at cosmological synthesis based on Newton's law of universal gravitation, which remarkably anticipates, on certain points, modern theories'.

The new cosmological revolution, which takes place at the dawn of the twentieth century, restores the notion of totality. Announced by Fitzgerald, Lorentz, Gustave Le Bon, it is systematised by Einstein. 'From cosmology to microphysics, Einstein has imposed his mark and modified the image of the world', writes Professor Louis Rougier in his *Traité de la connaissance* (Gauthier-Villars).[294]

Initially, however, Einstein did not seek to create a new theory of the universe. He only wanted to 'give the existing theories a more simple and secure logical basis'.

Everything began in 1881, when Michelson attempted to demonstrate, with the aid of light signals, the 'movement of the Earth in relation to aether', that is to say the 'absolute movement' of the Earth in space. The experiment fails — it appears to administer 'proof' that the Earth is immobile.

For a quarter of a century, physicists apply themselves rigorously to the problem. In 1905, Einstein discovers the solution. He formulates the theory of special relativity, which he will generalise ten years later.

It is the electromagnetic properties which explain the failure of the experiment. If the Earth seems immobile, it is because 'aether' does not exist. The speed of celestial bodies is limited to 300,000 km per second. It is isotropic, that is to say, it is the same for all observers whatever their movement will be. A traveller overtaken on a road by an automobile driving at the speed of light would be, in one second, 300,000 km from this vehicle, regardless of his own speed. And the result would be the same if he was crossed instead of being overtaken.

'Common sense does not appear to be accounted for', writes Pierre Marcenet in the *Cahiers universitaires*.[295] 'But it must take into account the

---

294 *Treatise of Knowledge.* — Tr.
295 *Academic notebooks.* — Tr.

simultaneity necessary for every observation'. We can say that a stick is thirty centimetres long if we can, at the same time, make the graduated increment of thirty coincide with a point situated at one of its extremities, and zero with a point situated at its other extremity. Now this simultaneity of observations taken at the extremities ceases to apply when two complexes are in 'relative movement' to each other, which is the case with all celestial bodies. This constant movement is translated by a spatial and temporal 'distortion'. The more the speed increases, the more time seems to slow down, the more distances seem to shrink.

The notions of 'absolute' space and time thus become inadequate. The two elements can no longer be separated. We will speak of *instances-localities*[296] localised in time-space. The Newtonian postulates, fundamental in physics and classical quasi-cosmology, must be abandoned.

Alongside this, Einstein demonstrates that it is possible to reduce mass to energy. Classical physics had already noted that a heated body is heavier. In atomic physics, four hydrogen atoms give helium with a mass weight proportional to the intervening loss of energy. Nature is transformed into energy according to the well-known formula: $E = mc^2$. The source of the radiance of stars is thus identified, which would be recreated artificially via atomic bombs.

The problem of the coexistence of matter and energy is resolved by this fact. Matter is the inertia of energy.

No Privileged Place

In 1915, general relativity extended the theses of special relativity to all possible observations, and not only to observations animated by a uniform movement. Gravitation then loses its mysterious character. Inert mass and heavy mass are identical, the laws of gravitation merely translate the inertia of matter. It is an effect of the 'curvature of space-time': masses (planets, for example, modify the properties of ambient space in the same way that hot bodies modify the temperature of the ambient milieu. Space is defined as a field of pure gravitation existing everywhere there is energy and whose characteristics vary. Outside of space, there is not a 'void', there is nothing.[297]

---

296 *instants-endroits.* — Tr.

297 Benoist uses the terms *vide* (void, vacuum, i.e. 'empty space') and *néant* (nothing, nihil, i.e. 'nonexistence'). — Tr.

'The sun, quite a massive body, "creates" in its vicinity a geometry whose fundamental curves are the trajectories of the planets. But elsewhere, in the vicinity of Sirius for example, another geometry will prevail'.

In the vicinity of a mass's interior, space is all the more 'curved' the greater and denser this mass is. 'If its size surpasses a certain limit, the curvature becomes such that space closes in upon itself in some way. Nothing, neither matter nor light, can escape it: this is a part of the universe completely separate from the rest'. Eddington (*Space, Time, Gravitation*, Hermann) has calculated that a globe of water with a 750 million kilometre radius would form a space of this kind. A luminous ray would turn around, returning indefinitely to its point of departure.

Gravitation affects all phenomena. In a gravitational field, rays of light are diverted, clocks slow down, etc. The universe is not Euclidean: 'At a very large scale', writes Merleau-Ponty and Morando, 'the distribution of matter in the universe is uniform. Not only is it verified that neither the Earth, the sun, nor the galaxy are the centre of the universe and that they do not occupy a remarkable place, but there is no centre in the universe at all, no notable place, no privileged location'.

Alongside the discovery of non-Euclidean geometries, the elaboration of non-Pythagorean arithmetic, non-Pascalian numbers, and non-Aristotelian logic, the birth of modern theories of knowledge are announced. All at once, the 'formal truths' of the ancient Greeks, the 'apriori world' of Descartes, the 'infinite space' of Newton, the 'noumena' of Kant, and the categories of the scholastics collapse.

The Big Bang Thesis

The 'cosmological revolution' has not yet come to its conclusion. The theory of relativity is succeeded, with Max Plank and Heisenberg, by the quantum theories of matter and energy, and then the theory of elementary particles. Theoretical cosmology has passed from the stage of the construction and study of particular 'models' of the universe, to research of general classes, such as the observational cosmology used to narrow these classes of models into more restrained sub-classes that agree as much as possible with the results of observation.

'One question divides the researchers: that of the "origin" of the universe. Two great hypotheses confront each other: the thesis of *continuous creation*, according to which the universe has existed for all time in a *dynamic* form, and the thesis of the 'primeval atom' (or Big Bang theory, to use the Anglo-Saxon expression).

The Belgian priest G. Lemaître (*L'hypothèse de l'atome primitive*. Griffon, Neuchâtel, 1946)[298] was without doubt the first cosmologist to reflect upon the question of *nucleosynthesis* in the universe. His theory may be summarised in the following way: 'the two principles of thermodynamics imply, from the point of view of quantum theory: (1) that energy exists in packets or distinct quanta and that the total remains constant; (2) that the number of these quanta grows without cease. As a consequence, if we go back through time, we must always find less quanta, until we have found all energy in the universe concentrated in a small number or in one single quantum'.

It is this unique quantum that Lemaître calls the 'primeval atom': the universe will be born from its sudden explosion, twelve or fifteen million years ago. The hypothesis is seductive. For the author, whose philosophical presuppositions are obvious, it has the primary advantage of restoring the notion of *causality*, which had been eliminated by the uncertainty principle. However, in the eyes of many cosmologists, the ideas of Lemaître are already outmoded. They do not allow us to explain the existence of the lighter elements: at best, the fragments of the primeval atom could only correspond to the heaviest nuclei. Some even consider that the idea of *beginning* and, as a result, that of an *initial singularity*, are meaningless — by the fact of the reevaluation which is imposed by the notion of time. In addition, we can also imagine a 'pulsating' universe, that is to say, passing in successive phases of *expansion* and *contraction*. (This hypothesis has been advanced by the British astrophysicist Fred Hoyle). From this perspective, it is the continuous creation of matter that fills the voids created by the expansion of the galactic systems. (But the problem of the formation of the galaxies themselves has still not received a satisfying solution).

A new worldview is to be born. But it is not certain if science, by its very nature, can *answer* (and, by consequence, give a *meaning*) to three final

---

298 *The Hypothesis of the Primeval Atom.* — Tr.

questions, which are but one: the existence of God, the freedom of man, and the origin of the universe.

*

La trois étapes de la cosmologie, a study by Jacques Merleau-Ponty and Bruno Morando.[299]
    Laffont, 316 pages.

*

In October 1976, 150 astronomers and astrophysicists gathered in Paris under the auspices of the CNRS and the International Astronomical Union to debate the formation and evolution of the universe. The expansionist cosmology, one of whose principal theoreticians, at the beginning of the century, was the American astronomer E. Hubble, had been strongly criticised. Within the framework of the law of uniform expansion of the universe, certain phenomena (notably the association of extra-galactic objects linked together by 'bridges of matter') indeed seemed unable to be explained. In addition, the constant of Hubble, deduced for each region of the universe by the relationship between speed of expansion and distance of galaxies, would prove to be inconstant. Now if there is continuous expansion in the universe, it is necessarily isotropic, that is to say, it is the same in every direction. There is thus a contradiction here.

During this same congress, Sandage and Taman have concluded to a new value for Hubble's constant ($H = 55$), notably smaller than that obtained to the present. As a consequence of this result (which inscribes itself in a model of a universe in expansion) the 'date' of the formation of the cosmos is pushed back considerably.

Finally according to two researchers at the Institute Henry Poincaré (Paris), H. Karoji and L. Nottale, there is room to think that the light issued from galaxies shifts differently towards red depending on whether or not it passes through some concentrations of matter. The crossing of a cluster of galaxies, for example, will be linked to an accentuated 'reddening'. This observation could give life again to theories of 'tired light', which base themselves on the fact that the energy of the photon (or 'grain of light') decreases throughout its journey because of its interaction with the matter that it crosses before reaching us.

THE ORIGIN OF LIFE

'We can only know the nature of things', said Heraclitus of Ephesus, 'when we know their origin and their evolution'. Today, the biologist no longer dreams of fabricating a man in a bottle. Nor even an amoeba or bacteria. He knows that these are the products of hundreds of thousands of years of evolution. But he still preoccupies himself with the problem of 'first causes': the origin of life.

'The traditional solutions to the problem of the origin of life point to two possibilities: either living beings emerge spontaneously from inert matter, or

---

299 *The Three Stages of Cosmology.* — Tr.

life existed in the universe for all eternity', recalls Christian Léourier, twenty-nine years of age.

Since the end of the last century, it has become impossible to remain content with these explanations. The discovery of microbes, and the experiments of Pasteur on the sterilisation of culture media (1862), put an end to the belief in 'spontaneous generation'. The theory of the 'panspermia', according to which life would be propagated from planet to planet by means of the 'aether', had also been refuted: no known germ could resist the high energy radiations of interplanetary space.

Alongside this, the theory of evolution formulated by Darwin has enabled the refutation of the 'eternalist' solution. From the instant that we admit that species have appeared one after the other, the question effectively arises of knowing where the first 'thrust' of evolution occurred.

Finally, evidence for the phenomenon of photosynthesis would appear as a challenge to scientific common sense.

It is by photosynthesis that solar energy intervenes in the great biochemical cycles of the terrestrial globe. Green plants (chlorophyll) absorb carbon dioxide from the air, and synthesise from it the organic substances that they need. Animals in turn receive these substances, either by directly absorbing the plants, or by nourishing themselves on herbivorous beings. All of these plants reject oxygen. Now it is precisely this that constitutes the breathable part of the atmosphere. Without oxygen: no life, no chlorophyll, no photosynthesis, no more oxygen.

In other words, the living systems are accounted for by organic substances, and organic substances by living systems. It is this contradiction, notably articulated by Lecompte du Noüy, who formulated the 'Lecomtian bind'[300] at the beginning of the century.

The Russian scientist A. I. Oparine observes: 'It was logical to think that living beings are formed by the evolution of the organic substances that compose them. But if such substances cannot be formed in natural conditions other than by the vital process of organisms, our deductions involuntarily fall into a vicious circle which appears inescapable. We realise that such ideas seemed to

---

300 *verrou lecomptien*, literally the 'Lecomtian lock'. — Tr.

raise insurmountable difficulties for solving the problem of the origin of life' (*L'origine et l'évolution de la vie*. Ed. de Moscou, 1960).[301]

It is precisely Oparine who, in 1924, allowed researchers to escape the impasse by advancing a 'revolutionary' hypothesis: the atmosphere of the earth has changed.

The 'Primordial Soup'

Astrophysics teaches us that the atmosphere of most planets is 'reducing'. That is to say, it is composed essentially of methane, ammoniac, hydrogen, and water vapour. Due to this, it is transparent to the ultraviolet radiation that emanates from the sun with great energy. On earth, by contrast, the atmosphere is 'oxydising': the ultraviolet rays are stopped by the twenty percent of oxygen in the atmosphere (and by the ozone layer which surrounds the globe at a height of 30 km).

Now, following Oparine, there is every reason to think that the primordial earthly atmosphere was also 'reducing' some three million years ago. It therefore allowed the ultraviolet rays to pass without filtering them. And it is this hyper-energetic radiation that could have provoked, on the surface of the earth and the sea, during powerful storms, some reactions of synthesis resulting in the formation of simple organic substances.

Our planet was probably formed at a relatively low temperature by the accumulation of cold, solid bodies of heterogeneous constitution. The difference of constitution and density of the solid matter of which it was formed has determined the 'non-homogeneity', that is to say it has provoked the appearance of *diversity*. This makes itself felt by a progressive reheating, principally due to the heat resulting from the disintegration of radioactive elements. The largest parts of the hydrocarbons detach themselves from the lithosphere and then combine themselves on the surface of the Earth with water vapour, ammonia, hydrogen sulphide, and the other 'reductive' atmospheric gasses.

'The primeval earth can be represented', writes Steven Rose, a thirty-nine year-old biochemist attached to London's Maudsley Institute, 'as a planet principally constituted by vast hot oceans, containing in solution different salts coming from rocks. Under these conditions, a certain number of organic compounds would have begun to form and spread themselves widely throughout

---

301 *The Origin and Evolution of Life.* — Tr.

the entire extent of the oceans. The formation of these compounds would have been conditioned by this 'reductive' atmosphere and by the constant influx of energy in the form of light and ultraviolet rays coming from the sun.

Initially dispersed in the form of solutions, the first organic substances would have then been combined to form macromolecular structures, which would be progressively differentiated, organised into 'coacervates' (a kind of 'drop of jelly' combined with salts, polymers, and organic compounds of weak molecular weight, studied by the science of colloids), before entering into exchange with the ambient milieu. These exchanges would have been complete by taking on the nature of the characteristic exchanges of life: self-renewal, self-regulation, self-reproduction. Finally, the current atmosphere would have replaced the early atmosphere, oxygen being successively freed by photosynthesis, produced by evolution, whereas a self-regulating 'carbon cycle' would establish itself between organisms, creating at the same time a new *phase* of life.

'At a certain stage of development', continues Steven Rose, 'the nucleic acids and proteins must have emerged in the form of interdependent molecules capable of mutual synthesis, thus giving birth to the proteinaceous DNA-RNA complex, currently responsible for genetic transfer.'

From its appearance, life profoundly modifies the conditions of the environment. Certain living forms, taking the upper hand in some way, destroy other less 'fit' forms. Animated matter thus 'chooses' more evolutionary and better-adapted paths. *Natural selection* begins.

It was still necessary to be able to reproduce this famous 'primordial soup' in a laboratory. This was achieved more than twenty years ago.

In 1953, the American chemist Stanley Miller produced a gaseous mixture comprised of 18% hydrogen, 26% methane, 26% ammonia, and 30% steam. He kept it all at 60° Celsius (representing the temperature of the earth billions of years ago) and submitted it to an intense ultraviolet radiation. A few hours later, dozens of amino acids were spontaneously formed in the flask, with a good number of other organic compounds, like formaldehyde. Submitting the resulting broth to ultraviolet rays again, Miller saw the nitrogenous bases, notably adenine, guanine, and some sugars like ribose and deoxyribose appear, that is to say, the bases and the sugars used in the DNA (deoxyribonucleic acid) and RNA (ribonucleic acid) of living cells.

It remains to be known if the sugar, the phosphate, and the nitrogenous bases could be linked in such a way as to form a nucleotide, that is, a complete element of the spiralled ladder of DNA and RNA, the celebrated 'double helix' of the genetic code, bearer of inheritance. Yet the true links of nucleotides have been able to be synthesised, always under the action of ultraviolet, by Dr. Schramm at Berlin's Max Planck Institute. (We have synthesised, for example, the ATP or adenosine triphosphate and smaller-sized proteins).

Numerous experiments of the same kind have been menées after Miller, both in the east (Pavloskaïa, Passynski) and the west (Ponamperuma, Sidney Fox). They have allowed us to recreate in laboratories the conditions of appearance of most of the compounds of fundamental biological interest existing in living matter in the free state (micromolecular) or the condensed state (macromolecular).

The importance of these works is obvious. The fact that, among the millions of a priori compounds susceptible to be formed under the action of ultraviolet radiation, only the amino acids specific to proteins (which are themselves the most specific constituents of living systems) are actually formed — this fact lets us suppose that life does not have the exceptional character that Lecomte du Noüy lent to it; rather, it is the logical, quasi-necessary consequence of environmental conditions which are probably not peculiar to our planet.

The consequences that can be drawn are not only of a scientific order. Christian Léourier also insists on the ideological 'benefits'.

Around the Notion of 'Emergence'

At first sight, a serious blow has been carried to 'vitalism', that is to say to the belief in a mysterious 'principle of life' radically foreign to the physical world. For the vitalists (who Jacques Monod calls the 'animists'), the appearance of life cannot be explained by a simple complexification of matter. For this reason, the most cannot come out of the least (cf. Claude Tresmontant, *Comment se pose aujourd'hui le problème de l'existence de Dieu ?* Seuil, 1968).[302] They even admit to creation *ex nihilo* when it comes to the existence and power of God.

Max Planck nevertheless affirms that 'a whole is always distinguished by something from the sum of its parts'. 'In fact', adds Professor Louis Rougier, experiment shows that every composed system manifests new properties distinct

---

302 *How is the Question of the God's Existence Posed Today?* — Tr.

from those of the elements composing it'. Thus, the chemical compound H20 manifests new properties (those of water) which are quite different from the hydrogen and oxygen that constitute it. To say that these 'emergent' properties were contained 'in potential' in the elements of the compound does not say anything significant. The characteristic taste of sugar is not 'potentially' in its three components, carbon, hydrogen, and oxygen, which are wholly devoid of flavor.

This philosophical-biological clash reaches its greatest intensity around the notion of *emergence*. For the "vitalists", emergence is an outbreak of an almost miraculous character. For the "reductionists", it simply refers to a link of a causal order, which a thorough study of biological phenomena shall allow us to determine with precision.

Among the anti-vitalists, some, like Jacques Monod, assert that the process by which the evolution of life began was initially the result of chance. The others, like Ernest Kahane (*La vie n'existe pas*, Ed. Rationalistes),[303] respond: 'Recourse to chance is almost as vain as recourse to metaphysics; it is a lazy conception which requires no confirmation, which does not lead to any hypothesis, and which leads to no experiment' (*Finalité en biologie*, in *Les Cahiers rationalistes*, December 1965).

The question is more fundamental than it seems. If compounds are "something more" than their parts, they are also something *other* than these parts (and not simply the same thing in another form). Can we say, under these conditions, that the passage from the inert to the organic, from the inanimate to the living, from the living to the conscious, is not equivalent to the passage from one *form of reality* to another? Living matter may well have *originated* from physical matter, but it is not *only* of physical matter. Born of the physico-chemical, it is not *only* physico-chemical (otherwise, *how* would it be alive?) And while it is true that the physico-chemical phenomena which manifest themselves in living phenomena have not gained anything specific, it is also true that their *organisation* is peculiar to living systems. Thus, are we actually in the presence of one and the same matter appearing in different forms? Of a matter which would not differ in *nature*, but in *degrees*? Which would not imply a qualitative "leap" but a quantitative "leap"? In short, as Steven Rose

---

303 *Life does not exist.* — Tr.

says, "where exactly does the border occur that separates flowers, dogs, and yeast cells, on the one hand, and molecules of salt, urea, or amino acids on the other?"

That this boundary will be, to a certain degree, somewhat blurred is demonstrated by the experiments on the tobacco mosaic virus that were simultaneously carried out in 1955 by Fraenkel-Conrat and Williams in the United States, and by Gierer and Schramm in Germany.

This virus consists of a small cylindrical stick with a central spiral of RNA surrounded by a sleeve of proteins. By simple methods, the RNA nucleic acid is separated from the sleeve and each of these two parts of the virus is broken down into hundreds of biologically inert components. Now, if all of the fragments are left intact, the basic structure of the RNA is reconstituted spontaneously. And the same is true of the protein sleeve. The complete synthesis of the virus is finally obtained. "Thus reassembled like a watch mechanism", writes the professor Louis Rougier, 'the virus recovers 50% of its original virulence: it comes back to life" (*Nouvelle Ecole*, 1968). Having isolated the virus from the mosaic pattern on the tobacco, Stanley will proceed to crystallise it into an ordinary chemical product, and then, having re-inoculated it to tobacco, makes it propagate and become infectious again. Thus, the experimenter can now progress at will from the organic to the physical-chemical, and then from a biologically inert body to one endowed with one of the essential characteristics of life: self-reproduction. (With this restrictive condition, however: that the body in question must be inoculated to an [innoculé à un] appropriate living being).

The problem of the relationships between *living* and *non-living* is not completely resolved. Thus, when Steven Rose declares that there is no more "essential" difference between the organic and the physical-chemical than there is "between a raw egg and a hard-boiled egg", he forgets that between the "raw egg" and the "hard-boiled egg", something *other than the egg* intervenes.

Charles Sadron, Professor at the National Museum of Natural History, Honorary Director of the CNRS's Centre for Research in Molecular Biophysics at Orléans-La Source, who was President of the Rationalist Union, at the same time that he sides with a reductionist conception of the phenomena of life, also recognizes that none of the manifestations of consciousness are reducible to a physico-chemical level. 'We cannot say that a pain or a pleasure is a magnitude, is a category of phenomena which falls within the physico-chemical. (*Les Cahiers rationalistes*, July 1975). The answers of the reductionist theorists are therefore no more satisfactory than those of the metaphysicians. And one wonders if the *language* of biochemistry is yet to be invented.

*

L'origine de la vie. Théories contemporaines, a study by Christian Léourier. Laffont, 172 pages.[304]

La chimie de la vie, a study by Steven Rose. Gauthier-Villars, 302 pages.[305]

*

On the problem of emergence, Pierre Thuillier published an important article (*Qu'est-ce que l'émergence ?*)[306] in the review *Atomes* (March 1968). He emphasises that the 'reduction-ism versus emergence' debate is not necessarily identical to the 'mechanism vs. vitalism' debate, and even less to the 'monism vs. metaphysics' debate. He also observes that discussions about the 'unity of science' (a theme cherished by the advocates of 'physicalism') are frequently distorted, for there can be a methodological unity of science without there being any unity (or reducibility by mutual conversion) of the different objects and levels of objects that scientific inquiry concerns itself with.

From a methodological point of view, we can say that effort of reduction is legitimate when it seeks to establish relations or correlations between different phenomena (or orders of phenomena), but ceases to be so when it uses the pretext of these relations and correlations to assert that such a phenomenon (or order of phenomena) is nothing other than some other phenomenon (or order of phenomena) constituted in another form.

OLD AND NEW LOGICS

Logic, in intellectual matters, is the form of honesty and rigor,' declared Léo Hamon, after leaving the Council of Ministers on 25 August 1971.

Traditionally, logic is the 'study of the conditions of truth'. Today, it is in fact much more than that: a true science whose object is the systematic study of the conditions in which a statement can be considered coherent, endowed with meaning, and susceptible to verification. Logicians do not deal with the content of statements. They do not indicate whether they are accurate or not. But they do tell us whether these statements are admissible from a formal point of view, that is to say, if the rules that allow reasoning are correctly observed.

---

304   *The Origin of Life: Contemporary Theories.* — Tr.

305   *The Chemistry of Life.* — Tr.

306   *What is emergence?* — Tr.

These rules differ from those of grammar and syntax. It is thus so, writes the British philosopher Alfred J. Ayer (*Language, Truth and Logic*), that certain grammatically correct statements are 'of an excessive modesty'. 'If I learn, for example', he adds, 'that lions are or are not carnivores, I know something true, but I do not fully know whether I will be eaten'.

It was long believed, with Kant, that logic was *geschlossen* und *vollendet* (closed and completed'). 'In reality', says Robert Blanché, a former Professor at the faculté des Lettres in Toulouse, 'it is the renewal of logic that has, over the past century, sparked as a reaction a renewal of its history'.

The old logic, bequeathed by Aristotle, was based on simple principles: the principle of identity (A = A), the principle of the excluded middle (all that which is not A is not A) and the principle of contradiction (the same concept cannot be defined as both A and not A). These principles were declared to be true a priori, at all times and places, and it was said that they pre-existed human understanding and reasoning. In this way, the distinction between the *truths of experience* drawn from observation, and *formal truths* deduced solely from intellectual connection to certain eternal laws, was introduced into western thought: the 'common notions', of Aristotle, and the 'evident principles' of Descartes.

Situated at the intersection of science, philosophy, and the analysis of language, modern logic breaks completely with this Aristotelian doctrine.

The rupture between what German logician Rudolf Carnap called 'the old and the new logic' is sometimes situated around 1850, a period when 'logic escaped the philosophers in order to be taken up by the mathematicians'. In fact, according to Blanché, the origins of modern logic (also called logicism or symbolic logic) go back to Leibniz, indeed even to the Presocratics.

'The Word Dog Does Not Bite'

The evolution of logic has followed that of physics and the life sciences. Blanché has outlined the principle steps. The logic of Aristotle is succeeded by that of the Stoics, which take a dialectic form, then by medieval logic, illustrated by Thomas Aquinas and the famous quarrel of Universals. The *Logique de Port-Royal*, 1662, embodies the Jansenist and Cartesian spirit. Leibniz, who discovered at the same time as Newton the bases of differential calculus, imagines the system of 'monads'. Meanwhile, the foundations of classical empiricism are laid by Francis Bacon, David Hume, and John Locke, and are furthered by Stuart Mill.

In the eighteenth century the 'evident principles' of Aristotle had taken refuge in mathematics. Independent of circumstances, it seemed that two and two always made four, that the sum of the angles of a triangle was always equal to two right angles, and that the shortest route from one point to another was always the straight line, etc.

The discovery in the nineteenth century of non-Euclidean geometries, non-Cartesian kinematics, and non-Pythagorean arithmetic, exploited by the theory of relativity, showed that this was not the case. The length and weight of a body change in space. If we draw a curvilinear triangle on a world map, the sum of its angles will be greater than two right angles. In a 'geometry of navigators', the shortest path from one point to another will not be the straight line, but the arc of the great terrestrial circle that passes through the two chosen points. In quantum mechanics, the logic of the excluded middle must be replaced by a weakened logic, practically devoid of contradiction. There is therefore a *plurality* of possible systems, and their choice depends on the conditions of the experiment.

At the beginning of the century, David Hilbert could write 'Mathematics is nothing more than a game played according to certain simple rules, with signs devoid of meaning written down on paper'.

It is to logicians such as Bertrand Russell, Gottlob Frege, Péano, and Couturat, that we owe the 'logicisation' of mathematics. That is to say, the reduction of mathematics to the fundamental laws of logic.

'The importance of Bertrand Russel's *Principles of Mathematics*, published in 1903, was such', notes Blanché, 'that Russell's symbolic writing has become the common language of the logicians'.

The development of mathematical logic dispelled many ambiguities. For years the logicians had wondered whether a statement such as 'the square circle is impossible' did not include the idea that the 'square circle' existed 'in some way' (otherwise one would not be able to speak about it). Russell and Whitehead, in *Principia Mathematica* (1910–13), showed that the problem disappeared as soon as the statement was transcribed in a more rigorous form. For example 'There is no x such that x will be both square and round'. Contrary to St. Anselm's belief (regarding God), the fact that one can *speak* of a thing does not imply that it *exists*. The definition of the unicorn is not enough to convince us of its reality. It is still necessary that the attributes given to it correspond to a *verifiable* reality. Words are not things. As William James says, 'the word dog does not bite'.

Thanks to symbolic logic, mathematical abstraction took on an extraordinary scope, whose limits (especially in Carnap, Russell, and Goodman) were studied by Jules Vuillemm, Professor at the Collège de France. We have developed not only several logics with two values, but logics of three, four, ten, or even an *infinity* of values, together with probability logics, modal logics, polyvalent logics, and so on.

Statements Void of Meaning

Ludwig Wittgenstein, author of the *Tractatus logico-philosophicus*, and the logicians of the Vienna Circle (Carnap, Reichenbach, Rougier) demonstrated that all statements were ultimately either of empirical, that is to say experiential, origin, or a truism (a 'tautology'), a statement that is *always true* under all circumstances, and which as such, teaches us nothing.

By saying, 'men are mortal; Socrates is a man; therefore Socrates is mortal', the ancients thought they had made a demonstration. 'For them', writes Bertrand Russell, 'such a proposition was true by virtue of its very form. Its truth, in its hypothetical form, depended neither on Socrates being a man, nor on the fact that all men die'. According to contemporary logicians, such a statement is insufficient. Indeed, it implies the prior demonstration that (a) Socrates is a man; (b) that men are mortal. Properly formulated, the statement becomes: 'If Socrates is a man and if men are mortal, then Socrates is mortal'.

The laws of logic thus appear as 'formal facilitators'. They are, in a sense, 'molds for statements', capable of operational transformations intended to facilitate reasoning, but which teach us nothing by themselves. At all times they must be faced with reality.

In 1954, Carnap could say: 'Logic is not a *theory*, i.e., a system of affirmations about certain objects, but a *language*, i.e., a system of signs with rules for their employment'.

'The problems which can be stated in the language of science, and which seem insoluble', writes Vuillemin, 'are apparent problems which result from an inappropriate play of language'. The same is true of many philosophical problems (or pseudo-problems). A statement such as 'Caesar is a prime number' is quite correct from a grammatical point of view. One cannot even say that it is 'false' because the opposite proposition ('Caesar is *not* a prime number') is no more acceptable. In fact, it is not grammar, but 'logical syntax', developed by the Vienna Circle, which tells us why it is not permissible: because 'the property of being a prime number belongs to the category of properties which can be attributed only to terms belonging to the category of names of numbers' (Reichenbach). Of such a statement, it will not be said that it is false', but that it is *void of meaning*.

This brings logic closer to the philosophy of science, which, as Vuillemin reminds us, 'being structural, cannot question the essence of things, but only the *types of relations* they allow to discern'. At the same time, logic interferes with mathematics, in all its forms. 'The consequence', notes Jean Piaget, 'is that in many countries, most of them French-speaking, philosophers do not know logic in its modern forms, the training of pupils at the bachelors level being almost nonexistent in this regard' (*Nature et methods d'épistémologie*, 1967).[307]

In logic, Bertrand Russell sees the very essence of philosophy. This is true to the degree that it 'provides an infinite number of possible hypotheses applicable to the analysis of any complex fact'. But we can also think, to the contrary, that logic no longer belongs to philosophy, to the extent that it now escapes purely speculative reflections — which makes it possible to preserve for philosophy its traditional role of elaborating worldviews by which man interprets the universe.

Relegated in the last century to the suburbs of the great scientific capitals, logic has since taken on a new dimension. 'The major event of recent decades', writes Blanché, 'is its definitive promotion to the rank of the positive sciences'.

*

La logique et le monde sensible, a study by Jules Vuillemin. Flammarion, 348 pages.[308]
La logique et son histoire, a study by Robert Blanché. Armand Colin, 366 pages.[309]
La méthode scientifique en philosophie, a study by Bertrand Russell. Payot, 150 pages.[310]

---

307 *Nature and Methods of Epistemology.* — Tr.
308 *The Logic of the Sensible World.* — Tr.
309 *Logic and its History.* — Tr.
310 *The Scientific Method in Philosophy.* — Tr.

EPISTEMOLOGY AND SCIENTIFIC DISCOVERY

'Suppose you are visiting a city for the first time. You use a map to guide you. Suddenly, you discover that the map does not correspond at all to the layout of the city's streets. You do not say, "The streets do not obey the law of the map". Instead, you say, "The map is wrong". This is precisely the situation of the scientist faced with the so-called "laws of nature". The laws constitute a map of nature drawn up by physicists. If one discovers a disagreement somewhere, one does not ask whether "nature" has disobeyed, but rather if the "physicists" have made an error'. This observation is made by the logician Rudolf Carnap in *Les fondements philosophiques de la physique*,[311] a work whose original edition appeared in 1966.

With this example, characteristic of the Vienna Circle (*Wiener Kreis*), Rudolf Carnap, who was born in Germany in 1891 and died in the United States in 1972, intended to show that 'natural laws' do not have the absolute character that is often attributed to them.

The work of the Vienna Circle is not yet well-known in France despite recent efforts to make them better-known, particularly by Armand Colin with the collection *Epistémologie*, directed by Pierre Thuillier.

In the 1930s, this school of scientific philosophy reached the height of its influence. Its leading representatives were Moritz Schlick, Rudolf Carnap, Hans Reichenbach, Otto Neurath, and Philipp Frank. They first taught in Germany, and then in the Anglo-Saxon countries.

The "Scientificity" of the Proposals

Heir to a long empiricist tradition going back to Hume, Locke, and Stuart Mill, the Vienna Circle situated itself in the continuation of the 'empirio-criticism' of Ernst Mach and Richard Avenarius, which Lenin maltreated in his *Materialism and empirio-criticism* (1905). He was also influenced by the early philosophy of Bertrand Russell and by that of Wittgenstein, as well as by early developments in modern physics, formal logic, and the analysis of language.

In reaction to the German idealism of Schelling and Hegel, the theorists of the Vienna Circle felt that questions as to the 'why' of things, inaccessible to the scientific method, were by this fact 'deprived of meaning'.

---

311 *The Philosophical Foundations of Physics.* — Tr.

For them, the only sensible question was the question of 'how'. Consequently, they distinguished two kinds of science: the empirical sciences (or natural sciences), and the formal sciences, like mathematics, logic, and so on. Only the first, they said, teach us something about the world. The second, whose propositions are so universal, and consequently always true, are nothing but conventional systems which *facilitate* reasoning, but they do not *instruct* in any way.

It is in contact with this circle, but on its margins, that the Austrian philosopher Karl R. Popper, now seventy-four, published his most famous book, *Logik der Forschung*,[312] which has been translated into French with a preface by Jacques Monod.

Born in Vienna, and emigrating to New-Zealand in 1937, Popper lived in Great Britain since 1946. It did not take him long to establish a position in intellectual circles, which lead him to chair, from 1959 to 1961, the British Society for the Philosophy of Science. He also taught at the University of London and the London School of Economics. His political philosophy is situated within the lineage of neo-conservative liberalism. In 1945, in his essay on *The Open Society and its Enemies*,[313] he identified Plato, Marx, and Hegel as the historical fathers of modern totalitarianism. In 1956, in *The Poverty of Historicism*,[314] he succeeded in rejecting, though not in a perfectly satisfying manner, all doctrines involving historical determinism. More recently, he opposed Herbert Marcuse in a debate that made great waves.

While still very young, Karl R. Popper takes an interest in the theory of relativity, which was receiving some brilliant experimental confirmations. At the same time, he closely follows the rise of Marxism and psychoanalysis, which Vienna was a 'capital' of in this period. 'But he also feels, very early', writes Jacques Monod, 'that the status of these powerful ideologies, which nevertheless believe themselves scientific, is profoundly different from that of the theory of relativity'.

---

312 *The Logic of Scientific Discovery.* — Tr.

313 German: *Die offene Gesellschaft und ihre Feinde,* French: *La société ouverte et ses ennemis.* — Tr.

314 Originally published in English; translated into French as *Misère de l'historicisme* (Plon). — Tr.

Popper then poses the question which will dominate his entire work: 'What criterion is applied to evaluate the scientificity of a proposition?'

It soon becomes apparent that 'Marxism and psychoanalysis lie outside of science precisely because, *by nature*, by the very structure of their theories, they are irrefutable'. The proof of facts has no effect on such doctrines. Pure beliefs, pure illusions, are *beyond* realities.

The first edition, in German, of *Logik der Forschung*, appeared in 1934–1935; the first English edition, in 1959. In the interim, Popper added a large number of remarks to the original text, corresponding to the period of his thought where he gradually diverged from the Vienna school. The French edition, achieved by the Commission of Translations from the International Institute of Philosophy, under the direction of Philippe Devaux, Professor at the University of Liège, takes all these additions into account.

This gives us a large book of considerable importance. For Monod, 'it is one of the rare works of epistemology in which a man of science can recognize, if not sometimes discover, the very movement of his thought, the true and rarely written history of the progress to which he could personally contribute'.

It has nevertheless taken forty years for this 'great and powerful book' to be published in France. 'This delay', adds Monod, 'is, like others, attributable to the "closed sociology" of French philosophy, which only seems to have been widely open, for many years, to the obscure extravagances of the German metaphysics'.

Verification and Causality

One of the problems studied by the Vienna Circle is that in a world where the relative seems to be the rule, what meaning should be given to the notion of 'law'? And first, what is a law?

In the last century, *universal* laws ('universal conditional statements' of formal logic), always true everywhere, were distinguished from *statistical* laws, which express strong probabilities. According to the Vienna Circle, such a distinction is erroneous. The 'universal' laws only express irregularities of repetitions (alternation of day and night, sensation of burning produced by fire, falling to the ground of objects released into the 'void', etc.) linked to *subjective* or *conventional* circumstances. In reality, there are no 'universal' laws, the universe is not governed in its *totality* by laws peculiar to the environment in which we live.

As a result, the notion of causality must be revised. Goethe once said: 'The thinker always misleads himself when he questions cause and the effect, for the two are but *one single* phenomenon'.

Carnap, former student of Gottlob Frege, Professor at the University of Chicago from 1936, shows in his *Logical Structure of the World* (1928)[315] that the idea of causality does not automatically imply the idea of *necessity*, with which it is often confused. If the 'general principles' are simple conventions which impose themselves on us by reason of structures ordained by our spirit, and not by the function of an absolute reality, then the 'explanatory' laws are always only those specifically involving an explanation of the 'if … then' type. The laws contain causality, but they do not have the virtue of a 'logical necessity'. (Following Mach and Poincaré, Rudolf Carnap and Moritz Schlick will say that this conception of causality is a *conditionalist* conception).

For the Vienna Circle, a meaningful proposition, to the extent that it cannot be validated by its conformity with 'general principles' alone, must be able to be verified. Conversely, what cannot be verified is considered to be meaningless; indeed, how does one separate pure speculation from inconsistent illusion? 'To give a meaning', says Philipp Frank (*Le principe de causalité et ses limites*, Flammarion),[316] is to show that there is a relation between a proposition and concrete realities'.

It was also necessary to say what the 'principle of verification' would consist in. Carnap constructed his theory of 'observation statements' (also called 'protocol sentences').[317] A proposition, he said, is *verified* whenever it can be reduced to 'observation statements', that is to say, to a small number of incontestable statements of observation — which Professor Louis Rougier has justly defined as the 'verbal process of received experience'.

In his *Logik der Forschung*, Karl R. Popper has no difficulty in demonstrating that such criteria are extremely insufficient. On the one hand, even false propositions can have meaning (a delusion, for example, reveals a mental illness). On the other hand, an idea may be correct without being verifiable

---

315 German: *Der Logische Aufbau der Welt*, French: *Structure logique du monde.* — Tr.

316 *The Principle of Causality and its Limits* — Tr.

317 German: *Protokollsätze.* — Tr.

experimentally (because the experiment cannot be materially realised, because it is a statement of a psychological nature). Taken in too restrictive a sense, the 'principle of verification' leads to a new form of dogmatism and reductionism, of which the 'physicalist' theory (sustained in particular by Otto Neurath) will be the culmination.

Popper also criticises the theories of the Oxford School, for which every philosophical problem traces itself back, in the final analysis, to the problem of language, and thus concerns the signification of words. In the desire to bring everything back to the *logical syntax of language*, Popper detects the illusory belief that it is possible to rationalise the formulation of *all* statements. Now, he remarks, the 'new languages' that we tried to create (models of the *languages of science*) revealed themselves to be highly non-functional.

Of the 'Negative Certainties'

He then proposes to replace 'proposition statements' with 'basic statements' bearing not only on actually realised perceptual experiences, but on observable processes expressing 'observations of *thinkable* facts'.

But he goes further. The idea that he defends, in the final analysis, is that it is *impossible* to 'prove' the validity of a hypothesis or an idea. For example, we can never verify that water 'always' boils at 100 degrees, for we can never boil 'all' the water existing in the universe. However, the same hypothesis, the same idea, can be *refuted* — verification is done *a contrario*. This means that a theory can be regarded as 'correct' as long as it resists the various refutations to which it is subjected.

In this sense, a 'proof' will only be 'provisional to refutation, the outcome of which is negative'. Instead of speaking of 'verifiability', one will speak of *testability*, that is, of the characteristics which enable us to submit a hypothesis to tests or experimental controls. Ultimately, the criterion of 'truth', will be replaced by the criterion of *falsifiability*.

Science, by nature, is therefore quite revisable and contingent. It gives only *negative certitudes*: it is as if it is sculpted in relief. A *fact* is an isolated occurrence, an 'event'. A law is not a fact — even if it 'becomes' one in current language: when we say, for example, that thermal expansion is 'one of the fundamental facts of physics'. Likewise, the function of research is not to establish an impossible 'truth', but, more simply, *to eliminate error*. As for scientific discovery, it can be considered as 'a refutation ... of the theory which excluded its possibility or occurrence'.

Jacques Monod summarises: '*Conjecture and refutation*, according to Popper, play the same logical role (as information source) in the enrichment of knowledge as *mutation* and *selection* respectively play in the evolution of the living world.

As Professor Pierre Dubois, Professor at Nanterre, reminds us, Karl R. Popper assigns to philosophy a well-defined object, which is the 'study of scientific methods'. In effect, he does not believe that there is a 'purely philosophical' question: nothing is immune to the demands of rigorous thought. But he does not deny speculation.

For as Jacques Monod reminds us, 'this is only the case because at the base of epistemology, a normative discipline, there must be a choice of *values*, an ethic'.

*

La logique de la découverte scientifique, a study by Karl R. Popper. Payot, 480 pages.[318]
Les fondements philosophiques de la physique, a study by Rudolf Carnap. Armand Colin, 285 pages.[319]
Langage et métaphysique dans la philosophie anglaise contemporaine, a study by Pierre Dubois. Klincksieck, 180 pages.[320]
Eléments d'épistemologie, a study by Car G. Hempel, Armand Colin, 184 pages.[321]

*

Leszek Kolakowsky, a Polish Marxist philosopher and Professor at Oxford, has published a study on *La philosophie positiviste* (Denoël, 1976),[322] in which he presents positivism as an antiphilosophy. For a more constructive approach, we will refer to the special issue on logical empiricism published by the journal *Nouvelle école* (Nr. 13, autumn–winter 1970), with articles by Louis Rougier, Philippe Devaux, and Alain de Benoist.

The journal *Erkenntnis*, one of the principal organs of the Vienna Circle, was republished in the Netherlands by D. Reidel (P.O. Box 17, Dordrecht). The same publisher also released a *Vienna Circle Collection* under the direction of Robert S. Cohen (Boston), Brian McGuinness (Oxford), and Henk L. Mulder (Amsterdam), in which the works of Otto Neurath (*Empiricism and Sociology*, 1973), Hans Reichenbach (*People, Politics, and Probability*, 1973),

---

318 German: *Logik der Forschung. Zur Erkenntnistheorie der modernen Naturwissenschaft*, published in English as *The Logic of Scientific Discovery*. — Tr.

319 *The Philosophical Foundations of Physics*. — Tr.

320 *Language and Metaphysics in Contemporary English Philosophy*. — Tr.

321 *Elements of Epistemology*. — Tr.

322 *Positivist Philosophy*. — Tr.

Ludwig Boltzmann (*Theoretical Physics and Philosophical Problems*, 1973), Rudolf Carnap (*Selected Essays*, 1974), Moritz Schlick (*Philosophical Papers*, 1975), Victor Kraft (*Foundations of a Scientific Value Theory, 1976*), Ernst Mach (*Knowledge and Error*, 1976), have appeared. A similar collection, the *Library of Exact Philosophy*, is in the course of publication by Springer-Verlag (Vienna-New York), under the direction of Professor Mario Bunge of Montréal. Herein we find studies by Lothar Krauth (*Die Philosophie Carnaps*, 1970), Victor Kraft (*Mathematik, Logik und Erfahrung*, 1970), Nicholas Rescher and Alasdair Urquhart (*Temporal Logic*, 1971), Richard von Mises (*Wahrscheinlichkeit, Statistik und Wahrheit*, 1972), Rudolf Carnap (*Bedeutung und Notwendigkeit*, 1972), Herbert Stachowiak, Joseph Horovitz, and so on.[323]

THE THREE MATTERS

'Energy, by virtue of its nature and its constitution, includes properties for the potentialisation and actualisation of its antagonistic dynamisms, each of them actualising themselves while potentialising the others'.

For any reader familiar with the work of Stéphane Lupasco, a physicist of Romanian origin and former researcher at CNRS, this sentence sounds like the synopsis of a theory.

Due to the apparent complexity, the layperson may admittedly become confused and feel like giving up. But this would be a mistake.

Since the beginning of the century, we have witnessed a sort of 'divorce between experience and human understanding'. The cause: microphysical experience obliges us to consider as real 'events' which, from the point of view of traditional logic, are 'impossible'.

This traditional logic is that of Aristotle. We know that it is based on the principles of identity, non-contradiction, and excluded middles. This means that a thing cannot be something other than what it is, that it cannot be in two different locations at the same time, and so on.

Now, following Einstein, physicists have shown that matter, in the final analysis, is identical with energy. The neutron, the electron, the atom, the molecule are 'energetic events'. The cosmos is made up of encompassing and overlapping sequences of systems within systems and structures within structures that destroy each other and mutually engender each other by constant transformations. In short, the universe is essentially *dynamic*. It is therefore 'incomprehensible' from the perspective of traditional logic, which is a *static*

---

323 *Carnap's Philosophy* (Krauth); *Mathematics, Logic, and Experience* (Kraft); *Probability, Statistics, and Truth* (von Mises); *Meaning and Necessity*, (Carnap). — Tr.

logic. In articulating his 'quantum' theory in 1900, Max Planck (1858–1947) demonstrated that radiant energy exists only in the form of tiny grains, the quanta, whose 'nature' is particularly disconcerting. The quantum can be regarded equally as a *wave* or a *corpuscle*, that is to say as an undulatory frequency, necessarily continuous, and at the same time, as a finite, necessarily discontinuous arithmetic quantity. For classical logic, this is a contradiction.

Now in microphysics, this kind of contradiction is not only possible, it is the rule; every quantum contains the potentiality of its transformation into a pair of electrons (drawn to orbit the nucleus of an atom by virtue of Coulomb's laws of electrostatic attraction).

Appearance of Diversity

After Planck, the physicist Wolfgang Pauli (1900–1958) made a number of observations which Lupasco has condensed into three principal laws:

1.   *The law of antagonism.* The principle indispensable to the formation of any system is a principle of antagonism: no atoms exist without simultaneous attraction and repulsion. The universe is a vast, tragic *conflict*: 'Everything within energy is a system by virtue of its constituting antagonism' (Lupasco).

2.   *The law of a contradiction that is constitutive of the homogenisation and heterogenisation of energy.* Electrons gravitate around the nucleus of the atom. Crucially, however, they do not all gravitate in *the same* orbit. Why? Because they are in accordance with Pauli's principle of quantum exclusion. 'The electrons', writes Lupasco, 'possess the property, which is quite disconcerting if one holds to the rules of classical logic, of excluding one another from the quantum state that they occupy'. This principle of exclusion is essential because it engenders an individualising diversification of energy, that is to say a *heterogenisation*: it explains the appearance of *diversity.*

'From the molecule', Lupasco adds, 'all systems therefore contain, by their very formation, the antagonistic competition of the two principles of homogenisation and heterogenisation'. This means that the more energy a system contains, the more *heterogeneous* and *differentiated* it is.

3.   *The law of the potentialisation and actualisation of each antagonistic dynamism.* By this it must be understood that for every dynamism, the

actualisation of a term (element) brings about by correlation the *potentialisation* of another term (anti-element).

The Law of Increasing Inequality

From these laws, Stéphane Lupasco draws many conclusions. The most important one takes into consideration the fact that, depending on whether the homogeneous or the heterogeneous will predominate within a system, we will see the development of structures (or more precisely the 'chains of structuring systematisation') of a different nature.

Three 'matters' can thus be identified:

1. *Physical matter.* (The only one that man has known and 'imagined' until recently). This is the matter of the *macrophysical* systems, i.e. of the world which surrounds us every day. Here *homogenisation* predominates, becoming actualised at the expense of heterogenisation (which is potentiated to the same degree as homogenization is actualised).

Physical systems obey the second principle of thermodynamics, articulated by Clausius, the principle of increasing positive entropy, that is to say, of the progressive degradation of energy. More and more accentuated, their homogenisation ends up destroying them.

2. *Living matter.* This is the matter of *biological* systems. It differs from the physical matter starting from the molecule. In this type of system, it is *heterogenisation* which dominates. As long as it is alive, an organism resists the 'entropic fatality'. More precisely, it 'inverts the classical entropic current by a negative entropy which has been aptly named negentropy'. Heterogenisation persists in it and acts as the theatre of perpetual *becoming* that keeps it alive.

'Accordingly', says Lupasco, 'biological death can be equated to a return to the physical system'. The living being is thus confounded, even in its most intimate structure, with the differentiated, the individualized, and consequently, the unequal. Every organism is characterised by its *personality*, which distinguishes it from all others, and (by virtue of the law of antagonism) by its *aggressiveness*, which allows it to place itself in opposition'. 'Histocompatibility antigens mark each of us with a personal seal', remarked Professor Jean Hamburger in 1973. It is only when they can no longer evolve, when they are no longer the locus of any *becoming*, that individuals or species, by 'materialis-ing', become homogeneous and 'equal': the final stage before *death*.

'Life', says Stéphane Lupasco, 'is nothing but *inequality* — a growing or increasing inequality'.

3.   *Microphysical matter.* This kind of matter defines energetic sys-tems in which the two contradictory principles (homogenisation and heterogenisation) are closely associated in a balancing antagonism (an 'equilibrating-antagonism').

In the atomic world, this type of system corresponds to the nucleus. The energies combine with such an antagonistic intensity that they can only be disintegrated in the laboratory by powerful bombardments. 'Curiously', notes Lupasco, 'this type of matter is found in the development of the *neuro-psycho-logical* system, particularly in man'.

Indeed one of the characteristics of man consists in the considerable devel-opment of his central nervous system, whose nervous substance attains such complexity that it allows *reflexive consciousness* (consciousness 'understands' itself). Now it certainly seems that, in this central system, as in the nucleus of the atom, the tendencies toward homogenisation and heterogenisation are also associated within an energetic systematisation differing from both the physical and biological systems. The mind of man is a *universe* unto itself.

It is this thesis which Lupasco develops in his essay on *L'énergie et matière psychique*.[324]

In the ordinary man, the two tendencies would be *simultaneously* potenti-ated and actualised in a perpetual tension forming the driving force of the mental life.

Taking the opposite view to most fashionable theories, Lupasco declares that 'it is not psychological contradiction and conflict that engenders mental illness, but, conversely, that the mentally ill suffer from a conflictual deficit, a lack of contradictions'. Psychoses and neuroses, for example, would be charac-terised 'by a paralysing hypertrophy of the non-contradiction which isolates the subject from the object and influences the dialectical mechanisms of the related systems of representation and of locomotion'.

---

324 *Energy and Psychological Matter.* — Tr.

A 'Dialectic of Death'

Also corresponding to the three matters are three cybernetics, the universe containing not one but three dialectics which are distinguished by the predominance within a given system of one or another kind of matter.

Every 'event' thus becomes *tripolar* at the same time as it induces a general tri-dialectic logic. The dialectics of life, which place the accent on energetic differentiation and therefore on increasing inequality, are opposed by the dialectics of physical systems, which place the accent on homogeneity.

'In essence', says Stephane Lupasco, 'the Marxist dialectic is a dialectic of death. Its approach is one of "materialisation" of society, which involves the gradual dissipation of its energy, its weakening, and ultimately its disappearance'.

It is therefore understandable why classical logic proves fruitful for analysing and describing physical systems: it operates in a domain where homogeneity and non-contradiction rule. 'The same is not true of biological phenomena. Here, it is an inverse logic, the antagonistic logic of the heterogeneous, that constitutes their energetic driving force'. This is what has probably been misunderstood by certain theorists of modern biology: as long as they remain within the bounds of classical logic, which is inadequate to their discipline, their science will not be able to escape its own limitations — and they will remain locked in the old alternative of 'mechanism' and 'teleology'.

The Secret Crisis of Our Old Understanding

Since 1935, the publication date of a thesis entitled *Du devenir logique et de l'affectivité* (republished by Vrin in 1973),[325] Lupasco has developed an entire tripartite 'cosmology' whose principal steps were: *L'expérience microphysique et la pensée humaine* (PUF, 1941),[326] *Le Principe d'antagonisme et la logique de l'énergie* (Hermann, 1951),[327] *Les trois matières* (Julliard, 1960),[328] *La tragédie de l'univers* (Casterman, 1969),[329] and so on.

---

325 *On Logical Becoming and Affectivity.* — Tr.
326 *Microphysical Experiment and Human Thought* — Tr.
327 *The Principle of Antagonism and the Logic of Energy.* — Tr.
328 *The Three Matters.* — Tr.
329 *The Tragedy of the Universe.* — Tr.

Figures as diverse as author Vintila Horia, scholar René Huyghe, painter Georges Matthieu, sociologist Edgar Morin, Professor Ernest Kahane, former president of the Rationalist Union, Eugène Ionesco, and others, have shown a great interest in these theses.

In Great Britain, George Melhuish published a study on *The Paradoxical Nature of Reality* which owes much to them.

An International Center for Research on the Logic of Antagonism[330] was formed in November 1973. It is chaired by Marc Beigbeder, head of the 'Lupascian' school and author of *Contradiction et nouvel entendement* (Bordas, 1972).[331]

'It is the resistance to the triple aspect of reality', asserts Lupasco, 'which via the secret crisis of our old understanding, provokes this general confusion and the intellectual malaise characteristic of our time'.

*

L'énergie et la matière psychique, et *L'énergie et la matière vivante*, studies by Stéphane Lupasco, Julliard, 327 and 356 pages.[332]
The Paradoxical Nature of Reality, a study by George Melhuish. St. Vincent's Press (St. Vincent's Priory, Sion Hill, Bristol), 196 pages.

*

On the work of Stéphane Lupasco, cf. the special number of the journal *La Tour de feu* (Nr. 85, March 1965): *Être et ne pas être avec Lupasco*;[333] and the text by Alain de Benoist, published by the review of the *Club français de la médaille* (Nr. 53, 2ème semestre 1976), on the occasion of the issuing of a coin (thanks to James Guitet) by the Currency Administration with the effigy of Lupasco. This text is accompanied by an article by Stéphane Lupasco on the *Trois orthodéductions qui se disputant le monde*.[334]

Centre international de recherches sur les logiques de l'antagonisme (CIRLA): 95 avenue Denfert-Rochereau, 75014 Paris.

CYBERNETICS AND ITS THEORETICIANS

In Stanley Kubrick's film, *2001, A Space Odyssey*, a robot that does not support the idea of being 'disconnected' becomes a murderer, thus violating the first of the 'laws of robotics' set out in 1941 by the novelist Asimov. In the film by

---

330 Centre international de recherches sur les logiques de l'antagonisme (CIRLA).

331 *Contradiction and New Understanding.* — Tr.

332 *Energy and Psychological Matter*, and *Energy and Living Matter.* — Tr.

333 *The Tower of Fire: Being and Non-being with Lupasco.* — Tr.

334 *Three Ortho-deductions which are Disputed by the World.* — Tr.

Joseph Sargent, *Colossus, the Forbin Project*,[335] a supercomputer methodically attempts to conquer the world.

From the point of view of cybernetics, this kind of situation is the very model of a false problem.

Norbert Wiener defines cybernetics as the 'science of information'; Ashby, as the 'rational science of machines'; Couffignal, as the 'art of the efficiency of action'.

A relatively recent discipline, cybernetics is therefore a threshold-science. Pertaining to both machines and living beings, it does not seek to realise a 'synthesis', but rather a comparative study: to see how far we can make machines and life coincide. In practice, it mainly deals with automatic mechanisms and neurophysiology.

Its 'inventor', Norbert Wiener (1894–1963), was a kind of Mozart of science. He learned to read at eighteen months, completed his bachelor's degree at fourteen, defended his doctoral thesis at eighteen. A former student of Bertrand Russell and David Hilbert, he was a professor of mathematics at the Massachusetts Institute of Technology (MIT). In 1948, he published a book entitled *Cybernetics: Or Control and Communication in the Animal and the Machine*. Four years later a new study appeared, this time aimed at the general public: *The Human Use of Human Beings*.[336] (There would be a second, revised edition in 1962, and a third edition including different variations in 1971, through Collection 10/18).

In these two books Wiener proposes an introduction to the 'human use of living beings'. More precisely, he attempts to determine what living organisms can teach us about the nature and possibilities of future machines.

'It is my thesis', he writes, 'that the physical functioning of the living individual and the operation of some of the newer communication machines are precisely parallel in their analogous attempts to control entropy through *feedback*'.[337]

---

335 Released in French as *Le cerveau d'acier* (The Steel Brain). — Tr.

336 Benoist is referring to the French translation which appeared in 1952: *Cybernétique et Société*; the English original appeared in 1950, two years after the previous book. — Tr.

337 Correcting *centaines* (hundreds) in the French citation for *certaines* (certain, some), per the original English edition. — Tr.

The word 'cybernetics' (which is found in Ampère in 1834) designates in Greek the art of conducting men in society, of 'piloting' them. It was chosen intentionally. Indeed for Wiener, the function of a ship's pilot is quite similar to the action of the regulatory organs of a mechanism.

'Between the captain, who says where the ship must go', he explains, 'and the steersman who maneuvers the helm, there is always an intermediary: the *pilot*, who chooses the route according to the orders received, and determines the best course to follow.'

Similarly, in a steam engine, the centrifugal governor controls the steam flow so that the velocity remains constant.

In the human body, it is the cerebellum which receives *information* from the brain and the nerves. It then determines the orders to be sent to the muscles, so that the movements they perform may be accomplished without affecting the equilibrium of the body. Thanks to the cerebellum, a true, built-in 'autopilot', we can hold an egg without breaking it, pick up something from the ground without falling, and so on.

The ship's pilot, the centrifugal governor, the cerebellum, and so on, are *cybernetic* organs which act by feedback. We do not tell them what to do, but what we want to happen. It is then up to them to 'perform'.

The Notion of Feedback

Whenever the 'autopilot' in the organism corrects the harmful effects of the variations of the external environment, whenever, in a mechanical system, the 'pilot' 'opposes' the tendency of the machine to deviate from the plan which should be its own, it is said that there is *retroaction*. Or, to use the language of the cyberneticians, there is *feedback*: the *effect* (the energy of the 'exit') acts 'retrospectively' on the *cause* (the energy of the 'entry').

Thanks to the notion of feedback, cybernetics accounts for innumerable phenomena interacting in time. Thus, Vito Volterra, the creator of functional analysis, has studied the 'oscillating balances' characteristic of predation phenomena: in the Canadian North, foxes feed almost exclusively on rabbits. The rabbits, for their part, are scarcely pursued except by foxes. Under these conditions, if the foxes eat too many rabbits, their food reserves decline excessively. Therefore the fox species declines. At the same time, the rabbit population, enjoying a renewed security, proliferates. In so doing, it automatically remedies the scarcity of foxes. And they multiply again, which puts the rabbits at risk. An 'oscillating equilibrium' is thus established by virtue of the feedback between the population of hunters and the population of the hunted.

In cosmology, the study of the processes of star formation reveals that, beyond a certain threshold, the mass and the density of the stellar sun ends up 'stabilizing'. 'This stability', explains Professor Louis Rougier, 'results from the cybernetic equilibrium between the thermonuclear energy (energy input) and the flux of energy lost to radiation (energy output)' (*Thermodynamique, cybernétique et évolution du cosmos*, in *Revue générale des sciences*, n° 5–6/1965).[338]

In economics, the same notion of feedback explains the interaction of supply and demand, prices and wages, liabilities and receivables, as well as cessations in expansion, reversals of trends, or the way in which a capital feeds upon its interest.

Need, for example, is a negative feedback that acts retrospectively upon its cause: the scarcity of products. It leads to an increase in demand, which, once satisfied, diminishes the need, and reverses the trend. We are thus witnessing the birth of a new cycle.

For the Ancients, economic equilibrium seemed 'miraculous'. The physiocrats celebrated it in dithyrambic language, as a providential order willed by God for the happiness of men. 'In view of this harmony', writes Bastiat in *Les harmonies économiques*, 'the economist may well exclaim, like the astronomer or physiologist: *Digitus Dei est hic!* (Here is the finger of God!)'. 'Today', writes Professor Rougier, 'we know that no providential order, no theological finalism, presides over these economic harmonies which so enchanted Bastiat. The secret agent of adapting supply to solvent demand is a cybernetic mechanism, the mechanism of price, which relies on feedback that subjects the formation of price in a free market to the decisions of the buyers and sellers'.

We still find the notion of feedback in the life of societies. Politically, a force, when it is in opposition, benefits from the deterioration of power that the regime in place undergoes. But, if it succeeds to this regime, it creates, by the very fact of its success, the conditions under which a new opposition will appear and develop at its expense. (It is therefore no exaggeration to say that one begins to lose power the day that one attains it).

---

338 *Thermodynamics, Cybernetics, and the Evolution of the Cosmos*, in *General Review of Sciences*. — Tr.

Most of the larger processes of interaction, alternation, 'oscillation', and so on, thus seem to be linked to 'cybernetic' movements. This may be the reason why history seems 'cyclical' or 'discontinuous', rather than unilinear.

Physiological Regulations

In his book on the history of cybernetics, Léon J. Delpech, president of the French Society of Cybernetics, Professor at the Sorbonne, cites the names of the great ancestors of cybernetics: Raymond Lulle, Leonardo da Vinci, Mersenne, Descartes (*Traité de l'homme*, 1635),[339] Leibniz, Vaucanson, and above all, Claude Bernard.

'The name of Claude Bernard', writes Delpech, 'ought to be placed on the same rank as the greatest in the history of science: Archimedes, Newton, or Einstein. But it took almost a century for the true significance of his work to be understood'.

Claude Bernard (1813–1878), a theoretician of experimental medicine, was the first to bring to light the importance of 'physiological regulation': thanks to *regulating* organs (lungs, liver, kidneys, digestive organs) the 'internal environments', that is to say, the set of physiological conditions for a given organism, are kept *constant*. In this way, the organism of man and other warm-blooded animals retains a certain independence from the variations of the external environment. And it is these cybernetic mechanisms that give physiology its unity.

'As varied as they are', writes Claude Bernard, 'all acts have but one aim: to maintain the conditions of life in the interior'.

When there is an external variation, the 'pilot' of the organism immediately brings the necessary 'corrections' to maintain internal temperature, blood pressure, hormonal regulation, oxygen regulation in the blood, and so on.

'If we move from a hot room to a cold room, notes Professor Rougier, the drop detected by our nervous system triggers an immediate correction; for example, it accelerates the respiration, which activates combustion, which has the retroactive effect of causing an increase in the internal temperature: or else the thermal control center triggers a corrective effect, a shiver. The shiver, like the increase in breathing, releases a surplus of heat which raises the temperature of the body to its normal level.

---

339 *Treatise on Man.* — Tr.

In the twentieth century, Charles Henry (1859–1926), director of the laboratory for the psychology of the senses at the Sorbonne, attempted to translate psychological and biological facts into the language of mathematics.

'I will only be understood in fifty years', he said.

Finally, in 1948, the English psychiatrist Gray Walther, a specialist in conditioned reflexes, succeeded in building small *synthetic animals*: 'electronic tortoises'. He obtained surprising results with them.

These 'tortoises' had two sensory organs: an organ of sight (photoelectric cell) and an organ of touch (electrical contact). It moves itself on motorised wheels. The cell, incorporated in the 'head', scanned the horizon while turning the steering wheel, looking for light rays. The electrical contact closed whenever the shell struck an obstacle.

With only these elements of 'assessment', the turtles already offered an impressive variety of behaviours: prospecting for light sources, discernment, stability, seeking optimal conditions for 'activity', and so on. They could even 'recognize' themselves in a mirror. 'This', notes Delpech, 'allowed them to distinguish between effective and ineffective behaviours. For example, they could circumvent obstacles blocking their path towards a light source — whereas butterflies, unequipped with this ability, will fly a whole day against a windowpane next to an open door'.

By adding to the 'system' an organ for hearing (microphone), Walther also succeeded in mechanising the processes of learning and memorisation. For the first time in history, machines have been endowed with the power to learn.

'We can then conceive of some experiments of the following nature: (1) we whistle and nothing happens; (2) we whistle and show a light: the turtle comes. This operation is repeated a certain number of times; (3) we whistle without showing the light: the turtle still comes. It has learned that a whistle means the likely presentation of light. But if one 'teases' the animal by making it come 'for nothing', memorisation acts negatively, and the call can be repeated: the animal no longer comes'.

Such behaviours involve only two elements, which correspond to seven 'mental experiences'. But the system can be improved.

'We can imagine', continues Delpech, 'how to give turtles language, and to provoke the appearance of various feelings in them (joy, sadness, generosity), or at the very least the external signs that relate to these feelings. Nothing would oppose the construction of turtles with artistic tastes, which would be sensitive to the harmony of sounds, lines, or colors. Nothing would prevent the mechanisation, in the same way that life does, of the processes of growth and death, etc. It is only the difficulties of practical realisation that limit the field of possible achievements, and rarely questions of principle'.

The human brain, however, contains some ten billion 'elements' (that is, nerve cells or neurons), each of which can have up to 10,000 different connections! The number of mental experiences and behaviors that can be furnished by such a system exceeds our understanding. Especially since 'the calculation produces this astounding observation: that ten elements alone would suffice to furnish to the whole of humanity, at the rate of twelve per second for each individual, different mental experiences during an extent of time figuring in the billions of years!'

In contemporary times, Pierre de Latil, Nicolas Schöffer, Stéphane Lupasco, Henri Laborit, and Raymond Ruyer have all been interested in cybernetics.

Authors and Great Doctrines

Numerous *models* of cybernetics have been conceived (that is to say, artificial mechanisms bearing certain analogies with real mechanisms, with the aim of developing others), as well as applications of cybernetics to pedagogy (Louis Couffignal, *Les machines à penser*, 1951), psychology (Abraham Moles, *Sociodynamique de la culture*, 1967), anthropology (P. Vendryès, *Déterminisme et autonomie*, 1956), biology (E. Huant, *Biologie et cybernétique*, 1954), economics, sociology, and so on.

Léon J. Delpech reviews these authors, whose names are sometimes ignored by the general public.

E. Huant, whose work is particularly interesting, has brought new light on the fundamental regulations among living beings. 'One of them', says Professor Delpech, 'results from genetic opportunities for the emergence of particular values of thought, provided that they can develop in a sufficiently evolved environment: it is the regulation of biological aristocratism, concomitant with the reception of the environment'. This regulation 'is the great opportunity that exists in the social environment to escape the entropic leveling. It therefore obliges man to constantly ensure sufficient *differentiation*, a sufficiently receptive and diversifying character for the biosocial environment'.

Previously, Delpech had already remarked: 'Human equality is a recent ideology (two centuries), founded on resentment, as Schiller has clearly shown. And all those who, like myself, have examined several thousand subjects, either biologically or medically, do not believe in it' (cited by Aurel David, *La cybernetique et l'humain*, Gallimard, 1965).

In a second work, yet to be published, Delpech will examine other cybernetic 'doctrines', including a particularly original one by Stéphane Lupasco.

In cybernetics, *information* occupies an essential place, in contrast to the other sciences, where this role generally comes back to energy. Yet, as Raymond Ruyer writes, 'there is never more information in the brain's output than in its input' (*La cybernétique et l'origine d'information*. Flammarion, 1954). Also it is not the 'gross' volume that counts most, but rather the way in which the information is *processed*, and then restored.

The machine, in this respect, far exceeds man, but it remains to be seen how far this machine (the artificial 'brain', the robot) will be able to imitate man and replace him.

Man in Equation?

Some cyberneticians seem to feed excessive expectations in this regard. Even by mechanising in the highest degree the phenomena of regulation and the behavioural-reflexes, and by taking account of the most statistically random elements, it is strongly doubtful whether a machine can ever reproduce on a strictly non-organic basis all the specific functions of living systems.

Nageotte said that 'the living being is a machine one of whose functions is to increase the machine' (*L'organisation de la matière par la vie*).[340]

Pierre Auger adds: 'We can easily imagine machine tools that could build similar machines by using the necessary potential for order (raw materials, energy). But here is where an insurmountable frontier appears: when we must recognise that the descendants of one of our living beings are not alike, but *identical*, while our machines along with their manufactured children, must inevitably degrade little by little without remedy. The machine can only reproduce a machine conforming to the plan, to the 'blueprint', that it contains, and as this is gradually altered, undergoing the common law of the masses

---

340 Usually given as: *L'organisation de la matière dans ses rapports avec la vie* (1922) (The Organisation of Matter in its Relationships with Life). — Tr.

of material subjected to statistics, they will alter themselves. In other words, the sons of our machines will necessarily be less perfect, no matter how little the amount. After a few generations, this drift towards disorder will render their functioning impossible and the lineage will die' (*L'homme microscopique*. Flammarion, 1951 and 1966).[341]

Pierre de Laid, who had planned to write a book called *L'homme en équation*,[342] in the end abandoned it. Professor Delpech, moreover, does not disguise the fact that, in many fields, Cybernetics appears 'without sail or compass'. This is the case in the field of reflexive consciousness: a machine can never *justify* in a *critical* way the principles which make it exist. 'It cannot, because it has no hypercritical knowledge of truth'. This is also the case in the domain of affective life, of aesthetic and moral judgments: a machine simulates feelings, but does not *experience* them. 'The work of art', notes Delpech, 'expresses itself in an affective conduct or behaviour of which it is the symbol, but it does not define itself'.

Whatever its *power*, the machine can never *will*. Only man, when he has created, can explain his creation by his *motivations*. To be the only one to define values, to observe an ethic, he is also the only one to manifest a will and to put the world in *form* according to his desire.

*

Cybernétique et ses théoriticiens, a study by Leon J. Delpech.[343] Casterman, 140 pages.

*

In *The Thinking Computer. Mind Inside Matter* (W. H. Freeman Co., San Francisco, 1976), Bertram Raphael addresses the problems of cybernetics from the perspective of artificial intelligence (the possibility for machines to recognise shapes, understand natural languages, solve problems, etc.). Unfortunately, he treats the problem without any critical distance, and is often content to express his faith in the beneficent virtues of the computer. Such an attitude has provoked criticism, sometimes fundamental, to which the laboratories have been sensitive. See, for example, the studies by H. Dreyfus (*What Computers Can't Do: A Critique of Artificial Reason*) and J. Weizenbaum (*Computer Power and Human Reason*, W. H. Freeman Co., San Francisco, 1975), which are currently provoking interesting debates among specialists.

---

341 *Microscopic Man.* — Tr.

342 *Man in Equation.* — Tr.

343 *Cybernetics and its Theorists.* — Tr.

Biological

CHANCE AND NECESSITY

*L*e hazard et la nécessité,[344] by Jacques Monod sold more than 150,000 copies. In 1965, Monod received the Nobel Prize in Medicine and Physiology, together with André Lwoff and François Jacob. Since then, Lwoff has published *L'ordre biologique* (Laffont),[345] and Jacob, *La logique du vivant* (Gallimard).[346] These two titles were also a success. This is a new occurrence.

Jacques Monod: thin lips, fine and sleek hands, the cold elegance of the clinician. He was a professor at the Collège de France where François Jacob also teaches. André Lwoff, 74, holds the Chair of Microbiology in the Faculty of Sciences in Paris. All three worked at the Institute Pasteur, where Monod led the cellular biochemistry department, Jacob the microbial genetics department, and Lwoff, since 1938, the microbial physiology department. Their Nobel Prize revealed the importance of the French School of Molecular Biology. He also brought this knowledge to the general public.

'Biology is really the science of the second half of the twentieth century', wrote the mathematician Lichnerowitz, a professor at the Collège de France and a directing member of CNRS. Publishers are not mistaken. The 'Science nouvelle' collection at Laffont began by publishing a bestseller called *The Double Helix*.[347] The author, James D. Watson, recounted, not without humor, how he discovered in 1953, with Rosalind Franklin and Francis Crick, the secret of the structures of DNA (deoxyribonucleic acid), which allowed the genetic code to be deciphered. After this there was *Molecular Biology of the Gene*,[348] also by Watson; *La genèse du vivant* (Masson),[349] by Albert Vandel;

344 English translation: *Chance and Necessity: Essay on the Natural Philosophy of Modern Biology* (New York: Alfred A. Knopf, 1971). — Tr.

345 English edition: *Biological Order* (Cambridge, MIT Press, 1962). — Tr.

346 English edition: *The Logic of Life: A History of Heredity* (New York: Vintage, 1976). — Tr.

347 I.e. the French edition: *La double hélice*. — Tr.

348 French edition: *Biologie moléculaire du gène* (Ediscience). — Tr.

349 *The Genesis of Life*. — Tr.

La révolution biologique (Laffont),[350] by Gordon Rattray Taylor, and so on. The movement was launched.

In *Chance and Necessity*, Jacques Monod not only speaks of biology. He intends to draw lessons in the order of religion and ideology. The subtitle of his book is 'Essay on the Natural Philosophy of Modern Biology'.

'Modesty', he says, 'befits the scholar, but not the ideas which inhabit him, and which he is obliged to defend'.

Immutable and Changing Systems

Chance and necessity develops a number of theses set forth by the author in November 1967, during his inaugural lecture at the Collège de France, which he already had occasion to summarise during a conference tour in the United States, as well as in interviews published by magazines such as *Raison présente* and *Atomes*. These theses are presented as a dissertation on the great 'paradox of living systems': the fact that these systems are both *immutable* and perpetually *changing*.

Immutable, because they are the theatre of phenomena that are indefinitely identical to themselves. Perpetually *changing*, because unforeseen events occur, which modify the course of things.

In the living world, reproduction is the principal operator. For the geneticist, the living being represents the execution of a program inscribed in its heredity. However, within this regular weave, unpredictable variations occur: *mutations*. On the evolutionary scale, these mutations allow the emergence of new species and branchings. But on the scale of individual life, they are almost always harmful.

'The mutation', says the biologist Jean Rostand, 'is, in sum, comparable to a slip of the tongue, a typo, a printer's error, which is obviously much more likely to spoil a beautiful text than improve it'.

Mutations occur at random, while heredity obeys laws. To these two properties, *chance* and *necessity*, which are defining characteristics of life, Monod gives more scholarly names: emergence and teleonomy. *Emergence* is 'the property of reproducing and multiplying highly complex ordered structures, and of allowing the evolutionary creation of structures of increasing complexity'. *Teleonomy* has a meaning close to 'purpose' or 'finality': 'Everything

---

350 *The Biological Revolution.* — Tr.

happens as if living beings were structured, organised, and conditioned for an end: the survival of the individual, but especially that of the species'.

In short, as the Greek philosopher Democritus (5th century BCE) had anticipated: 'Everything that exists in the universe is the fruit of chance and necessity'.

Monod classifies the great explanatory theories of living systems into two groups, according to whether they assert that teleonomy ensures and directs emergence or, to the contrary, that emergence precedes teleonomy.

In the first group are found the vitalist theories (generally abandoned today, which involve a mysterious 'vital force' specific to living matter), as well as causal explanations of a metaphysical or 'animistic' nature, from the physics of Aristotle to the biology of Teilhard de Chardin. Curiously, Monod asserts that it is also to this 'ideological family' that historical materialism is connected. Quoting Engels (*Dialectics of Nature*)[351] and Karl Marx, he attempts to demonstrate that Marxism is but one of the contemporary forms of 'universal animism'. An *idealism* all the more dangerous because it glorifies its 'objectivity'.

Monod reminds us that Engels rejected the second principle of thermodynamics and the selective interpretation of evolution.

'Marxist societies', he writes, 'profess a materialistic religion and dialectic of history. Their system is rooted in animism, outside of objective knowledge, outside of the truth, foreign and ultimately hostile to the science they want to use, but do not respect and serve'.

He adds: 'Even more than other animisms, historical materialism rests on a total confusion of the categories of value and knowledge. It is this conclusion which enables him, in a profoundly inauthentic discourse, to proclaim that he has 'scientifically' established the laws of history, to which man would have no other recourse and no other duty than obedience if he does not wish to enter into nothingness'. He concludes: 'Let us renounce this once and for all as an illusion, which is only puerile when it is not fatal'.

The 'Biological Order'

The second type of explanation: emergence precedes teleonomy. In other words: the structure of DNA varies as a result of fortuitous events (chance),

---

351 German: *Dialektik der Natur*, French: *La dialectique de la nature*. — Tr.

but once these variations are inscribed by nature, they propagate according to inflexible laws (necessity).

This conception has been imposed by Darwin. The decipherment of the genetic code, by allowing us to identify the physical support of emergence and to establish its structure, provides confirmation of this. 'It appears to us today', writes Monod, 'as the only rational, the only possible one'.

There is thus a 'biological order', but this order does not reflect any predetermined intention. Evolution indeed has a meaning, and yet there is no reason to abandon the basic postulate of the scientific world, according to which 'nature is objective'. Jacques Monod makes a comparison: 'In an automobile, the power of the engine is necessarily related to the transmission ratios in the gearbox. The car will only operate if there is a consequential modification in the power of the engine. And any mutation acting in one direction, at a certain level, can only be positively selected if it is mitigated by another mutation acting on another level. We will therefore see the automobiles evolve with a fairly constant ratio between their gearbox and the power of the engine. And we will say it is admirable, it is orthogenetic. In fact, it is controlled by the very structure of the system.

'Today', adds Jacques Monod, 'the physical support of emergence is identified, its structure established, and this structure accounts for its function'.

But can we consider as resolved the problem that philosophers and scholars have always clashed over: what is life?

According to some researchers, there is no fundamental difference between physical systems and living systems. There is only matter, more or less complexified, more or less differentiated according to the localities of space-time. Ultimately, they say, the question of the 'nature of life' is devoid of meaning. 'Life, as such, does not exist', says biologist Szent-Györgi. No one has ever seen it. The name of life has no meaning, for no such thing exists'.

According to other scholars, there is, on the contrary, a radical difference between the two great kinds of systems contained in the universe. Some 'revolutionary' characteristics make their appearance in the living cell. This is the problem of resistance to entropy.

The 'Counter-Selection'

Since Clausius, we know that matter is doomed to entropy, that is to say, to a progressive degradation of energy (second principle of thermodynamics). Now, as Stéphane Lupasco has written, 'starting from the molecule, certain atomic systems evolve towards a progressive homogeneity. Others differentiate themselves more and more. The first are *physical* systems. It is to these that the second principle of thermodynamics is applied, or the principle of entropy, as articulated by Clausius. The latter are *living* systems.

'The higher one climbs in the order of multi-cellular organisms', adds Lupasco, 'the greater the differentiation. It may well be said, therefore, that living matter possesses an anti-Clausius principle. Life is but increasing inequality'.

There is, however, an entropy that threatens evolved species: it is the peril of genetic degradation, a true 'qualitative entropy' attributable to the fact that natural selection has disappeared.

In the past, emphasises Monod, 'tribal or racial war played a very important role as an evolutionary factor. It is quite possible that the brutal disappearance of the Neanderthal man (around 35,000 years ago) was the result of a genocide committed by *Homo sapiens*, our ancestor. This pressure for selection may have favoured the expansion of races better endowed with intelligence, imagination, will, and ambition'.

Today, writes the biologist Jean Rostand, 'medicine, surgery, hygiene, philanthropy, social assistance, have consequently enabled the survival and procreation of multitudes of people who, from the genetic point of view, are unfit and would have otherwise been eliminated or in any case excluded from reproduction. Therefore, inevitably, by the channel of heredity, it contributes to an increase in the proportion of bad genes, and to their accumulation in the hereditary legacy. Since the species is no longer cleansed of poor mutational influences, its genetic level can only be lowered. Whether we like it or not, medicine cultivates disease. There is an essential contradiction between individual well-being and the genetic good. Civilisation, soft on unfit genes, increases the biological root of harm. Genetically, we pay dearly for medical and social progress'.

Anthropologist Ernst Mayr, former director of the Museum of Comparative Zoology at Harvard University, also insists on the danger of 'counter-selection' in his book *Populations, Species, and Evolution* (Hermann, 1974).[352] In the conception proposed by Lwoff, Jacob, and Monod, life is no longer the 'opposite' of death, as the *Encyclopaedia* would have it. Death becomes a 'necessity', prescribed by the genetic program from the 'chance' of birth. It is because organisms are mortal that there is evolution, that the atoms and molecules that form living systems can 'return to the mass, or ground', thus making possible new, more evolved expressions of the protoplasm. (Death, according to Maurice Marois, founder of the Institute of Life, is the 'servant' of life).

Yet if, in *Chance and Necessity*, life holds a special place, according to Jacques Monod, it is nevertheless almost a 'miracle'. In the beginning, he asserted, the chances that life would appear on earth and take the form it did were comparable to a monkey with a typewriter producing the works of Shakespeare — or water freezing in a hot saucepan.

'The universe was not pregnant with life, nor the biosphere with man. Our number came up in the game of Monte-Carlo.[353] Is it surprising that, like the one who has just won a million dollars, we should feel the strangeness and unreality of our condition?'

These remarks on 'improbability' of life have been exploited by some of Monod's opponents. Who could be persuaded, wrote the Jesuits Pierre Leroy (*Ecclesia, Project*) and François Russo (*Etudes*), that is it 'by chance' that the human machine, in all its complexity, has finally come to see the light of day?

One may also believe that Jacques Monod sins only by excessive pessimism. Why would the human phenomenon be a unique phenomenon? Millions of solar systems exist in the universe. Is it not reasonable to think that life has appeared and developed on worlds other than our own?

A Chance for Each Type of Necessity?

We now know that organic life exists outside our planet.

A few years ago, researchers from NASA examined a meteorite that had fallen in Australia in 1969. This meteorite contained amino acids (including five of the twenty amino acids present in living cells), the extraterrestrial origin of which could be established. They were 50% dextrorotatory and 50%

---

352 French edition: *Populations, espèces, et evolution.* — Tr.

353 Monte Carlo is a card game akin to Patience or Solitaire, but also a mathematical method using randomness to generate numerical results. — Tr.

levorotatory, that is to say, half of them deflected polarised light to the right, and the other half to the left. And yet, this proportion does not correspond to the amino acids constituting the proteins that we find on Earth.

Astronomers, for their part, have identified 'clouds' in interstellar space that contain the first specific constituents of living structures: formations of polymers corresponding, in sum, to anti-Clausius zones.

Under these conditions, one may wonder if the appearance of life, far from being *chance*, does not also emerge from a form of *necessity*. In this case we would be situated, as it were, at the 'intersection' of *two* universes, one governed, *with necessity*, by the expansion of *matter* into *space*, and the other, *with equal necessity*, by the expansion of *life* in *time*. Living structures should be considered *simultaneously* in terms of *invariance* and *differentiation*. The structure of the gene would appear, like that of the quantum, as *both* identitary and heterogenising;[354] it would be relatively antagonistic and contradictory, and so the notion of 'chance' should be revised.

Referring to the logic of Lupasco, Marc Beigbeder, author of *Contradiction et nouvel entendement*[355] and a study entitled *Le contre-Monod* (Grasset, 1972),[356] writes in *Nouvelle Ecole* (Nr. 25–26, winter 1974–75): 'Instead of chance, a notion that should be placed in the plural, since there would be a type of chance corresponding to each necessity, it seems more scientific, not only for words but for their content, to speak of relational indeterminations relevant to the antagonism of *two contradictory determinisms* always coexisting, according to a quantity of variable antagonism. (And we will say that each of the necessities here is the efficient, antagonistic cause for the indetermination of the other). On the level of logic, therefore, it seems entirely possible, and even recommended, to dispense with the word as well as the notion of 'chance', especially for the genetic phenomenon considered — and we can in part attribute the grip of traditional logic on the path of Jacques Monod, however highly scientific his mind, to the mythic structure of an absolute chance-contingency'.

If man is a pure product of chance, as Jacques Monod claims, should he despair the ability to give meaning to life? If he is a phenomenon which the

---

354 Fr. *identitaire et hétérogénéisante.* — Tr.

355 *Contradiction and New Understanding.* — Tr.

356 *Against Monod.* — Tr.

evolution of life could have done without, how should he conceive his place in the universe?

Monod has not evaded this difficulty. 'It must be recognised', he said, 'that it is impossible to establish or deduce an ethic of objective knowledge, and that it is impossible to live without ethics, and so, consequently, one must be formulated *axiomatically*'.

This new ethic is the *ethic of knowledge*, the true 'asceticism of objectivity', driven by research but not confused with it. 'The sole aim, the supreme value, the "sovereign good" in the ethics of knowledge', writes Jacques Monod, 'is not, let us admit, the happiness of humanity, still less its temporal power or its comfort, or even the Socratic "know thyself"; it is objective knowledge itself'.

What is the possibility of such an ethic?

Jacques Monod readily admits that it will be difficult for all men to adopt it, and that it presupposes values of reference that are far from universal. (Most are closely linked to the rise of Western Civilisation.) At the very least, he hopes scholars will support it.

This shows a 'naïve idealism'[357] taking place in the scientific world, replied Mr. Alfred Fabre-Luce in *La Revue des deux-mondes*.[358] For as experience has proven, scientists are far from being independent of fashionable ideologies.

Following the inaugural lecture given at the Collège de France by Monod, Fabre-Luce had already noted in *Le Monde*: 'Scientists remain men, and if they obey the ethics of knowledge in their laboratories, they are frequently inspired by other values as soon as they step out of them. In 1945, one such physicist, the inventor of the atomic bomb, permitted and prepared its use against certain yellows (the Japanese). In 1950, he no longer allowed it against other yellows (Koreans or Chinese), following another aggression. This distinction was not of a matter of professional morality, but of political conception'.

Another example: 'In 1951, a group of anthropologists and biologists gathered under the auspices of UNESCO launched a "declaration on race", which denied the existence of hereditary genetic differences. For the signatories, the differences between human groups were explained entirely by environment, culture, and history. But in 1964 another meeting of anthropologists and biologists formulated the 'Moscow Propositions', where, on the contrary, the idea

---

357 *angélisme*'. — Tr.

358 *Journal of the Two Worlds.* — Tr.

of a 'genetic capacity for intellectual flourishing' was admitted. Between the two documents there had been no scientific discovery, but only a change of atmosphere. In 1951, the concern was to respond to Nazism and colonialism. In 1964, nascent pride (notably 'négritude')[359] began to be taken into account, which asserted the existence of certain racial differences rather than denying them.

No Imperative Criteria

Professor Kastler, Nobel Prize winner, declared: 'I only conceive of the world with a creator, therefore a God'. François Jacob, Nobel Prize winner, asserts: 'God is no longer a problem for science'. Jacques Monod, Nobel Prize winner, remarks: 'God is a hypothesis that no longer concerns science'.

Pasteur said: 'When I open my laboratory, I close my oratory. When I open my oratory, I close my laboratory'.

Even when they agree in their work, researchers do not agree on the general conclusions to be drawn from it. Scientific knowledge strives to be objective, but how can we build a positive ethic upon it if something subjective always intervenes in behaviour? How can one objectively assess the world by being both judge and judged?

'The real debate', adds Alfred Fabre-Luce, 'is this: can simple objectivity provide the scientist (even a perfectly honest one), with the reasons for his choices outside his laboratory? The knowledge that science procures does not provide compelling criteria for any action. Let us suppose, for example, that we are able to intervene as we please in the mechanisms of heredity. What on earth would we do? What purpose would we follow?

He concludes: 'There is in Jacques Monod a Nietzschean who is unaware of himself!' The work of Monod nevertheless has the merit of clearly posing the problem. The solutions he proposes, the ethics he seeks to define at the dawn of the 'biological revolution', may not seem satisfactory. This is because they are *already* situated in a system of values. At the very moment that he speaks of 'objective knowledge', Monod has *implicitly* made a choice. But the system that he has built is necessarily incomplete, since, in scientific matters, one is never finished. When one closes a door, another soon opens.

---

359 *Négritude* is an anticolonial and African identitarian movement emerging in Francophone literature and philosophy since the 1930s. — Tr.

*

Le hasard et la nécessité, a study by Jacques Monod.[360] Seuil, 212 pages.

*

Jacques Monod died on May 31, 1976, in Cannes, after a long illness. On March 10, 1971, he took over the direction of the Institut Pasteur, without renouncing his philosophical and scientific work. On several occasions he had expressed his views in specialised publications. He had also signed various manifestos, including that of the *American Psychologist*, in favour of Arthur R. Jensen and research into psychological heredity.

At the 14th Nobel Symposium, held in Stockholm from the 15th to the 20th of September 1969, he explained his conception of an 'ethic of knowledge' in a presentation entitled *On Values in the Age of Science*. This appeared in: Arne Tiselius and Sam Nilsson (eds), *The Place of Value in a World of Facts* (Almqvist & Wiksell, Stockholm, 1970).

The publication of *Chance and Necessity* has given rise to numerous polemics, which are far from over. Religious circles, in particular, were incensed to see their beliefs reduced, like Marxism, to the common denominator of 'animism'. Some authors have endeavoured to reply to Jacques Monod from a strictly metaphysical point of view. Such is the case of Etienne Gilson (*D'Aristote à Darwin et retour. Essai sur quelques constantes de la bio-philosophie*. J. Vrin, 1971),[361] Emile Callot, (*Les limites de la philosophie naturelle de la biologie modern. Pensée universelle*, 1972),[362] Madeleine Barthélémy-Madaule (*L'idéologie du hasard et de la nécessité*. Seuil, 1972),[363] Georges Salet (*Hasard et certitude. Le transformisme devant la biologie actuelle*. Tequi, 1972),[364] Jean Martel (*Dieu, cet inconnu*. Emmanuel Vitte, Lyon, 1972),[365] and Joseph Chiari (*The Necessity of Being: A Philosophical Reply to Jacques Monod*. Paul Elek, London, 1973). The scientific value of these works is generally fairly low.

More interestingly, the essay by J. L. Boursin and P. Caussat, *Autopsie du hasard* (Bordas, 1970),[366] shows that the notions of absolute chance and absolute determination have a paradoxical tendency to become confused. It can be deduced that the most completely determined is also the most completely denuded of necessity; in other words, it is a kind of chance of the second degree.

---

360 English translation: *Chance and Necessity: Essay on the Natural Philosophy of Modern Biology* (New York: Alfred A. Knopf, 1971). — Tr.

361 *From Aristotle to Darwin and Back Again: An Essay on Some Constants of Biological Philosophy*. Translated into English with the following (sub)title: *From Aristotle to Darwin and Back Again: A Journey in Final Causality, Species, and Evolution* (University of Notre Dame Press, 1984) — Tr.

362 *The Limits of Modern Biology's Natural Philosophy*. — Tr.

363 *The Ideology of Chance and Necessity*. — Tr.

364 *Chance and Certainty: Transformism and Current Biology*. — Tr.

365 *God, This Unknown*.–Tr.

366 *Autopsy of Chance*. — Tr.

HISTORY / LOGIC OF LIFE

'A bacterium, an amoeba, a fern, what fate can they dream of, except to form two bacteria, two amoebae, two ferns?'

Punctual, faithful, patient, relentless reproduction. The logic of the living, says François Jacob, is to grow and multiply. There is a primordial operator in the world of life. A kind of biological Eternal Return. The scientists call it invariance or reproduction.

François Jacob, fifty-six year old professor of cellular genetics at the Collège de France, has been with the Institut Pasteur for twenty years. In 1965, with André Lwoff and Jacques Monod, he received the Nobel Prize in Medicine for his work on the genetics of viruses and bacteria.

To write the '*history* of heredity', is to trace its evolution. François Jacob attempts to do this by distinguishing four major phases of knowledge, which he compares to 'Russian dolls', nesting into each other and revealing each time a further 'level of reality'. To these phases, in which the world was intellectually decomposed and then recomposed according to new data, he assigns key names: *visible structure, organisation, time, gene,* and *molecule.*

The Laws of Heredity

The first stage is that of the 'visible structure'. It extends to the Renaissance. Biology is restricted to anatomy; the living being, to what one *sees.* We know that there is a strong chance that children will resemble their parents, but heredity is still the subject of the most fanciful assertions. Ambroise Paré speaks of 'the mare that bred a foal with the face of man' [la jument qui pouline d'un poulain à face de l'homme]. One believes in the existence of 'homunculi' and 'animalcules', or 'preformed' men and animals.

The second period: that of *classification.* It is realised that heredity has a *memory*, and one observes the lineages to discover its hidden architecture. Linné, Cuvier, Daubenton define the families, the orders, and the branches. Geoffroy Saint-Hilaire calls the sectors or areas that appear common to several species 'regions'.

We then realise that these species, described by anatomists and classified by naturalists, have not coexisted for all eternity, that we can compile the genealogical tree. This is the third major step: the discovery of *evolution.*

In *The Origin of Species*, the Englishman Charles Darwin identifies natural selection as the means by which species have differentiated and then stabilised: in the struggle for life, only the 'fittest', the most adapted to their environment, have survived. Selection is made from unexpected variations, entirely governed by chance. Necessity intervenes only afterwards.

'It took the genius of Darwin', says Jacques Monod, 'to impose the idea that teleonomy proceeds from emergence, which creates, sharpens, and amplifies it' (*Chance and Necessity*).

The naturalist Lamarck, however, advances the opposite hypothesis. According to him, living beings are ceaselessly 'readjusted' by the environment. The characters acquired by individuals during their existence are automatically transmitted to their descendants. Weismann's work shows that this is not the case. The environment does not have the means to 'teach heredity'. It influences the external constitution, the *soma*, but not the hereditary stock, the *germen*, which each individual receives by inheritance and transmits in turn.

This distinction of *soma* and *germen* suggests that reproduction, even in man, is not the expression of a conscious will. It is not man who decides to perpetuate himself, but life which perpetuates itself through him. The differentiation of the sexes is the detour which it employs for this purpose. Family structures, society, and individual attractiveness play only on the modalities. 'The germinal lineage forms the skeleton of the species upon which individuals form like excrescences. It is no longer the chicken that produces the egg. It is, in the words of Butler, the egg which has found in the hen a useful means for recreating an egg'.

At the same time, we realise that evolution has a *meaning*: the more evolved the species are, the more they move away from the undifferentiated world of amoebae and bacteria, the more they are specialised and individualised.

In the fourth stage, that of the gene, the scholarly world recognises that heredity is governed by interesting laws, not individuals, but populations. These laws are expressed in a rigorous fashion, under the form of significant statistical frequencies. 'What matters', explains Jacob, 'is knowing not which particles collide at a given moment, but how many collisions there are on average, and what is the probability of a particle participating in it'.

One evening in February 1865, a monk from the town of Brünn (now Brno), Gregor Johann Mendel, read a paper on the hybridisation of pea plants in front of members of the local society of natural sciences. There were about forty people there. Mendel is patiently heard, politely applauded. Upon his death a few years later, his memory will be completely forgotten. Today it is regarded as the birth of modern genetics.

By hybridising his peas in the garden of his monastery, Mendel had succeeded in following the mode of transmission of the hereditary characteristics contained in the *germen*. This does not happen at random, but according to rigorous statistical laws that concern not the individuals, but the populations, as Darwin had foreseen. 'With Mendel, biological phenomena suddenly acquire the rigor of mathematics'. (Gibbs and Boltzmann, at the same time, discovered the principle of calculating *probabilities*).

Finally, the gene structure shines for its part. In his laboratory, the biologist manages to decompose the living cells into inert physico-chemical constituents. Genes and chromosomes 'registered' [or 'inscribed'] in germ cells deliver their secret, and let the *molecule* of the nucleic acid appear. The notion of 'vital force' disappears. It is replaced by that of energy. The notion of heredity is expanded. The *genetic code* is deciphered.

The Secret of the 'Double Helix'

This code is a sequence of chemical patterns. 'It is a message written, not with ideograms, as in Chinese', notes François Jacob, 'but with an alphabet, like Morse'. Just as a sentence constitutes a segment of text, so too does a *gene* corresponds to a segment of the nucleic acid. In both cases, an isolated symbol does not mean anything; only the combination of signs takes on meaning'.

'Deoxyribonucleic acid (DNA), constituent of chromosomes, guardian of heredity, and source of evolution', writes Monod, 'is the philosophical stone of biology'!

In the space of twenty years, the structure of DNA, the famous 'double helix', has thus made a breakthrough. Biochemistry and then molecular biology made their appearance. 'Molecular biology', specifies Michel Foucault (*Les mots et les choses*),[367] also a professor at the Collège de France, 'locates

---

367 English edition: *The Order of Things: An Archaeology of the Human Sciences* (Vintage: New York, 1973). — Tr.

in the transmission of the genetic code (the link between nucleic acids and the proteins) errors, omissions, mix-ups, and likens them to the blunders or unintended findings of a scribe in a moment of distraction. All throughout life, chance plays with the discontinuous'.

Turning to the question of the 'nature of life', Mr. Jacob writes: 'The operational value of the concept of life has only been diluted and its power of abstraction has only declined. Life is no longer questioned today in laboratories. One no longer seeks to define its contours. We only attempt to analyse living systems'.

François Jacob understands that the question is, if not meaningless, at least beyond communicable scope. For those who work in a laboratory, to say what life is means to describe how it manifests itself. And to describe a living system is to study its history and its structure. The logic of organisation, the logic of evolution, these are the 'algorithms' of the living world.

The lessons that can now be drawn, however, are of direct concern to us. Societies *themselves* are organisms. 'There does not appear', writes André Lwoff in *L'order biologique*,[368] 'to be anything in common between a molecular society and a human society. And yet one cannot fail to be struck by a certain analogy between the phylogenetic evolution of organisms and the historical evolution of societies. Variation and selection have intervened in both cases. And then the interactions that govern the molecular and cellular order recall the phenomena that ensure the functioning of human societies: molecules and men are also subjected to harsh constraints. Finally, molecules in revolt and parasitic molecules also have their equivalents in human societies'.

New structures remain to be discovered. 'Today', writes François Jacob, 'the world is messages, codes, information. What dissection, tomorrow, will dislocate our objects in order to recompose them into a new space? What Russian doll will emerge?

'The dice govern us', said Michel Foucault.

*

La logique du vivant, a study by François Jacob.[369] Gallimard, 354 pages.

---

368 English edition: *Biological Order* (Cambridge, MIT Press, 1962). — Tr.
369 English edition: *The Logic of Life: A History of Heredity* (New York: Vintage, 1976). — Tr.

EVOLUTION

'When the masses hate the elites, they are as stupid as the woodcutter who saws the branch that he sits on. In striking them, they strike themselves, for everything that is contrary to the elite is at the same time detrimental to the entire collective. Egalitarianism is opposed to social and intellectual progress; it abolishes the motivation of the individual, desirous of acquiring more or better, suppresses the spirit of initiative and engenders a dense, black, stupid boredom. Stagnation sets in, social decadence commences. These are the fruits of a doctrine which draws its inspiration from an arbitrary *counter-evolutive*, and inhuman concept'.

Professor Pierre P. Grasse, aged eighty-two, a member of the Academy of Sciences, published these lines five years ago in the conclusion to a 'natural history of man' entitled: *Toi, ce petit dieu !* (Albin Michel, 1971).[370]

In this work, where he sketched the great lines of a philosophy of biology, he is also disturbed by the effects of the 'counter-selection': 'Our societies integrate the retarded, the alienated, the criminals; the pedagogues boost the least intellectually well-endowed, recuperating the mentally debilitated and all the abnormal enter the cycle of reproduction. The result is, necessarily, a fall of the intellectual, moral, even physical health of our contemporaries'.

He advocates a voluntary eugenics: 'Our species will retain the native qualities of the first *Homo sapiens* only by following the rules which assure the permanence of the animal species.'

It is indeed more than half a century since Professor Grassé has devoted himself to the research and teaching of biology. At the Sorbonne, he has occupied the Chair of Evolution for thirty years. Co-author of a monumental *Traité de zoologie* (Masson), an unrivaled work in the world of which some twenty-eight volumes have appeared between 1948 and 1970, he has overseen the *Zoologie* volumes published by the Pléiade Collection (Gallimard, 1963) and the large tomes of *La vie des animaux* (1968–1970), published by Larousse. In the domain of animal sociology, he has introduced such essential notions as 'social regulation' or 'group effect'. Thanks to his theory of 'stigmergy', he has been able to explain the collective and adaptive activities of social insects. His works on the structure of the cell are no less important.

---

370 *You, This Little God!* — Tr.

As early as 1943, he published an essay entitled *Evolution: Facts, experiences, theories*. 'Evolution', he writes today, 'is the major problem central to biology. Every attempt to understand the universe and man is influenced by the solution given to it. In addition, it is no longer considered as a hypothesis except by a handful of refractories, ignorant or blinded by dogmatic beliefs. For the atheist as for the practicing Catholic, evolution is a *fact*. Without taking it into consideration, the living world, the biocosm, remains unintelligible and no longer has any meaning'.

This much is obvious. Disagreement only arises among biologists when it comes to explaining the mechanism.

An Irreversible Fact, Unique Phenomena

Originally we find two theories. That of Darwin, which explains the variations within species by *natural selection*. By a kind of 'sorting' process that works through them, selection favours the individuals best suited to their environment and, consequently, to possible changes in this environment. To the notion of a 'struggle for life' resulting in the 'survival of the fittest', Darwin adds that of *sexual selection*, which determines a *differential fertility*, that is to say (and as would be confirmed by modern ethology) the strongest and most vigorous males fertilise the most numerous and most beautiful females. In the hypothesis of Lamarck, by contrast, it is the transformations of the environment which are translated *directly* by changes in the organisms of living forms. 'Need', writes Lamarck, 'creates the necessary organ, use strengthens it and makes it grow considerably; lack of use, on the other hand, leads to the atrophy and disappearance of the useless organ'.

With time, the debate became more subtle. In a strict sense, Lamarckism is no longer supported by anyone: since the discovery of the laws of genetics, it has been proven that there is no inheritance of acquired characteristics. Parallel to this, various experiments have made it possible to qualify and specify the scope of natural selection.

Transformism thus appears as an irreversible fact, 'marked by unique phenomena': the genesis of branchings, classes, and orders. Its *irreversibility* is due to: '(1) the low probability of reassembling the same objects again and subjecting them to the same physical and chemical conditions; (2) the variability of causes and their effects, which, becoming causes in their turn, change the nature and order of the whole'.

'The historical human phenomenon', writes Pierre P. Grasse, 'differs from the evolutive historical phenomenon because man does not passively undergo the action that the physical, social, and economic environment exercises upon him. He intervenes in events voluntarily, and by changing course with more or less success. Evolution impassively pursues its course, and neither an Alexander nor a Napoleon could change its direction.

On the basis of the work of the Dutch botanist Hugo De Vries (1848–1935), a new theory known as 'neo-Darwinian' recognised, along with *selection*, the role of *mutations* or sudden alterations of the genetic stock, that have no a priori selective value, but which are hereditary from the outset. According to this theory, also known as 'synthetic theory' or 'neo-mutationism', mutations 'create' genetic varieties, and natural selection is then applied to them.

Hence the formula of Jacques Monod: 'chance + necessity'. *Chance* presides over mutations, *necessity* (invariance) over the laws of heredity.

Most of the great biologists and geneticists of our time (J. B. S. Haldane, Julian Huxley, C. D. Darlington, Waddington, Fisher, Müller, Dobzhansky, Simpson, etc.) have supported the model that Crick and Watson's discovery of the genetic code in the 1960s appears to corroborate.

Thanks to the work of V. M. Ingram and E. Zuckerkandl on hormones, haemoglobin, and immunoglobulin, it was possible to reconstitute 'genealogical trees', both for certain animal species and for humans, which correspond precisely to those anticipated by the study of fossils; some convincing molecular explanations have been proposed.

Macro-evolution

But synthetic theory, although it explains the phenomena of *micro-evolution* well enough, that is to say, variations of small amplitude like the appearance of races and populations, is much less convincing in regards to *macro-evolution*: species formation and in particular the bush-like densification[371] of large *phylum* or lineages of development. 'To vary is one thing, to evolve is another', remarks Grassé. And we must also explain how we have been able to pass from 'micro-variations' to true evolution.

---

371 *buissonnement.* — Tr.

In the simple calculation of probabilities, taking into account the age of the Earth (and the fact that mutations do not occur simultaneously), it is almost inconceivable to attribute the development of a totality as complex as the genealogical tree of all living systems solely to the intervention of purely random variations. Certain facts, such as the adaptation of amphibian reptiles to terrestrial life, with the parallel modifications to the means of reproduction that this implies, are even blatantly inexplicable from such a perspective; likewise, the passage from aquatic or terrestrial life to aerial life and so on. The classical neo-Darwinian theory no longer satisfactorily explains the acquisition in the genotype, during the 'history' of the species, of innate behaviours whose existence is now verified.

Recourse to the notion of adaptation according to selective *advantage* (direct or indirect) does not solve the problem. Taken literally, this theory would imply the quasi-systematic disappearance of the oldest species. And yet, as the biologist Ludwig von Bertalanffy (*Theoretische Biologie*, 2 vols, Gebrüder Borntraeger, Berlin, 1932–42)[372] has remarked, 'the amoeba, the worm, the insect, the marsupial are as well adapted as the placental mammal; if they were not, they would have disappeared long ago'.

The mutations themselves pose as many problems as they solve. By making appeal to the concept of genetic assimilation, C. H. Waddington (*The Strategy of Genes*, London, 1957) introduced the surprising idea of 'virtual mutation'. It has long been observed that a population subjected to a disturbance begins by adapting somatically before adapting genetically. This is called the 'Baldwin effect'. Given that there is no acquired heredity, G. C. Simpson interpreted the fact as the result of a mutation coming to 'rescue' the somatic adaptation at the moment when it would be most useful. C. H. Waddington thinks, more precisely, that a specific *conditioning*[373] selects, from within the population, over a large number of generations, the most effective genetic combinations from existing genes — notably the unused alleles present at low frequency. If one accepts this interpretation, it is no longer possible to say that mutation is entirely random. At the most, we can consider that mutation 'randomly' intervenes to trigger a complex mechanism already underpinning it and 'kept in reserve'.

---

372 *Theoretical Biology.* — Tr.

373 *mis en condition.* — Tr.

One can also think, following Jacques Monod, that the input of new genetic information is not only due to the mutations themselves, but also to some of the recombinations that occur at the time of meiosis. The fundamental diversity of the living world (known as the *polymorphism* of individuals within a single species and the fact of polygenesis, that is to say, the determination of characteristics by several diversely inherited genes) would thus increase ever more, of its own accord, up to the 'qualitative bounds' that are equivalent to true mutations.

In addition, there is an obvious relationship of the cybernetic kind between heredity and environment; environmental transformations provoke the selection of genotypes, and the selected genotype, by its influence on behaviour, provokes in its turn modifications of the environment.

Finally, the mystery is reinforced by the fact that, from one great phylum to another, one detects a structural homology between the evolutionary lineages, even when they develop themselves separately. (Thus the vertebrates have earlier members built on the same *model*, be it man, dog, bird, whale, etc.) Arthur Koestler (*The Ghost in the Machine*)[374] cited the case of non-placental mammals in Australia. 'This continent', writes M. Quentin Debray, 'has been cut off from the Asiatic continent in the Upper Cretaceous at a time when mammals were tiny creatures like mice. This is why the mammals of Australia are different from ours: they are marsupials. And yet, despite this difference in detail and this complete isolation, Australia's mammals include moles, wolves, cats, and squirrels that appear to be copies of the corresponding placental mammals. Everything happens as if a complete evolutionary programme had been stored up in the ancestral mouse, determined to some close parameters'. (*Les mécanismes de l'évolution*, in *La Nouvelle Presse médicale*, 17 February 1973).[375]

An 'Outcry'[376]

All these considerations justify a certain skepticism against the certitudes of the 'ultra-Darwinists'. That is why Grassé resisted a chance that looked too much like providence, and asserted, not without reason, that recourse to the selection-mutation mechanism was unsatisfactory.

---

374 French edition: *Le cheval dans la locomotive* (Calmann-Lévy, 1968).

375 *Mechanisms of Evolution*, in *The New Medical Press*. — Tr.

376 Literally: a 'raising of the shields' (*une « levée de boucliers »*). — Tr.

'We regard as false', he writes, 'the dilemma "or chance or the supernatural" in which the biologists of randomness try in vain to corner their opponents. In fact, there is neither chance nor the supernatural, but laws which regulate living beings, laws whose research is the goal, the *raison d'être*, of science, which in this affair must have the last word'.

Rather than randomness, Professor Grassé thinks that *need* must play a role: as Waddington had foreseen, the living being would create 'needs' for itself that would play a positive role in evolution. He has this formula: 'To live is to react'. And to cite the work of neo-Lamarckian Paul Wintrebert (*Le vivant, créateur de son évolution*. Masson, 1962),[377] in which there occurs 'a grain of truth'.

Turning to the now classic debate on *finality* (the fact that the living world considered as a whole *appears* 'ordered' towards an end), Professor Grassé also takes up the opinion of Lucien Cuénot (*Invention et finalité en biologie*. Flammarion, 1941)[378] on the 'factual finality' present in life: life actually has a *tendency* to preserve and propagate itself. 'Immanent finality is an intrinsic property of living beings', he writes. 'Without it, they would not exist'.

Yet 'if one speaks the word "finality", there is an outcry. Probably because one does not distinguish the factual or *immanent* finality from the *transcendent* finality. On the latter, the biologist has little, if anything, to say: it belongs to metaphysics'. The factual finality that one detects in biology does not therefore imply a *finalist* or *teleological* explanation. This is but an anthropomorphic projection of the notion of causality.

Grassé quotes at length the recent work of H. M. Temin and S. Mitzutani (*Nature*, vol. 226, 1970, pp. 1211–13), S. S. Spiegelman (*Nature*, vol. 227, 1970, pp. 563–67), Hatanaka, etc. on 'replication', of viruses. These seem to demonstrate that information from RNA (ribonucleic acid) can sometimes be registered in DNA (deoxyribonucleic acid) and become hereditary. (This is the case, in particular, in the genesis of certain cancers).

In this one could see, says Grassé, a refutation of the 'central dogma of biology' formulated by Crick and taken up by Monod. (Cf. in the same order

---

377 *The Living Being, Creator of its Evolution*. — Tr.
378 *Creation and Finality in Biology*. — Tr.

of ideas *Mankind Evolving*[379] by Theodosius Dobzhansky, and the experiments of Waddington cited by Jean Piaget in *Biologie et connaissance*. Gallimard, 1967).[380] But is it so? According to the 'dogma', the important thing is not that one cannot switch from RNA to DNA (even if it is usually the reverse that occurs), but that one cannot ever pass from *nucleic acids* (RNA and DNA) containing genetic information to *proteins*, which determine the characteristics of the individual. And yet for now, there is no reason to believe that it is not to the nucleic acids, and to them alone, that proteins owe all of their information. (See Francis Crick, 'Central Dogma of Molecular Biology', in *Nature*, vol. 227, 1970, pp. 561–63.)

DNA Stabilises Evolution

At the end of the day, Professor Grassé sees evolution as the result of work being carried out 'at the level of infrastructures', triggered by internal and external factors, and which would have the effect of producing certain enzymes that would synthesize a new DNA, i.e. new genes. The *inscription* of 'information' in the genetic code would thus be an operation quite distinct from the *acquisition*, sometimes occurring at several generations of interval, in contrast to what happens in the case of a mutation: 'DNA registers, *stabilises* evolution, but does not *create* it'.

From this perspective, mutations would be used *secondarily* by organisms 'to produce the genotype best adapted to the conditions of the ambient environment' — mutagenesis becoming 'the main cause of the differences between individuals, races and species'.

The explanation of this cause, and even of this mutational necessity, is not to be sought in a vain metaphysics. It is more likely to be found in the *structural* conformation of life (what Jacques Monod calls the 'project of the organism'), in those organising forces and laws inherent to the system of life of which Ludwig von Bertalanffy (*Les problèmes de la vie. Essai sur la pensée biologique modern*. Gallimard, 1961)[381] speaks, and which constitute a complex whole, finding in itself the source of its regulation. As a consequence of this, it

---

379 English edition: Yale University Press: New Haven, Connecticut, 1962; French edition: *L'homme en evolution* (Paris: Flammarion, 1966). — Tr.

380 English edition: *Biology and Knowledge* (Chicago: University of Chicago Press, 1971).

381 *The Problems of Life: An Essay on Modern Biological Thought.* — Tr.

should be admitted that 'to chance is opposed a logical reason — independent of natural selection — which plays a different role according to the level at which it is exercised' (Quentin Debray, art. cit.).

This schema seems of the highest interest. It completes and clarifies the theses that we already know rather than fundamentally opposing them. An indispensable task in this field, perhaps more so than in others.

*

L'évolution du vivant, a study by Pierre P. Grassé.[382] Albin Michel, 477 pages.

*

In *La défaite de l'amour ou le triomphe de Freud* (Albin Michel, 1976),[383] Pierre P. Grassé has conversations in a philosophical way with individuals of a symbolic and ideological nature. Addressing at length the problem of the irrational in man, he examines the modern tendency towards the 'return of great myths' (from Jean-Jacques Rousseau to Lysenko). He also refers to the fundamental fact of biological disparity. 'Men', he writes, 'are born different from one another by their bodily and functional characteristics, by their intellect, and their sensitivity. Going against this truth of fact is either a mistake, or an act of bad faith'. He adds: 'Any ideology according to which the bodily and intellectual equality of men is a reality, descends into error, and must be combated without mercy'.

A very complete account of the neo-Darwinian doctrine of evolution can be found in Ernst Mayr's *Populations, espèces et évolutions* (Hermann, 1974),[384] described by Julian Huxley as the most remarkable essay published in this field since Darwin's *Origin of Species*. Reference can also be made to the special issue of *Nouvelle école* (Nr. 18, May–June 1972) on 'Evolution', whose introduction clearly situates the difficulties encountered in the study of macro-evolution.

THE LYSENKO AFFAIR

'That a fanatical, self-taught charlatan', writes Jacques Monod, 'was able, in the middle of the twentieth century, to obtain the support of all the powers in his country to impose in biology an inept theory and in agriculture ineffective and sometimes catastrophic practices; that this luminary has also succeeded in placing official prohibition upon the teaching and practice of one of the most fundamental biological disciplines, genetics, that is what stretches the imagination!'

---

382 English edition: *Evolution of Living Organisms* (New York: Academic Press, 1977). — Tr.

383 *The Defeat of Love or the Triumph of Freud.* — Tr.

384 *Populations, Species, and Evolution.* — Tr.

It is this, however, which has happened in the Soviet Union under the influence of Trofim D. Lysenko.

An Old Illusion

In the early thirties, a great controversy took place in Moscow. It concerned the problems of agronomy and general biology. The offensive is carried out by a small Ukrainian agronomist with tight lips and black eyes that seem to shoot lightning.

'Lysenko', remarks the Russian writer Zhores Medvedev, 'reminds one of a man with a toothache: God has given him health, but he looks sullen'.

In the course of his work, the Ukrainian is advised that the general principles of 'bourgeois genetics' did not conform at all to the Marxist theory that the individual is malleable at will under the influence of the environment. He therefore set himself the task of founding one based on miraculous hybridisations. In this 'new science', all the differences observed in living beings are accounted for by the environment (education, social environment, climate, etc.). By modifying the environment, Lysenko's hope is to be able to modify both the physical and psychological constitution, and to render the acquired characteristics transmissible.

This is a very old illusion. Popularised in the accounts of the Egyptians and Hebrews, the theory of the inheritance of acquired traits will be systematised in the nineteenth century by Jean-Baptiste Lamarck (1744–1829), a French naturalist born in Bazentin in the Somme. According to Lamarck, the function creates the organ by inheritance. That is to say, 'information' coming from outside can be inscribed in the genetic heritage of the species, as soon as it occurs with a sufficiently high frequency.

This seductive theory crumbles when the German biologist August Weisman demonstrates that 'the germinal *lineage* is sheltered from any variation that may occur in *individuals*'. This means that the events of everyday life only concern those who live them; they are not 'stored in the *memory* of inheritance' and then passed on to the descendants. Despite being settled in Africa for many generations, the Chinese do not acquire negroid characteristics 'from the influence of the environment'. The intellectual quotient of the imbecile does not improve when they are raised by the gifted. The one-legged person only gives birth to children with two legs. And circumcision, practiced in certain lineages for several millennia, has still not caused the congenital atrophy of the foreskin.

'The inheritance of acquired characteristics', writes François Jacob, 'is akin to a series of superstitions. More than any other, it has resisted experimentation. More than any other, it has contributed to the restriction of analysis of life in general, and of reproduction in particular. None of the alleged transmissions of acquired characteristics are resistant to analysis. It is possible, from birth, to systematically cut the tail of all the mice of a lineage. After five generations, the hundreds of small mice that stem from them will always be born with a normal tail, of the same average length as that of their ancestors. Heredity is separated from all local fantasy, from all influence, from all desire, and from every incident. It lodges itself in matter and in its arrangement' (*La logique du vivant*. Gallimard, 1970).[385]

It is this thesis, abandoned by all scientists, that Lysenko, on the eve of the Second World War, claims to renew in a 'revolutionary' form. Refusing to admit the existence of a genetic system located in the chromosomes, denying the action of genes, the material supports of inheritance, he attempts to state the laws of what he calls 'vegetative hybridisation'.

'In my system', he says, 'the characteristics of the graft influence the genotype of the rootstock!'

Lysenko claims to be a railwayman from the time of the Tsars who was converted into Michurinist forestry. To credulous scholars, and without ever providing evidence, he announced that he had created a new species and obtained miraculous harvests. Thanks to one of his experiments (the 'vernalisation of winter grains'), the increase in the germination of grains would have also been rendered inheritable.

In fact, the results obtained are perfectly consistent with the patterns of classical (Mendelian) genetics. 'New species' are simple variations caused by the genetic impurity of the material used.

'The style and background of Lysenko's statements', says Jacques Monod in the penetrating preface he wrote for Medvedev's book, 'prove that he was totally ignorant, not only of modern biology, but of scientific progress itself'.

---

385 English edition: *The Logic of Life: A History of Heredity* (New York: Vintage, 1976). — Tr.

His rapid rise is none the less striking. In 1938 he was appointed President of the VASKhNIL (Lenin All-Union Academy of Agricultural Sciences). The following year he entered the USSR's Academy of Sciences. In 1940 he became the director of Moscow's Institute of Genetics. He received three Stalin prizes. What are the reasons for this success?

'The real debate', explains Professor Monod, 'was not concerned with experimental biology, but almost exclusively with ideology or dogmatism. The essential argument (the only one in the long run), unceasingly reprised by Lysenko and his supporters against classical genetics, was its incompatibility with dialectical materialism. And on this point, he was not wrong. Dialectical materialism, in fact, is a philosophy of change based on 'contradiction'. This philosophy refuses to recognise in nature, and especially in living nature, the existence of invariant structures. Now, the theory of the gene is a theory of invariance. It presupposes a hereditary substance, the structure of which is now known, which in its normal functioning is invariant through generations and even hybridisations, not only with respect to the environment in which the organism is found, but even with regard to the internal environment of the cell'.

If the laws of life are such as 'bourgeois' science defines them, the great messianic dream of radically changing the world and the nature of man by acting on the 'superstructures' and on the environment, at the end of a history interpreted exclusively from the socio-economic point of view, is but a senseless chimera.

Failing to convince, Lysenko then attempts to break. From 1940, it was the triumph of 'ideological terrorism'. In August 1948, in a memorable meeting, the Ukrainian declared:

'A class enemy is always an enemy, scientist or not'.

And Stalin let out in a great laugh:

'Bravo, comrade Lysenko, bravo!'

Acquired heredity becomes an article of faith. Lysenko advocated the 'radical modification of soil': by ploughing to a depth of one meter! He also undertook to increase the fat content of Russian cows by hybridisation with Jersey milk. Such hybridisation, he assures, will only be successful, because a 'hybrid zygote' (i.e. a fertilized egg, the product of the union of two different sex cells) does not develop its characteristics according to the laws of heredity, but in a 'necessarily beneficial' way. To describe this unexpected phenomenon, Lysenko has this formula: 'The zygote is not mad'.

In the streets, one sings: 'Play cheerfully, my accordion / While I sing with my friend / The eternal glory of academician Lysenko'.

Bourgeois Genetics

At the same time, the NKVD closed laboratories and deportations commenced. The world-renowned agronomist and botanist Nicolas I. Vavilov, Lyssenko's predecessor as head of VASKhNIL, was declared an 'enemy of the people'. He was arrested and deported in August 1940 and died in a concentration camp on January 29, 1943. Other researchers are sent to Siberia or the Urals. It is a return to the Inquisition.

'They can lead us to the stake', says Vavilo, before disappearing, 'they can burn us alive. But they will never make us renounce our convictions'.

When they heard the news, the scientific world ran riot. In 1948, the great geneticist Hermann J. Müller resigned from the USSR's Academy of Sciences, of which he was an honorary member. Julian Huxley (*La biologue soviétique*, Stock 1950)[386] and Jean Rostand (*Les grands courants de la biologie*, Gallimard, 1951)[387] set the record straight.

'Scientifically', writes Julian Huxley, 'Lysenko can be described as illiterate'.

The British biologist J. B. S. Haldane, left the Communist Party loudly. In France, Professor Marcel Prenant, author of *Paléontologue et transformisme* (Albin Michel, 1950),[388] as well as Jacques Monod do the same. The latter will say: 'I am not ready to forget the delirious manifestations to which the publication of the documents relating to the case gave rise, in a part of the left intelligentsia and the French press'.

To defend itself, the French Communist Party launched a Society of Friends of Michurin and raised its voice against 'bourgeois genetics'. The arguments used are astonishing. In a special issue of the magazine *Europe*, the writer Aragon casts the imperative:

'Between a monk (Mendel) and a communist (Lysenko), choose!'

---

386 English edition: *Soviet Genetics and World Science: Lysenko and the Meaning of Heredity* (London: Chatto & Windus, 1949). — Tr.

387 *Major Currents in Biology.* — Tr.

388 *Palaeontology and Transformism.* — Tr.

Jacob Segal (*Mitchourine-Lyssenko*, ed. Françaid réunis)[389] coldly asserts that Weismann's genetics is 'modeled on the psychology of the Prussian Junker', while in *La Nouvelle critique* (November 1949) Francis Cohen writes: Lysenko is right because his theses have been endorsed by Stalin, 'the highest scientific authority of the whole world'.

When questioned about the conformity of their doctrine with science, Marxists react as *believers*.

Lysenko's omnipotence began to crumble as a result of advances in molecular biology in the United States in 1961, and also after the failure of the development of 'virgin lands' (1962) carried out according to his instructions. The fall of N. Khrushchev dealt him a fatal blow. On 21 October 1964, the *Komsomolskaya Pravda* ran the headline: 'Are we researchers or errand boys?' In February 1965, the Ukrainian had to abandon his duties at the Moscow Institute of Genetics.

The Minister of Agriculture, Volovchenko, is demoted. Vavilov is rehabilitated. Soviet biology, despite its setback, attempts to renew itself.

'But Lysenkoism is far from liquidated', said Medvedev. Many people still refuse to abandon the collection of primitive dogmas which they imposed with such vigour for so many years.

On 29 May 1970, at the very moment that his manuscript reached the west, Zhores Medvedev was arrested by the KGB. Interned in a psychiatric hospital, he was released on 18 June only upon the unanimous intervention of the Soviet scientists. In France, in *L'école et la nation*,[390] the Marxist Lucien Sève always maintains that 'gifts' (that is, psychological heredity) do not exist'. In *La Pensée* (August 1975),[391] Jean-Pierre Faure proclaims 'after the absolute reign of genetics, the return of the *environment*'. Pseudo-sciences have not disappeared from the field of knowledge.

*

Grandeur et chute de Lyssenko, a study by Zhores Medvedev.[392] Gallimard, 317 pages.

*

---

389 *Michurin-Lysenko.* — Tr.
390 *The School and the Nation.* — Tr.
391 *Thought.* — Tr.
392 English edition: *The Rise and Fall of T. D. Lysenko* (New York: Columbia University Press, 1969). — Tr.

Trofim Lysenko died on 20 November 1976, at the age of 78; but Soviet biology is still at an impasse. From 1966 there was a serious political-ideological conflict between Nikolai Dubinin, director of the Soviet Institute of Genetics, and Boris Astaurov, head of the Institute of Developmental Biology. It culminated in the disgrace of Astaurov, who died in December 1974 of a heart attack. Since then, with the help of Dubinin, the Soviet Communist Party has worked to reclaim most of the key sectors dependent on the Academy of Sciences. Alongside this, former 'Lysenkists', like Vasily Remeslon, have been rehabilitated. In 1975, the decision of the Soviet Council of Ministers to implement an 'important program for the research and teaching of genetics and molecular biology' has not been followed up by any practical results. In western scientific circles, it is believed that there is only one real geneticist in the USSR. This is Alexandre Bayev, who currently works in Siberia.

Apart from the books by Medvedev and Julian Huxley, the principal work consecrated to the 'Lysenko affair' is that of Conway Zirkle: *Evolution, Marxian Biology, and the Social Scene* (University of Pennsylvania Press, Philadelphia, 1959).

In the journal *Le Contrat social*[393] directed by Boris Souvarine, E. Delimars has also published a series of penetrating articles: *Nouvelle eclipse de Lyssenko* (March–April 1964), *La biologue en liberté surveille* (May–June 1964), *Le méfaits de Lyssenko* (May–June 1965), *Lyssenko ou la fin d'une imposture* (July–August 1965).[394]

The book by Dominique Lecourt, *Lyssenko: histoire réelle d'une science prolétarienne* (Maspéro, 1976),[395] is addressed to a Marxist public. Its author, disciple of Louis Althusser, develops a hypothesis *ad usum internum*[396] that attempts to explain the success of Lyssenko by Stalin's 'deviationist' views on epistemology and general theory of science. But as Maurice Fleury observes (*Lyssenko: un savant sur mesure*),[397] it is difficult to see why the 'cult of personality' must 'lead to the negation of the role of chromosomes and of Pasteur's work'. In reality, 'Lysenkoism owed its success to the fact that it appeared to be the only scientific doctrine that was ultimately in accord with the dialectical model' (*La Recherche*, February 1977).[398]

Lysenko's principal book, *Agrobiologuia*, published in Kiev in 1940, was translated into French in 1953 by éd. de Moscou: *Agrobiologie génétique, sélection et production des semences*.[399] It was subsequently withdrawn from sale.

---

393 *The Social Contract.* — Tr.

394 *New Eclipse of Lysenko; Biology in Monitored Freedom; The Misdeeds of Lysenko; Lysenko or the End of an Imposture.* — Tr.

395 *Lyssenko: The True History of a Proletarian Science.* — Tr.

396 Latin: 'for internal use'. — Tr.

397 *Lysenko: A Scientist Made to Measure.* — Tr.

398 *Research.* — Tr.

399 *Genetic Agrobiology: Selection and Production of Seeds.* — Tr.

TOWARDS BIOPOLITICS

In presenting the symposium 'Biology and the Future of Man', held from 18 to 24 September 1974 at the Sorbonne, Robert Mallet, Chancellor of the Universities, declared:

'The universal is generally better treated by *qualified individuals* than by *quantified nations*. A head of state ignorant of genetics and ecology is much more serious for the future of the world than a wealth of tradesmen who cannot read or write'.

Valéry Giscard d'Estaing responded to him on Tuesday 24 September, in the great amphitheater of the Sorbonne, by comparing society to an organisation:

'The fate *of men* is not distinct from the future *of man*: the spiritual inheritance of a collectively lived civilisation responds to the genetic inheritance of biological descent. And the natural *rejection* of any attack on either of these inheritances is a factor we must take into account when we are led to analyse the choices governing our future'.

One hundred and fifty individuals from thirty-six nations, including several Nobel-Prize-winners, came to Paris to investigate the new powers of science and the new responsibilities of man.

A Definition of Tomorrow's Revolution

This symposium, an initiative of the universities of Paris, made it possible to verify the important role that biology now plays in our everyday life. In the twenties, the queen of the sciences was *physics*. Today, *biology* reveals a new image of the universe to us. The discovery of the genetic code, the ensuing synthesis of cells, the prospects for viral transplantation and genetic 'engineering', the rise of neurobiology, molecular biology, eugenics, control of procreation, advances in immunology, haematology, organ transplantation, constitute the most striking aspects of a development which is now at the stage of 'technological' application.

Any policy today involves *biopolitics*.

'In the not-too-distant future, and in all likelihood, during the twenty-first century', declared Professor Jean Bernard, 'the execution of the genetic program, or even its structure, can be modified in order to correct its defects and to introduce supplements'.

Mallet anticipates a day when 'the genetic code could contribute to informing civil codes'.

'I have a feeling', said Giscard d'Estaing, 'that the scientific revolution of tomorrow will come to us from biology.

From such a symposium the best and the worst could emerge. The best: a presentation of the principal results of current research. The worst: a nebulous 'planetary' morality, replacing the responsibility of the scientist with a sort of castrating, apocalyptic discourse.

An important round table had been devoted to the biological foundations of behaviour. Professor Lhermitte, who presided over the meeting, had approached the problem of the process of acquisition of the brain. It had been brought up to critique ideologues giving too great an importance to the environment and neglecting the necessary complementarity between hereditary cultural factors. (In passing, he had even touched on the notion of acquisition *in utero*).

Any break between the psychosocial context and biology', says Dr. Escoffier-Lambiotte in *Le Monde*, 'is as stupid and archaic as the ancient distinction between "body and soul". The attitude of antipsychiatrists (who deny the reality of mental illness and attribute the responsibility for these disorders to the family and society) is "completely irrational" and constitutes an appeal to an equally archaic metaphysics for the explanation of behaviours that biology makes obvious to us'.

These remarks are similar to one of the conclusions reached during the International Pharmaceutical Meetings held a few weeks earlier in Paris: 'In biology, the brain and thought are two aspects of an indivisible *unity*'.

'Intelligence', Professor Lhennitte also pointed out, 'is significantly determined by heredity'.

And to recall this formula of René Zazzo: 'Just because social inequalities confuse the issue it does not mean we have the right to deny biological inequalities'.

Numerous data have been provided concerning the genetic, biochemical, or enzymological origin of certain mental diseases. Professor Kety (USA) has indicated that the correlation of the disease among adopted schizophrenic children is nonexistent with their adoptive parents, while it is very strong with their biological parents. On the other hand, the heredity of manic-depressive psychosis is now well established. 'Psychiatry has no future without biology', concluded Professor Freedman (USA).

The round table of 20 September was devoted to the problems posed by therapeutic trials on humans. Professor Mezey from the University of New Jersey recalled that experimentation on a healthy man is a necessity, provided it is carried out under strict control:

'If it had not been for the first kidney transplant, there would have been no such progress in immunology. There would not be so many thousands of people alive through haemodialysis'.

Many interventions have unfortunately been drowned in a universalist pathos, a cataclysmic 'pessimism' inspiring the utopias of the Pugwash Movement as well as the regressive and reductionist analyses of the Club of Rome. This chatter has given birth to a Universal Movement of Scientific Responsibility, which is concerned with 'foresight', but which will depart with difficulty from the vast domain of general propositions, lyrical flights, and 'generous' ideas.

'We are faced with a serious contradiction', one of the British participants declared at the end of the conference. Science rests on fundamental principles, such as reliance on the experimental method and the acceptance of results, whatever they may be. Yet scientists now claim to select such and such of these results according to their *desirability*, that is to say, their suitability with regard to dominant ideologies. They attempt, for example, to make believe that all problems must be 'globalised' and that a universal consciousness is in the process of being born in the laboratories. This is wrong. What they express is their personal opinion, and nothing more.

Against the Mythologies of this Time

The question is at the centre of a very current debate. It is claimed that science is not 'neutral'. In reality, it is the scientists who are not.

'Science tells us what is, not what *ought to be*', remarked a young biochemist. The belief in the unanimity of the scientific world is pure illusion. Giscard d'Estaing has stressed that: 'Progress will instead come from a collaboration between scientists and other men, especially politicians, rather than from a room of scientists contemplating among themselves'.

The influence exercised on researchers by ideological systems shows that, outside their specialties, they are only too vulnerable to the frame of mind and mythologies of their time.

In a joint essay by Dr. Watson Fuller under the title *Responsabilité scientifique* (Hermann, 1974),[400] Professor Geoffrey Beale points out that some scientists have argued for the elimination of affected research credits[401] whose results don't align with universalist beliefs or fashionable egalitarianism. (In the *Scientific American*, for example, Bodmer and Cavalli-Sforza proposed that research into racial psychometry be systematically discouraged).

Professor Jacques Monod from the Institut Pasteur replied: 'I cannot accept the idea of authoritatively ceasing research in a legitimate field where there is knowledge to be gained. I think that in attempting to get this, far from confronting our responsibilities, we instead try to escape them.

*

The proceedings of the World Symposium held at Sorbonne in September 1974 were published at the beginning of 1976 at Ediscience/McGraw-Hill under the title *Biology and the Future of Man*. The best pieces in the volume are those by Jean Hamburger, Paul Nez, François Lhermitte, Roger Gautheret, Jean Frezal, Henri Bequignot, and Georges Canguilhem.

A book devoted entirely to the current problems of biopolitics was published in 1976 under the direction of Professor Albert Somit of the State University of New York at Buffalo, *Biology and Politics* (Mouton, The Hague). It collects the papers presented at the conference *Biology and Politics*, held in Paris from 6 to 8 January 1975, under the patronage of the International Association of Political Science and the Guggenheim Foundation. Among the participants were Roger D. Masters, John H. Crook, Lionel Tiger, John Wahlke, etc.

---

400 *Scientific Responsibility.* — Tr.

401 *credits affectés aux recherches.* — Tr.

Ethology

THE INNATE AND THE ACQUIRED

He raises graylag geese and calls them by name. He knows the customs of jackdaws and Siberian wolves. He knows why ducks roll their eggs with their beaks, and why squirrels seem particularly 'kind' to us. Everyone recognises his silhouette: hair like snow, the white beard, his pipe, his laughing eyes.

His name is Konrad Lorenz.

With the ninety-one year old Austrian, Karl von Frisch, and the seventy year old Dutchman, Nikolaas Tinbergen, he was awarded the 1973 Nobel Prize in Physiology and Medicine for their work as a whole.

Konrad Lorenz, seventy-four years of age, was born in Vienna, where his father, Adolf Lorenz, a court adviser and friend of Emperor Francis Joseph, was an orthopaedic surgeon also interested in the problems of eugenics. In 1940, he became Professor of Comparative Psychology at the University of Königsberg. Imprisoned by the Russians, released in 1948, he founded the Institute for the Study of Comparative Behaviour in Altenberg the following year. In 1961 he became director of the Max-Planck Institute of Comparative Physiology in Seewiesen, near Lake Starnberg in the heart of Bavaria. Since 1957, he has been an Honorary Professor at the University of Munich.

Returning to his native village of Altenberg near Vienna for some years, he continued his work as director of the Institute for the Study of Comparative Behavior, an organisation attached to the Austrian Academy of Sciences. '

'Konrad Lorenz and Nikolaas Tinbergen can be regarded as the true founders of ethology, that is to say, of the science of comparative behavior', writes one of their disciples, Professor Irenäus Eibl-Eibesfeldt.

The Origin of Instinct

More precisely, ethology is the branch of scientific research which applies certain lessons learned from the theory of evolution to the analysis of the behaviour of men and animals; it treats, says Lorenz, 'animal and human behaviour as a *function of a system*'. That is, it tries ascertain why such a system presents such a character, and how this character has been acquired.

This new science developed from 1935, essentially under the influence of Lorenz, Tinbergen and the Englishman Julian Huxley. The first volume of the *Zeitschrift für Tierpsychologie* (Journal for Animal Psychology) appeared in 1937. The journal *Behaviour* was born in 1948; The *Revue du comportement animal* (Review of Animal Behavior), in 1966. In 1963, a book by Robert Ardrey, *Les enfants de Caïn* (Stock),[402] helps to popularise the works of Konrad Lorenz. A few years later, his works began to be translated throughout the whole world.

When presenting him with the Cino Del Duca world prize in Paris, the biologist Jean Rostand declared:

'Konrad Lorenz has renovated the methods of behavioural psychology by introducing direct observation of nature'.

Freud had been 'blinded by his sexual theories' because he had only observed animals in captivity. Lorenz chose the opposite approach. He respects the savagery of beasts, and wants them to remain themselves. He does not put them in cages. It is he who adapts to their lives.

For the ethologist, words like 'hate', 'anger', 'fidelity', 'respect', 'property' are translated by *aggressiveness*, *hierarchy*, *territoriality*, etc. Concepts considered as *innate behaviours*.

Innate behaviours are those that were once called 'instincts'. But while instincts seemed by their very nature to escape all analysis, innate behaviours became objects of study.

For the 'vitalists', instinct is a 'directive factor' resisting all causal explanation. For the 'behaviourists', it is a pure illusion: individuals are only supposed to learn under the influence of the environment.

Lorenz shows that not only does instinct exist, but that it is explained in a perfectly rational way, through innate mechanisms which are transmitted by heredity and which are formed in the course of evolution. 'Natural selection', he explains, 'generates *adaptation*, which is a *cogenitive* process by which the organism incorporates information existing in the ambient environment, extremely important for its survival (...) The existence of structures and

---

402 *The Children of Cain.* — Tr.

functions created by adaptation is characteristic of living beings. There is no such thing in the inorganic world'.

The American Charles O. Whitman as early as 1898, and the German Oskar Heinroth (*Beiträge zur Biologie*) since 1910, had hypothesised that behaviour was based on innate processes of more distant origin than we thought. The developments of contemporary science have confirmed these views.

The Vestiges of our Animal Past

Working from 1935 on the central nervous system, Erich von Holst has experimentally demonstrated that a sequence of innate movements can be coordinated in a *purely central* fashion, that is to say without the aid of any external 'stimulation'. These observations, first carried out on eels and fish, have been found among mammals and primates (see Erich von Holst, *Electrically Controlled Behaviour*, in *Scientific American*, March 1962). The explanation of 'reflexologists', according to which instinct will be produced by stimulation depending first and foremost on a nervous pathway from the afferent nerves (from the exterior) to the centre, is thus inadequate. The stimulations are in fact *spontaneously* produced by the central nervous system, and it is these which lead to the 'appetitive behaviour' necessary to the 'triggering' of the instinctive impulses.

The *physiological* nature of the instinctive movements thus finds itself identified: the behavioural sequences are not based on 'reflexes', but on an elementary ability of the central nervous system to spontaneously produce automatically regulated stimuli. At the same time, a causative physiological explanation of the spontaneity of certain movements is provided.

'Instinct is given at birth', writes Konrad Lorenz. 'It is independent of education, social influences, and experience. The instinctive act has nothing to do with acquired behaviour or intelligence'.

Among animals, the role of the innate in behaviour is extremely important: certain instinctive behaviours attested in the individual from birth have been 'programmed' (acquired) *phylogenetically*, that is to say, during the evolution of the species. 'A jackdaw, even if he has been deprived of all relations with his kind at an early age, practically possesses all the qualities and behaviours that would be his in the context of a normal society. (Studies in Animal and

Human Behaviour).[403] A cichlid fish 'knows' the colour of other fish species likely to attack it, even before it is removed from the egg. The greylag goose that has never seen a fox in its life 'knows, by reason of an innate triggering mechanism, that a furry, red-brown, elongated, form which creeps is dangerous for it' (*On Aggression*).[404]

Man does not escape the rule. He has *inherited* certain innate patterns of behaviour from his animal ancestors. 'He possesses certain qualities', writes Lorenz, 'because of his belonging to a species, and not because of his fortuitous membership in society determined by this species. And these qualities are not influenced by their formation in society'.

In the newborn, the existence of many innate behaviours are noted: rhythmic seeking for the teat, swimming and crawling movements, reflexive grip of the fingers, etc.

It is not the brain that dictates these movements: during the first two months of life, the behaviour of anencephalic children (lacking cerebral cortex) does not differ essentially from that of normal children. The environment no longer intervenes: Irenäus Eibl-Eibesfeldt has shown that in children born blind, deaf, and mute, reflex movements and expressions (anger, sulkiness, fear, sadness) are exactly the same as in other children.

For the grown adult, it is the domain of *emotions* (directly placing into question the relationship between the physical and the moral) that constitutes an area of choice for the ethologists.

Why do we tilt our heads to express approval? Why does the victorious athlete raise his arms as a sign of triumph? Why does the mistress of the house almost always raise her eyebrows when she welcomes her guests?

These 'spontaneous' gestures are vestiges of our animal past. They constitute a sub-verbal language.

In 1969, a zoologist from the University of Birmingham, Dr. Ewan C. Grant, analysed over one hundred human gestures and facial expressions, including eight types of smiles. It was noticed that most of these expressions are found in neighboring species. Thus, the habit of raising the eyebrows when asking a question seems to be a specific way to attract attention. This movement rounds

---

403 French edition: *Essais sur le comportement animal et humain.* — Tr.
404 French edition: *L'aggression.* Flammarion, 1969.

the eye and emphasises the importance of the look. Great apes use it to 'ask for communication'.

If a man wants to show arrogance and contempt, he adopts a rigid attitude, which consists of lowering his head and throwing it back slightly. He keeps his lips closed and expels the air he breathes through his nose. This attitude is found in baboons.

If a man erupts in anger, he reveals his teeth and raises the edges of his mouth, like a dog ready to bite.

If he wants to impress an interlocutor, he accentuates the size and width of his shoulders. Although he no longer has fur, the hair muscles of his back contract, giving him a thrill. In the chimpanzee who takes this posture, the figure seems enlarged.

The kiss, mark of tenderness or of simple social sympathy, derives from pecking. Laughter probably developed through the ritualisation of a threatening motion, reoriented. (To find the *same* things funny promotes collusion and strengthens mutual ties against outsiders).

'In analysing accelerated takes of people eating', Eibl-Eibesfeldt reports, 'we were struck by the fact that the individual, after one or two mouthfuls, raised their face and looked around, as if to explore the horizon. Baboons and chimpanzees have the same behaviour. It is probably a warning behaviour against enemies, which man still possesses in his phylogenetic heritage, which takes place automatically, even though there is not much danger today for man when he is eating'.

Konrad Lorenz has remarked that the characteristic features of infant morphology (prominent bulging forehead, head clearly too big compared to the body, eyes in the lower part of the head, rounded cheeks, short and chubby extremities) are found in the puppy as well as in the rabbit or chick, and that seeing them produces an *innate* protective behaviour in the adult, alongside a positive judgment that is always identical (the baby is declared 'cute').

This is what ethologists call the 'reaction to the baby'. It proves the biological origin of certain aesthetic or moral behaviours and judgments.

'All human beings', says Paul Ekman, director of the Human Interaction Laboratory in San Francisco, 'have a nervous and muscular program that binds a given emotion to certain movements of the facial muscles' (*Psychologie*, January 1976). This program is the same in all cultures. It therefore does not result from a process of learning. On the contrary, these human facial expressions lie in the direct prolongation of animal mimicry. (This is demonstrated again by Eibl-Eibesfeldt in *L'homme programmé. L'inné, facteur déterminant du comportement humain*. Flammarion, 1975).[405]

On Aggression

Like all higher primates, man is a *social* animal: he lives in a group. Better: his integration with a group conditions the discovery of his own identity, that is to say, the specific place he occupies within the group. As such, man is the seat of instinctive impulses that serve the formation and survival of the group: associative tendency, tendency to maintain individual and social distance, territoriality, sense of hierarchy.

'Since man is a social animal', Darwin observed, 'it is very likely that he inherited tendencies towards loyalty to his companions and obedience to the leader of his tribe' (*The Descent of Man*).

In *On Aggression*,[406] Lorenz points out that: 'In a community of higher animals, organised life cannot develop without a *principle of order*, a social hierarchy'.

In the primitive conditions of natural selection, 'rejection of the stranger' is another condition of the survival of the group: all animals, and chimpanzees in particular, attack those among them that they perceive as 'different' — even a monkey struck with polio whose behaviour seems strange to them.

In *On Aggression*, one of his first books published in France (the one that attracted the greatest attention), Lorenz demonstrates that aggression in all living species is a fundamental, innate impulse in the same vein as sexuality, hunger, fear, and so on. And it is the very expression of life: every organism, as it gradually develops itself, imposes itself to the detriment of the environment that it 'attacks'.

The philosopher Immanuel Kant wrote, as early as 1784, in his *Idea for a Universal History*: 'Thanks be to Nature, then, for the incompatibility, for

---

405　*The Programmed Man: The Innate, A Determining Factor in Human Behaviour*, being the French translation of *Der vorprogrammierte Mensch. Das Ererbte als bestimmender Faktor im menschlichen Verhalten*. Wien: Molden, 1973). I am unaware of an English edition. — Tr.

406　German: *Das sogenannte Böse. Zur Naturgeschichte der Agression* (Wien: Borotha-Schoeler, 1963) 1963), French: *L'Agression, une histoire naturelle du mal* (Paris: Flammarion, 1977). — Tr.

heartless competitive vanity, for the insatiable desire to possess and to rule! Without them, all the excellent natural capacities of humanity would forever sleep, undeveloped'.[407]

However, we must not confuse *aggression* (which is practiced within a species) with *predation* (which occurs between several species). The first, not the second, implies competition. The lion is no more in competition with the antelope that it devours than the cow is with the grass upon which it feeds. Conversely, it would be wrong to believe that aggression begins with the higher primates. 'Herbivores', says Eibl-Eibesfeldt, are by no means more peaceful towards their fellows. Bulls fight no less intensely than rabbits, sparrows, hamsters, or cats'.

Freud, who explained physiology through pathology, evoked the 'death instinct' (*destrudo*) to speak of aggressiveness.

Lorenz, who explains the pathology by physiology, rejects the Freudian interpretation: 'Attentive observation of the behaviour of children aged three to ten years', he writes, 'shows that they commit an average of a hundred aggressive acts per day, regardless of the culture to which they belong. The boys observed are much more aggressive than the girls, and this aggressiveness is greatest in toddlers (two to four years). It then decreases. Such a constant confirms its instinctive, innate character'.

Aggressive tendencies are neither good nor bad. Or rather, they are good and bad according to the circumstances.

'Aggression is not the diabolical and destructive principle that psychoanalysis discerns in it, but an essential part of the organisation of instincts for the protection of life'.

Not only is aggression the condition for the *survival* of societies (being understood that the imperatives for survival themselves impose limits to aggression), but it constitutes a *selection* that seems to be the origin of *social sympathy*. No personal *connection* appears in species without aggression: herring and finches, who live in very harmonious groups, are unaware of any familial relationship or even dependency. Nietzsche said: 'Great despisers are

---

407 German: *Idee zu einer allgemeinen Geschichte in weltbürgerlicher Absicht* (1784); English edition, Immanuel Kant, *Idea for a Universal History from a Cosmopolitan Point of View*, in *On History*, trans. Lewis White Beck (Indianapolis: The Bobbs-Merrill Co., 1963). — Trans.

also great venerators'. This goes even in the animal kingdom. We know *love* in proportion to which we know *hate*.

The Sense of Territory

'In man', specifies Eibl-Eibesfeldt, the suppression of aggression, 'an important driving force for cultural development', would very probably lead to the disappearance of the spirit of initiative. The spirit of competition, the taste for risk, the sense of honour, the will to undertake, and even industrial dynamism are all, like *war*, 'by-products' of an aggressive drive inscribed in the most delicate structures of the organism. To attack this pulse would be tantamount to depriving the species of its taste for struggle, its will to live. To condemn it to death.

By examining depth psychology, Sigmund Freud had the merit of seeking to identify some of our archaic impulses. But before long, it was the *sexual* impulse that his efforts centred upon. Recent studies, however, have shown that sexuality is not the principal preoccupation of species such as the gorilla, the baboon, or the chimpanzee. It forms the axis of their societies even less. For most species, the conquest of hierarchical symbols or plots of land is more frequently the object of *competition* than sexual partners. In the history of humanity, a small number of men have died for love. A great number have given their lives to defend their homeland.

The sense of territory (the *territorial imperative*) is of particular importance.

'Even within a family', writes Robert Ardrey, 'each person has his own individual domain. The boundaries of ownership for each family are even more clearly marked, and this "natural right" is recognised by legislators. No one may enter a stranger's apartment without specific authorisation, and if he does, he commits home invasion. Every crossing of the territorial boundaries requires special ceremonies in order to remain unpunished. Even when we visit friends, we follow a certain ritual ultimately destined to appease aggression, for example by bringing gifts, and we find the equivalent of this in the ceremonies of appeasement in animal greetings.'

'A car in urban life', he adds, 'is a very obvious form of *mobile territory*, as is confirmed by the resolve to defend it, manifested both by the driver and his dog. The territorial borders formed by fenders and bumpers isolate the car owners to the point that even in a common traffic jam, one sees a mosaic of territories whose owners, even if they do not get angry, ostensibly ignore each other' (*La loi naturelle*, Stock, 1971).[408]

After *On Aggression*, Konrad Lorenz published *Man Meets Dog*,[409] *Evolution and Modification of Behavior*,[410] *Essays on Animal and Human Behavior*,[411] and more. Authors such as Robert Ardrey (*African Genesis*),[412] Irenäeus Eibl-Eibesfeldt (*Programmed Man*),[413] Anthony Storr (*Human Aggression*),[414] Desmond Morris (*The Naked Ape*),[415] and others, cite him constantly.

The *Essays on Animal and Human Behaviour* are probably his most important work. This title brings together five studies published between 1935 and 1954. Lorenz talks about the formation of instinct, the habits of crows, and the manner in which graylag geese roll their eggs. Wrens, red-gorges, wolves, and muskrats: Konrad Lorenz lives in a world of paw sounds and birdsongs, like city children dream about. He knows all the animals. When they are with him, the jackdaws, the rabbits, and the bullfinches seem to speak. They tell their everyday lives. And the scholar draws the lesson from it.

A 'Specific Environment'

'I want to show', he writes, 'the heritage of the animal in contemporary man'. For if the animals are a little human, it is because humans are *also* animals. Lorenz warns us against 'anthropomorphism', which consists in judging our 'inferior

408 *Natural Law.* — Tr.

409 German edition: *So kam der Mensch auf den Hund* (Wien: Borotha-Schoeler, 1950), French edition: *Tous les chiens, tous les chats* (Paris: Flammarion, 1970). — Tr.

410 French edition: *Evolution et modification du comportement, L'inée et l'acquis* (Payot, 1970). — Tr.

411 German edition: *Über tierisches und menschliches Verhalten. Aus dem Werdegang der Verhaltenslehre. Gesammelte Abhandlungen aus den Jahren 1931–1963.* Band I und II (München: Piper, 1965), French edition: *Essais sur le comportement animal et humain : Les leçons de l'évolution de la théorie du comportement* (Paris: Seuil, 1970). — Tr.

412 Subtitled: *A Personal Investigation into the Animal Origins and Nature of Man* (New York: Atheneum, 1961), French edition: *Les enfants de Caïn* (Paris: Stock, 1963). — Tr.

413 German edition: *Der vorprogrammierte Mensch. Das Ererbte als bestimmender Faktor im menschlichen Verhalten* (Wien: Molden, 1973), French edition: *L'homme programmé. L'inné, facteur déterminant du comportement humain* (Paris: Flammarion, 1976). I am unaware of any English edition. — Tr.

414 French Edition: *L'agressivité nécessaire* (Paris: Laffont, 1969). — Tr.

415 English edition: (New York: McGraw-Hill, 1967, French edition: *Le singe nu* (Paris: Le livre de poche, 1971). — Tr.

brothers' according to criteria that is too-human. Biologically speaking, the ant is no more 'selfless' than the bulldog — and the cuckoo is as 'tender' as the squirrel. Their behaviour escapes moral categories. It is driven by instinct.

To explain the presence of identical, rudimentary *moral* behaviours in all human societies, three types of explanation have been advanced: the *metaphysical* explanation by 'natural right'; the *historical* explanation, which presupposes very ancient (and very unlikely) contacts between societies; and the *psychoanalytic* explanation, recently supported by Albert Ehrenzweig, which traces the 'sense of rightness' back to typical early childhood experiences.

Underlining the inadequacies of all these hypotheses, Konrad Lorenz argues that the 'mysterious feeling that distinguishes good from evil comes primarily from characteristic innate behaviours'.

'We can', he writes, 'consider as scientifically verified the fact that the *Homo sapiens* species possesses a system of highly differentiated behaviours which serve to eliminate parasites dangerous to society, and analogous to the defense system of cells through antibodies (…) In most cases, the original active impulsion is produced by the application of innate patterns and hereditary impulses'.

'What psychopathology calls "poverty of affect" (*Gemütsarmut*)', he adds, 'or blindness to respect for values (P. Schröder), most certainly rests on genetic foundations, and probably on the failure of relational, ethical, and aesthetic patterns'.

The influence of the biologist Jakob von Uexküll (1864–1944) is felt here on Lorenz's approach. Author of numerous works published since 1920 (*Umwelt und Innenwelt der Tiere*, 1921, *Theoretische Biologie*, 1928, *Streifzüge durch die Umwelten von Tieren und Menschen*, 1934 and 1940, etc.) and a famous essay on the 'Biology of the state' (*Staatsbiologie, Anatomie, Physiologie*, Pathologie des Staates, 1920 and 1933), von Uexküll is one of the principal theorists of 'organic epistemology'. We owe to him a very fruitful definition of the 'specific environment' (*Umwelt*)[416] of living systems.

In von Uexküll, the word *Umwelt* refers to the *individual environment*, the 'phenomenal' surroundings such as they are perceived, and therefore subjectively *constituted*, for every organism according to the sensory-motor

---

416 Benoist gives *monde spécifique* (specific, particular, or individual world) for von Uexküll's *Umwelt*, literally 'environment' or 'surrounding world'. — Tr.

abilities of its species. In effect, each species only perceives a particular and limited *form* of the world with its sensory organs. And it is these perceptions of their environment that serve to 'characterise' it for the individuals (to give it a *meaning*) and, as a consequence, to adopt such and such a behaviour. Man, of course, is no exception: he *perceives* the world in a way which is not that of the dog, which is not that of the bee, and so forth. (What we perceive as *colours* will be perceived in other species as *frequencies, rhythms*, etc.). Thanks to our instruments of measurement, we can refine our perceptions, but these do not become objective (or universal) for all. 'All the characteristics of objects', wrote von Uexküll, 'even if we decompose them into their ultimate elements, atoms and electrons, will always remain perceptual characteristics of our senses and *representations*'.

From this perspective, the universe, which is the *totality* of specific environments, appears as an interlacing of *lived worlds* and *perceived worlds*, where 'active space', 'tactile space', and 'visual space', while complementing each other, can also contradict. There are as many *worldviews* as there are *forms of life*.

Consequently, 'life' should no longer be understood as the whole that is formed by living beings, but rather as the whole that these living beings form with their *Umwelten*, their 'specific environments'. As for the environments, they are no longer studied according to the aspect that they have for us, but, for the first time, according to the aspect that they have for the studied species: comparing the organism to a 'house' and the specific environment to the 'garden' that surrounds it, von Uexküll strives to understand the garden only under the aspect that it assumes for the inhabitant of the house.

The Whole and the Part

Konrad Lorenz, in the same spirit, published a text in 1950 on *The Whole and the Part in Animal and Human Society*,[417] where he takes a firm stand against the mechanists and the behaviouralists, partisans of a purely analytical ('atomistic') and reductionist approach to biological reality.

'Their approach', he explains, 'consists in isolating the various elements of a system without seeing that the particularities of the whole are not able to be reduced to the sum of the peculiarities of the parts, but that they also

---

417 In *Studies in Animal and Human Behaviour* (*Essais sur le comportement animal et humain*). — Tr.

include those which *result from the arrangement of the parts*. By demonstrating their 'incapacity to grasp the nature of the organic totality as a system of practically universal reciprocal causal links', the adherents of reductionism are hard pressed to adequately explain 'emergent properties', and from this fact, implicitly consolidate the most irrational theses of 'animism' and metaphysics.

But Lorenz also criticises the equally excessive views of the proponents of 'Gestalt psychology', which have only tended to see the totality while neglecting the parts.

'Citing H. Werner, according to whom 'man, insofar as he belongs to a supra-individual unit, possesses qualities which are due only to his belonging to this totality and which are only comprehensible from the essence of this totality', he recalls that individuals are not interchangeable, and that it is still necessary to distinguish among 'collective traits' those that belong to the sociocultural environment and those which are innate.

It notably fails to fall into the Marxist type of conception, in which man would be the 'agent' of the masses — and the individual of the structures.

*

L'agression. Une histoire naturelle du mal, a study by Konrad Lorenz. Flammarion, 314 pages.[418]
Essais sur le comportement animal et humain, a study by Konrad Lorenz. Seuil, 483 pages.[419]
Ethologie. Biologie du comportement, a study by Irenäus Eibl-Eibesfeldt. NEB-Ed. Scientists (B. P. 3,78350 Jouy-en-Josas), 576 pages.[420]

*

Ethology has undergone considerable development in recent years. After Lorenz, a 'second generation' of ethologists have emerged, mainly in the German and Anglo-Saxon speaking countries. One of its principal representatives is Professor Irenäus Eibl-Eibesfeldt.

---

418 *On Aggression*, German: *Das sogenannte Böse. Zur Naturgeschichte der Agression* (Wien: Borotha-Schoeler, 1963) 1963). — Tr.

419 German edition: *Über tierisches und menschliches Verhalten. Aus dem Werdegang der Verhaltenslehre. Gesammelte Abhandlungen aus den Jahren 1931–1963.* Band I und II (München: Piper, 1965). — Tr.

420 *Ethology: The Biology of Behaviour* (New York: Holt, Rinehart and Winston, 1975). — Tr.

After Ethology: The Biology of Behaviour and *Against Aggression*,[421] he published *The Preprogrammed Man*[422] and *The Biology of Peace and War*.[423]

In *The Preprogrammed Man*, Eibl-Eibesfeldt writes: 'It is often said that man is an "instinctive being", which is true if we refer to the relation between the cultural tradition and the innate, but it is probably false in the absolute. In human behaviour, the role of phylogenetic adaptations is no less than in other higher mammals. In fact, the case of man even calls for a greater number of phylogenetic adaptations: one only has to think only of the disposition of man to learn languages. To attribute a negligible importance to the innate in human behaviour — as some still do today — would be to disavow scientific observations'.

He adds: 'Today in communities we are trying to raise children in groups without any connection to the parents, by departing from the mistaken idea that individualised relationships are at the origin of any egocentric attitude. One thus hopes to raise men without discrimination who are made for the collectivity, while completely forgetting that the child has a need to connect to his mother or a substitute, because he is phylogenetically programmed thus, and because a repression of the need to establish an individualised relationship has the effect of deprivation'.

In the same work, Professor Eibl-Eibesfeldt shows that the existence of hierarchies in human societies plays a powerful role in the inhibition of aggressive impulses. 'Hierarchisation', he says, 'seems to be a mechanism designed to neutralise aggression within a group; in this respect, it can be seen as an adaptation'. We can conclude that egalitarianism implies a greater intraspecific violence, and that its application would give social competition the form of merciless struggle.

On the origins and development of behavioural biology, see the special issue of *Nouvel école* (Nr. 25-26, winter 1974-75) dedicated to 'Ethology'. (This issue contains an important interview with Konrad Lorenz). On the œuvre of Lorenz, cf. the study by Heinrich Meier, *Konrad Lorenz* (in Criticòn, München, Nr. 37, September–October 1976); and the book by Alec Nisbett, *Konrad Lorenz: A Biography* (New York: Harcourt Bruce Jovannvich, 1977).

RITUAL BEHAVIOURS

On one hand, a lizard that inflates itself like an ox, the triumphal dance of a greylag goose, the prenuptial offering of a spider to its spouse. On the other, social conventions, children's games, voodoo, the symbolism of colours, and the United Nations. This is not a random inventory in the style of Prévert, but rather different aspects of a same reality: *ritualisation*.

---

421 French edition: *Contre l'agression.* — Tr.

422 German edition: *Der vorprogrammierte Mensch* (Wien: Molden, 1973), French edition: *L'homme programmé. L'inné, facteur déterminant du comportement humain* (Paris: Flammarion, 1976). I am unaware of any English edition. — Tr.

423 New York: The Viking Press, 1979; German edition: *Krieg und Frieden aus der Sicht der Verhaltensforschung* (München: Piper, 1975); French edition: *Guerre et paix dans l'homme* (Stock, 1976). — Tr.

Konrad Lorenz, in *On Aggression*, already insisted on the importance of the ceremonial.

'The formation of traditional rites', he wrote, 'certainly began at the dawn of human culture, just as, at a lower level, the formation of phylogenetic rites established the beginnings of animal social life'.

Every living society presents 'ritual' aspects. They constitute one of the preferred fields of ethologists, i.e., specialists in the biology of behaviour. Some essays have been collected by Julian Huxley in a book entitled *A Discussion on Ritualization of Behaviour in Animals and Man* (Papers presented at a colloquium of the Royal Academy in London).[424]

Philosopher and scientist, former director of UNESCO, Julian Huxley (1887–1975) was one of the most famous biologists of this time. To him we owe, among other things, the first serious book devoted to the Lysenko affair (*Soviet Genetics and World Science*),[425] a study on the spiritual crisis of the contemporary world (*Religion without Revelation*),[426] and innumerable articles and communications of a scientific nature. He was also one of the pioneers of ethology.

In 1872 Charles Darwin, author of *The Origin of Species*, devoted an essay to *The Expression of Emotions in Man and Animals*. 'He realises then', writes Huxley, 'that higher animals experience emotions, and that these aspects of subjective consciousness are not simple epiphenomena, but the active elements of an organisation with a unitary structure, combining material or physiological factors with mental or psychological factors'.

In 1901, Edmund Selous indulged in the observation of 'mutual parades' in a common bird, the crested grebe. In turn, Huxley, in 1914, studied sexual solicitations, 'signal-attitudes', the postures of threat or intimidation among mammals and birds. He observes that certain rites 'serve to establish an emotional link between the members of the group'.

All this work results in a triple conclusion. The vast majority of animal behaviour patterns have been ritualised. This ritualisation is the culmination of a particular *evolutionary* process. Finally, there are 'organs of behaviour',

---

424 London: Royal Society, 1966. — Tr.

425 Chatto & Windus, London; French edition: *La génétique soviétique* (Paris: Stock, 1950). — Tr.

426 French edition: *Religion sans révélation* (Paris: Stock, 1968) — Tr.

whose comparative morphology can be studied, exactly like that of the lower members or organs of the small pelvis.

According to Julian Huxley, ritualisation can be defined as 'the formalisation or adaptive channelling of emotionally motivated behaviour, under the pressure of natural selection'. It is therefore something quite different from mechanistic reactions, or pure reflexes, of which the American behaviourists have made the greatest abuses. This ritualisation fulfils three functions: it improves communication and signalisation, it limits losses or damages at the species level, it reinforces links within the group.

Sexual 'displays' respond to the first function. The peacock fans out its feathers. The male crested grebe takes the female's copulatory position — which leads its partner to take action.

In *territorial* animals, 'information' also bears upon the possession of land. The marking of borders is established by ceremonious flights, as in the woodcock, or by depositing excrement (of which the 'raised leg' of the domestic dog is a 'civilised' version).

Rites of appeasement or intimidation, substituted for real struggle, enable nature to reduce waste and save lives. The 'bluff' of the lizard, the panic of the octopus, bristling fur, shining fangs, grimacing faces: such are the 'forces of deterrence' in the animal world. Instinctive aggression is thus limited in its effects.

'In social predators such as wolves, losses resulting from aggression between members of the same species are almost totally avoided thanks to the special submissive attitudes that the animal adopts in situations of conflict. These attitudes trigger an *innate* inhibition mechanism in the strongest animal, which finds itself automatically prevented from attacking its adversary.

'In deer', Huxley adds, 'the antlers have a dual function: their arrangement is such that fighting is very rarely fatal or even dangerous, and their allometric growth gives them such prominent dimensions that their sight alone is enough to deter the adversary from engaging in combat'.

In man, the perpetual capacity to learn, historical consciousness, mastery of the environment, make the individual partly free from the constraints of the species. But the choices he must make are only more difficult. A mode of behaviour serves to institutionalise the relationships that one chooses to have with the environment. Ritualisation thus allows one 'to overcome affective ambivalence' (Erik H. Erikson). Its consequences then have a much greater scope.

None of the ancient rites have disappeared. They have only adapted to the imperatives of time. Calling the astrologer on the phone has replaced prayers to make rain.

A Range of Activities

A group that is too substantial to be consolidated solely by personal ties relies on a number of abstract principles and social conventions for its coherence and its 'mental unity'. 'Rites are an insurance against the danger of dissolution', writes Professor E. Shills of King's College, Cambridge. Their role is, in the proper sense, 'religious': they re-link (from *religere*) the members of the group to each other. Huxley, who maintains that 'the God of religions is dead, whereas religion is immortal', shows that the sense of the sacred is itself but a form of ritualisation. The same applies to 'good manners', which may (wrongly) seem useless, but which are in fact indispensable.

The present world thus provides the spectacle of *military* rites, from the duel to the Geneva Convention; the rites of *prestige*, such as Labour Day or the parades of Tianjin Square; of *medical* rites, ranging from the oath of Hippocrates to the traditional illegibility of scripts; of appeasement rites (the handshake); *funerary* rites, *liturgical* rites, *parliamentary* rites, and so on'.

'All these rites', writes Julian Huxley, 'cover a wide spectrum of activities, from the act of scratching the skull in case of perplexity, or lighting a cigarette when you feel slightly frustrated, to the game of golf that we play to avoid making a difficult decision'.

There are also *pathological* rites: rites of partial insanity and obsession. Delusions of interpretation and neuroses. And also *compulsive* rites (Huxley recalls that 'many people avoid walking on the gaps between the sidewalk slabs').

Spiders administered LSD begin to weave much more regular webs than normal: 'Like schizophrenics, they retreat, withdraw from exteroceptive stimuli, and the resulting reduction of conscious perceptions prevents them from adjusting their canvases to the irregularities of the site'. The 'psychedelic' effect of the drug would thus cause a disturbance of the rites of integration (inability to communicate within the group).

It is significant that the word 'rite', purely religious in origin (the 'reformed rite'), rapidly assumed a wider application. Marxists attribute a superficial character to 'ritual' behaviour, which they regard as the fruit of economic superstructures. Ethology provides a forcible denial to this belief.

'The iconoclast is mistaken', exclaims Konrad Lorenz.

'I do not believe', he adds, 'that the system of norms and social rites characteristic of cultures owes very much to the wisdom and imagination of men. It has been said that Moses had forbidden Jews to eat pork because of trichinosis. Assuming this to be true, he nevertheless preferred to trust his disciples' devotion more than their intelligence — since he pronounced a religious commandment rather than instituting a course of parasitology'.

*

Le comportement rituel chez l'homme et chez l'animal, essays published under the direction of Julian Huxley.[427] Gallimard, 419 pages.

*

Julian Huxley died in London on the 14th of February 1975 at eighty-seven years of age. In the course of his career, he had published major works not only on the genetics and biology of behaviour, but also on the history of religions, morals, and philosophy.

In 1961, during a conference organised by the University of Chicago, he stated: 'The evolutionary point of view must be global, but it must also be based on quality. This must be the dominant concept of our new belief system. Quality and richness versus quantity and uniformity. (…) A domain where individual variety comes to be particularly encouraged is education. In the majority of educational systems, under the pretext of alleged equality, the variety of gifts and talents are systematically discouraged. Our new system of thought must reject the myth of equality. Human beings are not born equal in gifts and in potentialities, and the progress of humankind is based on the very fact of their inequality. "Free, but unequal", such ought to be our motto — and the diversity of the heights, not conformity or adaptation to the middle, should be the aim of education'.

KONRAD LORENZ, THE MORALIST

'In correctly insisting on everyone's right to equal opportunities', affirms Konrad Lorenz, 'we have come, in a spirit of pseudo-democratic confusion, to the conviction that the aptitude for utilising opportunities is also the same for everyone, and that anyone could likewise do anything. In order to deny that

---

427 *Discussion on Ritualization of Behaviour in Animals and Man* (London: Royal Society, 1966). — Tr.

innate differences exist between men, it has been suggested that it is possible to condition them all. This, thank God, is not the case'.

The human species is currently going through a period of 'moulting' and 'transformation'. An ancient order is dead. A new order is yet to be born. It is the *interregnum*: the moment before the regeneration and the 'turning' (*Umschlag*)[428] of history.

The *aptitude for culture* is perhaps threatened the most. Now this aptitude, says Lorenz, is none other than the 'organ of civilisation'.

'We find', he explains, 'the duality of two *antagonistic* mechanisms, one of which tends to *fix* what has been acquired, while the other aims at gradually *suppressing* what is fixed in order to replace it by a higher reality. *Lack of fixity* causes the formation of monsters, both in the field of genetic inheritance and the domain of cultural tradition. *Lack of change* leads to the loss of adaptive power, the death of art as well as culture'. In other words: too much order ossifies, too much disorder destroys.

Conclusion: 'Each generation must recreate a new equilibrium between the maintenance of tradition and the rupture with the past'.

It is precisely because this mechanism is flawed that Konrad Lorenz, as a moralist, is concerned about the deterioration of the 'quality of life'.

A Being of Culture

In the book that he published in 1973, *Civilized Man's Eight Deadly Sins* (followed by *The Reverse of the Mirror* at the end of 1975),[429] Lorenz enumerates the eight principal 'mistakes' that not only threaten our immediate future, but the very existence of our species.

He has this formula: 'Humanity is, for the moment, a functional whole which has wandered completely astray from its path'.

Some of these 'deadly sins' cover threats that have already been noted by others: overpopulation and (especially) demographic imbalance, pollution and the sacking of natural resources, *stress* caused by the fear of 'no longer being in

---

428 Benoist gives *retournement* (reversal, turnaround) for *Umschlag* (transition, turnover). — Tr.

429 The dates given here are for the French editions: *Les huit péchés capitaux de la civilisation*, and *L'envers du miroir : Une histoire naturelle de la connaissance*. The German originals both appeared in 1973: *Die acht Todsünden der zivilisierten Menschheit*, and *Die Rückseite des Spiegels. Versuch einer Naturgeschichte menschlichen Erkennens*. The English editions appeared in 1974 and 1973 respectively. — Tr.

touch' (alienation), the nuclear threat, and so on. It is not on these dangers that Lorenz insists the most, but on other, less well known threats which appear to him all the more formidable because they correspond to 'disruptions of a behaviour that may have originally had value for the maintenance of the species'.

In the first place, there is the rupture of the equilibrium between aggressive impulses and traditional inhibitions.

In previous works, Lorenz had established that the aim of aggression, far from being a 'pathological' impulse, was the survival of individuals or groups at the expense of a reactive struggle against the environment. In a world where antagonism is the rule, the more an organism is deprived of aggressiveness, the more vulnerable and unfit for life it is.

Aggression, like most instinctive impulses, involves spontaneously triggered, affective emotional reactions (considered 'animal'). These have their seat in what physiologist Paul MacLean has called our 'old brain' (located in the hypothalamus) by contrast with the *neocortex*, the seat of rational and 'human' reactions.

In the normal individual, the impulses that are formed at the level of the *paleocortex* are generally more or less controlled by the *neocortex*. In the opposite case, the hypothalamus blocks the cortex, and reason is paralysed: which explains certain characteristics of mass psychology.

Within society, we find the same interaction between order and disorder, rational impulses and affective impulses.

'As Gehlen rightly said', remarks Konrad Lorenz, 'man, by his nature, that is, his phylogenesis, is a being of *culture*. In other words, his natural impulses and their conscious control, imposed by society, form a unique system in which these two factors are complementary'.

In *Natural Law*,[430] Robert Ardrey wrote: 'Without *order*, which only society can create, the vulnerable individual perishes. However, without a certain *disorder* allowing and favouring the full development of the diversity of its members, society declines and disintegrates into competitions of group selection'.

---

430 French edition: *La loi naturelle* (Stock, 1971). — Tr.

Usually, between these contradictory tendencies, an equilibrium is established by a phenomenon of internal regulation quite analogous to the principle of retroaction or feedback from cybernetics.

Konrad Lorenz thinks that this equilibrium is broken, and that we are going through 'oscillations' of a formidable magnitude.

'The opinion that rises against a widespread opinion is almost always right', he observes. 'But in this confrontation, the opposition adopts exaggerated forms, which it would never have taken if it did not have to compensate for the opposite opinion. If the reigning opinion suddenly collapses, which routinely happens, then the pendulum swings in the opposite direction towards an equally exaggerated position'. Passions and ideologies accentuate this phenomenon, which lead either to dictatorship or anarchy.

It is most likely in this sense that the problem of demography should be appreciated. For 'it is not only a matter of knowing how many men the Earth can feed, but of what density, and at what proximity, men begin to hate one another'.

What can be done to prevent aggressiveness from taking pathological forms? Lorenz emphasises that it is futile to hope to dispel it by removing the 'stimulating situations' in which aggressive behaviour is *triggered*, or by opposing it with a moral *veto*: 'The application of either of these two methods would equate to the desire to eliminate the increasing pressure in a boiler by closing the safety valve'.

It is better to *redirect* natural aggressiveness towards forms of activity that allow a 'cathartic discharge': scientific competitiveness, sport which provokes 'militant enthusiasm', and so on.

The 'Fatal Tepidness' of the Modern World

Another danger: the *deviation* of the innate sentiment that causes every normally constituted individual to protect the weakest and to revolt against injustice.

In the natural state, this sentiment also contributes to the survival of the group. In an evolved society, where natural selection no longer plays a role, it can also cause its disappearance.

In 1940, Konrad Lorenz wrote: 'In the prehistoric period of humanity, selection for hardness, heroism, social utility, etc., was solely achieved by hostile external factors. Today, this role must be taken up by a human organisation' (*Zeitschrift für angewandte Psychologie und Charakterkunde*).[431]

In a 1972 interview with Friedrich Hacker (*Aggression and Violence in the Modern World*),[432] he further remarked: 'The interests of the species are unfortunately opposed to humanitarian requirements'.

In 1973, he adds: 'The feeling of humanity which we ought have for each person in particular is opposed to the interests of the human species as a whole. The compassion we feel towards the antisocial among us, whose inferiority perhaps stems from irreversible wounds dating from early childhood, or from hereditary defects, prevents us from protecting normal beings. Moreover, we can no longer use the qualifications "superior" or "inferior" when speaking of men, without being suspected of pleading for the gas chamber'.

Example: 'In his lectures at the Menninger Clinic in Topeka, Hacker cited the case of a young murderer subjected to psychotherapeutic treatment, considered cured, and then released. He immediately committed another murder, followed by three others. It wasn't until the criminal killed his fourth victim that a society imbued with democratic and behaviourist humanitarian principles admitted that he represented a public danger'.

'The conviction, elevated to the rank of religion', continues to Lorenz, 'that all men are born equal, and that the defects and flaws of the criminal are due to a neglect in education, undermines and annihilates the natural sense of good and evil, first of all in the culprit, who feels sorry for himself and is considered a victim of society (…) The individual who is deficient in the affective and social domain is an unfortunate, an unhealthy person worthy of compassion. But deficiency is evil in itself'.

Lorenz, then draws attention to the 'fatal tepidity' (*Wärmetod*, the 'warm death') which reigns in the present world.

In nature, 'each learning of a behaviour that is confirmed by a reward pushes the organism to accommodate itself to painful situations in order to obtain pleasure. In other words, the organism accepts without flinching situations which, prior to training, would have provoked reactions of aversion and inhibition. A wolf or a dog, for example, in order to catch an enticing prey, does many things that they would normally loathe. They run through thorns,

---

431 *Journal for Applied Psychology and Character Studies*. — Tr.

432 *Agression et violence dans le monde modern* (Calmann-Lévy, 1972). — Tr.

leap into cold water, and expose themselves to dangers which they notoriously dread.

In short, the more one wants something, the more one is willing to pay to obtain it. This balance between 'pleasure' and 'displeasure' is the basis of every economy.

Over the centuries, men too have given all the more value to things that they had more difficulty procuring. 'Harsh weeks, pleasant holidays', said Goethe. This time has passed. 'Due to the progressive domination of its environment, modern man has, by dint of circumstance, displaced the pleasure-displeasure balance in favour of a *growing hypersensitivity to any painful situation*, to the point where his capacity for enjoyment is blunted'.

'We are hardly aware of the degree to which we depend on modern comfort, so much that it goes without saying. The most modest servant would violently revolt if a room were put at their disposal with the heating, lighting, bedding, and conveniences that seemed decent to Goethe or the Duchess of Weimar.

Alongside this, the least social inequality is perceived as 'injustice': by *contrast* (for the all-penetrating *media* provides *everyone* with a means of a comparison) it appears doubly 'scandalous', and gives rise to ideologies of resentment ('what about me?').

Hypersensitivity to displeasure renders one *incapable of joy*: 'Helmut Schulze has pointed out the surprising fact that neither the word nor the concept of joy appears in Freud.[433] He knows pleasure, but not joy. When one reaches the summit of a difficult mountain, remarks Schulze, with sore muscles, damaged fingers, and the prospect of soon confronting the greater risks and difficulties of the descent, it is not a question of pleasure, but of the greatest imaginable joy'.

Thanks to the manipulation of *fashion*, a certain industry tends to encourage this desire for *instant gratification* by creating false needs and producing objects with 'built-in-obsolescence'.

'Intolerance to pain, which never ceases to increase in our day, transforms the natural ups and downs of human life into an artificially levelled plain, and this tendency engenders a fatal *boredom*'.

---

433 Ironically, the German word for joy is *Freude*. — Tr.

The man whose pleasure is dulled by habit and ease is effectively com-pelled to seek ever *renewed* sensations, always *stronger*, so that very soon he will desire that which exceeds norms: drugs, perversions.

'Men', says Lorenz, 'have today reached a state of dangerous softening, which probably leads to the ruin of a culture'.

The unhealthy love of novelty is called 'neophilia'. A pathological 'cultural' exaggeration of this specifically human trait can be seen in *neoteny*. The de-mand for the *immediate satisfaction* of every desire *in nuce*, remarks Lorenz, is, moreover, a characteristic feature of childhood. Previously, the adolescent learned patience by becoming an adult. Today, patience has become useless: 'psychological' childhood lasts longer than 'physiological' childhood. And egalitarianism, which brings everything to the lowest level, adds even more to the *infantilisation of adults* by gradually tracing the outlines of a 'fool-proof' civilisation (where even 'imbeciles' can occupy the first ranks).

'The question is therefore knowing whether the infantile characteristics of the genetic program are not being developed in disastrous proportions'.

The Erosion of Tradition

Here Konrad Lorenz observes some great analogies between the development of individuals, the evolution of civilisations, and the phylogenesis of species.

The ideology that *dominates* today, he remarked, is an ideology of the least effort, which refuses all hierarchy and all constraint. Now, the acceptance of constraint, in all its forms, is already one of the characteristics of maturity. In egalitarian doctrines there is, on the contrary, a puerile utopianism which finds a natural prolongation in the cult of the infantile ('the child in power'). According to Rousseau, man in the natural state is instinctively good; society corrupts him. According to certain fashionable theses, the moods of the child are naturally good; the adult corrupts them. The dispute of generations thus took an unforgiving turn.

'The current youth's revolution is founded on *hate*. Rebellious youth react against an older generation like a cultural unit reacts against a foreign race'.

Konrad Lorenz emphasises, however, that the 'revolt of the young' is not an evil in itself. The adolescent, like the crab, must reject his 'shell' in order to grow: in order to reveal his own personality, he must distance himself from the world with which, as a child, he had first identified. The time of the 'just measure' comes after. What is abnormal, therefore, is not that youth revolt, but that their revolt is taken *for something other than what it is*; and that adults, subjugated by their rhetoric, demonstrate a complacency towards them that indicates a loss of energy and proves that they now have the same *mental age* as their progeniture.

'At the age of puberty, young people turn away from parental tradition. Their function is to criticise old ideals, to throw overboard all that is outdated and to discover new tasks (...) But at the same time, the coherence of tradition must never be truly broken'.

It is the parents who have given up that bear the responsibility for the erosion of tradition, according to Lorenz; those who have found 'anti-authoritarian education' a good pretext for evading the responsibilities of a well-understood authority.

'Thousands of children', he asserts, 'have become unfortunate neurotics because of the famous "anti-authoritarian" education designed to prevent frustrations'.

He explains: 'The child brought up within a non-hierarchical group is in an absolutely *artificial* situation. Not being able to repress its instinctive tendency to assume first place, the child tyrannises its parents without resistance and is obliged to assume a role of *leader*, which it does not feel at ease in at all. When the child tries to annoy its parents to provoke a justified reaction of indignation in them, it does not receive the aggressive response that it unconsciously expected, but runs up against the rubber wall of beautiful speeches and hollow, pseudo-rational phrases.

'Yet no man has ever identified with a poor slave, and no one is willing to admit the cultural values respected by this slave. It is only if one loves someone from the depths of the heart and is admired at the same time that one can adopt his tradition. Such an "image of the father" is manifestly lacking in most teenagers growing up today'.

Faced with a challenge of affirming the irreducible antagonism of authority and love, Lorenz proclaims: 'The recognition of a hierarchical situation is not an obstacle to love. Everyone should remember that as a child he did not care less for the people he admired and to whom he was subject. On the contrary, he loved them more and better than his equals and inferiors'.

'A man whose social behaviour has not reached a sufficient degree of maturity', he adds, 'remains at a stage of *infantilism* and can only become a *parasite* of society. He wishes to continue enjoying the consideration of adults proper only to the child. Countless young people today stand up against the social order and, also, against their parents. Despite this attitude, they expect to be nurtured by this very society and by their parents. It is a sign of unthinking, childish behaviour. If these frequent states of infantilism and the growing progress of juvenile criminality are based, as I fear, on genetic anomalies among civilised man, we run a very serious danger'.

In the end, says Lorenz, the 'eight deadly sins' are the most visible signs of a process of *dehumanisation.* And this process is favoured by this 'pseudo-democratic doctrine according to which the social and moral behaviour of man is not absolutely determined by the *phylogenetic* evolution of his nervous system or its sensory organs, rather it is influenced only by the "conditioning" it has undergone during its *ontogenesis*'.

'It is senseless', he writes again, 'to suppose that it is enough to destroy a forest in order to automatically make a new one grow. And yet we are witnessing in our day the continuous weakening of the factors which ensure the transmission of tradition and the strengthening of factors which rupture it. By destroying the institutions and the old data, we risk the triumph of true regression (...) If this evolution continues to be maintained in an uncontrolled way, if no mechanism, no institution for conservation appears, this phenomenon could very well mean the end of civilisation and, I think very seriously, the regression of man to a pre-Cro-Magnon stage'.[434]

Such remarks led the Marxist Jean-Michel Goux, a Professor at the University of Paris VII, to blame the author of *On Aggression* for 'treating as biological phenomena' those 'phenomena which are manifestly linked to capitalist competitiveness' (*L'Humanité*, November 2, 1973)!

For Konrad Lorenz, the solution to current problems will never occur by 'ideological speculation' but rather by the 'patient work of inductive research', which consists in identifying and acting upon real causes.

To begin with, it would be necessary to better understand the realities of life.

---

434 Reading *pré-cromanien* for *pré-Cro-Magnon*— Tr.

'I consider it in no way utopian', says Lorenz, 'to give every sensible human being sufficient knowledge of the essential facts of biology. Biology is a fascinating science, provided it is intelligently taught in such a way that the pupil realises that, being himself a living creature, what he is told is directly relevant to him. (…) The qualified teaching of biology forms the only foundation on which to establish sound opinions concerning humanity and its relations with the universe'.

As Robert Ardrey already said:

'What is dramatic is not that Rousseau was mistaken, but that two centuries later we were still following him; that the progress made by biology since Darwin has not influenced our way of thinking; that today's modes of thinking proceed from Rousseau's errors, as if the natural sciences had never existed'.

*

Les huite péchés capitaux de la civilisation, a study by Konrad Lorenz.[435] Flammarion, 170 pages.

*

In *Behind the Mirror: A Search for a Natural History of Human Knowledge*,[436] a work which is a kind of follow up to *Civilized Man's Eight Deadly Sins*, Konrad Lorenz attempts to give an overview of the cognitive mechanisms in man. He stresses that this task is the indispensable prerequisite for a 'self-analysis of civilised man based on biological knowledge'.

Overwhelmingly ethological in order to establish anthropology and sociology on new foundations, he reminds us that the knowledge we have of the world is closely linked to the physiological apparatus (the human 'mirror') in which it is reflected. This perceptual and cognitive apparatus rests on innate foundations inherited from evolution. Thus neither 'reason' nor 'knowledge' exists autonomously: the relations between the perceiving-man and the perceived-world form an organic system of interactions. Likewise, there is no 'a priori experience': evolution itself is a storehouse of information to which man adds his own acquisitions. Gradually, all the spiritual, intellectual and technological activities of humanity are thus seen to be situated in a phylogenetic perspective.

The theory of perception and the theory of knowledge proposed by Lorenz refer back to both the rationalists, who claim to be able to know the world 'objectively', and to the idealists who claim to study 'human nature' without taking into account the world of which it is the 'reflection'.

---

435 *Civilized Man's Eight Deadly Sins* (New York: Harcourt Brace Jovanovich, 1974), German: *Die acht Todsünden der zivilisierten Menschheit* (München: Piper, 1973). — Tr.

436 French: *L'envers du miroir : Une histoire naturelle de la connaissance* (Paris: Flammarion, 1975), German: *Die Rückseite des Spiegels. Versuch einer Naturgeschichte des menschlichen Erkennens* (München: Piper, 1973). — Tr.

THE HIDDEN DIMENSION

We live in an invisible bubble. This bubble is our 'personal distance', our intimate and vital space. This is our hidden dimension. All these bubbles form a 'super-bubble'. When it is too compressed, it bursts. And we burst with it.

Published in the United States in 1966, the study entitled *The Hidden Dimension* constitutes a long dissertation on 'proxemics', which the author defines as 'the science concerning man's use of space as a specialised elaboration of culture'. That is to say, it concerns the way man uses the space that he maintains between himself and others, and the one he builds around him.

Edward T. Hall, attached to the Department of Anthropology at Northwestern University, has been cited at length by Robert Ardrey. He himself cites the works of Konrad Lorenz and Nikolaas Tinbergen. Indeed, proxemics owes very much to ethology.

'My training as an anthropologist', emphasises Professor Hall, 'has accustomed me to seek in biological infrastructures the origin of such and such an aspect of human behavior. This approach highlights the fact that man, like other members of the animal kingdom, is, from beginning to end, an irremediable prisoner of his organism'.

Vital space (*Lebensraum*) is a concrete reality, necessary for the equilibrium of every individual. In nature, this balance is normally assured by *predation* (destruction of the surplus population of one species by members of another species). When predation no longer plays a role, *self-regulation* intervenes, which is not only linked, as Malthus believed, to the presence or absence of food reserves, but also to 'physiological mechanisms of reaction to density'.

The Scandinavians have observed for centuries the suicidal march of lemmings (a rodent closely related to voles) into the sea. Similar suicidal behaviours were observed in rabbits.

In other cases, self-regulation is effected by a *glandular* path: the mean weight of the adrenals increases in proportion to the density of the population, leading to a fatal endocrine reaction. In the course of the 1950s, Professor John Christian showed that the average weight of the adrenal glands in marmots increased by 30 to 60% during periods of 'overpopulation'.

Placed in overcrowded conditions, and with the impossibility of committing suicide, some animals adopt aberrant behaviour.

This is the case with humans. The increase in population density leads to a *qualitative* change in lifestyle. Beyond a certain threshold, the most common activities become impossible: to teach a course to students, to maintain relations with neighbours, to use public transport. The laws of mass psychology take precedence over the individual principles of behaviour. This is reflected in the rise of anxieties and neuroses, the succession of trends, the whirlwind of exoticism. *Stress.*

Plurality of Mentalities

At the beginning of the century, when they began to study the language of the Indians and the Eskimos, linguists realised that 'the Indo-European languages were not the model of all other languages'. Since language is only the reflection of thought, Edward T. Hall deduces that, from one population to another, the way of seeing the world is also not the same. 'Our thesis', he writes, 'is that the principles established in regards to language are equally valid for the rest of human conduct and, in fact, for any cultural phenomenon. Individuals from different cultures not only speak different languages, but, more importantly, *live in different sensory worlds*'.

For any single period, therefore, there is a *plurality of mentalities*. Each society has its own way of 'conceiving' human relationships, individual movements, the layout of dwellings, the structures of cities, the boundaries of intimacy.

Among animals, zoologists distinguish 'contact' species, such as the parrot and hedgehog — or the great Antarctic penguin, which maintains its heat by snuggling against its fellows — and 'non-contact' species, like the horse, the dog, the cat, the rat, or the seagull. Even among man there are people more inclined than others to *contact* and promiscuity.

Within European culture, which places great importance on the individual, 'critical distance' seems to be particularly important. At the dawn of history, our ancestors formed small, highly fluid communities with human dimensions. At the same time, in the Near East, there were cities like anthills, administered by scribes and royal officials: Babylon, Sumer, Ur in Chaldaea.

Tactical, Visual, and Olfactory Spaces

Today, Europeans use their leisure time to move away from urban concentrations.

The notion of 'crowding' is not felt everywhere in the same way. A fixed space in one society is not necessarily fixed in another.

'In the United States', remarks Edward Hall, 'people move from one room to another, or from one part of a room to another, to satisfy each particular activity, whether it be to eat, sleep, work, or to make social contact. In Japan, the walls are mobile: they are discretely opened or folded up according to the various domestic activities. The Chinese behave in an even different manner, by assigning fixed characters to elements that Americans consider to be fixed. A guest in China is not supposed to move his chair unless he is invited by his host. To do so would be tantamount to moving a screen or a partition in a foreign house'.

The shape of the rooms, the position of the doors, the thickness of the walls, and the weight of the seats vary according to whether *promiscuity* is more or less well supported. Everything depends on the 'critical distance', that is, on the size of the bubble. 'The door is of great importance to the Germans. Those who come to the United States find the doors light and fragile. In their offices, the Americans work with open doors. The Germans close them. The closing of the door preserves the integrity of the room and ensures the reality of a protective border that preserves them from contacts that are too intimate'.

This bubble is larger in Great Britain than in the United States; larger among the Nordic than in the Mediterranean; larger in Europe than in the Third World.

'For the English, to be overheard is to intrude on others, a failure in manners and a sign of socially inferior behaviour. However, because of the way they modulate their voices, the English in an American setting may sound and look conspiratorial to Americans, which can result in their being branded as troublemakers'.

Hall then examines the different categories of space: *tactile* space, *visual* space, *olfactory* space.

'During World War Two in France', he recalls, 'I observed that the aroma of French bread freshly removed from the oven at 4:00 a.m. could make a speeding jeep scream to a halt. The reader can ask himself what smells we have in the U.S. that can achieve such results'.

In the Middle East, Americans find that the Arabs are 'pushy' because they 'shove and jostle in public'. The Arabs, on the other hand, find the Americans lacking education, 'because they stand apart'. 'Americans and Arabs', writes Edward T. Hall, 'live in different sensory worlds much of the time. They interpret their sensory data differently and combine them in different ways. American women who have married Arabs in this country and who have known only the "learned American" side of their personality have often observed that their husbands assume different personalities when they return to their homelands where they are again immersed in Arab communication and are captives of Arab perceptions. They become in every sense of the word quite different people'.

In light of these observations, man appears as an 'organism who creates his extensions' to the point of substituting them for nature.

The consequence: man conflates himself with the world, and by modifying the world, modifies himself. By constructing his *biotope*, he determines the organism that he *will be*. Proxemics returns here to the preoccupations of ecology. In large, overpopulated cities, a new type of man is formed.

To Live According to his Rhythm

In this regard, Professor Hall denounces the traumatising nature of contemporary architectural achievements aimed at eliminating differentiation in the habitat. 'With the anarchic urbanisation that is developing today', he writes, 'it is less the overcrowding that threatens us than it is the *loss of our identity*'.

'He demolishes', writes Françoise Choay in his preface, 'the *universalist* pretension of the tradition of spatial planning derived from Fourier, and taken up by Gropius, Le Corbusier, and his disciples'.

In the cities of tomorrow, man must be able to live according to his own pace or rhythm. And yet the optimum dimensions of *lived* or *experienced space* depend on the 'intensity of relations', a criterion that varies vastly from place to place. 'There is therefore no universal urbanism'.

'Because of our a-cultural bias', Edward T. Hall concludes, 'we believe only in the superficial differences between the peoples of this world. For this reason, we miss much of the richness which comes from knowing others'.

The richness of the world is its *diversity*.

*

La dimension caché, as study by Edward T. Hall.[437] Seuil, 253 pages.

*

What Edward T. Hall says about space in *The Hidden Dimension*, he also demonstrates about time in a second study entitled *The Silent Language*.[438] Each culture, in effect, formalises and orders temporal spaces in a unique way. From this results a different perception of the notion of time, which is expressed, among other places, in the structure of language. (Here E. T. Hall converges with the observations of Benjamin Lee Whorf observations on the mental system revealed by the formation and development of different language families).

He gives this example: 'I remember an American agriculturalist who went to Egypt to teach modern agricultural methods to the Egyptian farmers. At one point in his work he asked his interpreter to ask a farmer how much he expected his field to yield that year. The farmer responded by becoming very excited and angry. In an obvious attempt to soften the reply the interpreter said, "He says he doesn't know". The American realised something had gone wrong, but he had no way of knowing what. Later I learned that the Arabs regard anyone who tries to look into the future as slightly insane. When the American asked him about his future yield, the Egyptian was highly insulted since he thought the American considered him crazy. To the Arab only God knows the future, and it is presumptuous even to talk about it'.

E. T. Hall develops the idea that culture, which is intimately linked to social communication, is not a thing, but a set of things — which means that 'there is no one basic unit or elementary particle, no single isolate for all cultures'. Likewise, there is no independent experience of culture that makes it possible to 'calibrate' it: experience is 'something man projects on the outside world as he gains it in its culturally determined form'. The conclusion: 'There is a principle of relativity in culture, just as there is in physics and mathematics'.

NATURAL LAW

'A society', Says Robert Ardrey, 'is a group of *unequal* beings organised to meet common needs. In every species founded on sexual reproduction, the equality of individuals is a natural impossibility. Inequality must therefore be considered as the first law of social structures, whether in human societies or otherwise'.

Citing Jefferson, according to whom 'all men are created equal', Henry Allers Moe, former director of the Guggenheim Foundation, said one evening in 1965:

---

437 *The Hidden Dimension* (Garden City, NY: Doubleday, 1966). — Tr.
438 French edition: *Le langage silencieux* (Mame, 1973). — Tr.

'There are not many absurd statements that have done as much harm as this one. Everyone knows it, but no one says it'.

Robert Ardrey, sixty-nine years of age, says it. And even writes it. An American living in Rome, a dramatist (he is the author of *Thunder Rock*, a play that was performed in Paris as *Tour d'Ivoire* under the direction of Jean Mercure), a successful screenwriter and novelist (*Khartoum*), he abandoned literature in 1955, after a series of conversations with Professor Raymond Dart.

Like L. S. B. Leakey and Robert Broom, Dart belongs to a generation of anthropologists and palaeontologists who have shown that the evolution of man 'from some ancestral monkey from the forests was not what was believed in the time of Darwin'. In 1924, in the Transvaal, he discovered the remains of one of our 'great predatory ancestors': the African Australopithecus.

This biped with a small brain but strong canines lived two or three million years ago. A carnivorous hunter, he used tools to slaughter his prey. He is one of the direct ascendants of the human branch: we are indeed the 'children of Cain'.

'With one or two exceptions', says palaeontologist Alfred S. Romer in 1968, 'all the specialists examining the question today believe that Australopithecines are the true ancestors of man'.

Raymond Dart had already sustained the view twenty years ago (*International Anthropological and Linguistics Review*, 1, 1953, 201): man essentially distinguishes himself from other primates by the fact that he is first a hunter, and a large part of his physical and psychic peculiarities are explained by his predatory mode of life. This thesis has been confirmed by P. R. Thompson in a study published in the *Journal of Human Evolution* (4, 1975, 113) which furnishes 'irrefutable proofs of the convergence of human behaviour with carnivorous behaviour'.

Thompson's study concerns fifteen species of primates and eleven species of the most well-known carnivores, and distinguishes seven distinct behavioural traits in which the two categories oppose. It shows that the behaviour of man is identical to that of carnivores and different from that of primates on six points: sharing of food within the social group, storing food, occasional cannibalism, killing more prey than necessary (surplus killing), aggression against non-prey species, and the way of feeding the young. (The seventh point concerns the defence of the group, which, in man as in other primates, is principally assured by males; Thompson sees this as a consequence of the division of labour).

'The union of the carnivore and the big brain', states Ardrey, 'there lies the origin of man'. Our oldest ancestor was a killer. His murderous ways are the most certain in our heritage. Man is not descended from a fallen angel, but from an evolved anthropoid. He is an animal of prey.

Immediately after his meeting with Dart, Robert Ardrey, who remembers having studied natural science in Chicago, returned to his first vocation. He obtained some grants and embarked for Africa. In 1961, in *African Genesis* (French title: *Les enfants de Caïn*, 'The Children of Cain', Stock, 1963) he took up the conclusion of Raymond Dart again, but this time deepened them.

The question that he poses is this: 'What have we *inherited* from our hunter ancestor?'.

The answer imposes itself: If the first hominids are not peaceful baboons, but carnivorous killers, then Rousseau, Marx, and Freud are wrong. 'And with them', writes Ardrey, 'all those who believe in man's first innocence, in his innate lack of aggression, who deny that violence forms part of our nature, and who believe that it is solely determined by the contingencies of the environment'.

A second book was published in 1966. *The Territorial Imperative* (*Le territoire*, Stock, 1968). Ardrey underscores the significance, in most societies, of the 'territorial impulse'.

As soon as an individual enters the age of adulthood, he explains, he begins to 'establish himself', to 'settle down'. He demarcates his zone of influence, marks his borders, and creates his routines. In short, he *takes possession* of a territory, that is to say, of part of his specific environment.

The quicker this space is demarcated, the quicker he will establish normal social relations—provided that the territories are well differentiated. In the United States, Gerald B. Suttles (*The Social Order of the Slum*) and Edward T. Hall (*The Hidden Dimension*) have shown that delinquency increases in direct relation to the anonymity of the large concrete hives.

A 'territorial instinct' therefore exists, which is essentially defensive. 'If we defend our homeland and our country', writes Robert Ardrey, 'it is for *biological* reasons—not because we choose to do it, but because we must'.

From the outset, *African Genesis* and *The Territorial Imperative* knew a smashing success.

In *The Social Contract*, Ardrey pushes his reasoning to its ultimate consequences. Referring principally to Konrad Lorenz, he not only shows, in a lively and colorful style, that 'aggression is the main guarantee of survival', he also attacks the egalitarian myth.

Sociologists and politicians have long pointed out that egalitarian systems, far from conforming to societies that are fundamentally homogeneous, conserve (and even occasionally resurrect) the inequalities that they denounce. Hence the idea that these inequalities are not due to the influence of the 'environment' or to 'class relations', but that they correspond, in the social field, to an inequality in the distribution of aptitudes.

'Diversity', explains Ardrey, 'is the very substance of evolution, for it is from the diversity of beings that natural selection makes its choice'.

He adds: 'The question of inequality can be displaced, but there was a time, the Victorian era, when sexuality was also displaced. If we have transferred the taboo of sexuality to its consequences, perhaps this is but an evolution of the Puritan spirit'.

The Errors of Jean-Jacques Rousseau

One afternoon in New York, Robert Ardrey was feeding the birds. It is cold, the ground is covered with snow. Half a dozen titmice fly around, but they do not approach, even though they are probably hungry. Suddenly, a seventh titmouse appears and alights upon the edge of the plate. All the others then join it. The 'alpha' has arrived.

In the farmyard, 'each chicken has the right to peck those who are inferior to it in the hierarchy, but these have no right to return the favor'. Such 'phenomena of domination' have been observed among birds (Eliot Howard, then Lorenz), fish, and reptiles (G. K. Noble), as well as among primates (Carpenter).

Every society thus has its born leaders. They are the *alphas*. They play the simultaneous role of chiefs, sentinels, and guardians.

Contra Freud, the psychoanalyst Alfred Adler argued that the will to power, not sexuality, governs behavior. 'His conclusions', assures Ardrey, 'are now confirmed by the study of the natural world of which man is a part'.

The French edition of Ardrey's book is entitled *La loi naturelle* (Natural Law), but the English original is called *The Social Contract*. Here, the celebrated

Discours sur l'origine et les fondements de l'inégalité parmi les hommes (1754),[439] by Jean-Jacques Rousseau, is in fact revised and corrected.

A century before Darwin, Rousseau understood that man is rooted in nature. But his 'nature' resembles the green paradise of infantile love. It is an *ideal* nature, which does not take into account either the realities of life or what is *specifically human* in man. It is also the *projection*, into an imaginary past, of a *moralising* point of view: what society *should* be according to Rousseau. In *L'Emile* he writes: 'Nature has made man happy and good, but society makes him depraved and miserable'. It therefore inaugurates what Robert Ardrey calls 'the era of the alibi'. ('If I fail in my undertakings, it is the *fault of others*'). And rejoining the use, by Judeo-Christianity, of 'resentment' as a driver of morality — and as a formative principle of American 'good conscience' (cf. Nietzsche, *The Genealogy of Morality*).

The German philosopher Ernst Cassirer would remark: 'All contemporary social struggles have the same origin. They proceed from the consciousness of the responsibility of society, which Rousseau was the first to have and which he bequeathed to posterity'.

Is it really society that corrupts man, or man that corrupts society?

The Foundations of a New Social Contract

According to Robert Ardrey, many of the disappointments that man has encountered are explained by his refusal to admit the existence of a 'natural law' applying to his innate relationship to living systems taken in their entirety. From this emerges his dream of an 'impossible philosophy'. Because he tends to master the universe, man believes he can make a clean slate of the past. But to *master* the world is not to *change* it. The existence of supersonic aircraft does not negate the laws of gravity.

'We have tried to dominate nature as if we ourselves were not a part of this nature. And we have pursued the dream of human equality as men of centuries past pursued the Holy Grail'.

One consequence, among many others: 'We are still waiting for the day when the scientist will be free to explore racial differences in total freedom without having his life threatened'.

---

439 *Discourse on the Origin and Foundations of Inequality Among Men.* — Tr.

Professor Sol Tax, from the University of Chicago, has written: 'We are egalitarian, not because we can prove the existence of absolute equality, but because we are certain that the differences that may exist within vast populations are irrelevant on the plane of the politics of nations. This conviction proceeds from our knowledge, but it equally satisfies us as citizens of the world'.

Comments Robert Ardrey: 'These remarks are not those of a free man. Nor do they say what the discipline of a free science should be'.

What we lack most today is an 'evolutionary philosophy'. The society of equals is a utopia. But the *just* society, where everyone has their chances *at the beginning*, is an accessible goal.

'The just society as I see it', writes Robert Ardrey, 'is a society in which a sufficient order protects the members, whatever the diversity of their gifts, while a sufficient disorder offers each individual every opportunity to develop these genetic gifts'.

This balance between order and disorder, unity and diversity, constitutes the new 'social contract' that he intends to propose.

'We are not gods, and Jean-Jacques was right. We are a part of nature, he said so, too. But the fundamental difference between my social contract and Rousseau's lies in the fact that his was an agreement between fallen angels, while mine is between evolved apes'.

*

La loi naturelle, a study by Robert Ardrey.[440] Stock, 447 pages, 26 Francs.

*

The classification of the Australopithecus continues to be the subject of a certain number of debates. A new diagnosis has been proposed by M. H. Wolpoff and C. O. Lovejoy in the *Journal of Human Evolution* (4, 1975, 275). It incorporates the genera 'Paranthropus', 'Plesianthropus', 'Meganthropus', 'Zinjanthropus', and so on. Its authors defend the thesis (which they had already previously revealed) of a single line of African Plio-Pleistocene hominids. In this thesis, there is continuity and direct filiation between *Homo africanus* (Australopithecus), *Homo erectus*, and *Homo sapiens*. In addition, the two Australopithecus morphologies (slender and robust) are grouped together: we only distinguish morphotypes due to individual variations (and without doubt also to sexual dimorphism).

According to other orders, by contrast, only the 'slender' Australopithecus would be placed among the ancestors of man: the 'robust' Australopithecus would constitute a distinct

---

440 *The Social Contract: A Personal Inquiry into the Evolutionary Sources of Order and Disorder* (London: Collins, 1970). — Tr.

branch corresponding to the Paranthropus. This is the thesis sustained by J. T. Robinson, in *Early Hominid Posture and Locomotion* (Chicago: University of Chicago Press, 1972).

Some controversies have also resulted in *Homo habilis*, a taxon created in 1964, which some consider to be a simple extension of the 'slender' Australopithecus morphology.

In March 1976, Robert Ardrey published a new book entitled *The Hunting Peoples* (New York: Atheneum). It is an ethological approach to the phenomenon of the primitive hunter. A French translation is anticipated.

IS MAN ONLY AN ANIMAL?

What is man's place in nature? Is man an animal? If so, is he nothing else?

For centuries, anthropomorphism has governed our minds. Under the influence of beliefs and dogmas. It seemed self-evident that man, 'king of creation', was also the *centre*. His 'nature' was said to be radically distinct from that of other living beings.

It was also self-evident that the sun and the stars revolved around the Earth. In his *City of God* (XVI, 9), St. Augustine deduces the impossibility of the antipodes from the fact that 'on the day of Judgment, the men who would be on the other side of the Earth could not see the Lord descending through the air'.

This vision of the world collapsed on 24 May 1542.

On that day, the German astronomer Nicolas Copernicus published a work entitled *De revolutionibus orbium coelestium*. Herein he resurrected the ancient theory of Aristarchus of Samos (270 BC), who first sensed that the Earth and the other planets of our system revolve around the sun.

On 5 March 1616, the Sacred Congregation of the Index suspended Copernicus's book. But it was already too late. The *libido sciendi*,[441] which the Fathers of the Church and the Doctors of the Middle Ages had expressly condemned, resumed its rights.

First speculative and theoretical, the research became operative and descriptive. Leonardo da Vinci (1552–1619) declares: 'The interpreter of the Nature's artifices is experience'.

Returning in its turn to the monistic conception of the first physicists of Ionia, Galileo (1561–1643) establishes the physical reality of heliocentrism: it is now the Earth that revolves around the sun. Ruining the cosmology of Aristotle, it renders the work of Newton and his successors possible. 'For the

---

441 Latin: *desire to know, lust for knowledge.* — Tr.

closed and finite world of the ancients and the Scholastics, he substitutes the open and infinite world which enthuses Giordano Bruno and scares Pascal' (Louis Rougier).

The German Kepler (1571–1630) demonstrates that the planets describe ellipses, and that they do not move uniformly in their orbits. Henceforth, the Earth is only one planet among others. The world becomes an infinite universe, 'whose center is everywhere and whose circumference nowhere'. In the eighteenth century, Fontenelle, the French philosopher, would hold forth on the 'plurality of worlds'.

In his *Scienza nuova* (1725–1730), the Neapolitan Jean-Baptiste Vico affirms that humanity, in the west, is the only one compatible with its destiny. Lavoisier (1743–1794) declares: 'Man is a new Prometheus, a second creator'.

Vertical Ape

In 1859, Charles Darwin published *The Origin of Species*. He demonstrated that 'man is the co-descendant with other species of some ancient, lower, and extinct form'.

The animal origin of man was sensed at the end of the eighteenth century by Buffon and Linnaeus. In 1809, Lamarck had suggested that the characteristics of human organisation could have been produced by the 'changes in habits of an ape' (*Philosophie biologique*).

Darwin goes further. Using evidence of a taxonomic, morphological and embryological order, he establishes the fact of *evolution*, whose mechanism is explained by natural selection (which eliminates the weakest) and selective fertility (which favours the multiplication of the best). It shows that species derive from each other, and that man, if he is the last cry of evolution, is not necessarily the last word.

In certain traits of the anatomy of human beings he observes traces of an ancient kinship. The small point on the helix of the ear comes from the primates.[442] The semilunar fold of the eye (the 'third eyelid') connects us to birds. Darwin cites again the coccyx, the appendix, the large root of the canine teeth, the atrophied muscles of the scalp: all of these are so many *vestiges* corresponding, in the cultural domain, to the decorative buttons that we wear

---

442 The auricular tubercle, also known as Darwin's tubercle. — Tr.

on our sleeves which have not been used for buttoning for a long time, or the ribbons of hats which become simple ornaments over time.

As soon as Darwin's works were published, we see what Jean Rostand has called 'hominid pride'.[443]

'Is it truly believable', asks Wilberforce, bishop of Oxford, 'that the favourite varieties of turnips could ever become men!'

At a meeting of the British Association, Wilberforce, opposed to Huxley, a disciple of Darwin's, asked his interlocutor if it is by his grandfather or grandmother that he descends from the ape. Unperturbed, Huxley replied:

'I would rather descend from an ape than from an imbecile who takes pleasure in confusing a question of which he does not understand the first word'.

A part of the public refuses to suffer the 'zoological humiliation,' just as it had refused, in the time of Galilee, the 'cosmological humiliation'. This was the beginning of the 'war of the ape'.

The transformist idea would nevertheless rapidly make its way. Broca in France, and Haeckel in Germany, are its first defenders. Today it is unanimous among scholars, even if they are still divided in their evaluation of its scope.

It is now known, as Jean Rostand has written, that 'in a certain family of small placental mammals, transformations appeared which would lead to the *vertical ape*, whose forehead would rise towards the stars, and who would seek meaning in the universe' (*Charles Darwin*, Gallimard, 1947).

Since the discovery of the remains of Neanderthal man in 1857, human palaeontology has itself made immense progress.

It is commonly believed that the primates appeared at the beginning of the tertiary era, around seventy million years ago, from a primitive strain of insectivores represented today by the genus *Tupaia* (treeshrews native to Southeast Asia).

The apes (the species apparently closest to ours) come from a strain that separated from the primates twenty or thirty million years ago.

By 1960, the earliest Hominin were still being traced back to the beginning of the Quaternary, that is, about a million years ago. More recent findings (and the implementation of dating methods such as potassium-argon) have

---

443 Reading *hominiote* as *hominide*. — Tr.

led to new assessments. Hominin fossils found north of Kenya, near Lake Turkana, have been dated to five millions years. In 1974, in a field in Hadar in Central Afar (Ethiopia), the three-million-year-old skeleton of a 'slender' Australopithecus was unearthed, and named 'Lucy' — and in 1975, in the same location, the bones of hominin that lived 3.5 million years ago. Other fossils, such as the 'Ramapithecus' (uncovered at Fort Ternan, East Africa), which is *fourteen or fifteen million years old*, have also been added to our human ancestry.

According to Konrad Lorenz, one can speak of hominisation when three conditions are present: (1) *The central representation of space*, developed (especially in climbing) from the prehensile use of the hand, which constitutes the principle of all thought. (2) *A permanent attitude of curiosity and active exploration*, characteristic of a 'non-specialised' species. (3) *A 'cultural' aptitude for self-domestication*, creating new degrees of freedom in action.

'As man possesses the same senses as the lower animals, his fundamental intuitions must be the same', wrote Darwin, thus paving the way for modern ethology, i.e. the biology of behaviour.

Today, the ensuing theoretical and ideological significance of these discoveries appears considerable.

Against the Philosophies of the Impossible

In *L'Humanité*, (21 June 1974) Luce Langevin wrote: 'What distinguishes and privileges the action of man is work'.

Yet we know now that private property is not the result of the division of labour or of a 'contradiction' in the relation of the forces of production — as Karl Marx purported. It is, like all phenomena of *possession*, a *natural* institution whose origin is lost in the labyrinth of a pre-human heritage.

'The philosophies of Rousseau, Marx, or Freud', observes Dr. Pierre Debray-Ritzen, 'have not yet grasped the explosive importance of what contemporary anthropology and ethology brings: how could Marx have known that *property* has been marked for hundreds of millions of years in evolution? How could Freud imagine that *hierarchy* is an institution common to all animal societies and that the tendency to dominate his peers, to become an 'alpha', is an ancient instinct which is also hundreds of millions of years old? Would Rousseau have imagined that the *Australopithecus africanus*, from which we are undoubtedly derived, was a carnivore, and therefore a killer?

Recently, a 'second school' of ethologists (almost all American) have attempted to substitute the thesis of the inherentness of the aggressive impulse with another conception, inspired by psychoanalysis, in which aggressiveness is simply a *reaction* to the 'frustrations' of the surrounding environment.

This thesis, which seemed to prevail in the seventh meeting held at Rueil-Malmaison in May 1974, merely resumes the arguments of the old 'reflexologists'. It is very unconvincing: we know now that the repeated frustration undergone by individuals or groups can lead to total passivity as well as endemic violence.

Other criticisms of Lorenz and Ardrey came from proponents of the 'philosophies of the impossible' (existentialism, neo-Marxism, structuralism, the Frankfurt School, anti-psychiatry), by those who *moralise* the world and only accept existence under the condition that it be *justified* — forgetting that it is only in death that the *selfsame* is perfect.

For L. Berkowitz (*Aggression*, McGraw Hill, 1962), the conclusions of classical ethology revert to saying that 'civilisation and the moral order must ultimately be founded on strength and not on love and charity'. According to B. F. Skinner, who is the principal theorist of behaviourism, these conclusions 'encourage an attitude of resigned passivity'.

Robert Ardrey responds with a smile:

'It must be admitted that no one obeys the territorial imperative as much as a professor of sociology contesting the intrusive hypothesis of biology, according to which man is a territorial animal!'

In *The Human Imperative*,[444] Alexander Alland, Professor at Columbia University, seemed to fuel the debate by claiming to defend man against 'absolute biological determinism'.

'Numerous recent, successful works', he wrote, 'wanted to convince us that aggression, territoriality, and other sad human behaviours, already exist in lower animal species. Certain biological continuities between man and animal were then overestimated and used as an explanation for the worst aspects of

---

444 French edition: *La dimension humaine: réponse à Konrad Lorenz* (Paris: Seuil, 1974). — Tr.

humanity. On the basis of such statements, wars and conflicts eventually appear inevitable'.

In fact, on reading his book, one realises that Alland's preoccupations are mainly of a social and political nature: his main criticism of Ardrey is that he has shown his hostility 'to progressives, Marxists, and Freudians'. He explicitly claims 'the message of Marx' and asserts that the Soviet system has proven to be 'stunningly effective'.

Moreover, his tract is largely deficient in its purpose, for neither Robert Ardrey, nor even Lorenz, have ever declared that the study of animal behaviour allowed us to explain *everything* about man.

Alland himself admits that Lorenz 'tries to establish a synthesis between the biological heritage and its cultural expression'. As for Ardrey, he writes: 'The human mind is free, for it neither strictly nor directly obeys instinct. Among all the instinctual problems that rage in man, there is always one which wants to dominate others and win acceptance'.

Nevertheless, the question remains: Is man only an animal — and nothing else?

The Specifically Human Level

The reality of our pre-human heritage is undeniable. It is expressed in the most deeply buried layers of our brain (the *palaeocortex*). Beyond the species that preceded it, man is the heir to three billion years of life. This immense past corresponds to his *biological dimension*.

This, however, is not sufficient to characterise the human being. To say that man is an animal is a fact. But how does he differ from other animals?

After centuries of anthropomorphism (even theomorphism), it is important not to fall into pure zoomorphism or biologism.

Regarding the 'reality' of man, one can say that it can be apprehended and decomposed into four levels: the *microphysical* level (*energy*); the *macrophysical* level (*matter*); the *biological* level (*life*), and finally a specifically *human* level, characterised by *culture* and *historical consciousness*.

Man shares his belonging to the first *three* levels of the universe with increasingly restricted 'parts'. Only the last one properly belongs to him.

Certain fashionable ideologies attempt to reduce these different levels to one another by erasing the *emergent* qualities that characterise and differentiate each level. These are the ideological *reductionists*.

All the Instincts

Materialism reduces man to his material dimension. Its logic is that of physical systems, governed by the second law of thermodynamics: it is a logic of homogeneity, and therefore, in the final analysis, a logic of the growing entropy and of death.

Pure biologism (or *biological materialism*) has the merit of placing the accent on aspects of the human being that are far too underestimated today: heredity, ethnicity, and animal inheritance. It also remains, however, beyond what can and must be a complete description of the human phenomenon. It does not, *on its own*, allow interpretation.

In their work, ethologists note a number of striking analogies between the animal and human kingdoms. However, sometimes they compare man to the chimpanzee, sometimes to the Ugandan kob, sometimes to the giraffe and the gudgeon, if not to the squirrel or the seagull. These comparisons show that man is less the descendant of one branch of evolution than the heir of the *totality of the animal kingdom*. Man is not 'devoid of instincts', as the American Ashley asserts. On the contrary, he has *all* the instincts. This forces him to make *choices* — to *actualise* this or that instinct to the detriment of others.

After having shown that man, *in his biological dimension* (and in no other) is subject, like the other animals, to the 'natural law' of living systems, Konrad Lorenz (whatever his opponents have said) has always taken care to show that this is what makes the *specificity* of the human phenomenon.

He also refers to one of the masters of 'philosophical anthropology' (*philosophische Anthropologie*), the sociologist and philosopher Arnold Gehlen, who died in 1976, and was author of seminal works which unfortunately have not been translated into French: *Der Mensch. Seine Natur und seine Stellung in der Welt* (1940 and 1966), *Urmensch und Spätkultur* (1956), *Die Seele im technischen Zeitalter* (1957), *Anthropologische Forschung* (1961), *Moral und Hypermoral* (1969), *Einblicke* (1975), etc.[445]

---

445 *Man: His Nature and his Place in the World*; *Early Man and Late Culture*; *The Soul in a Technical Age*; *Anthropological Research*; *Morality and Hypermorality*; *Insights*. — Tr.

Arnold Gehlen

According to Gehlen, whose thought lies at the antipodes of Rousseau's, one of the characteristic traits of man is that he is not adapted to a particular environment, but to *all* environments. This enables him to be 'open to the entire world' and to *build his environment himself*. To use one of Ernst Jünger's expressions, it can be said that this 'openness' is oriented towards the 'total mobilisation of the world'. Man, therefore, has the possibility of choice, and by consequence a *freedom* which belongs only to him. In this he is distinguished from other species, which, being subject to their own environment, are narrowly *specialised*. Man, however, is the 'specialist of non-specialisation'.

'Imagine', writes Konrad Lorenz, 'a *triathlon* whose requirements were a thirty-kilometer run, a four-meter climb, a dive twenty-meters deep with the task of bringing an sunken object back to the surface: there is no mammal that performs these deeds, which are within the capacity of any average citizen.

Even the term instinct is inappropriate when it concerns man.

What characterises instinct in the animal is that its *object*, as well as the way it is expressed (that is, the *sequence of events* arising from the execution impulses), are 'programmed' in advance: the wolf, the tiger, and the baboon know instinctively how and upon what their aggression should be exercised, the food they need to eat, how and on whom they must exercise their sexual power, etc. For man, this is not the case. The plurality of instincts within him correspond to a certain number of *impulses* without a predetermined object. It is still necessary for him choose which of these he can possibly dominate; and he can give an almost infinite number of concrete expressions to them.

'The response to an *impulse*', writes Alexander Alland, 'is not as rigidly modelled as the response to an *instinct*. The fact that a man has an impulse dictated by hunger, for example, tells us nothing about how he will get food, or what he will eat'.

While the animal is completely *subject* to its belonging to a given species, man, on the contrary, is 'partially free from the constraints of the species' (Spengler). His *neocortex* can superimpose his will upon the impulses, emotions, and the moods produced by the *palaeocortex*. The domestic, reasoned consciousness in him feels it. His freedom of choice is preserved at all times.

Nietzsche's remark is thus authenticated: 'Man's sickness is man, he suffers from himself: the consequence of a violent divorce from his animal past'.[446]

On the other hand (and Lorenz quotes Gehlen again), man is an '*incomplete* being': his non-specialisation is explained by the fact that his capacity for adaptation endures throughout his whole life, whereas in other species it is restricted to the short period of infancy.

The small animal, left to itself, can very quickly manage on its own. He knows instinctively what he needs and what he must avoid. At thirteen weeks a chimpanzee begins to masticate pieces of solid food. At seventeen or eighteen months he is familiar with all the 'techniques' of adults. The small human is very different. It has to learn everything. When we raise a three-month-old baby with a small monkey of the same age: in every area, the monkey outperforms the child.

The higher one climbs the scale of organised beings, *the longer the maturation*, the more time it takes to make a *complete* individual.

Great apes reach the age of puberty between seven and twelve years (for a lifespan of forty to fifty years). It occurs in men between eleven and fifteen years — up to seventeen years in the Nordic countries. (It should be noted that in men, maturation lasts longer than in women).

The precocity of the animal world goes hand in hand with a development that 'locks in' more rapidly. 'The proverb', writes Lorenz, 'that an old dog does not learn new tricks also applies without restriction to all inquisitive, non-specialised animals. An old black crow, or an old rat, has absolutely nothing of the openness to the world which, in young animals, resonates so closely with the "human"'.

Man is therefore a *persistently juvenile* being. For him, the 'learning' period is prolonged almost indefinitely. His mind remains an 'open system' until his final moments. We become men only because we have benefited from a very long childhood.

To describe this 'persistent juvenility', which is peculiar to humans, zoologists speak of *foetalisation* or *neoteny*.

---

446 *Genealogy of Morality*, II, 16. — Tr.

'The distinctive character of man', writes Lorenz, 'the preservation of an active and creative capacity for adaptation to the environment, is a phenomenon of *neoteny*'.

This superiority is responsible for both the *greatness* and also the extreme *fragility* of the human race. When the crayfish is moulting, it must abandon its shell: at that moment it is more vulnerable than ever. Man is continually 'moulting' his whole life. He can always imagine *differently* and want *better*. He creates, accomplishes, and surpasses himself, but perpetually puts himself in danger. 'Man', says Gehlen, is a '*risky* being': he has 'by his very constitution, a chance of losing himself'.

There is also a close connection between the *neoteny* and the enduring nature of *curiosity* and *imagination*.

Human thought is essentially imaginative. It develops without the aid of concrete objects, and 'builds' by simple curiosity. Man can learn new motor coordinations, for example, without having practiced the exercise himself. He can express feelings that he has not felt himself. His knowledge is nourished not only by experiences, but also by intuitions, analyses, deductions. We *play* with the concepts that our mind contains. ('Man is perfectly man only when he plays', says Schiller).

Ultimately, man is the only being who is *conscious of being conscious*. Animals know that they exist, but they do not know that they will die. They are conscious of death only when it seizes them. Men, and by extension cultures, know that they are mortal. Their 'double consciousness' is a *historical* consciousness: it puts time into *perspective*.

Man Draws Everything from Himself

Darwin said 'free will is to mind what chance is to matter. This is our arrogance, our deep admiration for ourselves'.

The behaviours which are purely instinctive and *predetermined* in the animal are found in 'thought' in the human species, and *historicised*. From sexuality, man makes eroticism; form work, organised action; from aggression, a strategy; from the 'word', a discourse; from a series of events, a history.

He is the only one to be able to say *I* with knowledge, he is also the only one to be able to *capitalise* the ancestral *inheritance*, to *reactualise* it at any moment, to enrich it by *renewing it*. It is this in which his 'free will' consists.

'Free, man draws everything from himself, including his own end', writes Professor Pierre P. Grassé — 'whence his immense responsibility with regard to the species. He *finalises everything*, including the future of his species. Condemned to be the worker of his destiny, he weaves his future and gives life the meaning that his will and his desire suggest to him (…) The finality presents itself completely differently among animals than it does for us, for the determinants of their conduct differ radically from ours. More precisely, in man, the immanent biological finality which dominates our bodily structure and our organic functions is overlaid by the finality created by our will in the field of freedom' (*Toi, ce petit dieu !* Albin Michel, 1971).

Whereas the animal is born *already trained*, man must train himself. He is a 'being of dressage' (Gehlen).[447] Hence the importance of *education* and the need for *discipline* in order to create *circuits of habit*. To want to escape from all constraint, and, above all, from that which the individual must impose on himself, is to return to the lower limit of humanity. To be *less* human.

Organiser of his own destiny, man in the final analysis is a profoundly *cultural* being.

His potential abilities are innate. But they are developed or thwarted by the environment, and then constantly reoriented by learning and cultural heritage. The latter determines the knowledge system (the group's own worldview), which consists of classifications allowing the division, analysis, and comprehension of the surrounding environment (including the human environment), and consequently, the statement of norms and rules of action. Man inherits a tradition. But within it, he innovates constantly: a subtle dialectic, where permanence and change are combined. As Alland writes: 'Man is born with the faculty of assimilating culture, not with culture'.

For a 'Return to Culture'

Culture itself has a biological origin. Better: 'Every change in our environment gives rise to new selective pressures, which continue to operate, both genetically and culturally' (Alland). But this biological basis is one factor, while the possibilities and modalities of cultural expression vary immensely.

---

447 The term *dressage*, from the verb *dresser*, means 'to train', or 'to straighten', with an implied sense of 'final correction', much as in 'finishing schools'; cf. the English use of dressage as the 'highest expression of horse training'. — Tr.

It remains to be seen, however, to what extent *self-mastery* is innate. This is a crucial detail, since it is precisely this quality which enables man to act independently of his impulses (see Arnold Gehlen, *Moral und Hypermoral*, and Irenäus Eibl-Eibesfeldt (*The Preprogrammed Man*).

Thanks to evidence from ethology, it is now possible to initiate a radical critique of the philosophies stemming from Rousseau's thought. Man is not 'naturally good'. At birth, he is neither 'free' nor 'equal' to anyone. But to deepen this criticism, it is necessary, as Arnold Gehlen has done in *Der Mensch*, to substitute for the doubtful (and often reductionist) slogan of 'return to nature' that of 'return to culture'.

Nature, say the philosophers of life, tells us what we *are*, but not what we can *become*.

In an essay published in 1973, *L'anti-nature*, Clement Rosset rightly denounced 'deep and ineradicable illusion' in the very idea of 'nature'.

Claiming in turn Empedocles, the sophists and atomists of antiquity, as well as Machiavelli and Nietzsche, he notes that what is man's own, that is to say *culture*, corresponds precisely to the part of him which, not belonging to 'nature', can be considered 'artifice'. He therefore denounces the '*naturalist* ideologies', and among them, the 'ecological' challenge that, regardless of its legitimate aspects, is essentially *anti-cultural* (hence 'anti-human') insofar as it suggests that man must not 'defy' nature, that he must stop his growth and *cease to be a man,* rather than engaging himself in new confrontations.

Rossez, to the contrary, proposes that man should fully assume his specificity 'by renouncing the idea of nature, which can be regarded as the principle of all ideas tending to "divinise" existence and to deprecate it as such'.

'Thus', he continues, 'man, freed from the idea of nature, will be able to recover his true … nature: a "denatured" and *properly human* nature'.

Here we find the necessity of a tragic conception of life: 'To affirm existence is to *affirm tragedy*: to consent to the impossibility of seizing existence in general. The tragedy of existence is to dispense with any ontological framework. The affirmation is tragic or it is not (…) This is the constant paradox of tragic philosophy: to celebrate without reason and to detail all the horror of the world for the sole pleasure of placing the inalterable character of its *joy* in relief'.

And Rosset concludes: 'The distinction is imposed between the formula of *morality and religion* ('Be first humble and you will see happiness follows') and the formula of *joy* ('Be first happy and you will necessarily be humble'). The second formula is more certain than the first: for joy guarantees humility (Nietzsche), whereas humility does not guarantee joy (Pascal). The chronological and psychological nuance is important, for it signifies that the deepest wisdom does not recommend to be humble first, but happy first'.

*

La dimension humaine, a study by Alexander Alland. Seuil, 190 pages.[448]
L'anti-nature, a study by Clément Rosset. PUF, 330 pages.[449]

*

Human ethology has been combined with scientific ecology, genetics, and the study of population dynamics to give rise to a new discipline, sociobiology. It is defined as a 'systematic study of the biological foundations of all forms of social behaviour, both in man and in animals' (*New Scientist*, 13 May 1976). Its principal theorist is Edward O. Wilson, a Professor at Harvard University, whose great work, *Sociobiology: The New Synthesis* (Belknap: Harvard, 1979) was a sensation in the United States.

Sociobiology is part of the ('elitist') neo-Darwinian theory of evolution. It takes into account the fact that there is a high degree of interactions between individuals in the same population resulting from preferential associations not exclusively linked to habitat. It shows that individuals of the same population are not random, interchangeable units. What is more, it proposes a re-examination of the notion of natural selection by shifting its emphasis from the individual to the parental group (kin). In this hypothesis, 'altruistic behaviours' are no longer in contradiction with the 'Darwinian fitness' of the gene — a notion according to which the main biological function of the organism is not the reproduction of other organisms, but the reproduction and multiplication (through other organisms) of the 'best' genes from the point of view of selection and adaptation.

Professor Wilson's theories have been particularly well received by ethologists. However, in the United States, they have provoked a campaign of systematic denigration on the part of the left-wing 'radical scientists' gathered around Richard C. Lewontin. They formed a 'Sociobiology Study Group' whose aim was to denounce the 'implicit political message' of sociobiology. A book has even been published emanating from this circle: Sahilins, *The Use and Abuse of Biology: An Anthropological Critique of Sociobiology* (University of Michigan Press, Ann Arbor, 1976.)

To these critiques, E. O. Wilson replied (*New York Review of Books*, 11 December, 1975), that his opponents distort his views in order to propagate a purely environmentalist ideology, and for his part he never denied the specific importance of cultural factors.

---

448 *The Human Imperative* (New York: Columbia University Press, 1972). — Tr.
449 *Anti-Nature*. — Tr.

Inspired by Marxism or Behaviourism, the attacks against Lorenz, Eibl-Eibesfeldt, and Ardrey also continue to grow. In the space of a few years, the criticisms of John P. Scott (*Aggression*, Chicago: University of Chicago Press, 1958 and 1970), Ashley Montagu (*Man and Aggression*, London: Oxford University Press, 1968 and 1973), Walter Hollitscher (*Kain oder Prometheus?* Frankfurt/M: Marxistische Blätter, 1972), Jospeph Rattner (*Aggression und menschliche Natur*, Frankfurt/M: Fischer, 1972),[450] Wolfgang Schmidtbauer (*Die sogennante Aggression*, Hamburg: Hoffmann und Campe, 1972),[451] and Kurt Gerhardt (*Aggression und Rassismus — elementare Verhaltensweisen?* Körsel, München, 1973),[452] Rolf Denker (*Aufklärung über Aggression*, W. Kohlhammer, Stuttgart, 1975),[453] Ulrich Erckenbrecht (*Mensch, du Affe*, Kübler: Lampertheim, 1975),[454] Gerhard Roth (*Kritik der Verhaltungsforschung*), C. H. Beck, München, 1976),[455] Gunter Pilz and Hugo Moesch (*Der Mensch und die Graugans. Eine Kritik an Konrad Lorenz*. Umschau: Frankfurt/M, 1976),[456] etc. These studies, which all seem to reiterate each other, are on the whole not very convincing.

---

450 *Aggression and Human Nature.* — Tr.

451 *So-called Aggression.* — Tr.

452 *Aggression and Racism — Elementary Behaviours?* — Tr.

453 *Clarification on Aggression.* — Tr.

454 *Man, You Monkey.* — Tr.

455 *Critique of Behavioural Research.* — Tr.

456 *The Man and the Greylag Goose: A Critique of Konrad Lorenz.* — Tr.

Psychological

INTELLIGENCE, INHERITANCE, AND IQ

'The results of numerous carefully conducted surveys unquestionably lead to the conclusion that IQ (intelligence quotient) tests, suitably designed and administered, yield results that coincide remarkably well with the child's successes (...) In a very summary way, let us say that any child with an IQ. of 115 can hope to enter high school, that if he has a quotient of 125 he will enter university, and that he has every chance to graduate at the top of his class if his quotient is between 135 and 140'.

According to Professor Hans J. Eysenck, the prospects of 'democratising' education are more limited than we would believe.

Born in Berlin in 1916 and established in Great Britain since 1936, Professor Eysenck studied at the Universities of Dijon, Brussels, and Exeter. He was appointed in 1942 to the Mill Hill Emergency Hospital and then to the Maudsley Hospital in London. In 1950, he took over the Department of Psychology at the Institute of Psychiatry of the University of London. He is probably the British psychologist most well-known to the public. We see him regularly on television. Almost all of his books have been bestsellers (*Know Your Own IQ, Crime and Personality, Sense and Nonsense in Psychology, Uses and Abuse of Psychology, Psychology and Politics*). In total, sales of his works have exceeded 1.5 million copies.

In *Know Your Own IQ*, he surveys intelligence tests and allows the reader to 'evaluate' themselves.

It was the Frenchman Alfred Binet who, in 1904, first noticed that mental capacities and functions could be measured by tests which required these capacities and functions in order to pass.

Psychometry soon developed, especially in the Anglo-Saxon countries, where, unlike France, psychology is regarded as a *science* and not as a branch of speculative philosophy.

Mental Age / Actual Age

Today there are a whole host of 'tests', some more generalised and some more specialised in scope (tests to evaluate a particular aptitude, tests for children, tests used in psychiatry, etc.). Professor Eysenck's 'game-book' consists in eight series of forty questions. Their peculiarity is as follows: it is by discovering the method that allows one to pose the problem that one also discovers the solution.

An example of 'verbal' test: 'Black is to white as high is to: (1) low; (2) green; (3) ascending; (4) distant'. The right answer is obviously 'low'. 'Green' is an aberrant answer. 'Ascending' and 'distant' indicate bad comprehension.

An example of a 'progressive logic' test: 'What is the missing number at the end of the series: 3, 7, 16, 35 ...' The answer is 74. (Each number is the double of the preceding, plus one, plus two, plus three, etc.).

Other tests consist of comparing sets of words and forms, noting similarities and differences. Within each series, the exercises grow increasingly difficult.

Through these kinds of tests, psychologists evaluate the *mental age* of a subject. Having a mental age of three means that the tests that are passed are successfully completed (statistically speaking) by three-year-olds. But this mental age is not necessarily the *real* age: a child who passes the tests of the eight-year-old, but is tripped up by tests of the nine-year-old, has a mental age of eight years, whether he is nine or ten chronologically.

By deriving an arithmetic ratio between mental and chronological ages (a ratio multiplied by 100 in order to eliminate decimals), we obtain the *intellectual quotient* (IQ), 'one of the best-known concepts', writes Eysenck, 'among anyone who is concerned with psychology in any capacity'. Three children with a mental age of eight years, but a chronological age of six, eight, and twelve years, will have an IQ of 133 (8/6 x 100), 100 (normal IQ) and 67, respectively.

In the European population, there are approximately 50% of people with an IQ between 90 and 110, 25% having a higher IQ, and 25% a lower IQ Among the best, Eysenck says, 'there are about 14.5% with IQs between 110 and 120, 7% between 120 and 130, 3% between 130 and 140, and 0.5% above 140'. There is an international association called Mensa, founded by Sir Cyril Burt, which groups people whose quotient exceeds 148 (after they have passed various tests). It has 20,000 members in some 15 countries. (La Mensa-France was created on the initiative of Robert Lehr).

Individuals whose IQ is less than 70 are considered as 'mentally deficient'. Among these, *imbeciles* (IQ 25 to 50) and *idiots* (less than 25) are usually entrusted to specialised institutions. *Morons* (from 50 to 70) are capable of carrying out, under surveillance, certain *concrete* operations (as opposed to *formal* operations, which require a capacity for abstraction).

Of course, the distinction between mental age and chronological age is only valid for children year-to-year, when intellectual development is not stabilised. For adults, when year-to-year growth no longer has a different value, psychologists introduce 'corrective weights'. 'What we actually tell an adult when we tell him his IQ', says Professor Eysenck, 'is that if the concept of IQ was still applicable at his age, that is the IQ he would have actually obtained'.

Studies carried out according to professional categories show that, from a *statistic* point of view (there are of course exceptions), there is a very clear correlation between social position and successful results in intelligence tests. We find individuals of all IQs in each social class, but the *average* of these IQs varies according class. A British study, for example, has highlighted six social classes, from the 'higher professional' to the 'unskilled', whose average IQs are 140, 130, 116, 108, 90, and 85 respectively.

Predictive Value

The misuse that certain 'reductive' industrial psychologists (the 'deluded psychopaths'[457] denounced by de Montmollin in a book published in 1972) have made of intelligence tests have sparked criticisms that are sometimes justified. It is certainly very difficult to *quantify* intelligence or character. On the other hand, an assessment (of an 'analytic' kind) of the *sum* of different personality traits gives us an incomplete picture of this personality regarded as a whole. Nevertheless, it is also certain that IQ evaluation has a *predictive* value: it allows us, statistically speaking, to *predict* what socio-educational level an individual is most likely to reach. 'The connection between IQ and academic achievement continues throughout the course of the studies', says Jean-Louis Lavallard (…) 'the students with higher than average IQs apply more frequently for entry into

---

457 The term is *psychopîtres* is a neologism which seems to condense *psychopathes* (psychopaths) and *pîtres* (fools, clowns).

bachelor's degrees and are more often accepted. They have also gone into more reputedly difficult sectors (*Le Monde de l'éducation*, October, 1975). Lastly, the misuse of a thing does not imply that the thing itself is bad.

In his book, Professor Eysenck responds to numerous objections.

Contrary to a widespread belief, therefore, the Professor's opinion of his pupils does not decisively influence the grades he gives them. Indeed, 'if one compares the assessments of a teacher of a pupil with the results obtained by the same pupil during an IQ test, one sees that there is a close correlation between the two'.

Of course, there are always exceptions. A very bright child can get bad results at school. But that does not mean that he is 'less intelligent' than he thought — or that the professors 'want' this. His failures are more likely due to character traits that have nothing to do with intelligence: the ability to work in groups, assiduity, accuracy, personal interest, among other things.

'To criticise a measure of intelligence on the pretext that it does not teach us anything about non-intellectual qualities is not an acceptable attitude'. But the reverse is not true: 'Those who have low IQ cannot succeed in intellectual or academic careers'.

Can we say, however, that there are many kinds of intelligence?

During the 1920s, the *nature* of intelligence was the subject of debates that are somewhat outdated today: we call intelligence the set of mental faculties that prove best suited to existence in an evolved society: speed of comprehension, a spirit of analysis and synthesis, aptitude for logic, abstract reasoning, sense of adaptation.

The subjective aspect of this definition should not surprise us: intelligence is not an absolute fact — it varies from culture to culture. But its 'subjective' nature does not prevent it from being evaluated. The sensation of 'hot' and 'cold' is also subjective. This does not prevent heat being measured 'objectively' by means of the thermometer. 'Despite greater complexity', says Eysenck, 'intelligence tests are comparable to the thermometer: they give objective indications on something that is not objective'. Moreover, when the thermometer was invented, little was known about the nature of heat'.

Experimented, revised, and refined since the beginning of the century, these tests have proven their worth. Their results can be expressed in the form of curves and equations with a 'reliability' of 90 to 95%.

It should not be forgotten, however, that these measures are only *statistical* data. In scientific matters, 'true' only means 'endowed with a very high degree of probability', except in the field of mathematics, whose propositions are always true precisely because they tell us nothing about the realities that they describe. IQ itself is an average: from one category of tests to another, the disparity in 'performance' often reaches ten points.

By knowing our IQ, we do not know how we will respond to this or that particular circumstance any more than knowing our average life expectancy (determined, in particular, by insurance companies) will tell us when we shall die.

On the other hand, character traits, too often neglected, can model in a determinate manner the way intelligence expresses itself. Certain qualities, for example, may partly compensate for a very average IQ: extraversion, level of personal attraction, initiative, commercial sense, obstinacy. Here we enter the domain of character analysis.

Hereditary Intelligence to 80%

The general public often asks whether intelligence is innate or whether it can be acquired through education. In this connection, Hans J. Eysenck relates experiments not only on parents and children, but also on brothers and sisters (or, better, twins) separated at birth and raised in different environments. 'This kind of research', he writes, 'testifies more in favour of the importance of heredity than to that of environmental influence'.

Conversely, it is also possible to keep the environment *constant* by varying heredity, for example by studying the IQ of children raised in an orphanage. 'If it is the environment that determines intelligence', says Eysenck, 'then all these children should have very similar IQs, and if these IQs differ, the cause can only be imputable to heredity. Now, when this experiment was attempted, it was found that in these orphans, the degree of intelligence was just as variable as in other children under the influence of the most diverse environments. This is why, here again, heredity appears to be the decisive factor in determining the differences of intelligence that exist between individuals'.

'Around 80% of all factors contributing to individual differences in intelligence are hereditary', Professor Eysenck concludes, '20% come from the environment. In other words, heredity is four times more important than the environment'.

*

Exercez votre intelligence, by Werner Kirst and Ulrich Diekmeyer. Casterman, 127 pages.[458]
Comment calculer votre quotient intellectuel, by Hans J. Eysenck. Mercure de France, 185 pages.[459]

*

Several books have criticised psychometric methods, sometimes virulently. In *Les tests en procès* (Dunod, 1970),[460] Dominique Beriot and Alain Exiga protest against 'the abuse of psychometrics'. Michel Tort, in a pamphlet on *Le quotient intellectuel* (Maspéro, 1974),[461] affirms, quoting Mao Tse-Tung in support, that the practice of testing is a tool 'at the service of the bourgeoisie'. See also: Jean Gobet, *Les tests démystifiés* (Aubier-Montaigne, 1976).[462] Hans J. Eysenck, in his various works, notably *The Measurement of Intelligence* (Medical and Technical Publishing Co., Lancaster, 1973), has done justice to these assertions, whose ideological bias is almost always evident.

Since 1974, the international presidency of Mensa has been held by R. Buckminster Fuller. (Mensa-France: B.P. 114, 75825 Paris Cedex 17).

RACE AND PSYCHOMETRY

'This book is only the beginning. A necessary start. Those who do not appreciate it are those for whom race has replaced sex as the main taboo!'

This quote from the renowned botanist and geneticist Cyril D. Darlington, a former Professor at the University of Oxford, appeared in the *Sunday Times*, about a book by Professor Hans J. Eysenck entitled *Race, Intelligence, and Education*.

What is it about?

Originally, the debate is a simple one. The results obtained by blacks in psychometric tests for measuring the intelligence quotient (IQ) have always been clearly below those obtained by whites in both England and the United States. The *mean* difference is about fifteen points, the 'normal' IQ (the 'standard deviation') is established at 100.

---

458 *Exercise your Intelligence.* — Tr.
459 *How to Calculate your Intellectual Quotient.* — Tr.
460 *Tests on Trial.* — Tr.
461 *The Intellectual Quotient.* — Tr.
462 *The Tests Demystified.* — Tr.

With a few exceptions, all psychologists admit this fact. But they obviously no longer agree when it comes to explaining the causes. For some, this difference is due to hereditary differences. For others, there are 'environmental' differences such as education, social milieu, standard of living, and so on.

It is the age-old conflict between heredity and the environment, the innate and the acquired. Nature and nurture, as the Anglo-Saxons say.

In *Race, Intelligence, and Education*, Hans J. Eysenck, after presenting the case, affirms that the theses of the 'environmentalists', partisans of the influence of the environment, are unsustainable; that the differences in performance between blacks and whites in IQ result from a difference in genetic makeup; and that 90% of scientists know, but they prefer not to talk.

Opinions waver. For Hans J. Eysenck is not just anyone. The *Sunday Times* says that he is 'one of the most influential scholars' in England. In 1934, he fled Nazi persecution. It is therefore difficult to accuse him of 'racism'. (This has not stopped the British extreme-left, however).

His demonstration is principally based on three observations.

(1) All experiments carried out on homozygous twins (that is, 'true twins'), separated at birth and raised in different environments, show that their intellectual quotient remains substantially the same, a few points apart. This attests that the intelligence is strongly hereditary.

(2) The average difference in IQ is found entirely in the selection of blacks and whites raised under the same conditions, frequenting the same establishments, and enjoying the same socio-economic status. It still exists if we put the whites of the lowest social strata in competition with wealthy blacks. The 'environment' is therefore not the determining explanatory factor.

(3) The Chinese, whose social status in the United States is generally much lower than that of whites, obtain the best results from the tests. Conversely, the average IQ of American Indians, who are discriminated against much more heavily than blacks, is higher than the latter.

Professor Eysenck's conclusion: 'There are racial differences in terms of anatomy, physiology, and even biochemistry. Why would the brain be an exception? We must face the facts. Intelligence is determined by heredity'.

A Discussion on 'Jensenism'

The controversy is not new.

In the United States, the first 'psychometry' experiments were carried out in the army to evaluate the intellectual capacities of new recruits; they are found in the work of Yerkes, which date back to 1916. Between 1935 and 1950, Professor Frank C. J. McGurk, from Villanova, completed some sixty-three surveys of comparative racial psychology. All lead to the same results. (Audrey M. Shuey gives a detailed presentation in *The Testing of Negro Intelligence*, Social Science Press, New York, 1966).

At the end of 1968, Professor Arthur R. Jensen, Vice-President of the American Educational Research Association, Professor of Psychology and Education at the University of Berkeley, published a long study in the *Harvard Educational Review* (winter 1968–69) on the reasons for the failure of the school catch-up programs. He stressed the 'inability of blacks to pass the tests of conceptual intelligence'.

This study caused a large backlash. A 'Jensenist heresy' was spoken of. Two years later, on 17 and 18 August 1970, Professors Jensen and Eysenck met in London during a symposium on the theme 'Human Differences and Social Problems'.

In his book, H. J. Eysenck speaks at length about Professor Jensen. 'His works are quite remarkable', he wrote. 'They deserved better than the polemic they provoked'.

The validity of psychometric tests has sometimes been debated. They were accused of being 'culturally impregnated', that is to say, they have been programmed according to the criteria of 'middle class American whites'. Professor Eysenck's response: 'The results are no better with "non-verbal" performance tests dealing with aptitude in abstract reasoning. Indeed, black schoolchildren still achieved their worst results in this category'.

In fact, if discrimination is to be avoided, it is time to recognise that there are various forms of 'intelligence' among peoples and races. Wanting to reduce all human diversity only to the European model is a particularly hateful form of racism. Different peoples have a different *mentality* according to their given lifestyle, the worldview that conforms to their thought, and the character traits with which they have been endowed during evolution under the pressure of natural selection. We cannot therefore say that there are 'superior' or 'inferior' races. There are only different races, which are *all* superior to each other *in relation to their own values and rhythms.*

'There is no theoretical obstacle to genetic differences between races', writes Jean-Louis Lavallard. 'Why should blacks and whites not be distinguished by intellect as by skin colour? Certain races would not necessarily be inferior to others (...) The qualitative differences of intelligence between races would explain the existence of different civilisations. Each of these would be the reflection of the intellectual capacities of its members. The notions of inferiority or superiority then lose all meaning. The so-called inferiority of certain races is only the consequence of a bad adaptation of a community to a civilisation for which it is not made and which is imposed on it' (*Le Monde de l'éducation*, October 1975).[463]

Against Discrimination

In black Africa, psychometric surveys using (non-verbal) 'performance' tests were carried out by R. A. C. Olivier (Kenya, 1929), Niessen and Kinder (Nigeria, 1934–35), J. D. Clarke (Mozambique, 1946–49), R. Maistriaux (Belgian Congo, 1953–54), etc. (See J. R. Clark, *Performance Tests of Intelligence in Africa*, Overseas Education, London, 1948). In the *Revue de Psychologie des peuples*, published in Le Havre with the assistance of the CNRS, Gérard Wintringer writes: 'The difference between the intelligence of blacks and whites is not only of a quantitative order, but also of a *qualitative* order. The intellectual 'inferiority' of the black is explained by mental behaviour which is deeply conditioned by a concrete, intuitive attitude, and riveted to the syncretic perception of sensible reality. Among blacks, sensible knowledge seems to have a preponderance over intellectual knowledge, and efforts that are willed and directed by reflection are less frequent among them than among the white man'.

This distinction was taken up by the President of the Republic of Senegal, Leopold Senghor, when he declared to the *Monde*: 'Negritude is characterised by a power of emotion leading to the intuitive assimilation of the object, of the outside world. This *intuitive* reason is opposed to the *discursive* reason of the white European. Blacks proceed by induction and intuition; others, by analysis and deduction'.

Hans J. Eysenck also emphasises that that observations like those of Jensen only have a *statistic* value. To speak of differences in racial IQ of a value of around fifteen points does not mean that *all* blacks perform less well than *all*

463 *The World of Education.* — Tr.

whites. On the contrary, about 40% of blacks have a higher IQ than the average IQ of whites. The comparison is only valid for average values. Therefore, one cannot base an argument for any individual discrimination upon it.

'What causes racism and hatred,' writes Eysenck, 'is stupidity and ignorance. The role of the scientist is not to create morals, but to describe reality and increase knowledge'.

A few years ago, Professor William B. Shockley (Stanford University), Nobel Prize winner, inventor of the transistor, asked the American Academy of Sciences to appoint a mission for gathering facts to determine the respective importance of heredity and environment in the formation of intelligence. His proposal was rejected by 200 votes to 10, with 640 abstentions.

'The members of the Academy are like the adversaries of Galilee', said Professor Eysenck. 'They refuse to look in the telescope for fear of seeing what they have been told'.

*

Race, Intelligence, and Education, a study by J. Eysenck. Maurice Temple Smith (37 Great Russell Street, London WC 1), 70 pages.

*

The 'Jensen affair' and its consequences have aroused polemics of considerable magnitude. Several dozen books have been published on the subject, mainly in Anglo-Saxon countries. Currently, the controversy continues to rage in the columns of specialised journals (*American Psychologist, Psychology Today, Science*, etc.). In France, a complete dossier on the affair has been published by Jean-Pierre Hébert, *Race et QI*, (Copernic, 1977).[464]

The journal, *Nouvelle école* (Nr. 18 May-June, 1972) also published an interview with A. R. Jensen — who is the author of a dozen works, including *Individual Differences in Learning: Interference Factors* (U.S. Office of Education, Washington, 1965), *Understanding Readiness* (University of Illinois Press, Urbana, 1969), *Genetics and Education* (Methuen, London, 1972), *Educability and Group Differences* (Methuen, London, 1973), *Educational Differences* (Methuen, London, 1974).

GENETICS AND PSYCHIATRY

Rats, which have many weaknesses, were thought to be quite sober. Medical doctors have debunked this reputation. 'As early as 1940, Richter and Campbell found that rats recognise a 2% alcoholic solution, and that they prefer it to water. Moreover, the descendants of 'drinkers' tend to be 'drinkers' significantly

---

464 *Race and IQ*. — Tr.

more than the descendants of 'non-drinkers' do, that is, they prefer alcoholic beverages.

'Alcoholism therefore seems partly hereditary', says Dr. Quentin Debray, 'and it is not only through family influence. A depressive tendency, especially among women, is strongly associated with this defect'.

If we are to believe 'anti-psychiatrists', there are no mental illnesses, but only 'social alienations' and 'psychoses of civilisation'. 'Anti-psychiatrists thus make the environment solely responsible for mental disorders', says Dr. Abramow. They thus deny the role played by *constitutional* factors, by the way in which the brain is formed during its development. And yet recent research shows that certain mental illnesses can be transmitted to the offspring not by psychological dysfunctionality of the family environment, but rather by the laws of genetics' (*Le Soir*, Brussels, 23 September, 1972).

It is these factors that Dr. Debray, an intern in the psychiatric hospitals, reviews in a book on *Génetique et psychiatrie*,[465] which received the second prize of the *Confrontations Psychiatriques Special* in 1972.

The laws of genetics determine the functioning of genes, to which most physical and mental characteristics correspond; they are carried by the chromosomes in cell nuclei.

In the human species there are forty-six chromosomes. Coupled two by two, in twenty-three pairs, they are all identical with the exception of the two *gonosomes*, or sexual chromosomes. These may be of two kinds: either XX, characteristic of the female sex; or XY, characteristic of the male sex.

When these chromosomes are 'defective' (due to hereditary disease, malformation, 'breakage', presence of an extra chromosome, etc.) the organism is generally affected by a defect. This defect is said to be constitutional or innate.

'If we find', says Dr. Abramow, 'a disease that affects different members of the same family by precisely following the (highly complex) path of certain characteristics called 'genetic markers', that is to say if any person possessing the marker(s) is affected by the disease under study and if the persons to whom the markers have not been transmitted are not affected by the disease, it can be said that this disease is linked to a defective gene, that the gene is located

465 *Genetics and Psychiatry.* — Tr.

in the same chromosome as the marker, and the closer it is to the marker the more the transmission will have corresponded.

To carry out such work, experiments on *twins* prove to be crucial. We distinguish 'true twins' (homozygotes), derived from the same egg, and the 'false twins' (heterozygotes), which are born at the same time, but come from two different eggs. (Twins with different gender are necessarily heterozygotes). Only the former are the bearers of the same material heredity. By following them in the course of their existence, specialists can accurately measure the respective importance of heredity and environment in the formation and development of their personality.

The most serious mental illness is perhaps *schizophrenia*, which was once called 'premature dementia'. It exists in all races, all cultures. The schizophrenic refuses (or neglects) the reality that surrounds him. He lives in a distorted *inner* world, where intellectual discord reigns. He will say, for example, 'I am not going to walk under the trees, because I am too young to die'. The idea of tree being associated, here, with that of wood, and 'therefore' a coffin.

In the general population, the proportion of schizophrenics is only 0.9%. However, 'according to Kallmann, a child whose parent is schizophrenic is 16.4% more likely to be schizophrenic. If both parents are affected, the percentage will be 68.1%'.

An Obsessive Neurosis

'As yet, there is no precise, verified theory on the biochemistry of schizophrenia', writes Dr. Debray. But numerous, irrefutable facts indicate that a metabolic pathway appears to be disturbed in schizophrenics; that it is even more the case in the periodic catatonic; it is less so in paranoid delirium. In other words, the day approaches when schizophrenia finds a biochemical and genetic explanation'.

Authors such as Malacarne and Dallapicola have already detected immunological abnormalities in the serum of schizophrenics.

Dr. Georges Heuyer, author of a remarkable essay on *La schizophrénie*, also points out 'the very high probability of hereditary transmission' of the illness.

Another example is *manic-depressive psychosis* or *bipolar disorder*. This affects mood. The patient is unable to control bouts of unbridled joy followed by crises of total depression. Suicide is common. In the United States, the average frequency is 0.4%. According to Kallmann, the illness, when present, occurs simultaneously in 'false twins' in 25.5% of cases, and 100% among true twins.

Recent work has been done at the Columbia-Presbyterian Medical Center in New York by a researcher from the Free University of Brussels, Dr. Mendlewicz and his team. Their results were presented in August 1972 at a scientific congress held in Copenhagen. In many cases, manic-depressive psychosis is associated with some form of color blindness (color confusion) and blood group XgA. Since these two characteristics depend on a defective gene in the sex chromosome X, women (XX) are twice as likely as men (XY) to be affected.

Dr. Debray also cites the case of two twins (whom he designates as A and B), aged twenty-four, who presented exactly the same symptoms of obsessive compulsive disorder in regards to cleanliness.

'A has not been on the bus for fifteen years. He cannot touch a floor, which could be contaminated by unknown feet. He makes complicated calculations in order to avoid all the objects that may have been contaminated: he cleans or washes coins and banknotes that appear suspect. If he feels contaminated, he immediately washes his hands, his body, and his clothes according to laws prescribed by B. Defecation is done naked and followed by a bath or a shower. Complicated precautions are taken regarding the cleanliness of the bed. Obsessive doubts occur about the perfection of rituals, so much so that during a stay in the United States, A called his brother across the Atlantic by phone to enumerate the details of his bathroom. He refused an excellent opportunity because he had heard that a dog had entered the establishment'.

'B is undoubtedly still more affected. He cannot talk to a contaminated friend for several months, even by phone. If this happens, it is washed completely. He cannot empty his rubbish himself. Like his brother, he keeps his room perfectly clean and forbids access to anyone'.

In 1965, a study by a Scottish doctor, Patricia Jacoba, on a population of serious offenders, revealed that a much higher proportion of ordinary criminals than could have been expected were suffering from a 'chromosomal aberration', the XYY syndrome, characterised by the presence in the organism's cells of an extra ('masculine') Y gonosome.

Dr. Quentin Debray comments and clarifies this study, which at the time caused great controversy. (One spoke, a little hastily, of the 'chromosome of the crime'). He compared the illness in question with Klinefelter syndrome, characterised by an absence of the Y chromosome in a male subject of ambiguous sexual appearance. 'Klinefelter's syndrome', he writes, 'a non-inherited chromosomal aberration, is accompanied by a tendency to delinquency and criminality. There is an imbalance to the perversions, which are not just any perversions, because the frequency of sexual assault and child killing is more pronounced than in average offenders and criminals'.

Each mental condition is so reviewed. At the end of the book, Dr. Debray offers the reader a small concluding diagram. In black, the parts corresponding to diseases where the genetic element intervenes without doubt. In white, what seems conditioned (the circumstances that can precipitate the disease on a predisposed ground).

Treatable Diseases

In the first of these categories we must place schizophrenia, intellectual retardation, manic-depressive psychosis, then anxiety, psychopathic imbalances, homosexuality (there is an innate homosexuality, of genetic origin, alongside an acquired, reactive, often neurotic homosexuality). In the second: anorexia nervosa, neurotic depressions, and especially hysteria.

'Not everything is genetically determined in psychology', writes Professor Jerôme Lejeune in his preface. 'Far from it. But what is truly surprising is that so many things are, and that so little of it is perceived'.

'The objections to genetics', adds Debray, 'do not exist in medicine, because there is no disputing the experiments and the statistics'. In fact, with the exception of the anti-psychiatrists, reluctance only comes from Marxist theorists, who believe that the individual can be transformed by eroding social differences (psychometric tests aimed at measuring intelligence have been prohibited in the USSR since 1936). And psychoanalysts, who doubtless remember the word of Freud: 'The doctrine of drives is, so to speak, our mythology'.

The public should still be properly informed, but this is not always the case. Many, for example, believe that 'genetic' means 'inevitable'. But the opposite is true. 'For the geneticist', explains Professor Lejeune, 'the knowledge of the transmission mechanism of diseases is only a first step, indispensable to the precise delimitation of a morbid entity. For, when this individualisation has been achieved, it becomes possible to thwart the pathological mechanism, since in the end any genetic defect necessarily implies a precise metabolic disorder'.

The way is thus open to eugenic information and prevention, as well as to genetic prophylaxis. (In Germany, the first clinic for genetic disorders opened in Marburg). The disorder becomes accessible to treatment when it can be determined with precision. In the immediate future, research is oriented towards the development of biochemical tests upon blood, urine, and the cerebrospinal fluid (which bathes the central nervous system). We thus hope to be able to detect the metabolic symptoms of the principal disorders.

Biochemistry is therefore called upon to play an essential role in the identification and treatment of mental illnesses. 'Psychiatry', says Dr. Abramow, 'will then resolutely emerge from esotericism and magic, where it has been relegated for far too long'.

*

Génétique et psychiatrie, by Quentin De-bray. Fayard, 237 pages, 45 francs.[466]
La schizophrénie, by Georges Heuyer. PUF, 230 pages, 32 francs.[467]

PSYCHIATRISTS IN THE ASYLUM

'There is a man who walks around a public garden. From the *outside*. Now and then he shakes the garden's fence and cries: 'Why have they locked me up?''

Normal people love stories about crazy people. This could be used to introduce anti-psychiatry.

'The insane asylum, the psychiatrist, psychiatry — all flourished and prospered with bourgeois capitalist society in the second half of the nineteenth century, and a little at the beginning of this one. All of this is in the process of deteriorating, but it is a little foolish to die late'.

It is in these terms that Roger Gentis, author of *Murs de l'asile* (Maspéro, 1971),[468] a psychiatrist and adept at anti-psychiatry, sets out his convictions. Since the great era of structuralism (1967–1970), intellectual leftism crystallised around two poles: anti-pedagogy and anti-psychiatry. The same influences are found: Rousseau's utopianism, existentialism and phenomenology, 'Freudo-Marxism' (Wilhelm Reich), neo-structuralism (Foucault, Lacan), and

---

466 *Genetics and Psychiatry.* — Tr.
467 *Schizophrenia.* — Tr.
468 *Walls of the Asylum.* — Tr.

the inevitable 'Frankfurt school' (Marcuse, Bloch, Adorno). The affair is no longer in its infancy. It is necessary to pay attention.

'Social Alienation'

It all began in London during the sixties. A group of 'neo-psychiatrists', apparently more expert in philosophy than medicine, decided to 'disrupt' the profession. Three names immediately stand out. David Cooper (*Psychiatry and Anti-psychiatry*. Paladin, 1967),[469] Aaron Esterson (*Sanity, Madness, and the Family: Families of Schizophrenics*. Penguin, 1964),[470] and especially Ronald D. Laing.

'It was Laing who opened our eyes' says Harold Heyward. Fifty years old, tired eyes, black shoulder-length hair, Mr. Laing has the curiously asymmetrical face of the first offender. He began by studying psychoanalysis and schizophrenia. He then plunged into Jean-Paul Sartre, before leaving for Kathmandu.

At first glance, anti-psychiatry seeks to present itself as a more 'humane' therapy. A praiseworthy concern; but it collapses as soon as we discover the two great postulates which inspire it: (1) There are no mentally ill people; (2) it is society that makes us mad.

The word 'crazy' (mad, foolish), vulgarised by common language (to be 'madly in love', to 'act the fool'),[471] corresponds to a precise reality for clinicians. Beyond the wall of psychosis, there is a rupture between the 'normal' brain and the brain of the mentally ill. A complete rupture. For anti-psychiatrists, on the contrary, the boundaries of 'normality' are purely conventional.

'The mental state of those who are called "normal"', writes Silvio G. Fanti, 'is almost the same as those who are locked up'. Cooper claims: 'It is often when people start to become healthy that they enter a psychiatric hospital'.

Here, anti-psychiatrists use the theory of 'alienation' (Karl Marx), which they seek to renovate by speculating on the 'repressive nature' of the modern institutions of family (Freud), society and politics (Marcuse, Reich).

---

469 French edition: *Psychiatrie et antipsychiatrie* (Seuil, 1970). — Tr.

470 French edition: *L'équilibre mental, la folie et la famille* (Maspéro, 1971). — Tr.

471 *Fou* in French means 'crazy, mad, insane, foolish, wild' etc. He cites the common expressions: *amour fou* (mad love) and *faire le fou* (act the fool). — Tr.

Accordingly, madness is therefore not a *state*. It is at most a status. A 're-sponse' to existing society. A means of 'defending' oneself against a 'repression' which is even subtler because it advances in a masked form. And since this re-action is ultimately very healthy (from the point of view of this contestation), all accepted realities must shift into their opposites. 'The "normal" are thus truly "insane", that is, *alienated* from a false reality', writes Gilbert C. Rapaille, 'whereas the "insane" are those who resist this alienation'.

The insane person thus becomes the accuser par excellence, and even an index for the madness of 'others' (normal people). For they are only alienated by society, whereas the 'normal' are probably alienated by their normality (which is a madness that ignores). In short, we cannot escape it.

Anti-psychiatrists make extensive use of quotation marks. They always place them around 'madness'. 'Mental illness and all the social practices that it involves', says Hayward, 'is fabricated in every instance from the *myth* of mental illness'. Schizophrenia, in particular, far from being a hereditary illness, will be 'the consequence of a whole series of repressions perpetrated by family and society' (special issue of *La Nef* on *Anti-Psychiatry*, January–May 1971).

A Major Project for the Union of the 'Marginal'

In 1965, anti-psychiatrists in London set up an 'experimental community cen-tre' at Kingsley Hall. Patients and doctors lived together. On equal footing. 'In this hospital', says Jean-Michel-Palmier, 'no constraint is imposed on the sick, there are no tranquilisers, we get up and eat when we want, we make love with who we want. There are no longer any sick people, but individuals who have sought refuge in this community because life has become impossible for them'. But very quickly, difficulties magnified. One of the 'boarders' took up the habit of keeping her excrement and smearing it on the wall of her room, which adjoined the kitchen. 'There were meetings', indicates one of the doctors of the center, 'to decide whether or not that person had the right to do this, as well as to do whatever she wanted in her room. It was then found that the extent of the smell was greater than the extent of the room. She was asked to reduce the extent of the smear of her excrement' (*La Nef,* op cit.)

The 'experiment' ended in 1969. A hundred patients found themselves on the street. 'Such innovations', says Palmier, 'have not only raised the indignation of psychiatrists, but also of the residents of the neighbourhood, whose children had become accustomed to stoning the walls of the hospital'.

This is just the beginning. In all western countries, especially in the United States, the anti-psychiatrists wage war against the 'order of caregivers' (Maud Mannoni, *Le psychiatre, son « fou » et la psychanalyse*, a work dedicated to Jacques Lacan).[472] Diagnostic practices, which are equivalent to 'medicalisation' of social violence, and the resort to medications, which would be a 'chemical straightjacket', are denounced as a desire for 'psychiatric segregation'.

The rest follows suit. The family 'represses'. Society 'spreads inequality'. The asylum 'imprisons', etc. The psychiatric hospital is a 'concentration camp', where doctor-supervisors and nurse-wardens 'create schizophrenia'. Internment allows society to eliminate its 'accusers' — and doctors provide it with 'alibis'.

Of course, psychiatry is 'racist': 'One says insane like one says negroes, North Africans,[473] or Portuguese. From here to extermination, there are only a few short steps' (Roger Gentis).

It is also castrating. 'Psychiatrists cut off the speech of the patients, who are transformed by being psychiatrised (which effectively *makes* them insane), just like we cut off the willy' (Jean-Paul Dollé).

This politico-mystical approach to the problem, all these dissertations on 'individual shipwreck', the 'difficulty of being', and the closed universe, do not come without a cost. The enterprise of anti-psychiatry is part of a large 'Marcusian' project which consists in uniting all the 'marginalised' (eternal students, foreign workers, sexual minorities, residents under house arrest and in psychiatric asylums) because, being the only ones who are 'non-integrated', the only ones *born of revolution* that are still available in society, they can become the spark of revolt and the engine of subversion. Hence the slogan 'Asylums-prisons: same battle!'

In France, the anti-psychiatrists have several journals at their disposal: *Cahiers pour la folie, Tankonala-santé*, etc. They are 'militant' organs, where the mad 'reclaim speech'. We read observations like: 'The only difference between

---

472 *The Psychiatrist, his 'Madness', and Psychoanalysis.* — Tr.

473 *Bougnoles*, a pejorative term for North Africans. — Tr.

a man and a lobster is that a man cannot masturbate with its claws'[474] (*Cahiers pour la folie*, nr. 8), etc.

Dr. Yves Pélicier, forty-four years of age, an Associate Professor of neurology and psychiatry (University of Paris-V) is the complete opposite of an antipsychiatrist. He belongs to the 'Algerian school' (Jean-Claude Scotto, Marcel Delpretti, Maurice Porot, Henri Luccioni, Henri Dufour, and Robert Escoute, co-authors of a recent manual on psycho-pharmacology) headed by Professor J.-M. Sutter. His aim is to react against 'the literary fashions and mannerisms of the time'. He has twenty years' experience.

A Dive into Obscurantism

His book, *La psychiatrie comprehensible*,[475] inaugurated a collection directed by Professor Pierre Debray-Ritzen with the publisher Fayard. He attempted to break free from the 'bondage of animism' and to bring clarity where others compounded confusion.

'With verbose ignorance', writes Debray-Ritzen, 'akin to that which surrounded fevers before bacteriology, a proliferous interpretation spread through psychology and psychiatry through the influence of Freud, the philosophical digression, and, more recently, the sophisms of anti-psychiatry. But in the years to come, genetics, biochemistry, experimental psychology, and the identification of unsuspected correlations will demolish these castles of word and sand'.

'Among certain contemporary psychiatrists', remarks Professor Léon Michaux, 'the obscurity of exposition, far from indicating depth of thought according to the coquetry of their intention, only translates to inconsistency'.

Reviewing the various categories of mental illnesses (schizophrenia, paranoia, delusions, dementias, retardations, neuroses, phobias, hysteria, psychoses, depressions, etc.), Dr. Pélicier formally contests the position that society does violence to the patient. 'In truth', he writes, 'it forgets that illness is the first violence, that it actually exists even where no physician can be found to detect it, and that not so long ago, when most mental illnesses were considered a sign of sin, debauchery, of diabolical pacts, of atavism, the fate of patients was scarcely enviable'.

---

474 Playing on *homme* (man) and *homard* (lobster). — Tr.
475 *Comprehensible Psychiatry*. — Tr.

Forgetful of the lessons of Hippocrates, psychiatry had fallen back into obscurantism in the Middle Ages. 'This era, as fierce as it is grandiose', says Michaux, 'is essentially anti-scientific. For psychiatry, it is marked by the return to the *supernatural* conception of mental illness. The insane person is not sick, he is bewitched, possessed by the devil; deserving no pity, he must be exorcised, even tortured and burnt. It is the time of the witch trials and the Sabbaths. It is also, thanks to collective suggestion, the epoch of epidemics of hysterical religious madness'.

These superstitions will disappear in time. Philippe Pinel (1745–1826) had to wait until 1793, at the height of the Terror, to liberate the residents of Bicêtre Hospital from their chains.

Far from having oppressed the patient, the 'medicalisation' of psychiatry has thus marked the beginning of its liberation — the anti-psychiatrists preach a genuine step backwards by declaring the insane 'possessed' by society in the same way that the theologians of the Middle Ages called them 'possessed' by a demon.

Dr. Pélicier also denounces the myth of 'good drug' and the 'trinket of artificial paradises'. 'As far as the long-term effects of hashish are concerned', he writes, 'they may be summarised by a progressive desocialisation, a detachment from reality, a more or less rationalised homelessness justified by foolish or puerile principles'. He adds: 'What would Marx think of this *opium*, proposed to the people to deliver them?

In a joint essay published under the direction of Dr. Cyrille Koupernik (*L'antipsychiatrie, sense ou non-sens ?*),[476] Dr. Jean-Paul Charrier affirms that the failure of anti-psychiatry is largely due to its schizolatry'.[477]

In the eyes of anti-psychiatrists, the schizophrenic manifests a particularly *exemplary* attitude. By seeking to 'escape' (internally) from a 'corrupt' external world, he gives: the most 'obvious' signs of his good health. He becomes the objective *ally* of 'subversion'.

'Schizophrenia', declares Gilbert C. Rapaille, 'is only a *label* given by those who are said to be normal to those whose behaviour seems strange and bizarre to them'.

---

476 *Anti-psychiatry: Sense or Nonsense?*–Tr.

477 *Schizolâtrie*, formed after *idolâtrie* (idolatry): 'worship of schizophrenia'. — Tr.

'All the ambiguity of antipsychiatry', observes Jean-Michel Palmier, 'wavers between a radical negation of the disorder (there are no schizophrenics, says Cooper), and a mystical conception of it (the schizophrenic is a 'foreign poet in our time', his illness is a 'transcendental experience'), asserts Laing.

'Speculation', wrote Dr. Marcel Eck (in *La Nouvelle Presse médicale*)[478] 'seems to support this observation. One has wanted to systematically reject the psychiatric at the expense of the philosophical theories. The nostalgic sense has been lost and the very concept of schizophrenia has been effaced'.

This statement is in line with that of Professor Georges Heuyer: 'The study of schizophrenia, like that of all other diseases, must be clinical. It must begin and end with the patient. The smallest fact is preferable to all the theories. Bergsonian, phenomenological, and existentialist concepts have contributed nothing to the emergence of the etiology of symptoms, to clinical forms, to evolution and treatment of schizophrenia. Moreover, 'since Freud, there has not been anything new in psychoanalysis'. Only 'a pretentious literature and insignificant prattle'.

Thanks to Chemotherapy

Conclusion: insane people exist, everybody has met them. And the only way of *effectively* tending to them is by recognising that 'they themselves are the cause of themselves' — and that psychopathic personalities require appropriate treatment.

In all serious cases, *chemotherapy* proves indispensable. 'Far from representing a "chemical straightjacket"', writes Dr. Pélicier, 'chemotherapy, handled with precision and method, makes for extraordinary progress which can be measured by comparing it to the previous situation'.

Perhaps there are patients that should be released from the asylums. But there are also anti-psychiatrists that should be locked up.

*

La psychiatrie compréhensible, by Yves Pélicier. Fayard, 254 pages.[479]
Une antipsychiatrie ?, by Harold Heyward and Mireille Varigas. Ed. Universitaires, 144 pages.[480]

---

478 *The New Medical Press.* — Tr.
479 *Comprehensible Psychiatry.* — Tr.
480 *An Anti-Psychiatry?* — Tr.

Le fou est normal, by Silvio G. Fanti. Flammarion, 216 pages.[481]
Laing, by Gilbert C. Rapaille. Ed. Universitaires, 118 pages.
L'équilibre mental, le folie et la famille, by Ronald D. Laing and Aaron Esterson. Maspéro. 230 pages.[482]
Les degrés de la folie, by Léon Michaux. Hachette. 304 pages.[483]
L'antipsychiatrie, sens ou non-sens ?, essays published by Cyrille Koupernik. PUF, 240 pages.[484]

*

Although its success has been largely confined to politico-literary circles, the anti-psychiatric movement, since its inception, has only grown and prospered. Its leaders remain Ronald Laing (*The Politics of Experience and the Bird of Paradise*. Penguin, 1967; *The Divided Self*. Penguin, 1960; *Knots*. Penguin, 1970; *The Self and Others*. Tavistock, 1961. *The Politics of the Family and Other Essays*. Tavistock, 1971)[485] and David Cooper (*Psychiatry and Anti-Psychiatry*. Paladin, 1967; *The Death of the Family*. Penguin, 1971).[486] But we must also cite the studies of Thomas Szasz (*The Myth of Mental Illness*. Harper & Row. 1961; *The Manufacture of Madness*. Harper & Row, 1970),[487] Gérard Hof (*Je ne serai plus psychiatre*. Stock, 1976),[488] and so forth.

In his last book, *Grammar of Living* (Penguin, 1974),[489] David Cooper again denounces medical psychiatry as the 'CIA of the individual psyche', and claims that experiments with drugs or 'schizoid regression', far from being signs of failure in the eyes of society, are on the contrary the surest index of the bankruptcy of this very society. The book is also bathed in a mixture of diffused religiosity and pre-Freudian phenomenology, interspersed with incantations of a 'new sexual morality' and appeals to a vaguely Buddhist 'meditation'.

Christian Delacampagne, in *Antipsychiatrie. Les voies du sacré* (Grasset, 1974),[490] attempts to free the 'philosophy' of the movement. On the other hand, Chantal Bosseur (*Clefs pour antipsychiatrie*)[491] introduces a useful distinction between the English school of

---

481 *The Madman is Normal.* — Tr.

482 *The Psychiatrist, his 'Madness', and Psychoanalysis.* — Tr.

483 *Degrees of Madness.* — Tr.

484 *Anti-Psychiatry: Sense or Nonsense?* — Tr.

485 French editions: *La politique de l'expérience* (Stock, 1969); *Le moi divisé* (Stock, 1970); *Nœuds* (Stock, 1971); *Soi et les autre*. Gallimard, 1971; *La politique de le famille* (Stock, 1972). — Tr.

486 French editions: *Psychiatrie et antipsychiatrie* (Seuil, 1970); *Mort de la famille* (Seuil, 1972). — Tr.

487 French editions: *Le mythe de la maladie mentale* (Payot, 1975); *Fabriquer la folie* (Payot, 1976); *Idéologie et folie* (PUF, 1976). — Tr.

488 *I Will No Longer be a Psychiatrist.* — Tr.

489 French edition: *Une grammaire à l'usage des vivants* (Seuil, 1976). — Tr.

490 *Anti-Psychiatry: Paths of the Sacred.* — Tr.

491 *Keys for Anti-Psychiatry.* — Tr.

anti-psychiatry (Laing, Cooper, Esterson) and the American school, less known but ultimately more important.

This second school, of which Thomas Szasz, born in Budapest in 1920, was a founder, is centred in Palo Alto, California, and devotes itself mainly to the 'study' of schizophrenia. Independently of his references to Jean-Paul Sartre and Zen Buddhism (in the 'popularised' version of Alan Watts), it is essentially reduced to a new form of environmentalism and behaviourism. Rejecting most Freudian concepts (the unconscious, intrapsychic conflict, etc.), it attributes almost every disturbing factor to the environment (familial, social, and institutional). Mental illness thus becomes a 'logical' response to an 'aggressive stimulus' produced by society. On this Palo Alto school, see P. Watzlawick, J. Helmick-Beauvin, and D. Jackson, *Pragmatics of Human Communication* (Norton, 1967),[492] and P. Watzlawick, J. Weakland and R. Fisch, *Change: Principles of Problem Formation and Problem Resolution* (Norton, 1974).[493]

PSYCHOANALYSTS WITHOUT COMPLEXES

'They do not realise we are bringing them the plague', Freud whispered on the boat that brought him to America.

It was a few months before the Second World War. Since then, the epidemic has spread. The 28th Congress of the International Psychoanalytical Association was held from 22–27 July 1972 at UNESCO. 1,600 participants from thirty-two countries were attending this 'summit', where the American delegation, emanating from the emigration of the 1930s, accounted for almost two thirds of the audience. Among the topics for discussion: 'transference' and hysteria.

In reality, the meeting mostly revealed contradictions. For the great Freudian church is divided into sects. And the popes excommunicate themselves by citing quotes.

In the case of France alone, there are four denominations corresponding to different stages of dissent. There is the Paris Psychoanalytical Society, born in 1926, presided over by Dr. Evelyne Kestemberg (who publishes the *Revue française de psychanalyse*); the Psychoanalytic Association of France, of Dr. Jean-Baptiste Pontalis, created in 1953 (which publishes the *Nouvelle revue de psychanalyse* through Gallimard); the Freudian School of Paris, founded in 1963 around Jacques Lacan (journal: *Scilicet*, published by Sueil); and the fourth group, born in 1969 (journal: *Topique*). In total: 265 adherents — of which 57 are not medical practitioners.

---

492 French edition: *Une logique de la communication* (Seuil, 1972). — Tr.

493 French edition: *Changements, paradoxes, et psychothérapie* (Seuil, 1974). — Tr.

Only the first two companies are affiliated to the International Association, whose creation dates back to 1910. The other two are dominated by the personality of Jacques Lacan, a neo-Marxist theorist who became fashionable in certain circles of L'Ecole normale supérieur, and who, under the influence of Ferdinand de Saussure, undertook to re-read Freud in the light of structural linguistics.

Between the two splits, the psychoanalysts officiate behind closed doors. They recruit by co-opting.

Their clientele consists of agitated or delirious psychotics, patients with neuroses, personality disorders, phobias, obsessions, depression and, of course, the full spectrum of sexual difficulties.

The engine of psychoanalytic cure is *transference*, that is to say, the privileged, 'decomplexing' relationship which is established between the patient and the analyst. The latter combines the advantages of the priest and the doctor. We can tell him everything. He accepts everything. He erases the blame. He is the intermediary between an atrophied will and a mysterious universe, that of the unconscious, whose arcana does not hold secrets from him; he predicts the 'drives' and draws out their 'true' causes. He gives alibis and keeps on chattering. He makes it possible to talk about oneself in good conscience.

This gives psychoanalysis a surprisingly considerable success. Dr. Yves Pélicier, author of *La psychiatrie compréhensible*, speaks of a 'cultural phenomenon': a sign of the times.

Conditioned by the mass media, and especially by the women's press, the public at large questions its complexes and frustrations with a delicious thrill.

'The analysis of works of art and literary criticism have opened to psychoanalysis an unlimited career', says Dr. Pélicier. 'It is enough', writes Raymond Ruyer, 'to look through the weekly women's magazines to see that popular psychoanalysis is to the feminine *intelligentsia* what Marxism is to the masculine *intelligentsia*' (*Les nuisances idéologiques*. Fayard, 1972).

Little by little, psychoanalysis has infiltrated ethnology (Lévi-Strauss), anthropology (Ruth Benedict, Franz Boas), psychosociology (Kurt Lewin), pedagogy (Benjamin Spock), linguistics, marketing, and so on. Its latest avatar, anti-psychiatry, is far from having a consensus. But as Roland Jaccard acknowledges in *Le Monde*, 'it is already necessary in our day for a young psychiatrist to have a distinct courage and a singular nonconformism in order to refuse psychoanalysis'.

Resentment

The paternity of concepts such as the 'unconscious', 'repression', 'psycho-therapy', and so on are generally attributed to Freud by the public. This is a serious mistake.

'In Freud's doctrine, what is new is not true', says a Parisian psychologist. 'And what is true is not new'.

In a work of considerable erudition, *The Discovery of the Unconscious* (published in a French translation by the editor of the *Cahiers médicales lyonnais*), Professor Henri F. Ellenberger from the University of Montreal has traced, in eight-hundred pages, the history of 'dynamic psychiatry'. Freud's name only appears in the last third of the book.

The origin of 'depth psychology' goes back to Greek and Roman antiquity. We find certain manifestations in primitive societies. From the Middle Ages, religious 'counselling' contributed to its development, along with the effusive role of *confession*. In the eighteenth century, in France, Mesmer and Puységur laid the foundations for a true doctrine and for a therapy of the unconscious. It is this doctrine, enriched by the observations of Schopenhauer, Fechner, Bachofen, Darwin, Nietzsche, etc., which will be re-covered around 1880 by Bernheim and Charcot, and especially by Pierre Janet, whose importance and memory Ellenberger happily strives to demonstrate and rehabilitate.

In fact, Freud's originality lies mainly in his rigid *interpretation* of the disorders of the unconscious, which almost exclusively emphasise sexuality and the emotional conflicts of early childhood.

For Freud, the notion of *repression* holds the sacred role, which in Marx, is played by *alienation*. It is always a matter of finding excuses for those whose 'performance' in the domain of social competition is mediocre. And to fuel the ideology of *resentment*. In the *system* of psychoanalysis, man is practically never able to affirm his *ego* completely. He endures himself, when he does not endure others. He is the plaything of inner drives and latent *desires*, which are *realised abstractions* similar to medieval allegories. Freud thus 'modernises' the old theory of the 'scapegoat' — whose *practice* is like the ancestor of release.

It is remarkable that at a time when the general public seems totally won over to psychoanalysis, the specialists gradually move away from it.

'We find ourselves today in a rather curious situation', says the English psychologist H. J. Eysenck, 'in the sense that psychoanalysis is widely accepted by the layman and those who have no notion of what psychology is, whereas it is rejected by those who possess serious knowledge of the field'.

In the United States, according to the National Institute of Mental Health, only 2% of mental patients are treated with psychoanalysis.

'The psychoanalytic movement is becoming an insignificant branch of psychiatry', admits Dr. Judd Marmot, former president of the American Academy of Psychoanalysis.

'Psychoanalysis is disappearing', notes Dr. Thomas Szasz with sadness.

It is because the actual *therapeutic* bankruptcy of psychoanalysis is more and more clearly recognised.

Has psychoanalysis ever *cured* anyone? The question ultimately does not make much sense.

'There is no method', remarked Hans J. Eysenck, 'from prayer to cold baths, from hypnosis to dental extractions, which has not obtained "good" results. In this field, suggestion, the interpersonal relationship, play a particularly important role. A patient who believes he can be cured is cured all the more easily. This is especially true in the field of mental disorders.

A study conducted by Dr. Deniker of five hundred individuals with severe neurosis, reveals that two out of three subjects recovered normally, without having received any treatment. Thus the rate of 'healing' obtained by psychoanalysis not only does not exceed that of other methods of treatment, it is not even better than remissions obtained spontaneously.

'The subjects treated by psychoanalysis', writes Professor Eysenck in the journal *Nouvelle école*, 'cure rather less well and more slowly'.

He adds: 'I will say, in weighing my words, that Freud has pushed psychiatry back more than fifty years'.

*

La science contra Freud. Science versus Freud, essays published under the direction of Quentin Debray. Special issue of *Nouvelle-école* (B.P. 129–07, 75326 Paris Cedex 07), 130 pages.[494]

---

494 *Science Versus Freud.* — Tr.

A la découverte de l'inconscient, by Henri F. Ellenberger. SIMEP-Editions (47–49, rue du 4 août, 69611 Villeurbanne), 772 pages.[495]

FREUDIAN SCHOLASTICISM

'Freud was never a scientist' declared Dr. Debray-Ritzen in a talk given in Toulouse in December 1972 under the auspices of the association G.R.E.C.E. (Group for the Research and Study of European Civilisation).[496]

Dr. Pierre Debray-Ritzen, 54 years of age, white coat and bow tie, leads a double professional life. He is both a child psychiatrist and an accomplished writer. He is a 'somnambulist', says Arthur Koestler, using the term in the sense given to it by Charcot and Janet. A hospital physician and a professor at the Faculty of Medicine in Paris, he specialises in the problems of neuropsychology and directs the child patient unit within this discipline. As a writer, he has published (under the pseudonym of Quentin Ritzen) *Les nervures d'être* and *Un final venetien*,[497] as well as essays on Chekhov, Koestler, Hemingway, and Simenon — before taking on Sigmund Freud.

In the preface to *La scolastique freudienne*, Arthur Koestler writes: 'These devastating pages have the ardor and the irony of a Renan attacking holy scripture'.

The comparison is quite accurate. 'Scholasticism', says Dr. Debray-Ritzen, 'is a logical and systematised reasoning that aims to penetrate minds with *revealed truths*, that is to say, postulates or assertions which have not received scientific verification'. This is the opposite of the experimental method, defined by Claude Bernard.

In 1938, Etienne Gilson wrote: 'Articles of faith can be proven in theology by a rational and necessary demonstration; that is to say, they can be proven on the condition that they are first believed'. The same goes for psychoanalysis.

For Freud, 'revealed truths' bear names such as *id* and *ego*, the unconscious, drives, the Oedipus complex, object relations, infantile sexuality, and the interpretation of dreams.

---

495 English edition: *The Discovery of the Unconscious: The History and Evolution of Dynamic Psychiatry* (New York: Basic Books, 1970). — Tr.

496 *Groupement de recherche et d'études pour la civilisation européenne.* — Tr.

497 *The Veins of Being. One Last Venetian.* — Tr.

The Role of the Sexual Function

As opposed to the overused notion of the *unconscious*, Dr. De bray-Ritzen prefers that of 'non-conscious'. 'Consciousness', he explains, 'is something relative. We can imagine it a little like a theater. Clear, verbalised, consciousness is centre stage, in the spotlight. And then there are the wings, and in these wings, everything unused, everything non-conscious that we have accrued. The non-conscious can come on stage if we call upon it, but it can also come by itself, depending on emotional circumstances, sensory provocations, or associations of ideas'.

Dreams are part of the unconscious. Freud took to them with delight. For him, the *meaning* of the dream is also the *cause*. This led him to announce gravely that they were 'almost like the *Vermot* almanac' but in the style of the *Key to Dreams* of the Babylonian diviners.[498]

Thus we come to the fundamental subject of the role of the sexual function. 'Freud', says Koestler, 'restored Eros to his legitimate place, which the Victorians had refused'. Unfortunately, by restoring it to its place, psychoanalysis seems to have made it vicious.

Infantile sexuality, however, is not a myth. The child is not the paragon of innocence imagined by angelic parents. Nor is it a 'perverse polymorph'. On this subject, Dr. Debray-Ritzen declares:

'Infant sexuality is a reality that varies according to the individual. Above all, it does not explain everything. As a paediatrician, I can say that there are children, especially girls, who escape sexual curiosity right up until advanced ages, that is, until about eight or ten years old. It is therefore truly absurd to derive it from a 'fixation', as they say in the jargon of psychoanalysis, at one of the stages of infantile sexuality, the origin of which is called (in a far too imprecise manner) neurosis.

For his part, Professor Lhermitte states: 'It is not impossible that an infant has an emotional life, that it is sensitive to certain situations or events, and that it can be marked. But to maintain that the personality is determined at this age or even earlier, even in the intra-uterine life, according to a process of escalation in which the various psychoanalytic schools have been engaged

---

498 The *Vermot* is a French almanac devoting one page to each day of the year; the *Clef des songes* (Key to Dreams) were medieval guides to interpreting dreams inspired by the second century *Onirocritica* of Artemidorus of Ephesus. — Tr.

since Freud, is an exaggeration, no doubt even a biological impossibility — especially for those who have observed the brain of the newborn or even the small child in optical and electronic microscopy, in histoenzymology and histochemistry' (*La Revue médicale de Picardie*, November 1975).

Therapeutics

Doctors call medicines without any therapeutic value, but which nevertheless exercise a beneficent action because the patient believes they are real, 'placebos' (sugar pills, distilled water shots). The patient *feels* relieved because he thinks he has *been* relieved. On the mental plane, the 'therapeutic value' of psychoanalysis is about the same. The relationship upon which it is based is a kind of secular confession, an avatar of the Coué method.

'To question the therapeutic value of psychoanalysis', says Dr. Debray-Ritzen, 'is ultimately to pose the problem of the interpersonal relationship, of the action that one being can exercise over another through dialogue, example, emotional ties, natural influence, and so on (…) Subjugation, sacrifice, abandonment, three or five times a week over three years on the couch are well worth the effort, regardless of the theme: Buddha, Jesus, Marx, or Oedipus. It is open to the Freudians to see in their enterprise only the distinctiveness of the transference. It is open to us to find only a kind of asceticism and the suggestion of a personal consultation'.

Neurosis is the major issue for Freudians. But in this rather vague concept, psychoanalysis coagulates disorders of a different nature: hysterical conversion, anxiety, angst, phobic and obsessional conditions, and so on. It can obtain results for the treatment of anxious and phobic neuroses, but it is almost powerless to cure hysteria, which Freud, in 1890, had made the cornerstone of his system. As Dr. Debray-Ritzen notes, 'a well-enacted isolation more easily controls hysterical contracture than the long psychoanalytical confessions, which may ultimately exacerbate the problem'.

Of course, psychoanalysis has never cured any psychosis, adult or infantile, no addiction, no psychopathic personality, no chronic delirium, no manic-depressive psychosis, etc.

A Torrent of *Logos* upon the World

To the methods used by Freud, Dr. Debray-Ritzen gives the names of *hyperformulation*, *hyperreduction*, *hypersynthesis*, and *hypersymbolisation*. This 'hyper' consists in giving to *particular* observations a *general* scope or significance that they do not have.

'I have cited the example of the gentleman who collected the hulls of boats. It is probable that this person has a nostalgia for the sea, where he had perhaps lived as a child. The psychoanalyst, for his part, will seek a symbol. He thinks that the hull of the boat is the belly of the mother, and that the gentleman collects the hulls because he suffers from an Oedipus complex. This is foolish!'

Another example: 'For Freud, the gentleman who has a phobia of door knobs is not afraid of microbes at all; rather he sees the door knob as the symbol of his father's penis! Similarly, for the psychoanalyst, the crisis of epilepsy will be the 'symbolic equivalent' of orgasm, etc. We are fully in the domain of magical thinking'.

And yet Freud had a sense of humour. One day, when he was fiddling with a cigar, he declared to a disciple who raised his eyebrow: 'You see, sometimes a cigar is just a cigar'. Arthur Koestler adds: 'I know a few contemporary analysts who would prefer to castrate themselves before admitting this'.

In the ideological posterity of Freud, Mélanie Klein occupies an important place. It was she who, in the twenties, began to apply psychoanalytic theories to the young infant (less than thirty months). This translated into blatantly delusional theories at the extremes of unintelligibility.

'For all little boys', writes Mélanie Klein, 'a moving car represents masturbation and coitus; two cars that meet each other also represent coitus, while the comparison between two cars of different dimensions expresses rivalry with the father and his penis' (*Le psychanalyse de l'enfant*).

Claims of this kind at first provoke a smile. Until the moment that psychoanalyst René Spitz undertook to 'update' them by affirming, notably, that the whole development of the adult is explained by the nature of the relations between the mother and the child during the first months!

This theory, which senselessly exploits a reality well-known to ethologists (the fact that *imprinting*, i.e. emotional 'imprint', is particularly strong during the 'sensitive period' following birth), has had the most serious consequences.

'To say, for example', emphasises Dr. Pierre Debray-Ritzen, 'that mental debility is due to the fact that a child was unloved by its mother during the first months of its life, is absolutely outrageous. It is vile ignorance. First because it is not true: the causes of mental debility are varied and are coming to be well known (there are metabolic dysfunctions, hereditary defects, diseases of the egg during pregnancy, etc.). In addition, it is an abuse of confidence, because it is claimed that psychotherapy will improve the child's condition. And at the end of a year or eighteen months we see the mothers *blamed*, and they come in and complain that they have been deceived'.

Dr. Debray-Ritzen does not hide his pessimism. 'A torrent of *logos*', he writes, 'spreads over the world without any kind of scientific rigor, which openly turns its back on knowledge and stirs up senseless concepts in exactly the same way that one would turn prayer wheels'. And to quote the terrible words of Chekhov: 'It is said that truth will triumph in the end, but it is not true'.

*

La scolastique freudienne, by Pierre Debray-Ritzen. Fayard, 272 pages.

*

The appearance of the book by Pierre Debray-Ritzen, which has aroused numerous echoes in the press, seems to have given the launch of an anti-Freudian campaign by the public at large (cf. for example the article by Eric Chamberlain, *Bye bye, docteur Freud* in *Jacinte*, February 1976).

In October 1974, a polemic in the columns of the *Figaro* contrasted Professor Debray-Ritzen to the psychoanalyst Bruno Bettelheim, founder of the 'orthogenic' school of Chicago, which was featured on television in a series of particularly laudatory programs. Bettelheim (who is neither a medical doctor nor a psychiatrist) has claimed, in *The Empty Fortress (The Free Press, 1967)*[499] that autism (a particularly serious childrens' disorder which completely cuts the child off from the exterior world) was exclusively the product of psycho-affective factors induced by the environment. Debray-Ritzen has responded that these claims are 'outrageously ignorant'. He clarifies: 'I refute the permanent reference of psychoanalysis to the supposed responsibility of the parents. In the current state of our knowledge of autism, only biochemical, genetic, and psychopharmacological research allows us to make progress'.

---

499 French edition: *La forteresse vide* (Gallimard, 1969). — Tr.

FROM OEDIPUS TO MOSES

During a trip to Athens in 1904, Sigmund Freud visited the Acropolis with his brother. Thirty years later, in a letter to Romain Rolland, he confessed to having been seized that day by a 'temporary feeling of alienation'.[500] A revealing episode of an ambiguous life.

Was it necessary to be Jewish in order to invent psychoanalysis? In a letter to Pastor Pfister, Freud replied in the affirmative. Marthe Robert, an accomplished Germanist, a Kafka specialist, a translator of Goethe and Nietzsche, wanted to clarify the meaning of this response.

That Freud felt himself to be, in a certain way, the heir of Jewish culture seems to be certain. And we know that until his death he was a member of the Free Lodge of the *B'nai B'rith*. And his letters are revealing.

In 1908 he wrote to Karl Abraham: 'Remember, I beg you, that affinities of race bring you closer to my intellectual temperament'. In 1928, to Enrico Morselli: 'Although I have long been detached from the religion of my ancestors, I have never lost the feeling of solidarity towards my people'.

After the death of the English psychoanalyst David Eder in 1936, he wrote to his sister-in-law: 'We are Jews, the both of us, and we both knew too that we had in common what I know of the miraculous, hitherto inaccessible to analysis, which is characteristic of the Jew'.

The vast majority of Freud's disciples were also Jewish: Otto Rank, Karl Abraham, Sandor Ferenczi, Theodor Reik, Alfred Adler, Mélanie Klein, Tausk, Stekel, etc.

One exception, however, is Carl G. Jung. When he separated from him, Freud wrote to the psychiatrist Ludwig Biswanger: 'In all this there is only one serious thing: the Semites and the Aryans or anti-Semites, which I wanted to bring together in order to fuse them in the service of psychoanalysis, are once again beginning to separate like oil and water'.

A Persistent Discomfort

Talmudic thought has often been reconciled with the approach of psychoanalysis. For Manès Sperber, Freudianism is 'psychologisation of the Old

---

500 German: *Entfremdungsgefühl* (feeling of alienation or estrangement), French *dépersonnalisation* (de-personalisation). — Tr.

Testament' (*The Achilles Heel*. Doubleday, 1960).[501] In 1964, Professor David Bakan of the University of Chicago published an essay entitled *Sigmund Freud and the Jewish Mystical Tradition* (D. Van Nostrand, 1958).[502] More recently, Dr. Percival Bailey presented Freud as a 'lay rabbi', whose attitude regarding sex is that of the Kabbala (*Sigmund der Unserene: A Tragedy in Three Acts*. Charles C. Thomas, 1965).[503]

This opinion is shared by Ernst Jimon: 'The resemblance between the world of the Talmud and the spiritual world in which Freud lived is not due solely to the similarity of form on the level of the association technique. It is in Judaism that we must seek the secret of Freud's work'.

Hence the sentiment of Kafka, as reported by Marthe Robert: 'Freud's work, rather, is a chapter in Jewish history written by the present generation, and in a way it forms the most recent of the commentaries on the Talmud, and any extension to which it is prone resides in this'.

However, this does not explain the (re)emergence, in an unbelieving Jew, of an inheritance which he only seems to have received in scattered pieces.

Freud's mother spoke a German still indistinct from Yiddish. His father, Jakob, from the Hasidic circles of Galicia, probably preserved the distinctive allure of a pious western European Jew. Originating from Hasidic circles, he had nevertheless abandoned ancestral Judaism, and upon his death in 1896, he left 'the most gifted of his sons in an ambiguous position, midway between a logical rupture and an impossible fidelity'.

All throughout his life, Sigmund Freud was necessarily divided between 'two stories, two cultures, two forms of thought: on the one hand, that of the Jewish people, nourished by the Bible and the Talmud, the source of an intensely lived tradition; on the other hand, western humanism, Classical and Germanic culture. In a word, the "other side"'.

In his work, innumerable biblical references exist alongside quotations from his favourite authors: Goethe, Lessing, Shakespeare, Virgil, and Sophocles.

But at home, this duality does not give rise to a harmonious synthesis. On the contrary, it provokes a persistent *discomfort*.

---

501 French edition: *Le talon d'Achille* (Calmann-Levy, 1957). — Tr.

502 French edition: *Freud et la tradition mystique juive* (Payot). — Tr.

503 French edition: *Sigmund le tourmenté* (La Table ronde, 1972). — Tr.

Engaged in *two* cultures without belonging exclusively to any one, he finds in this interior suspense a certain intellectual freedom as well as additional knowledge, but also a rending, and here Marthe Robert comes close to seeing the inception of the Freudian edifice.

The same ambivalence exists towards the surrounding society: 'While on the Jewish side, people, for Freud, form a familiar reality that reassures with its warmth and proximity, on the other side there is something occult and even harmful; it is the Sphinx, the absent one, who there is every reason to fear as soon as he appears on the historical scene'.

In 1926 Freud declares at a *B'nai B'rith* gathering: 'As a Jew, I was prepared: join the opposition and renounce any agreement with the united majority'.

The high places of European culture attract him even as they repel him. For years, a kind of *inhibition* prevented him from going to Rome, a city with which he had formed a 'singular love affair', but where the Arch of Titus remained the symbol of an abhorrent power. ('It is because he is Jewish that he cannot go to Rome', writes Marthe Robert).

The analysis of his 'Roman dreams' (and some others) reveals a certain tendency towards *repression*: 'He redacted the sexual content of his dreams'.

Thus Freud never ceased to play two characters. The *carnal* son of Jakob, he would have liked to have had a father like Hamilcar, who made his son swear to fight Rome until his last breath. The *spiritual* son of Goethe, he would like to be, as Napoleon was, the son of his works alone.

Two fathers is one too many.

A veneration mingled with terror and perhaps a secret jealousy: this feeling of the Hebrews in regards to Yahweh defines the *relationship to the father* as Freud feels it — and as he will present it in his theory of the *Oedipus complex*.

The same theme, it is true, is found in the Jewish tradition as well as in the Hellenic tradition. But in different forms: that of a *patricide* in the kingdom of Laius (Oedipus kills his father, thus fulfilling destiny), that of a (deferred) *infanticide* among the Hebrews (Abraham, to comply with Yahweh, agrees to sacrifice Isaac).

Naturally, Freud prefers to take his inspiration from the Greek narrative: by endowing it with a new lineage or *parentage*, it raises him, like Oedipus, 'to a kind of royalty'.

The theme of patricide is present in *The Interpretation of Dreams*. It is presented again in *Totem and Taboo*. It culminates in *Moses and Monotheism* (1934), a 'historical novel' where Freud, towards the end of his life, made Moses a noble Egyptian who was initiated into monotheism by the pharaoh Akhenaton and ultimately put to death by the Jews.

As Freud declared to Arnold Zweig: 'It is Moses who *made* the Jew'. If Moses himself were only an adoptive Jew, there would no longer be a problem.

We thus begin to see the portrait of a double-faced Freud: at once bourgeois and revolutionary, respectful of conventions and deeply subversive (in the sense that the Prophets were the 'subversives' of their time), whose theories, though 'born from a humanistic culture which, at the turn of the nineteenth century, formed the pride and power of the ruling class, nevertheless represents the most radically destructive act against which the bourgeoisie has ever had to defend itself'.

This is what brings Freud close to Karl Marx.

On Responsibility

The first was raised in the philosophical spirit of the Enlightenment (*Aufklärung*). The second grew up in the spiritual milieu of leftist Hegelianism (Feuerbach, Moses, Hess). In relation to German society, they feel both assimilated and different *at the same time*. And it is not until the bond linking Marx and Engels that the relationship of Freud and Wilhelm Fliess is evoked.

Can we also say, in terms of psychoanalysis, that they both *assumed* and *interiorised* the paternal responsibility on the basis of an identification?

Karl Marx was the grandson of Rabbi Marx Lévy and the nephew of Rabbi Samuel Marx. But his father had converted to Protestantism to escape the situation of the Jews after the annexation of the Rhineland to Prussia. And yet his book, *On the Jewish Question* (1843),[504] written at the age of twenty-five, will be considered one of the classics of 'leftist anti-Semitism'. (It is only later that Marx will combine philosophical materialism with an idealistic pauperism strongly tinged with Messianism).

In *Marx et la question juive* (Gallimard, 1972),[505] Robert Misrahi, a lecturer at the University of Paris I, writes: 'The origin of Marx's anti-Semitism is

---

504 German: *Zur Judenfrage*, in the *Deutsch–Französische Jahrbücher*. — Tr.
505 *Marx and the Jewish Question*. — Tr.

Marx himself'. 'Marx's identification with his father', he adds, 'is the reflexive interiorisation of a negation operated by the model (the father) with respect to his own negative model, the Jewish religious family'.

Likewise born out of Freud's desire to escape from a father whom he venerated consciously but feared and even hated unconsciously, psychoanalysis is probably the most imposing system of *repression* and *self-justification* ever conceived: Freud is delivered from his phantasms by *projecting* them onto humanity. He has generalised this *particular* case, which was his own, by making it no longer appear as such — and by creating at the same time the conditions for its *redemption*. (If the legs of ordinary people were cut off, dwarves would no longer have complexes). Psychoanalysis is a 'family saga' — written impersonally.

Freud proceeded undercover, undermining his era from within, just as he placed man in question by departing from himself. This is how he was able to gain credibility, and how he was able to win the victory of his dreams over eternal Rome.

'Thus', writes Marthe Robert, 'psychoanalysis does not have the sole purpose of making the conscious life communicate with the unconscious part of the *psyche*; it also serves as an intermediary between two forms of culture and thought by founding a distinct and independent order of knowledge that breaks radically with the religious and philosophical tradition of the west. Henceforth, whenever western civilization, concerned with all that stirs the foundations of everything it has created, formed, and thought, will be driven to interrogate its spiritual infrastructure, it will be necessary for it to pass through the new law which denounces the old or at least declares it obsolete'.

And Freud, supremely skilful, will leave centuries 'perplexed before the mystery of his identity'.

*

D'Oedipe à Moïse, by Marthe Robert.[506] Calmann-Lévy, 279 pages.

*

On the ambiguous attitude of Karl Marx on the place of Jewish culture, cf. the book by Jacques Hermione, *La gauche, Israël et les Juifs* (Round Table, 1970),[507] which places the po-

---

506 *From Oedipus to Moses: Freud's Jewish Identity* (Garden City, NY: Anchor Books, 1976). — Tr.
507 *The Left, Israel, and the Jews.* — Tr.

lemics raised by the publication of *On the Jewish Question* in the more general context of an 'anti-Semitism of the left'. Marx writes that 'Jewish emancipation consists in emancipating humanity from Judaism'. He adds: 'We recognise in Judaism a generally present antisocial element which, through the development to which the Jews have actively participated in this bad relationship, has been pushed to its highest point in the present time, a height where it can only necessarily disintegrate'. M. Hermione concludes that for Marx, 'everything is reduced to the will to suppress the Jew, and therefore to the search for what can lead to his suppression'. An opposing view is expressed by Robert Mandrou, in his preface to the latest French edition of *On the Jewish Question* (*La question juive*, UGE-10/18, 1968).

Examining her 'relationship with Freud', Hélène Cixous declares: 'In my last texts, I situated Moses as a typical male character, that is, a limited power, a phallus threatened with castration. Castration, the Bible, in fact, is brimming; this is so much the world of threat that it is not by chance that Freud comes from it: psychoanalysis is the Bible of the phallus' (*Les Nouveaux cahiers*, autumn 1976).

Pedagogical

THE THESES OF JEAN PIAGET

' At the age of thirteen months', remark Rémy Droz and Maryvonne Rahmy, 'one of Piaget's daughters designates a dog by *vouaou*, then, within a few months, this term is applied to the owner of the dog, to geometric drawings, a horse, two horses, a baby carriage with a baby and a lady, chickens, cyclists, etc. At the age of sixteen months, this term seems definitively reserved for the dog.

The observation seems insignificant. It verifies, however, the validity of one of the propositions of a fundamental science: the psychology of the child.

At the end of 1966, Jean Piaget's work encompassed more than twenty thousand pages of published text. Considerable, but not flashy, and covering several domains (biology, psychology, pedagogy, sociology, 'genetic epistemology') it has continued to remain at the forefront for forty years — without ever being fashionable.

Born in Neufchâtel in 1896, a doctor of science at the age of twenty-two, Piaget oriented himself before long towards psychology. His first works made him known immediately. In 1952, he became professor of genetic psychology at the Sorbonne. He is currently co-director of the Institute of Educational Sciences, a Professor at the Faculty of Science in Geneva, and director of the Centre for Genetic Epistemology, which has gathered international researchers since 1955.

Differences in Structure

His works are divided between purely experimental studies and works of popularisation. Among the first are: *The Child's Construction of Reality* (1937),[508] *Judgement and Reasoning in the Child* (1947),[509] *The Child's Conception of*

---

[508] English edition: (London: Routledge and Kegan Paul, 1955); French edition: *La construction du réel chez l'enfant* (Paris: Delachaux et Niestlé, 1937). — Tr.

[509] English edition: (London: Kegan Paul, Trench, Trubner & Co, 1928); French edition: *Le jugement et le raisonnement chez l'enfant* (Neuchâtel, Paris: Delachaux et Niestlé, 1924;

Geometry (1948),[510] *Biology and Knowledge* (1967).[511] And among the second: *Six Psychological Studies* (1964),[512] *The Psychology of the Child* (1966),[513] *Genetic Epistemology* (1970),[514] and *Psychology and Epistemology* (1970).[515]

Droz teaches at the University of Lausanne. Rahmy is a school psychologist. Both worked with Piaget. 'There exists only one way', they remark, 'of being introduced to Piaget's thought. It is to read the texts he has written'.

As early as the eighteenth century, it had been sensed that people did not have quite the same 'brain' as little people. In other words: the intelligence of the child differs from that of the adult, not only from a quantitative point of view, but also qualitatively.

'Much research has already helped to confirm this point of view. But Piaget goes further: he discovers the differences and analyses their consequences for the view of the world and the explanation of physical phenomena. He tries to sketch the *world of the child* by detaching himself, as much as possible, from the norms of the adult' (*Understanding Piaget*).

During the twenties, Jean Piaget undertook the analysis of the different developmental stages of children's thought. He notes that this development is affected by 'successive balances and stratifications'. He then divides the *genesis* of the brain into four 'slices' or 'stages': the *sensory-motor* stage, the '*egocentric*' stage, the '*social*' stage, and the stage of *formal operations*. Alongside this, he develops an appropriate investigative method, consisting at once of experimental psychology and psychiatric interviewing.

---

third edition 1947). — Tr.

510 English edition: (London: Routledge and K. Paul, 1960); French edition: *La géométrie spontanée de l'enfant* (Paris: Presses univ. de France, 1948). — Tr.

511 English edition: (Chicago: University of Chicago Press, 1971); French edition: *Biologie et connaissance: essai sur les relations entre les régulations organiques et les processus cognitifs* (Paris: Gallimard, 1967). — Tr.

512 English edition: (New York: Random House, 1967); French edition: *Six études de psychologie* (Genève: Ed. Gonthier, 1964). — Tr.

513 English edition: (New York: Basic Books, 1969); French edition: *La psychologie de l'enfant* (Paris: Presses Univ. de France, 1966). — Tr.

514 English edition: (New York: Columbia Univ. Press, 1970); French edition: *L'épistémologie génétique* (Paris: Presses universitaires de France, 1970). — Tr.

515 English edition: (New York: Grossman, 1971); French edition: *Psychologie et épistémologie: pour une théorie de la connaissance* (Paris: Gonthier-Denoël, 1970). — Tr.

'He is not content simply to observe, he provokes the child's behaviour with appropriate *situations* in order to understand, as far as possible, the inner mechanisms (schemes or patterns) ruling child behaviour.

In the first two years of his life, the child acquires a predominantly practical intelligence: he finds that some objects break, while others bend or tear. There is sucking of the thumb, and movement of objects.

Contrary to what the partisans of classical empirical ('associationalist') psychology thought, the earliest knowledge that the little person has of the world is therefore not due solely to its perceptions. But also, and above all, the discoveries he makes by *acting* upon things, combining them, articulating them, transforming them. These 'activities' (in the 'Piagetian' sense of the word) teach him that certain *properties* of things are linked to the actions that are exercised upon them.

At the age of two, and up to the age of seven, the child enters the first stage of concrete operations. It learns the difference between the home, the street, and the school. But he confuses the objects contained in these different sets. He creates 'symbols': the stick becomes a rifle, cane, or telescope. He makes analogical comparisons: 'a piece of grass contained in its seed is like a pair of glasses in their case'. The cause-and-effect relationship is misunderstood. 'How does the bicycle work?' With the wheels. And the wheels? Because they're round. But how do they turn? 'It's the bicycle that turns them'.

The child brings everything back to him. It takes a long time to understand that 'Spot' is also called 'dog', and that the grocer may be a 'monsieur' without necessarily being a 'dad'.

Substance, Volume, and Weight

It is in the field of 'spontaneous geometry' that this type of reasoning is most striking. Droz and Rahmy cite an example. 'It consists in presenting to the child a square placed on one of its sides, then to make it undergo a rotation of 45 degrees so that it rests on the point. The child is then asked if the object is the same. All the young subjects (up to the age of six or at least seven), or almost all of them, claim that the square placed on the point is not a square, and that it is not even the same individual object'.

Identical results are obtained by deforming a ball of modelling clay, or by transferring an equal quantity of liquid into different vessels. The child does not establish the ratio that could exist simultaneously between size, volume, substance, weight, and so forth.

At around seven or eight years old, the child enters the *operative* period properly speaking. Under the influence of the school and group games, he is 'socialised': his conception of relations with others is more relative, less egocentric. *Causes* are identified. The child realises that 'certain properties of a situation or object are *invariable* in relation to the action which is imposed on them'. If he transfers the contents of a champagne flute to a mug of beer, he understands that the volume of the liquid remains the same 'because nothing has been added or removed'. He also distinguishes *categories*, and admits that if 'all ducks are birds', then '(only) some birds are ducks'.

The notion of conservation of weight is acquired at nine or ten years; the notion of conservation of substance, towards eight years, that of conservation of volume, towards twelve years.

Finally, in a last stage, starting at eleven or twelve years, the child gains access to the notion of *abstraction*. He represents objects or situations that are not available for immediate action.

'Then we see proportions appear', writes Jean Piaget, 'as well as the ability to reason and represent according to two systems of references at the same time, and the structures of mechanical balance' (*Problems of Genetic Psychology*).[516] The child may appreciate, for example, the relative movement of a snail on a board moving in the opposite direction. 'He becomes capable of operating on *propositions* and *hypotheses*', not only on objects. Finally, he arrives at a hypothetico-deductive style of reasoning, such as: 'If my hypothesis is correct, then such object must react in such a way to such manipulation'.

An Adapted Teaching

This is, of course, a *typical* pattern. In practice, there may be variations, depending on location, in the speed and duration of development. Piaget reports that in Martinique, he found up to four years of 'delay' in the answers obtained for his tests. 'It was, however, children enrolled according to the French primary school curriculum, which goes toward the certificate of studies. In spite

---

516　*The Child and Reality: Problems of Genetic Psychology* (New York: Grossman, 1973); French edition: *Problèmes de psychologie génétique: l'enfant et la réalité* (Paris: Denoël Gonthier, 1972). — Tr.

of this, the little Martiniquans are up to four years late in acquiring the notions of conservation, deduction, and sequencing' (*Problems of Genetic Psychology*).

Thinking, Piaget reminds us, is *given* by heredity only in the form of a potentiality. The brain at birth is neither a 'blank slate' nor the receptacle of a universal 'reason' equally distributed among individuals. The psyche *constructs itself* by a series of reciprocal assimilations and adaptations between the individual's innate dispositions and the exterior environment. It does not emerge in a single stroke, but in stages. It flourishes like a flower.

Piagetian concepts prove particularly fruitful when they are related to pedagogy. It is indeed evident that teaching must be adapted to the different stages of child mental development. We can therefore conceive of programs that are 'sensory', 'conventional', 'intuitive', 'concrete', 'rational', and so forth. Piaget himself has spoken for an '*active* pedagogy' taking into consideration the child as it is, not as one would wish it to be. 'It would be of the highest interest', he wrote in *Psychology and Pedagogy* (1969),[517] 'for those responsible for directing educators to be in possession of objective studies on the relations between social life and education'.

'This *adapted* teaching requires that the adult world should not be brutally *imposed* on the child, but that the child should be progressively lead as it gradually passes through the stages of its development. This theory highlights the errors of the hyper-authoritarian method ('we shall train them!'), without falling into the exaggeration of 'child value' as practiced by Alphonse Ferrière (*L'école modern française*, 1922; *L'école active*, 1947–59)[518] or Célestin Freinet (*Pour l'école du peuple*, Maspero, 1971).[519]

Descriptive for children, Piagetian psychology becomes *explanatory* for adults. It helps us to better understand the mechanism of the Child's mental operations.

Piaget insists in particular on the 'unconscious cogenitive', on the fact that the genesis of thought is not clearly perceived by the subject. The adult, in fact, 'forgot' that his 'logical' actions originally come from the *interiorisation* of operations that were at first material and concrete. The structures of his mind have been balanced, 'crystallised'. To him they seem to have been there the

---

517 *Psychologie et pédagogie* (Paris: Denoël, 1969). — Tr.

518 *The Modern French School; The Active School.* — Tr.

519 *For the School of the People.* — Tr.

whole time. He imagines, quite wrongly, that they correspond, not to a practical experience that he shares with his kin, but to logical necessities — that which is given for a priori understanding. He thus believes that his vision of the world reflects the absolute reality of things.

Adaptation

Such a mechanism explains why mental development can be 'arrested' at an earlier stage. Piaget quotes Spencer, who in his *Traité de sociologie*[520] recounts 'the story of a lady who was traveling with a long suitcase rather than a square suitcase, because she thought that the dresses weighed less when spread out than when folded'.

'For Piaget', Droz and Rahmy conclude, 'intelligence essentially appears as an activity of an organism that allows the subject to *adapt* his behavior (including his knowledge and his thoughts) to the modifications of the environment'. 'Intelligence', he writes, 'constitutes the state of equilibrium towards which all the successive adaptations of a sensory-motor and cognitive order tend, as well as all the assimilative and accommodating exchanges between the organism and the environment'. (*The Psychology of Intelligence*, 1967).[521] This definition is accepted by most specialists, who connect intelligence to three essential qualities: the ability to adapt to ever-changing situations, the approximation of the real, and the aptitude for abstraction (logical and formal operations).

In *Insights and Illusions of Philosophy* (1965),[522] Jean Piaget vigorously denounces the 'false ideal of a supra-scientific knowledge'. He also asserts the autonomy of *genetic* psychology, a positive science auxiliary to epistemology, against literary and philosophical currents (Bergsonism, phenomenology, existentialism), which would like to make it a mere appendix to philosophy.

Bertrand Russell said: 'Science is what we know. Philosophy is what we do not know yet'. With psychology, we know.

*

---

520 *Treatise on Sociology*. — Tr.

521 English: (London: Routledge and Kegan Paul, 1951); French: *La psychologie de l'intelligence* (Paris: A. Colin, 1947). — Tr.

522 English: (London: Routledge and Kegan Paul, 1972); French: *Sagesse et illusions de la philosophie* (Paris: Presses Univ. de France., 1965). — Tr.

Lire Piaget, by Rémy Droz and Maryvonne Rahmy. Charles-Dessart, Brussels, (distr. Sedim), 244 pages.[523]

Epistémologie des sciences de l'homme, by Jean Piaget. Gallimard, 380 pages.[524]

Problèmes de psychologie génétique, by Jean Piaget. Denoël-Gonthier, 174 pages.[525]

Orientations actuelles de le psychopédagogie, by Jehanne Deloncle. Privat, 150 pages.[526]

*

There are many books on Jean Piaget, notably those by G. Lerbet (*Piaget*. Ed. Universitaires, 1970) and P. C. Richmond (*An Introduction to Piaget*. Routledge & Kegan Paul, London, 1970). The most recent we owe to Jean-Claude Bringuier (*Conversations libres avec Jean Piaget*. Laffont, 1977), who brings together a series of interviews conducted in 1969 and 1975–76. Here, in a relaxed and lively manner, Jean Piaget explains the principal aspects of his work.

In recent years, Piaget has devoted himself above all to 'genetic epistemology', which is 'the study of the successive states of a science in the function of its development'. This new discipline proposes to examine the history of the sciences, to reveal its roots and formative mechanisms 'up to the prescientific or infrascientific field of common knowledge'. In other words, it seeks to identify the morphisms (or correspondences preserving structure) that can exist between the individual development of intelligence and the history of scientific progress. One of the collaborators of Jean Piaget, the physicist Rolando Garcia, declares in this connection: 'The intention of genetic epistemology is to give a sort of description and global explanation of knowledge. This means finding the unity between the human being as a biological being, the child and current, unsophisticated man, and scientific man — to find the unity of development not through a unifying, reductive theory, but through the discovery of common mechanisms'.

The works of the Centre for Genetic Epistemology (33 volumes published between 1957 and 1975) are published by the Presses universitaires de France (PUF), in a collection directed by Jean Piaget. They have also published an *Epistémologie des sciences de l'homme* (*Tendances principales de la recherche dans les sciences sociales et humaines*, vol. 1. Unesco-Mouton, 1970),[527] corresponding to the first three chapters of a systematic study of the human sciences.

Piagetian concepts have begun to provide the substance of many psychological tests: they are already applied to inter-ethnic psychometry. These tests place the accent on the quality of the reasoning more than the veracity of the answers. In Canada, the Institute of Psychology at the University of Montreal has been working for some years in this vein (cf. 'Piaget et le QI', in *Psychologie*, February 1973). Cf. also the paper by Read D. Tuddenham from Berkeley University ('A Piagetian Test of Cognitive Development') at the Symposium on Intelligence by the Ontario Institute for Studies in Education (8 May 1969).

523　*Understanding Piaget* (New York: International Universities Press, 1976). — Tr.

524　*Epistemology of the Human Sciences*. — Tr.

525　*The Child and Reality: Problems of Genetic Psychology* (New York: Grossman, 1973). — Tr.

526　*Current Orientations of Psycho-Pedagogy*. — Tr.

527　*Epistemology of the Human Sciences (Principle Research Tendencies in the Human and Social Sciences)*. — Tr.

PEDAGOGICAL RESPONSIBILITY

'To dominate a child', says Dr. Dreikurs, 'is to impose on him what he must do and have him revolt. To be firm is to *choose* what you want to do, and have him execute it'.

A tenacious propaganda tends to assimilate relations between generations to a dialectical relationship of the Hegelian 'master-slave' type. The break-up of family structures, the challenging of authority and hierarchy, the degradation of the university, and the (ideological and commercial) myth of the 'child-king' accentuate the unrest and add to the anguish of parents.

Dr. Rudolf Dreikurs, eighty years of age, frameless bifocals, finely trimmed mustache, is a specialist in child psychology. Born in Vienna, he was the organizer of the first Austrian Mental Hygiene Committee. In 1937, he moved to the United States. He teaches psychiatry at the Chicago Medical School.

This old-fashioned 'Herr Doktor' is an advocate of avant-garde pedagogy. 'Authority is dead', he says. 'And yet', he adds, 'resignation is more intolerable than ever'.

Educating Parents

Neo-pedagogy, nourished by psychoanalysis and behaviourism, practically reigned supreme in the early fifties. Launched in America before establishing itself in Europe, it has produced a generation of inadequate, 'neo-communists' and hippies.

Pampered children of the post-war period, protestors fail to understand that life does not show them the solicitude to which they have been accustomed. Inadequately armed for competition, they react according to the classic pattern: revolt and secession. Secluded away from the world, they believe to be able to solve collectively problems that they have been unable to face on their own. They seek to replace by the group (the 'community') the family which they lacked.

Apparently struck with amnesia regarding their own childhood, parents, for their part, have a hard time understanding their offspring. Clashes result. It is a vicious circle.

'Jerome, five years old, opposes everything his mother asks. He breaks his toys, his plates, and his furniture in violent fits of anger. His mother is the very model of someone who fulfils her obligations. The father, who hates the drama, yields to the aggravated pressure of the mother in order to have peace'. The diagnosis of Dr. Dreikurs: 'Jerome observes and admires the power of his mother. He feels that the force is of prime importance, and he tries to obtain a similar power. Using anger as a means of asserting himself, he imitates his mother. She thinks that by punishing him, she has the upper hand, without realising that the next manifestation of immoderate conduct will be a revenge, and the beginning of another *round* in the fight for power'.

To 'avoid the scuffle', most adults are ready to evade their responsibilities. Dr. Dreikurs takes them to task. 'Like all children', he writes, 'the parents need to be educated'.

From birth, the child observes his surroundings. And what he learns first is the weaknesses of those who lecture him. Very quickly, he knows where to find the chinks in their armour.

The parents, unconscious, commit the first error: to speak (whether positively or negatively) of children in their presence — under the naive pretext that they are 'too small to understand'. Repository of attention, pet sayings, barrages of kisses, hugs and tickles, the dear little one triumphs. He is put on a pedestal. When he grows up, he will hardly understand that the star is being taken away from him, and his anger will be deferred to those around him.

Divide and conquer: the child, little king, learns this by himself. He shelters behind the weakness of the father to avoid the reprimands of the mother. Or vice versa. 'Look at what your daughter has done'. The child provokes discord and benefits from it.

The problem here is not so much whether it is necessary to use firmness but to learn to avoid using it at the wrong time. The worst thing is to get nervous. 'If we explode abruptly', says Dr. Dreikurs, 'our children will listen to us only when we are violent with them'. ('If you get in such a state about me', they will think, 'then I am just as strong as you').

'Mother surprised Laurent, four years old, in the process of climbing on the kitchen table to get sweets: "Not now", she says, "it's almost time for lunch". The child insists, starts to cry, and stamps his foot. Anger intensifies. "Laurent, stop! I'll give you one, but, for heaven's sake, stop screaming". Conclusion: Mother first refused, but Laurent forced her to give in. He has thus won, and his confidence in his own power strengthens'.

The Courage to Say 'No'

To yield once is to yield always — for firmness asserted late or rarely will appear unfair. The 'good mother', under these conditions, quickly became a slave. She is brought easily under the (moral) whip, which the dear little one uses without any difficulty. The Hegelian relation is then reversed.

Omegas dominate *alphas*. The 'anti-authoritarian' education of children by parents means not less than the hyper-authoritarian education of the parents by the children.

The 'boyfriend style' is based on an illusion: it supposes that the child has a mode of understanding things that is actually completely foreign to him. In this way of educating their progeny, parents actually put themselves *beneath* their children: they are the ones who regress in mental age. And most frequently, the effects of the family environment reinforce those of heredity. The parents speak to their children like they do to little dogs, and give them ridiculous diminutives. 'Baby language' and tickles. Nothing in all this creates strong souls. ('I like strength', said Stendhal, 'that strength that can be shown by an ant as much as an elephant.') Without character, intelligence is nothing.

In conflicts of authority, parents are always the strongest. But the children are the most beaten. Dr. Dreikurs shows the need to avoid such conflicts without giving in to undue demands. This 'third way' consists in developing personal experience. Its basic principle: 'Use natural and logical consequences'.

'Ruth, three years old, dawdles. She needs to prepare to go out for her usual Saturday night walk. Finally, Dad and Mum climb in the car, and say to her: "Apparently, you do not want to walk; but we do. Good-bye, darling, we'll be back soon". The following Saturday, Ruth is ready ahead of time'. Commentary: 'Mum and Dad make no effort to coerce Ruth, but take responsibility for their own attitude. They maintain their plan, and apply the principle of logical consequence'.

Another example: Eric, seven, refuses to eat stew under the pretext that he does not 'like it'. The two disastrous solutions are weakness ('then, what do you want to eat?') and conflict ('you're going to eat like everyone else'). The middle way: 'We are having stew tonight. If you don't want any, you can leave the table. You won't have anything else of course. The choice is yours'.

Again we must remain firm: 'If after the meal he has refused, Eric comes and asks for milk and bread, do not yield': "The house is not a restaurant, I only serve at mealtime".

As a rule, parents talk too much and do not act enough. The child thus learns where the 'threshold of irritability' falls, which he can abuse without risk. Trial and error allow him to translate into his personal language expressions such as: 'wait a little, you'll see' (still waiting), 'now that's enough' (implying: before was not enough), 'speak to your father' (I am not able to settle the matter by myself), 'if I get up, you are going to cop a spanking' (threat not followed by effect). Dr. Dreikurs calls it 'chasing flies'.

'The child', he writes, 'provokes an annoyance in his parents similar to the sound of a fly. Exasperated by the irritating behaviour, we tend to chase the child around, saying: "don't do that, stop it, no, no, hurry up, keep quiet", etc., as if we were getting rid of a blowfly. And in each case, the parents eventually let themselves get caught up in violent reactions'. Hence the classic cycle: irritation, punishment and reprimand, injustice, rebellion.

Dr. Dreikurs points out that it is necessary to have 'the courage to say no'. Do not give in to blackmail (tears, screams, fear of the dark, anger) or provocations. 'Oh ! I must be at home at five o'clock', a mother said to her friend. 'Why?' 'Because I told Elizabeth I'll be there. She must watch me out the window. When I'm not on time, she's absolutely terrified. She weeps and puts herself in all sorts of states'.

'Elizabeth has trained her mother well', says Dr. Dreikurs. 'The girl holds the hoop, and her mother jumps right through. Fear is used to dominate the mother'.

Nor is there 'any reason to buy a child every toy that he sees and thinks he wants. This favours his caprices, and makes him believe that these gifts are owed to him'.

Do not soften needlessly. The phenomenon of the child who only begins to cry after a fall if he knows he has been *seen* is well-known. Hospital staff know what to expect. 'Doctors and nurses who work with children with disabilities are amazed at the courage that they have and the cleverness with which they can compensate for or overcome their difficulties. They are very aware of the *danger* of pity. Fully advanced children collapse because of sympathy or pity given by misguided parents or neighbours'.

Dr. Dreikurs concludes: 'It is much easier to get the child to respect the order once the firmness of the parents is recognised and respect for the child is proven'.

Despite some unnecessary concessions, especially in vocabulary (the author refers to Adlerian psychology), the work of Dr. Rudolf Dreikurs helps to bridge the generation gap by knowing that *lectures* will never be as valuable as *examples*. But also for parents, the education of a child can be a good opportunity — to learn to behave like adults.

*

Le défi de l'enfant, by Rudolf Dreikurs. Laffont, 298 pages.[528]

*

Dr. Benjamin Spock, whose book *Baby and Child Care (Comment soigner et éduquer son enfant*, Laffont, 1957) served as a 'Bible' for millions of parents, is recognised today for having advocated 'anti-authoritarian methods' that completely deceived them. 'Because of people like me', he writes in the New York magazine, *Redbook* (January 1974), 'a wealth of parents have been led to believe that only Psychiatrists, psychologists, paediatricians and social workers know how to care for children. It was a mistake'.

'Obviously', he adds, 'I had said all this with a good intention. But it is a fact that children need authority. In America, parents are not firm enough. They imagine that if they show authority, children will be angry with them or will love them less. It is enough to see everything that an unbearable child can obtain simply by shouting: "I hate you!" Parents give in immediately. Generally speaking, parents are guilty: they think that everything the child does wrong is their fault, because they have given them "complexes", that they have "traumatised" them, that they did not listen to the "specialists", etc. By accusing them of incompetence and ignorance, we have accentuated this feeling of guilt. And now it is I who repent'.

A no less firm condemnation of 'libertarian' pedagogy can be found in Claude Alzon's book, *La Mort de Pygmalion* (Maspero, 1974).[529] Denouncing both the 'worship of youthful incompleteness' and 'the regression of parents to the infantile stage', Alzon writes: 'those who were most difficult to integrate into society were the strongest beings, whose personality was developed by an uncommon education urging them to contest a society in which they did not find a place to their measure. Today, it is the young people who have received the most infantile education who are incapable, by their very childishness, of integrating. And so the protester is no longer the same. Yesterday he was the most sophisticated worker. In our day, young people are the weakest. Yesterday, one could expect everything from a revolt by solid men. Today, all we can fear is the sterile agitation of backward adolescents (...) Once again, the adult will not be changed by creating an immaturity even greater than his own, but by asking him, quite simply, to win back his own maturity'.

---

528 *Children: The Challenge* (New York: Hawthorn Books, 1964). — Tr.
529 *The Death of Pygmalion*. — Tr.

CHILD BEHAVIOURAL DISORDERS

A child is not an adult in miniature, but a developing being, a different being whose emotional development and intellectual activity unfold according to particular laws.

This thesis of Jean Piaget, Dr. Pierre Debray-Ritzen (fifty-four years of age, Professor at the Faculty of Medicine in Paris), and Dr. Badrig Mélékian (forty-nine years of age, head of the Paediatric Clinic), is illustrated by demonstrating its sound foundations.

Composed in a direct style without concession to the jargon of psychoanalysis or to what Jean Giono calls speculative 'philosophications', their study of *Les troubles du comportement de l'infant*[530] forms a useful and precise collection. It describes disorders such as sphincter misconduct, motor function disturbances, sleep and eating disorders, tics, rhythmic disorders, instabilities, and so on. But it also provides clarifications on etiology, that is to say, the causes and the genesis of disorders.

Our 'Three Brains'

Besides the attacks and disturbances of the environment, the authors bring back the role of the constitution, indeed of heredity.

'In view of the accumulation of our knowledge concerning the hereditary causes of the different encephalopathies', they write, 'it would be absurd to deny the truth of genetics (…) Moreover, who can claim that many behavioural disorders currently attributed exclusively to the ambient environment and to psychogenic causes, are not in fact due to yet-unknown hereditary and biochemical factors'.

They also insist on the lessons to be drawn from the most recent work of cerebral schizophysiology.

Following the British scholar Paul MacLean, the specialists now distinguish 'three brains':

1.   The *palaeocortex* or 'reptilian brain', some two hundred million years old, situated in the hypothalamus. It is the seat of our most elementary impulses: control of awareness, sensory stimulation, monitoring of the neuro-vegetative respiratory and cardiovascular centres, aggressive tendencies, etc.

---

530 *Child Behavioural Disorders.* — Tr.

2. The *mesocortex*, or 'palaeomammalian brain', appeared a hundred million years ago and is located in the limbic lobe (which adjoins the brain stem). It is the seat of affective reactions and sexual desires, it monitors the regulation of the olfactory function, emotional behaviour, etc. 'Unconscious emotional set, like all automatisms whose palaeocephalic seat remains' (Henri Laborit, *L'agressivité détourné*. UGE / 10–18, 1970), it is this brain which 'emotionally colours' aggressiveness and gives elemental urges their emotional tone: the search for sexual domination, the need to be favoured, admired, or loved.

3. The *neocortex*, which corresponds to the part of the brain that biologists have always known. Appearing as a distinctive feature among simians and primates, it is, in *Homo sapiens*, the seat of conceptual intelligence and reason.

Following Debray-Ritzen and Mélékian, many behavioural disorders come from poor coordination between the three 'stages':

'On the one hand, the *neocortex* speaks with a language that the old brain cannot understand. On the other hand, and to the contrary, the lower, archaic behaviours (sexual, aggressive, gregarious, ecological) remain the masters: they communicate emotions and moods to the *neocortex* and the latter, even though conscious of these emotional reactions, remains unconscious of their phylogenetic signification as well as of the ancestral purpose that guides them. Thus the *neocortex* adopts these behaviours, and gives them the appearance of reason by ultimately being their dupe. Man believes that his consciousness has been suddenly given to him as a new nature, whereas it is only a new foam emerging from the depths of the tertiary era. Due to this, many ideologies and philosophies are built on this ignorance'.

Among the 'external' annoyances, the lack of authority is not forgotten: 'Few children are able to bear it. The absence of firmness, of rule, of sanctions puts them in a situation that is ultimately *anxiety-provoking* for them to constantly have to ask how far they can go in terms of permission and dispute'.

When asked about this in 1974, Konrad Lorenz stated: 'A social system in which the child is *alpha* and mother *omega* is not a normal system. It is an unhealthy system. On the other hand, a German psychologist has demonstrated in a magisterial way how complete frustration and complete absence of frustration produce exactly the same pathological effects on the child. If you give the bottle to a child before it has cried or done anything to get it, you will arrive at the same result as if you give it to him by forcing him to cry to have it. In both cases, the child is unable to practice reaching a goal. Now, in the first months of his life, the child must learn that he must *work* to obtain something. If he gains the habit of getting what he wants without working, it has the same pathological consequences as if he were working without ever getting anything. The absence of obstacles to overcome is therefore just as dangerous as the existence of insurmountable obstacles. (It suffices to transpose this principle into the adult world to understand the nature of one of the defects of modern societies)'.

'In addition, the presence of a familial community is necessary, because it allows the transfer of authority to be created. The man of thirty years understands perfectly well that the advice of his fifty-five year-old father is valid, and he respects him. The five-year-old boy cannot yet comprehend the superiority of his grandfather, but he admires the ten-year-old boy who has already been allowed to take on small responsibilities. For the ten-year-old child, these responsibilities are privileges, not duties, and he understands very well that in order to benefit from them, he must submit to a certain discipline. As a result, he can give explanations to his five-year-old brother. This creates a hierarchy of admiration and discipline, with the ancestors at the top' (interview with *Nouvelle école*, winter 1974–75).

Unambiguous Process

In Debray-Ritzen and Mélékian's book, the explanations of a 'Freudian' inspiration (Freud, Melanie Klein, Otto Rank, René Spitz, etc.), which 'model all personalities on a precocious and stereotyped chronology, which follows an unambiguous process based on sexuality alone', are firmly rejected.

These theories, says Professor Debray-Ritzen, 'are hardly based on facts, but rather on the singular propensity of a certain language to generalise itself, and a strong tendency to interpret by analogy'.

Freud's disciples, he continues, artificially dissociate emotional development from intellectual development. They postulate an implausibly premature organisation, to which only emotional dynamics would lead. They affirm, however different individuals may be, that this dynamics is the same for everyone. Finally, they 'automatically reduce a whole range of symptoms to a single interpretation' — namely, sexuality.

To Rousseau, Freud, and Marx, Professor Debray-Ritzen opposes Arthur Koestler, Konrad Lorenz, and Robert Ardrey.

'Philosophies', he concludes, 'have still not grasped the explosive importance of that which is provided by anthropology and ethology today'.

*

Les troubles du comportement de l'enfant, by Pierre Debray-Ritzen and Badrig Mélékian.[531]
Fayard, 192 pages.

*

In 1976, Pierre Debray-Ritzen published an encyclopaedia of child psychology (*La psychologie de l'enfant*. Retz).[532] Instead of ideologies, he advocates 'separative eclecticism', a method of judging problems (behavioural disorders, debilities, aggressiveness, etc.) 'in their own nature and original singularity'. 'The word eclecticism', he says, 'is taken here in an original sense: the refusal to be informed by a single doctrine and an informed choice of what is good to take from the different branches of knowledge; the word 'separator' is used according to the sense that it has in the expression 'separative power' (for example of the microscope), that is to say, the quality which makes it possible to distinguish two points which were hitherto confused)'.

THE GIFTED

On May 29, 1975, Victor Serebriakoff, President of Mensa International, on passage to Johannesburg, declared to the *South African Financial Gazette*: 'Western countries waste and neglect their most valuable capital: gray matter'.

He added: 'while we do not hesitate, for good reason, to spend considerable sums of money on providing better education to mentally handicapped children, there is no provision for children with above average intelligence to flourish to the best of their abilities. This is a scandalous situation'.

Does modem society assassinate its geniuses?

Yes, claims Rémy Chauvin, in a study entitled *Les superdoués*. 'Their childhood', he writes, 'is a burden. Many commit suicide mentally, in order to regain a world that does not want their talent'.

---

531 *Child Behavioural Disorders.* — Tr.
532 *Child Psychology.* — Tr.

'Creatives' and 'Savants'

Professor at the Sorbonne, specialist in animal psychology and sociology, Chauvin has published numerous books on biology and ethology. At a Congress held in Monaco from 30 June to 4 July 1975, he was elected Vice-President of the International Association for Psychotronic Research (which deals with parapsychology from a scientific point of view).

'There are', he observes, 'geniuses by right of birth'. For example, the Irish mathematician Hamilton, who at the age of five could read Greek, Latin, and Hebrew; at seven, Italian and French; and at nine, Sanskrit and Arabic. Or the philosopher Jeremy Bentham, who at three years old, wrote letters that a cultivated adult would not have disavowed. There are also more recent cases. At twenty-six months, a little girl named Millie could already read 700 words. Madeline's IQ (intelligence quotient) reached 192 at the age of seven.

Interest in gifted children is old. Plato, in *The Republic*, recommends a vigorous selection. In the last century, after studying 997 eminent men, Sir Francis Galton, a cousin of Darwin, who was one of the first to apply the teachings of statistics to the study of heredity and individual differences, discovered that they had a total of 535 prominent parents, while the same number of 'average' men had only four. He also discovered that great men were often elder sons, which corroborates the observation that, on average, the level of intelligence decreases with the rank of birth.

According to Rémy Chauvin, there are two types of gifted children.

First, the brilliant subjects: the 'strong learners' of the classical variety. They are essentially characterised by a much higher than normal IQ. Then come the 'creatives'. These are innovators, 'originals'. They do not correspond to the traditional idea that we have of the elite. But they are the ones who change the world.

Many great men were 'creative': like Goethe, who composed and performed plays at the age of six, or Pascal, who at twelve rediscovered the laws of geometry.

Up to an IQ level of around 120, the correlation between *intelligence* and *creativity* is very strong. Above it, it decreases rapidly. For creative children, the difficulties of adapting are obvious. They are often challenging children and difficult to raise. Generally, they bewilder their acquaintances.

Their precocity is especially evident in the domain of reading: they 'devour'. Endowed with a strong sense of humour, determined to 'do nothing like the others', they borrow, in their way of reasoning, surprising 'shortcuts', and at any time they can display a 'mischievousness' and a frustrating flippancy.

In class, they have excellent grades in what interests them, very bad in what bores them. They are students who are often 'noticed'. The professors either love them or loathe them with the same vigour. They go to the extreme. They are repelled by the 'average'. In every sense of the word.

This curious way of working earns them occasional or repeated academic failures. This may lead to a loss of equilibrium in regards to the milieu that surrounds them.

At the age of sixteen, the mathematician Evariste Galois was failed at the entrance examination to the Polytechnic: he had insulted the examiner because the questions he had been asked were 'too simple'.

In terms of character, creative people are nonconformists, with all that it this entails for brilliance, charm, but also fragility. Uneasy, even anxious, and tending to live alone, they are prone to 'affectionate' yet dangerous indulgences in everything that departs from the norm and which feeds the fantasies of their vivid imaginations. 'Revolutionaries' of heart and vulnerable in soul, they also tend to become easily crestfallen.

'The characteristic traits of the gifted', writes Chauvin, 'are the same everywhere: anxiety, insecurity, a feeling of isolation, an incessant desire to read, a preference for self-direction, etc'.

Among the gifted of the 'classical' kind, the difficulties are of a different order. At six, a child with an IQ of 180 has an intellectual level of eleven years. At ten or eleven years, he is at the level of an 'average' student. In relation to his acquaintances, this is translated by a feeling of rupture.

Mr. Chauvin goes so far as to say: 'the stronger the IQ, the more severe the problems of social adjustment, and the more serious the persecutions at school'.

The result: according to a survey by Ralph Goldberg and Passow carried out in 1966, about 40 of the gifted (54% of boys and 33% of girls) have grades so bad from high school that they cannot enter into higher education. And their failures only multiply once they reach adulthood.

Throughout their existence, many will still be victims of what Pierre Viansson-Ponté called 'democratic egalitarianism'.

Potential Aptitudes

Chauvin relates: 'In a large number of American establishments, the teachers have claimed that they do not have any particularly gifted children in their class, which is obviously impossible. Either the problem did not interest them, or they were under the influence of an absurd democratic prejudice'.

Once again it is the dispute between heredity and environment. Both factors must be taken into consideration. But heredity is given *first*. Then the environment exerts its influence. *Genetics* has primacy.

Numerous ideologues claim, however, that all men are equal and mouldable at will. 'One recognises here', observes Chauvin, 'a theory of Marxist inspiration. But if we leave *metaphysics* aside and confine ourselves to facts, they lead us to a different opinion'. He adds: 'Elitism exists even in nature'.

However, it should not be forgotten that aptitudes, even hereditary ones, are only potentials. If no opportunity is given for them to be expressed, they atrophy, like a muscle that is no longer used. 'It is a grave mistake', says Victor Serebriakoff, 'to believe that in gifted children, "genius" is automatically expressed. In order to express themselves properly, the gifted require an appropriately favourable environment. Whence the need for detection, selection, and constant and sustained assistance'.

In passing, Rémy Chauvin dispels several other misconceptions. He points out, for example, that strong intellectual quotients are recruited in all environments, even if the least favoured social classes are also those with the highest proportion of below average IQs — in the highest social classes, the chances for an individual to be gifted at birth with a higher IQ are greater.

An explanation: the genetic law of 'regression to the mean', which ensures the circulation of the elites. And the fact that the 'middle' or disadvantaged classes are also the most numerous. (One gifted child is born for every 10,000 people.)

Contrary to a relatively widespread idea, it is inaccurate for gifted children to be generally physically ill. According to a Terman survey carried out over forty years among 1,528 people of different races and backgrounds, all with an

IQ above 150, their physical characteristics are almost always above average. In early childhood, they learn walking and speech earlier. From this point of view, there is a certain psychosomatic solidarity.

Likewise, prodigious calculators are, furthermore, not necessarily dumb. The mathematician Henri Poincaré (*La science et hypothèse*) made all his calculations in his head. Gauss, at three years old, carried out complex operations. Ampere did the same at four, with beans and pebbles.

Chauvin also suggests that gifted children inform us of the meaning of evolution, which continues not at the level of *volume* but of the *structural functioning* of the brain.

'Are higher intelligences', he writes, 'really only the end of the classical Gauss curve, or are they something else?' And what would happen if the Gauss curve shifted over the centuries to the great intelligences? In any case, when we speak of the possible paths of man's future evolution, I firmly believe we overlook a major one. This way is shown to us by gifted children, even though they are not conscious of it themselves.

To avoid the 'waste of grey matter', two methods exist: *accelerated study*, which allows the most gifted to 'jump' classes or to do two classes in a single year; and *regrouping*, which gathers the gifted under the wing of specialised teachers.

A Program for Detection and Information

Chauvin is quite supportive of the second formula. But he emphasises that there is a great difference between what could be an education for the gifted, and different schools of a 'higher level' which currently exist, which are primarily centres of *forcing*. He therefore proposes the development of a genuine 'detection' and information program.

This raises the problem of training the teachers. It also poses the problem of the dominant ideology: as long as l'Education nationale continues to regard it as an article of faith that 'gifts do not exist', gifted children will be condemned. And society, which helps to perfect children who are gifted at skiing, tennis, or swimming, will continue to do nothing in the field of intelligence and creativity.

In the *Revue des deux-mondes* (November 1968), a Professor at the Sorbonne thus characterised the reforms of higher education introduced by the general law and simultaneously adopted by Parliament: 'The guiding idea that inspires these reforms is that all children are gifted by nature of an equal intelligence and that all also have the appeal to undertake higher studies'.

In the Soviet Union, where since July 1936 the use of intelligence tests has been forbidden, mathematicians organise a lecture every year aimed at recruiting the most brilliant minds. In France, in the spring of 1972, Mensa tried to open a school for the gifted in the Nice area. They had to give it up for failure to obtain the necessary authorisations.

*

Les surdoés, by Rémy Chauvin.[533] Stock, 216 pages.

*

The first International Conference on Gifted Children was held in London in September 1975. At the end of the proceedings, four hundred specialists from fifty-five countries were able to compare their points of view, and an international council was established. Its presidency was entrusted to Dan Bitan, who is responsible for gifted children in the Israeli Ministry for National Education.

In the United States, a Council for Exceptional Children (Box 6034, MidCity Station, Washington DC, 20005), attached to the National Education Association, was established in the aftermath of the war. It publishes the journal *Exceptional Children*. In France, there is a National Association for Gifted Children (ANPES)[534] headquartered in Nice and chaired by Jean-Claude Terrassier.

THE UNIVERSITY PLAGUED BY BEASTS

National education is a great whale stranded on the shore of the world, devoured by small beasts. 'Yes', writes Roger Ikor, 'the great beast is prey to beasts, but first to the biggest of all, which is itself'.

'That things have been denied in the university', he continues, 'no one doubts, even, and above all, those whose profession it is to pretend that they are doing well. What things? But all, parbleu! Or almost'.

Roger Ikor, sixty-five years of age, an Agrégé of Literature,[535] Assistant Professor at the Sorbonne, has been teaching since 1937. As a novelist, he

---

533 *Gifted.* — Tr.

534 Association nationale pour les enfants surdoués. — Tr.

535 An *agrégé* is a holder of the *agrégation*, the highest teaching diploma in France.

received the Goncourt Prize in 1955 (for *Les eaux mêlées*).[536] Politically he is quite socialist.

'Psychoanalytic Purgation'

His book, *L'école et la culture*, is subtitled *L'université proie aux bêtes*.[537] It bears the following dedication: 'To my effectively practicing colleagues, to avenge the pedagogues who do not practice'. It provides a means of opposing abstractions and chimeras with concrete reality.

The French university, claims Ikor, has become a field of experiments for uninspired pedagogues. This is the domain of Father Ubu. Clochemerle plus Kafka.

'The standard procedure', he explains, 'consists in: (1) multiplying the experiments, which amounts to willingly sacrificing a number of children used as guinea pigs; (2) making two steps forward in the chosen direction; (3) then a crab step half back; (4) then a small, timid mini-reform; (5) which will soon be replaced by another; (6) then ... I abbreviate: after ten years, twenty years, the landscape, by callous swipes, is thus transformed'.

An example: a well-meaning spirit once thought that numerical grading was 'traumatic' because it encouraged emulation (hence bringing out the best) and gave 'complexes' to those who received bad marks. The scale of 0 to 20 has thus been replaced by five 'levels': A, B, C, D, E. 'The system was tremendously revolutionary: it has been practiced for many years in the capitalist United States! And it was also used, I believe, by the Jesuits in the nineteenth century'.

After this, because the 'levels' lacked precision, they were usually given a 'plus' sign or a 'minus' sign.

'Five times three makes fifteen, and the end result is a slight shortening of the 0 to 20 old scale. Only by a little, because 20 and 19 were actually quite rare, as were 0 and 1. And thus an important verbal revolution is realised!'.

Another example: 'free expression'. This was the subject of the commission for the reform of French teaching, chaired by Pierre Emmanuel. Ikor resigned in order to express his disagreement with the so-called theories of 'creativity', which he sees as a 'psychoanalytic purgation'.

---

536 *Mixed Waters.* — Tr.

537 *School and Culture: The University Plagued by Beasts.* — Tr.

'The child expresses himself'? he writes. 'By god, yes: like a lemon! The juice, moreover, is succulent for the adult who tastes it: like surrealist poetry still fresh to the mind! I, myself, affirm that it is a criminal violation to the integrity of the child's soul, that is, to its very freedom. The fact that violation is perpetrated without violence does not change the fact that it is a true misappropriation of the minor'.

The result: 'In a society which demands beings that are conditioned to its functions, the University will deliver goods to those who are good for nothing, who know nothing but farfetched specialties, while having everything to learn, beginning with spelling and the mathematical rule of three'.

A disillusioned reflection: 'It is better for an educated person to be taught well by a backward or perhaps 'conservative' teacher, than to be educated badly by a perfect or even 'revolutionary' teacher.

For behind the dance of reforms and *continuous experimentation*, there are fashionable ideologies and 'new educators'.

'I have always been seized with terror', writes Ikor, 'before these saints, these inflexible inquisitors, who never raise their voices, who constantly carry an unchanging smile upon their faces, bathed in certainty, who never seem to have the demeanor of order-givers, but who are blissfully obeyed … Today, certain 'advanced' reformers strongly remind me of these men'.

The credo of 'cultural and social paedogogicomania' begins with the refusal of *selection*. Of the pupils as of the teachers. Some educators (like the scholastics that were replete throughout the Middle Ages, says Ikor) find it quite normal that the society which employs them considers them perfect.

'If we listen to them, anyone would have the right to teach anything in any way without having to account to anyone, and they wouldn't need academic titles (the hide of an ass, how revolting!) — and the first man who came along would seize the children and manipulate them as he pleased, simly because it is his personal vocation! If this is not delivering the University to the beasts, then what is it?'

'Now, whatever way one takes things, education remains a matter of authority. (Obedience is *correlative* of command). 'Since the education of the young is inscribed in animal reality, it obeys deep laws which, originally, depend on our bodies and belong to our biology. From such laws, which are natural, we cannot escape'.

In short, education is a 'dressage'.

'What I dare to put forward here is not very fashionable. The word *dressage* shocks those who are delicate. Too bad! It says exactly what it means: that the human being walks upright'.[538]

Previously, French mothers said to their offspring: 'Don't touch the matches, you'll burn yourself'. The young Englishman, however, was left to himself: 'You want to play with matches? Play! When you burn yourself, you will understand! (On one hand, it was theory, on the other, practice). Today we give matches to the child. Then he is consoled without explaining why he was burned.

The Misdeeds of the Core Curriculum

Roger Ikor, who remains suspicious of the notion of the *elite*, considers that 'gigantism of the university is irreversible'. He quotes, however, the words of Montaigne: 'When men are assembled, their heads shrink'.

This is because the spirit does not like the masses.

Between a class of twenty-five pupils and a class of fifty, there is not simply a difference of degree: 'It is impossible to know with precision at what moment a gathering of grains becomes a pile. Nevertheless, from a certain moment, the pile exists as such and is worked with a shovel, or even a digger. The same goes with school'.

Ikor also denounces the misdeeds of the 'core curriculum'. We know the principle: in middle school,[539] everyone receives the same teaching. Having become state law, the 'core curriculum' reigns over the whole cycle of compulsory schooling. And yet, 'it is difficult to see how the same mould could receive a future Einstein or a future Diafoirus at fifteen years of age without disaster'.

This is the trend that dominates. The 'social situation' is supposed to take the place of intelligence and give rise to higher education. In a 'homogeneous' education system, everyone can be rendered intelligent. Here we find the egalitarian postulate.

---

538 In French, the word *dressage* generally means 'to train' (especially of an animal, i.e. to 'rear' or 'raise'); the word also has a strong sense of 'straightening', or 'standing' (being 'erect', 'upright'), which is what the author is playing on here. This sense is also evident in the verb form: *dresser*: 'to train, prepare, establish, raise, erect', etc. — Tr.

539 In France, *collège*, or grades 6–9 (age 11–15). — Tr.

The latter proceeds from 'two rival philosophies, which, despite opposing premises, culminated, in matters of instruction, in the same conclusions. It is a matter of French *Cartesianism* and English *empiricism*: the Cartesians consider reason to be identical in all men, the empiricists maintain that mind is a *tabula rasa* at birth, offering the same opportunities for development in all children' (Louis Rougier, *L'égalité dans l'éducation*, in *Le Spectacle du monde*, March 1969).[540]

On the first page of the *Discourse on Method*, Descartes, a former pupil of the Jesuits, declares, 'Good sense or reason is naturally equal in all men'. Bossuet, Bishop of Meaux, writes in his *Logic*: 'To be a man is equally suited to the wisest and the most foolish, without ever being able to say, speaking properly and exactly, that one man is more man than another'.

From the empiricism of the 'clean slate', which sees the newborn's mind as a 'sheet of white paper' (according to Locke's expression), Helvetius asserts that 'spirit, genius, and virtue are the product of instruction', such that from the smallest shepherd of the Alps, a Newton or Lycurgus can be drawn at will' (*De l'esprit*).

Ikor responds: 'The best of us are blind to this deplorable but incontestable reality that men are unequal in strength, quality, and value. Or rather their intelligence knows, but their heart, content, speaks louder. The conclusion: 'To each according to his quality, his value, his strength. To restrain the most gifted is as unjust as restraining the least gifted'.

Ikor, finally, speaks at length about the reform of French. He particularly denounces the method which replaces, under the guise of 'simplification' (as usual, the less gifted should not be given 'complexes'), the study of the literary work (considered a *masterpiece*, thus made by an *elite*), with that of the 'text', and more specifically the 'non-literary text': a popular song, a 'fashionable' poster or advertising flyer, etc., made by the *masses* — in short, to substitute the 'French which we speak' (*basic French*) with the French we *have to* speak.

'How can you say', he asked, 'that a thought can be sharply formulated unless it has rubbed against good models?'

---

540 'Equality in Education' in *The Spectacle of the World*. — Tr.

If the University is to stop being plagued by beasts, it must be restored to men. And preferably to sensible men. This is obvious, of course. 'But would de La Palice not be the greatest revolutionary mankind has ever produced?'

*

L'école et la culture, by Roger Ikor. Castermann, 139 pages.

*

At the beginning of 1976, a Study Group for a New Education (GENE)[541] was created that proposed to develop a global education project as an integral part of the conception of the world and life. GENE, which claims to situate itself 'beyond the sterilising past of certain traditional pedagogy like derealising the utopianism of certain conformist pedagogy', wishes to gather around it all those who, by the fact of their competences or their functions (professors, teachers, psychologists, doctors, parents of pupils, etc.), are concerned about the problems of education. It publishes the journal *Nouvel éducation* (130 rue de la Pompe, 75116 Paris).

---

541 *Groupe d'études pour une nouvelle education.* — Tr.

OTHER BOOKS PUBLISHED BY ARKTOS